ENGAGING DECONSTRUCTIVE THEOLOGY

Engaging Deconstructive Theology presents an evangelical approach for theological conversation with postmodern thinkers. Themes are considered from Derrida, Foucault, Mark C. Taylor, Rorty, and Cupitt, developing dialogue from an open-minded evangelical perspective. Ron Michener draws upon insights from radical postmodern thought and seeks to advance an apologetic approach to the Christian faith that acknowledges a mosaic of human sources including experience, literature, and the imagination.

ASHGATE NEW CRITICAL THINKING IN RELIGION, THEOLOGY AND BIBLICAL STUDIES

The *Ashgate New Critical Thinking in Religion, Theology and Biblical Studies* series brings high quality research monograph publishing back into focus for authors, international libraries, and student, academic and research readers. Headed by an international editorial advisory board of acclaimed scholars spanning the breadth of religious studies, theology and biblical studies, this open-ended monograph series presents cutting-edge research from both established and new authors in the field. With specialist focus yet clear contextual presentation of contemporary research, books in the series take research into important new directions and open the field to new critical debate within the discipline, in areas of related study, and in key areas for contemporary society.

Engaging Deconstructive Theology

RONALD T. MICHENER
Evangelische Theologische Faculteit, Belgium

ASHGATE

Scripture taken from the HOLY BIBLE, NEW INTERNATIONAL VERSION.

Copyright © 1973, 1978, 1984 International Bible Society. Used by permission of Zondervan Bible Publishers

Published by
Ashgate Publishing Limited
Gower House
Croft Road
Aldershot
Hampshire GU11 3HR
England

Ashgate Publishing Company
Suite 420
101 Cherry Street
Burlington, VT 05401-4405
USA

Ashgate website: http://www.ashgate.com

British Library Cataloguing in Publication Data
Michener, Ronald T.
    Engaging deconstructive theology. – (Ashgate new critical thinking in religion, theology and biblical studies) 1.Deconstruction 2.Postmodern theology
    I.Title
    230'.046

Library of Congress Cataloging-in-Publication Data
Michener, Ronald T.
    Engaging deconstructive theology / Ronald T. Michener.
        p. cm. – (Ashgate new critical thinking in religion, theology, and biblical studies)
    Includes bibliographical references and index. ISBN 0-7546-5581-4 (hardcover : alk. paper)
    1. Theology. 2. Deconstruction. 3. Postmodernism–Religious aspects–Christianity. I. Title. II. Series.

    BT83.8.M53 2006
    230'.046–dc21

2006011545

ISBN   978-0-7546-5581-7

Printed and bound in Great Britain by MPG Books Ltd. Bodmin, Cornwall.

Contents

Acknowledgements

I thank my colleagues at the Evangelische Theologische Faculteit in Leuven, Belgium, for their fraternal support, kindness, and gentle prodding to finish this work. I am equally grateful for my students who have charitably listened and engaged these ideas at various levels through the years. I also want to express appreciation to my student assistant, Mr. Maarten Zijlstra, who has diligently helped in the preparation of the index.

I offer many thanks to my former professors at the Faculté universitaire de Théologie protestante de Bruxelles, Dr. Anne-Marie Reijnen and Dr. Bernard Hort for their academic support, verbal encouragement and valuable criticisms from the inception of this work. Both are fine examples of patient, open-minded, interactive scholars seeking the type of academic dialogue this book is advocating.

I owe a debt of thanks to my dear friend, Musuvaho Paluku, who has been a tremendous source of encouragement and help through various stages of the writing process these past years.

Additionally, I would like to express my gratitude to the late Dr. Stanley J. Grenz who inspired and challenged me through his words and works to engage postmodern thought and theology. His loss is felt deeply by many who have been inspired by his scholarship and piety.

Finally, I want to express my appreciation and love to my longsuffering wife Sandra and to my son Nathanaël for their enduring care when my mind has at times been "elsewhere" in the course of this project.

Preface

Some believe postmodernism is no longer a viable intellectual force. Yet D.A. Carson claims, "rumors of postmodernity's demise are greatly exaggerated."[1] Carson submits that no other worldview has displaced that which is asserted by postmodernity; and also, the diversity of western culture itself nourishes a sort of *de facto* postmodernity.[2] In agreement with Carson, I am writing as one who assumes that postmodernity is still a prevalent intellectual movement, hence quite relevant for our current study.

I am writing, in a sense, as a "displaced" American. I readily acknowledge that I write with the limited interpretive lenses of one living as a foreigner in Belgium. Yet, I trust this personal "marginalization" of sorts, will help me to perceive the issues at hand in a distinctive way as an observer of postmodern influences from my own cultural background, within the culture I am living, and from the perspective of my own Protestant evangelical subculture. My personal interest in the subject of postmodernism and its relation to theology indeed stems from my background and current ambitions to understand the culture and subcultures in which I live. As an ordained Protestant minister, and ongoing student of theology, I have chosen a vocation that is preoccupied with the notion of truth and the presentation of truth to the world of today.

My perception of the need for continued Christian apologetic analysis in view of postmodern deconstructionism also stems from my personal commitments as an evangelical Protestant Christian minister. I am compelled to communicate the gospel, the Christian message of the grace of God in Jesus Christ. At times, apologetic activity is needed to effectively communicate this gospel. But through this activity, it is my desire to exhibit an open mind to learn from non-evangelical perspectives, without making relative the claims of evangelical Christian belief and practice. Definitions on the meaning of "evangelical" can be varied and complex, but I would concur with others who have suggested the following general emphases:

1. The Reformation doctrine of the authority and primacy of Scripture
2. A focus on conversion and personal spiritual devotion
3. An emphasis upon the historical person of Jesus Christ and his death and resurrection
4. A concern for evangelism and mission (sharing the gospel message with others).[3]

---

1 D.A. Carson, *The Gagging of God: Christianity Confronts Pluralism* (Grand Rapids: Zondervan, 1996), p. 22.

2 Ibid.

3 See McGrath, *A Passion For Truth*, p. 22; Carson, *The Gagging of God,* p. 444; and Pierard, "Evangelicalism," p. 311.

Unfortunately, evangelicalism has often taken a defensive posture in both North America and Europe, commonly expressing itself reactively, rather than actively engaging a genuine vision for theology. As a result, evangelicalism is at times viewed as narrow-minded fundamentalism.[4] Others insist, however, that evangelicalism may be quite tolerant and accepting of diversity where it does not concern the central issues of the Christian faith.[5] Stanley J. Grenz, for example, pictured evangelicals as those standing between fundamentalism and liberalism, remaining open to dialogue and engagement with other viewpoints.[6] Donald G. Bloesch's perspective is a bit different with his employment of the term "centrist evangelical." Bloesch submits that being a centrist ought not be confused with the "middle road" between liberalism and fundamentalism, as Grenz seemed to imply. Rather, it embraces truth where it is found in both, and rejects untruth in these positions as well.[7] My perspective is to take Bloesch a step further. Rather than simply rejecting untruth, I am recommending dialogue concerning the nature of the motives *behind* these notions of "untruth." More on this will be said later.

Further, I am writing from a "progressive" evangelical perspective. "Progressive," of course, may hold different shades of meaning to those who support this notion with respect to evangelicalism. Non-evangelical theologian Gary Dorrien, has chronicled in his book, *The Remaking of Evangelical Theology*, that a progressive evangelical is one who is in favor of dialogue which promotes a "generous orthodoxy."[8] I would agree. Progressive evangelicals realize that much of postmodern thinking may lead to nihilism, but they also recognize the "dethronement" of the cultural hegemonies of many modernist assumptions. Grenz was a "progressive" evangelical who heartily concurred with this in *Renewing the Center: Evangelical Theology in a Post-Theological Era*:

---

4   See Donald G. Bloesch, *Essentials of Evangelical Theology: God, Authority, & Salvation*, vol. 1 (San Francisco: Harper & Row, 1978), p. 20. Bloesch claims that evangelicalism has struggled to present a credible witness (particularly in America) because it has concerned itself with insignificant and peripheral details, which has isolated it from its own heritage and contemporary theological discussion. Timothy George points out that fundamentalism ignores great dogmatic tradition in favor of simple biblicism, while evangelicals celebrate the great orthodox doctrines of the faith as essentials to the gospel and everyday life. See Timothy George, "If I'm an Evangelical, What Am I?," *Christianity Today* August 9, 1999, p. 62.

5   McGrath, *A Passion For Truth*, pp. 20–23.

6   Grenz, *Revisioning Evangelical Theology,* pp. 25–6. For a helpful examination of the "two party" philosophical bifurcation of "liberal" and "conservative" in American Protestant Christianity, see Nancey Murphy, *Beyond Liberalism & Fundamentalism: How Modern and Postmodern Philosophy Set the Theological Agenda* (Valley Forge: Trinity Press International, 1996).

7   Donald G. Bloesch, *God The Almighty: Power, Wisdom, Holiness, Love* (Carlisle: The Paternoster Press, 1995), p. 12.

8   Gary Dorrien, *The Remaking of Evangelical Theology* (Louisville: Westminster John Knox, 1998), p. 185ff. Cf. Stanley J. Grenz, *Renewing the Center* (Grand Rapids: Baker, 2000), pp. 21, 331.

The postmodern condition calls Christians to move beyond the fixation with a conflictual polarity that knows only the categories of "liberal" and "conservative," and thus pits so-called conservatives against loosely defined liberals. Instead, the situation in which the church is increasingly ministering requires a "generous orthodoxy" characteristic of a renewed "center" that lies beyond the polarizations of the past, produced as they were by modernist assumptions – a generous orthodoxy, that is, that takes seriously the postmodern problematic. Therefore, the way forward is for evangelicals to take the lead in renewing a theological "center" that can meet the challenges of the postmodern, and in some sense post-theological, situation in which the church now finds itself.[9]

As a progressive evangelical, I would affirm the authority of Scripture and its expression of doctrinal truths through narrative, poetry, and other literary genres. I believe in a real personal God, who can modestly and partially be described by, but not fully contained in propositions of Scripture. Although rational inquiry is important, I affirm a spirituality that is also personal, emotional and relational.

Accordingly, I will not fully embrace modernity or postmodernity, but suggest that we learn from both, critique them both, and oppose and defend elements from both, in order to help create new approaches to Christian apologetics in response to and in dialogue with postmodern deconstructive theology.

It would be presumptuous to attempt an evaluation or summary of the postmodern movement as a whole. This would be virtually impossible without making sweeping generalizations and assumptions. Neither will I simply provide a critique for or against postmodern deconstructionism. Most works that address postmodern deconstructive theology seem to either embrace it without limits (as one may see in the works of Mark C. Taylor and Don Cupitt), or relentlessly criticize it.[10] Those in a more radically critical vein portray postmodern thinking as a monstrous "boogeyman" threatening all we know to be true.[11]

Although there are several works that are extremely helpful in the analysis of postmodernism, there does not appear to be a work that has specifically examined deconstructive theological themes found in Lyotard, Derrida, Foucault, Taylor, Rorty and Cupitt with the expressed purpose of developing apologetic renewal and dialogue from an evangelical perspective. My desire is to provide these "case studies" as introductory examples of such an "interactionist engagement" which I trust may prompt a continued development of a Christian conversational apologetic methodology among evangelicals and non-evangelicals alike. Most books addressing radical postmodern concerns are either too highly technical or too simplistic to reach

---

9   Stanley J. Grenz, *Renewing the Center*, p. 331.

10   See R. Albert Mohler's essay, "Contending for Truth in an Age of Anti-Truth," in James Montgomery Boice and Benjamin E. Sasse (eds), *Here We Stand: A Call From Confessing Evangelicals* (Grand Rapids: Baker, 1996), pp. 59–76; and Dennis McCallum, "Evangelical Imperatives," in *The Death of Truth* (Minneapolis: Bethany House, 1996), p. 244.

11   See Merold Westphal, "The Ostrich and the Boogeyman: Placing Postmodernism," *Christian Scholar's Review* 20/2 (1990): 114–17.

the broad range of theological students and educators desiring to fairly interact with such concerns. This book attempts to target those in between these extremes.

While I do not endorse all of its conclusions, I do suggest that the postmodern critique on theology can generate and propel further theological investigation in the apologetic arena. The specific contribution of this book centers on an attempt to glean insights and criticisms from various strands of postmodern deconstructionist thought in order to suggest a person-centered, dialogue-based apologetic.

Ronald T. Michener

PART 1
Introduction and Historical Context

Chapter 1

Introduction

Perhaps the most ambiguous, elusive, and controversial word of the past two decades is *postmodernism*. It has had and continues to have multiple meanings and contexts. It has been used in politics, popular culture and media, architecture, science, history, literature and theology. Often it is perceived that the ideas and movements presented in postmodernism are uniquely reserved for abstract discussions among the academic elite in the halls of the university. However, one will see that this is not the case. Instead, these ideas and influences present us with revolutionary challenges to our faith and practical living. They challenge the way we believe, the way we view ourselves in the world, the way we view God, and the way we do our thinking, research and teaching. Postmodern epistemological shifts have significantly impacted philosophical and theological thinking, stimulating a variety of new formats and conceptions for theological method.[1]

Apparently, the term "postmodern" may have been first used in the 1870s by an English artist named John Watkins Chapman in the context of his critique of Impressionistic art. Later, in 1917 a German writer named Rudolph Pannwitz used the term "postmodern men" to describe those who were amoral and nihilistic in their lifestyle and values, apart from modern European civilization at that time.[2] In 1934 the word *posmodernismo* was said to be used by the Spanish writer Federico de Onis, to refer to an "exhausted and mildly conservative modernism."[3] In 1939, British Historian Arnold Toynbee is said to have described the era of devastation following World War I as "Post-Modern." The tragic, horrific effects of this war brought a sudden end to the progressive, optimistic outlook of liberalism. In turn, this opened the door to new perspectives in viewing reality.[4] Apparently, Toynbee later discussed his notion of a "postmodern age" in 1954. In this context, Toynbee's analysis was based on his perception of the social instability, industrial growth, and

---

1 See Nancey Murphy, *Beyond Liberalism & Fundamentalism.* Note especially her concluding comments on pp. 152–3.

2 Glenn Ward, *Teach Yourself Postmodernism* (London: Hodder Headline Plc, 1997), p. 6.

3 Barry Smart quotes M. Calinescu in Barry Smart, *Postmodernity* (London and New York: Routledge, 1993), p. 19 as cited in David West, *An Introduction to Continental Philosophy* (Cambridge, Mass.: Blackwell, 1996), p. 195. Cf. Stanley J. Grenz, *A Primer On Postmodernism* (Grand Rapids: Eerdmans, 1996), pp. 15–16.

4 R. Albert Mohler, "The Integrity of the Evangelical Tradition and the Challenge of the Postmodern Paradigm," in *The Challenge of Postmodernism: An Evangelical Engagement*, ed. David S. Dockery (Grand Rapids, Baker, 1997), p. 68.

loss of the middle class in the mid–1870s.[5] The term *postmodern* gained widespread attention in the 1960s and 1970s, at first referring to a new unique artistic style of architecture.[6] The political events of the late 1960s and the disillusionment with Marxist and Leftist thought devastated previous utopian ideals, setting the scene for the ambivalence of postmodern thought.[7]

The term moved to the forefront of the academic world in 1979 with the publication of *La Condition Postmoderne* (The Postmodern Condition) by Jean-François Lyotard. Lyotard broadly defined postmodernism as *"l'incrédulité à l'égard des métarécits"* (incredulity toward metanarratives).[8] This "incredulity" describes a mood or as Lyotard's title submits, a condition of the post-industrial modernist legitimations of history and science typified in mainstream Enlightenment thought.[9] More on Lyotard will be discussed later in relation to the roots of deconstructionism in Europe.

Domains of Postmodernism

In many ways, the word "postmodernism" defies description. This is due to the fact, as mentioned above, that a myriad of disciplines have adopted various ideas about postmodernism and made them their own. "Postmodern" may refer to a particular abstract film, a piece of art, or to a particular historical context. As Glenn Ward submits, the term may refer to a *state of affairs* in society, a *set of ideas* which explain a state of affairs, an *artistic style*, or simply a *word* that is used to describe these stated aspects.[10]

David West suggests that postmodernism developed into two different, but not unrelated domains. The first is the radical skeptical critique of modernism and the Enlightenment project confronting the basic ideals of western metaphysics. The second is the postmodernism which highlights the cultural and social theory of current western society. A tension may be seen in these two approaches. The second domain of postmodernism would necessitate some kind of philosophical account

---

5   Cf. West, *An Introduction to Continental Philosophy*, p. 196; also Glenn Ward, *Teach Yourself Postmodernism*, p. 6; and Stanley J. Grenz, *A Primer On Postmodernism* (Grand Rapids: Eerdmans, 1996), p. 16. Grenz recommends Margaret A. Rose's discussion of Toynbee's use of the term and its meaning in Margaret A. Rose, "Defining the Postmodern," in *The Postmodern Reader*, ed. Charles Jencks (New York: St. Martin's Press, 1992), pp. 119–36.

6   See West, *An Introduction to Continental Philosophy*, pp. 195–6; and Grenz, *A Primer On Postmodernism*, p. 2.

7   West, *An Introduction to Continental Philosophy* , p. 196.

8   Jean-François Lyotard, *La Condition Postmoderne*, Collection Critique (Paris: Les Editions de Minuit, 1979), p. 7. This was later published in English as *The Postmodern Condition*, trans. Geoff Bennington and Brian Massumi (Minneapolis: University of Minnesota Press, 1984).

9   Cf. West, *An Introduction to Continental Philosophy*, pp. 197–200.

10   Ward, *Teach Yourself Postmodernism*, p. 4.

of history, whereas the radical, skeptical domain would attempt to deny such an account.[11]

In circles of American Protestant evangelical theology, "postmodernism" is sometimes used as a catch-all term for the ills of contemporary degenerate society, seen as the end result of a supposed pernicious French philosophy. This popular conception, along with the failure of many authors to distinguish particular postmodern philosophers and/or theologians from cultural degeneracy at large, creates much confusion. Andrew Gustafson helpfully distinguishes between two broad arenas of postmodernism, that which he calls "crass societal postmodernism" and "academic postmodernism."[12] It is not that this "crass societal postmodernism" has no basis or relation with academic postmodernism, but its modes of expression are certainly different.

Gustafson's description of "crass societal postmodernism" or, as I prefer to simply call it, "cultural postmodernism," expresses itself through a radically eclectic, image-driven culture. As Mark C. Taylor states: "In the multiple worlds of postmodernity, there is nothing that is not virtual because everything is always already mediaized."[13] Although it is beyond the scope of our study to carefully examine the various expressions of cultural postmodernism, it is evidenced in everything from television, the internet, virtual reality, MTV, and even body piercing and tattooing.[14] These cultural elements mark a plurality of expression, presentation, and information, stemming from a diversity of sources not linked to some ultimate authority structure. As evidenced with television music videos, this image-driven culture appeals not only to one or two of the senses, but to several of the senses at the same time. Tattoos and ornaments placed on or through the body display the complex variety and plurality of dissonant voices of expression. Such cultural images suggest a worldview where the identity of the self is not fixed, but is culturally driven and defined.[15] The younger, "Generation X" (often called simply "Gen X"), born in the mid–sixties, to late seventies, is often associated with shaping cultural

---

11 Cf. West, *An Introduction to Continental Philosophy*, pp. 196–7.

12 Andrew Gustafson, "Apologetically Listening to Derrida," *Philosophia Christi* 20/2 (1997): 15–42. Cf. Lawrence Cahoone who also makes an interesting distinction between what he calls *historical* postmodernism, *methodological* postmodernism, and *positive* postmodernism. Historical postmodernism is an historical claim that modernity is ending and bringing about a major social, cultural, etc. transformation. Methodological postmodernism is more ideologically based—critiquing the notion of truth and undermining rational inquiry. Positive postmodernism offers alternative "positive" perspectives or visions in response to methodological postmodernism. See Lawrence Cahoone in his "Introduction" to *From Modernism to Postmodernism*, ed. Lawrence Cahoone (Cambridge, Mass.: Blackwell, 1996), pp. 17–18.

13 Mark C. Taylor, *Hiding* (Chicago: University of Chicago Press, 1997), pp. 333–4.

14 For visual examples of this cultural movement with philosophical commentary, see Taylor, *Hiding*.

15 Douglas Groothuis, *Truth Decay: Defending Christianity Against the Challenges of Postmodernism* (Downers Grove: InterVarsity, 2000), pp. 54–5.

postmodernism. It is a generation which is said to be disillusioned and marked by chaos, even pessimistic about their chances for survival.[16] Again, Mark C. Taylor astutely and artistically describes the nature of this disenchantment in a postmodern, media driven, "web"-driven, culture:

> When webs expand to become worldwide, both their strengths and weaknesses grow exponentially. Paradoxically, the networks that sustain us are also the structures that threaten us. As we struggle to negotiate the tensions within which we are suspended, it is necessary to resist every temptation to view these networks in either utopian or dystopian terms. Between the real and the ideal lies the strange spacing of the virtual. Neither real nor nonreal, the virtual is something else, something other, something that remains fraught with opportunity as well as danger.[17]

However, it is academic postmodernism which will be our primary concern in this work. Academic postmodernism in general addresses the intellectual concerns seen in the break from Enlightenment ideals. As previously noted, academic postmodernism affects not only philosophy and theology, but also literary criticism, sociology, history and a host of other fields of study. Some consider postmodernism to be an effective term to describe our position on the historical chart.[18] Others would consider it to be a useful term to describe a radicalization of the modern period, that is, an *ultra-modernism* or *hyper-modernism*.[19] Even others would consider it better described as an attitude, instead of a trend or paradigm.[20] For the purposes of this book I will be referring to postmodernism primarily as an intellectual movement challenging modernism and the Enlightenment project. I would not be so impetuous as to purport that modernism as an intellectual movement has ceased and a completely new postmodern era or movement has emerged. Modernism and many of its Enlightenment ideals are still very much alive and well in various contexts. But I would argue that a postmodern ethos has emerged in our current era which has indeed radically challenged basic modernist assumptions.

---

16 See David S. Dockery, "The Challenge of Postmodernism," in *The Challenge of Postmodernism: An Evangelical Engagement*, ed. David S. Dockery (Grand Rapids: Baker, 1997), p. 15.

17 Taylor, *Hiding*, pp. 334–5.

18 See, for example, Dockery, "The Challenge of Postmodernism," p. 13. Dockery says postmodernism "primarily refers to time rather than to a distinct ideology." Others, such as Antoine Vergote, would claim that the term "postmodern" is a vague, unhelpful designation. He denies that we have entered into any age that should be properly called "postmodern." According to Vergote, we are still ingrained in modernism. See Antoine Vergote, *Modernité et Christianisme: Interrogations critiques réciproques* (Paris: Les Editions du Cerf, 1999), pp. 7, 28, 41–2.

19 See, for example, Thomas Oden, *After Modernity What? Agenda for Theology* (Grand Rapids: Zondervan, 1990), esp. pp. 71–99. Also see *Entretien avec Marc Augé* in Pierre-Olivier Monteil, *La Grâce et le Désordre* (Genève: Labor et Fides, 1998), p. 97.

20 J. Wentzel Van Huyssteen, *Essays in Postfoundationalist Theology* (Grand Rapids: Eerdmans, 1997), p. 187.

The Problem Stated

As Christians move into the 21st century, amidst all these cultural and intellectual movements and changes, they must learn to effectively meet new challenges. Although I disagree with David S. Dockery when he asserts that the modern mode of thinking is obsolete, I would heartily agree when he equally claims that postmodernism presents Christians with a new set of challenges and "rich opportunities" for witness to the gospel message. If Christians are to continue to communicate and incarnate the gospel in a world with postmodern assumptions, then they must seek to understand their culture and seek relevancy. Postmodernism, both intellectually and culturally, has challenged basic worldviews and assumptions of ethics, self-perspective, and theological expression. Postmodernism has often forfeited the notion of absolute truth in favor of radical pluralistic expression.[21] Such pluralism or, as postmodern theologian David Tracy calls it, "plurality," is now typical of intellectual thought in most countries in the western world. Diversification and syncretistic thinking is gaining ground, and "*relative* cultural homogeneity" is declining among western nations.[22] It is amidst these postmodern assumptions where one seeks the pertinence and "truth" of confessional Christianity. Should Christians be threatened by such seemingly radical postmodern perspectives? Is postmodernism, even deconstructive postmodernism, seen only as a theological assault bringing relativistic doom, or may it possibly be heard as a prophetic voice beckoning us to appropriate new insights? It is these questions to which I will seek to respond in this book.

Types of Postmodern Theologies

Just as postmodernism is expressed in a myriad of disciplines, it is also expressed in a variety of ways in theology itself. Diogenes Allen describes four major "streams" of postmodern theology which provide a critique of modern liberal theology. First is confessional theology, characterized by Karl Barth's neo-orthodox attack on liberal theology. The second "stream" is existential-hermeneutical, based on both Heidegger and Schleiermacher. The third is theological deconstructionism (which I will be addressing) indebted both to Heidegger and Derrida. The last "stream" is that of process theology, based on the process philosophy of Alfred North Whitehcad and Charles Hartshorne.[23]

Postmodern theologian, David Ray Griffin, is perhaps the one most noted for describing four basic types of postmodern theologies: 1) Conservative or Restorationist theology; 2) Liberationist theology; 3) Constructive, Revisionary, or

---

21 Dockery, "The Challenge of Postmodernism," pp. 13–15.

22 Carson, *The Gagging of God,* pp. 13–17.

23 Diogenes Allen, *Christian Belief in a Postmodern World* (Louisville: Westminster/ John Knox,1989), p 6.

Process theology; and 4) Deconstructive theology.[24] In my estimation, as helpful as classifications may be, such breakdowns are more convenient and useful for establishing starting points for research than they are definitive. Echoing the words of theologian Terrence W. Tilley: "contemporary theologies are as fluid as wild rivers running in the spring ... no pattern is final or definitive."[25] Theologians such as Tilley, Roger E. Olson, and Swiss theologian, Klauspeter Blaser, also justifiably include "post-liberal" theology (such as that of George Lindbeck) in the categories of postmodern theology as well.[26] As Tilley purports: "Like the deconstructive postmoderns, postliberals find the humanism of religious liberalism to be religious pretense."[27]

At this point, it will be helpful to summarize the basic themes of the four most commonly considered postmodern theologies.

Conservative or Restorationist Theology

The first type mentioned, conservative or restorationist postmodern theology, seeks to conserve or restore many positive elements within the premodern and modern worldviews.[28] This type is most commonly associated with Roman Catholic theologians, for example in the work of former Pope John Paul II, current Pope Benedict XVI (especially seen in his writings as Cardinal Ratzinger), and George William Rutler. Rutler advocates a revivalist Roman Catholic position based on pre-

---

24 David Ray Griffin, "Introduction: Varieties of Postmodern Theology," in David Ray Griffin, William A. Beardslee, and Joe Holland, *Varieties of Postmodern Theology* (Albany: State University of New York Press, 1989), pp. 3–5. Other authors would follow Griffin in these classifications. For example, Carson, *The Gagging of God*, pp. 79–80; Dockery, "The Challenge of Postmodernism," pp. 16–17; Millard J. Erickson, *Christian Theology*, 2nd edn (Grand Rapids: Baker, 1998), pp. 167–8; and Patrick Evrard and Pierre Gisel, "Présentation," in *La Théologie en postmodernité*, eds Pierre Gisel and Patrick Evrard (Geneva: Labor et Fides, 1996), pp. 8–9. More recently, Kevin J. Vanhoozer's edited work, *The Cambridge Companion to Postmodern Theology* (Cambridge: Cambridge University Press, 2003), identifies seven distinctive postmodern theologies.

25 Terrence W. Tilley, ed., *Postmodern Theologies: The Challenge of Religious Diversity* (Maryknoll: Orbis Books, 1995), p. 115. Tilley argues for an atypical approach to the classification of postmodern theologies, which he claims shows a clearer connection across traditions and denominations, see pp. 115–18.

26 Postliberalism is distinctively an American/British movement originally associated with Yale Divinity School that seeks to reverse accommodations of modernism into Christianity. It emphasizes the value of narrative as a hermeneutic for biblical interpretation and the importance of language over experience. It is very much associated with postmodernism in its rejection of Enlightenment meta-narratives. See Roger E. Olson, "Back to the Bible (Almost): Why Yale's postliberal theologians deserve an evangelical hearing," *Christianity Today*, (May 20, 1996): 31; Klauspeter Blaser, "Variété des théologies postmodernes et crise des 'fondationalismes,'" in *La Théologie en postmodernité*, pp. 194; 203–11.

27 Tilley, *Postmodern Theologies*, p. viii.

28 See Dockery, "The Challenge of Postmodernism," pp. 16–17.

modern life. He does not even consider ecumenical ideals, and his comments on Protestantism are quite negative. For Rutler, we must restore the unifying Catholic worldview which was destroyed with the Enlightenment and Protestantism. We must restore full papal infallibility and return to the immutable doctrines of the faith.[29]

The restorationist position, however, is not only limited to Roman Catholic theologians. Griffin mentions that affinity to this form of postmodern theology is also evidenced by Lutheran theologian Richard John Neuhaus in his work, *The Catholic Moment: The Paradox of the Church in the Postmodern World* (San Francisco: Harper & Row, 1987).[30] Although not mentioned by Griffin, this perspective is also expressed in the work of Methodist theologian Thomas C. Oden, who advocates a return to classical spiritual disciplines in the face of disillusionment with modernity. Oden submits:

> But in this present ecumenical environment it seems most fitting to focus primarily on current evangelical strains of the postmodern rediscovery of ancient ecumenical Christianity. The European and American old-line Reformed and Lutheran traditions have already had their go at theological renewal in the five decades of Reformed neo-orthodoxy of the period from 1920–1970. But those days were never celebrated heartily by other more marginalized American evangelicals or the heirs of the revivalist or sanctificationist traditions.[31]

Christopher Hall also expresses a kindred restorationist spirit with Oden in his plea to return to patristic studies. He claims that the "tradition embodied in the reflections of the church fathers on Scripture possesses the flexibility and responsiveness to meet the interpretative and ethical challenges the contemporary world poses."[32]

Liberationist Theology

A liberationist postmodern theology emphasizes pluralistic values and the transformation of oppressive social and political structures. A primary representative of this approach would be the African American, neo-Marxist, pragmatic theology of Cornel West, as well as other theologies of communal praxis.[33] This would include certain feminist theologies (as seen for example in the work of Sharon Welch), the Latin-American liberation theology of Gustavo Gutiérrez, and even the Baptist

---

29 Griffin, "Introduction: Varieties of Postmodern Theology," pp. 5–6.

30 Ibid., p. 5

31 Thomas C. Oden, "The Death of Modernity and Postmodern Evangelical Spirituality," in *The Challenge of Postmodernism*, ed. David S. Dockery, pp. 22–3. See also Oden, *After Modernity What? Agenda for Theology* (Grand Rapids: Zondervan, 1990).

32 Christopher Hall, *Reading Scripture with the Church Fathers* (Downers Grove: InterVarsity, 1998), p. 31.

33 See Griffin, "Introduction: Varieties of Postmodern Theology," p. 4 in David Ray Griffin, William A. Beardslee, and Joe Holland, *Varieties of Postmodern Theology*, and William A. Beardslee, "Cornell West's Postmodern Theology," Ibid., pp. 149–53.

theology of J.W. McClendon, Jr.[34] Although these expressions of postmodern liberation theology are quite diverse in their traditions and their use of language, they each emphasize a liberation community. As Tilley comments:

> The communities of solidarity, resistance, and fellowship are not composed by people unattracted by the charm of the cultures which valorize dominance, exclusivity, and comfort. The community of struggle is where eternal rest is found and where perpetual light can be found—if rest and light are available anywhere in a postmodern world.[35]

Liberation theologies emphasize the reconciliation of doctrine and ethics, theology and sociology. Modern theologies have often bifurcated systematic theology from theological and social ethics. Consequently, theological doctrines have been expressed outside the crucible and immediate context of the sin-marred world in which we live. A truly postmodern liberation theology does not simply articulate general truths about reality, but expresses them in relation to the pragmatic issues at hand.[36]

Constructive, Revisionary or Process Theology

This third type of postmodern theology understands that western culture is still very much indebted to modernism, while recognizing that a shift is taking place. Abandoning many modernist metaphysical assumptions, it attempts a new postmodern worldview through process theology. This view is characteristically represented by David R. Griffin and William A. Beardslee in the Protestant vein, and David Tracy and Joe Holland in the Roman Catholic vein. Thomas Berry, Matthew Fox, Schubert Ogden, and Gordon Kaufman are other names of scholars who may be associated with this position.[37] Griffin contrasts his "contructive" postmodern theology with "deconstructive" (eliminative) theology:

> Revisionary postmodernism resists the nihilistic conclusions of eliminative postmodernism, not by reaffirming the supernatural God, but by rejecting the premises about nature and perception that were formed under the influence of belief in that God.[38]

In this view, the key concept is *creativity*. The actual world is made up of creative events and societies which are formed by those events. The human soul (or mind, according to Griffin) is one such society which is made of a series of creative events at a high level. The human body is also a society which is made of a variety of

---

34 See Tilley, *Postmodern Theologies*, pp. 115–51.

35 Ibid., p. 151.

36 See Griffin, "Postmodern Theology as Liberation Theology: A Response to Harvey Cox," *Varieties of Postmodern Theology*, pp. 81, 82.

37 See Patrick Evrard and Pierre Gisel, "Présentation," p. 9; Griffin, "Introduction: Varieties of Postmodern Theology," p. 3; and, Tilley, *Postmodern Theologies*, p. 28.

38 David Ray Griffin, "Postmodern Theology and A/theology: A Response to Mark C. Taylor," in *Varieties of Postmodern Theology*, p. 42.

many low level creative events of various stages. Consequently, Griffin purports, there is not a mind-body problem since both are made of creative events which exercise both final and efficient causation. There is also no problem with the modern notion of an isolated self because, in Griffin's view, "completely real individuals" occur as occasions of experience which arise from relations to prior occasions of experience.[39]

Griffin's Whiteheadian notion of God, of course, is by no means omniscient or omnipotent. As Griffin states: "Whether we will destroy our planet prematurely is not yet knowable, even by God. Whether we will do so is up to the present and future decisions of creatures."[40] According to Griffin, God is naturally related to the world. The basic principles of existence apply to God as they do to other things. God cannot interrupt natural, causal processes at any time. Instead, God is to be considered the "soul of the universe." As Griffin states: "What exists necessarily is not God alone, but God–and–a–world."[41]

Deconstructive Theology

The efforts of this book will be specifically directed towards engaging postmodern deconstructive theology. It is perhaps this "deconstructionist" position which has been most adamant in refuting the modernist position.[42] As previously mentioned, Griffin calls this type of postmodern theology "eliminative postmodernism." It is a type of theology that attempts, through subversion, to bring about the self-destruction of the modern worldview into an non-worldview through its denial of objectivity. This is also directly applied to the context of theology.[43] It is due to such adamant denial of objectivity and radical questioning of the nature of truth that I have have found the deconstructionist position the most provocative for theological investigation today.

Focus and Limits of Study

I have chosen to limit my discussion to six thinkers with respect to postmodern deconstructive theology. The first three are characteristic of postmodern deconstructionism and its European roots: Jean-François Lyotard, Jacques Derrida, and Michel Foucault. The next two are representative of deconstruction in the United States: Mark C. Taylor and Richard Rorty. Finally, I will discuss deconstruction in Britain with Don Cupitt. Of these six thinkers, only two (Mark C. Taylor and Don Cupitt) may be properly considered "theologians," and neither of these two actually

---

39 Griffin, "Postmodern Theology and A/theology: A Response to Mark C. Taylor," pp. 42–3.

40 Ibid., p. 50.

41 Ibid., p. 48.

42 See Carson, *The Gagging of God,* p. 21.

43 Griffin, "Postmodern Theology and A/theology: A Response to Mark C. Taylor," p. 29; and Griffin, "Introduction: Varieties of Postmodern Theology," pp. 3–4.

hold formal positions in departments of theology. Nonetheless, each of the above authors has produced works which are often cited in current theological works and have greatly impacted postmodern deconstructive theology. In this respect one may consider each of these thinkers "makers of theology" even though several of them are not properly theologians themselves.[44]

I will briefly discuss Lyotard because much of postmodern deconstructionist theology is based on his dissolution of meta-narratives. Deconstructive theologian Mark C. Taylor shares Lyotard's parting from established patterns into a life of "directionless movement."[45] However, the term "deconstruction" is most properly associated with the prominent figure of Jacques Derrida. Although Derrida was certainly aware of the religious characteristics of deconstruction, "Christian theology does not form a distinctive part of his intellectual history."[46] Yet, there are many theological considerations which Derrida addressed in his works.

Mark C. Taylor, Richard Rorty, and Don Cupitt are included because they are most often associated with postmodern deconstructive theology derived from the French-based, poststructuralism of Derrida. It may be argued that there are better representatives of postmodern deconstructive theology than Rorty in North America. For example, one may rightfully include John D. Caputo, Charles E. Winquist, Carl A. Raschke, and Edith Wyschogrod, among others from the list of those who would be worthy representatives of work done in postmodern deconstructive theology in America. However, for the purposes of this investigation of contributions and insights of deconstructive theology for evangelical apologetic methodology, I will limit the discussion to two of the most often cited authors in contemporary theological works: Mark C. Taylor and Richard Rorty.

Although Foucault is certainly considered "postmodern," he is not always associated with deconstructionism. I have included Foucault because of his "deconstruction" of systems of power and discipline that have greatly affected theological and religious thinking. Theological edifices which seemed immovable with modernism, are seen as eroded and dissolved.[47] I agree with Millard Erickson who lists Derrida, Lyotard, and Foucault as deconstructive, "radical, postmodernist

---

44 As Stephen D. Moore points out, "Derrida took elaborate 'precautions' (his term) to avoid coming off sounding like a theologian, or a negative theologian, or even a negative atheologian." Yet, as he continues, "Foucault took few such precautions; ..." In fact, Moore instructs us that Foucault actually twice even compared his work to that of negative theology. See Stephen D. Moore, *Poststructuralism and the New Testament* (Minneapolis: Fortress Press, 1994), p. 93 and Ibid., note 38.

45 William A. Beardslee, "Christ in the Postmodern Age: Reflections Inspired by Jean-François Lyotard," in *Varieties of Postmodern Theology*, p. 67.

46 Kevin Hart, *The Trespass of the Sign* (Cambridge: Cambridge University Press, 1989) p. x.

47 Tilley, *Postmodern Theologies,* pp. vii–viii.

philosophers" who have influenced theologies which have eliminated or deconstructed doctrines as traditional as God.[48]

As one can see, Rorty has been greatly influenced by the work of Derrida. Griffin includes Rorty as a thinker typical of deconstructive or eliminative postmodern thought.[49] Preferring the term "ultra–modern" to the term "postmodern," Methodist theologian Thomas Oden claims that both Richard Rorty and Jacques Derrida are "ultra-modern" writers characteristic of "deconstructionist literary criticism and relativistic nihilism" which demonstrate philosophical commitments to the despair of relativism.[50] Some would contend, as Oden, that deconstructive theology does not fit the postmodern label. Rather, such "theories of dissolution" are better considered "ultramodern" or "mostmodern" because of their denial of any unity at the heart of today's world of plurality. It is argued that such a denial is a main constituent of liberal modernism.[51] Although deconstructive postmodernists seek to undermine modernist Enlightenment structures, they paradoxically use Enlightenment methods, some suggest, in order to argue their points. Deconstructionists, theologian Nancey Murphy argues, "share too many assumptions with their modern predecessors to count as truly postmodern."[52] In a similar fashion, Graham Ward claims that they represent the "apotheosis" of liberalism—with thinking "rooted in the liberal ethics and anthropology of modernity ...."[53]

I can agree that not all deconstructive thinkers would necessarily accept the title 'postmodernist'."[54] For example, Michel Foucault is most often considered "postmodern," but he himself questions the use of this term:

> What are we here calling postmodernity? I'm not up to date ... neither do I grasp the kinds of problems indicated by the use of this term—or how they would be common to people thought of as being "postmodern" ... I do not understand what kind of problem is common to the people we call postmodern or post-structuralist.[55]

---

48   Erickson, *Christian Theology*, p. 167. In this sense as well, I am not intending to restrict the term "deconstruction" simply to the field of literary criticism. I would, as Erickson's term suggests, affirm the broader meaning of deconstruction as "radical postmodernism."

49   See Griffin, "Introduction: Varieties of Postmodern Theology," p. 3.

50   Thomas C. Oden, "The Death of Modernity and Postmodern Evangelical Spirituality," in *The Challenge of Postmodernism: An Evangelical Engagement*, p. 26.

51   Tilley, *Postmodern Theologies,* p. 164. Nancey Murphy and James Wm. McClendon, Jr also argue for this perspective in Nancey Murphy and James Wm. McClendon Jr, "Distinguishing Modern and Postmodern Theologies," *Modern Theology* 5/3 (1989): 199–212, see especially pp. 211–12.

52   Murphy, *Beyond Liberalism & Fundamentalism*, p. 87.

53   Graham Ward, "Introduction, or A Guide to Theological Thinking in Cyberspace," in *The Postmodern God: A Theological Reader*, ed. Graham Ward (Oxford: Blackwell, 1997), p. xl.

54   See Tilley, *Postmodern Theologies*, p. 41–2.

55   Michel Foucault cited in Andrew Gustafson, "Apologetically Listening to Derrida."

Although these criticisms have merit, I will not attempt to change the nomenclature in this study. Rather, I will suggest that the terms "postmodern" and "deconstruction," although inadequate in several respects, are terms which have been generally applied to the thinking of the aforementioned authors. There are certainly evident marks of modernist thinking rooted in postmodernist thinking. However, there are significant intellectual differences, at least in the works of these writers, that in our opinion still merit the term "postmodern." Since these terms have been used to describe, critique and evoke certain styles and modes of academic thought, for heuristic purposes, I will continue to use them.

These prolific authors address far too many issues for any presumption of exhaustive treatment or criticism, nor is this the intention of this book. Instead I wish to specifically address several crucial theological claims and/or implications from each author in order to provide a critical appropriation. I hope to achieve enough familiarity with the authors to identify the roots of major concerns expressed in deconstructive theology. It is my desire to locate, from these "case studies," crucial points for conversational contact available for apologetic dialogue. I will discuss positive insights with each thinker, while abnegating others. I readily acknowledge that a project of this nature cannot be comprehensive, but must be selective in choosing authors and positions.

This book will also limit itself as to the depth to which it will pursue the philosophical backgrounds of the authors considered. Much can be said regarding how Hegel, Nietzsche, Habermas, Gadamer, and many others have influenced deconstructive authors and much of postmodern thought. But due to the scope of this study, only cursory explanations and backgrounds will be provided where appropriate. I have attempted to identify those which most crucially and integrally relate to postmodern deconstructionism, are most often cited in evangelical theological literature, and more specifically those authors whose works have the most direct implications for theology and the development of interactional insights for Christian apologetics.[56]

---

56 I readily admit that my reading is colored by my own cultural and geographical perceptions. Additionally, I should say that awareness and influence of postmodern philosophy and theology extends far beyond the borders of Continental Europe, Great Britain and the United States. By way of example, note the works of V.Y. Mudimbe, African scholar and Professor of Romance Languages and Comparative Literature at Duke University. In his award–winning book, *The Invention of Africa: Gnosis, Philosophy, and the Order of Knowledge* (Bloomington and Indianapolis: Indiana University Press, 1988), Mudimbe attempts to "deconstruct" the meaning of "Africa." He presents, in a manner reminiscent of Foucault, an "archaeological" investigation pertaining to power and knowledge in discourse about Africa. (p. xi). Mudimbe claims that "it is important to note that African ideology, as a body of reflexions and questions, springs from the same lines of dissolution that, in the kingdom of the Same, allowed Lévi–Strauss's and Foucault's crises" (p. 43). Mudimbe demonstrates how postmodern deconstructionist trends in Western scholarship have indeed made an impact on African thought (see pp. 165–68, 175). Also see Mudimbe's sequel, *The Idea of Africa* (Bloomington and Indianapolis: Indiana University Press, 1994). This book as well keenly demonstrates deep postmodern concerns. In his preface he maintains that African

Although some readers may not agree with my conclusions or presentations, it is my desire to present a fair critique of the issues considered.

Finally, this book is not simply a critique or analysis of the deconstructionist movement as a whole, influencing a broad range disciplines, most notably in circles of American literary criticism. Instead, as I have stressed, I am more specifically attempting to examine the implications of deconstructionist theology for Christian apologetic discussion and thought. I will attempt to discover, through critical interaction with postmodern deconstructive theologies, insights on how one may sustain or modify Christian apologetic work through engagement with such theologies. It is not my desire to be combative, but interactive. This work will not provide substantial arguments for belief in Christianity, although it is inextricably assumed throughout. Instead, I am primarily speaking to the ongoing creation of an environment for apologetic engagement and dialogue. At times I will strongly express disagreement and opposition, yet I will also acknowledge strengths in opposing perspectives and learn lessons from points of disparity. Before beginning an examination of postmodern deconstructive theology, however, I will first attempt to lay some brief descriptive groundwork of its historical context.

---

discourses have been "silenced" or "converted by conquering Western discourses." Mudimbe contends that this "will to truth" in the "Western order" has for centuries been "inventing Africa" (pp. xiv, xv).

Chapter 2

Historical Context:
From Modernism to Postmodernism

In order to express the context of postmodern deconstructive theology, a brief historical overview on the progression from modernism to postmodernism as an intellectual movement is essential.[1] I admit the risk of oversimplification and trivialization. Obviously, the entire historical, cultural and theological development from modernity, the Enlightenment, and into postmodernity cannot be described or developed in view of the scope of this chapter. Significant figures and complexities of the authors addressed will be noticeably omitted. Also, it is not my intention to homogenize each of these complex authors into some monolithic "postmodern project." I simply wish to demonstrate the broad range of influences and issues evident in these thinkers significant in the development of deconstructive theological thought.

The Enlightenment to Modernity: Historical and Philosophical Roots

Francis Bacon (1561–1626)

The Renaissance thinker Francis Bacon is considered a pivotal figure between the Renaissance and Enlightenment. Bacon paved the way forward through his iconoclasm of past, misplaced scientific allegiances which led to hasty generalizations with former thinkers. Instead, Bacon insisted on the value of inductive reasoning

---

1 I would offer a caveat at this juncture. Mark C. Taylor offers the pessimistic claim that "amid the debris of Western philosophy – history, thematics, and geneaology are impossible." Mark C. Taylor, *Altarity* (Chicago: The University of Chicago Press, 1987), p. xxx. I am less pessimistic than Taylor, but would agree that a strict genealogical tracing of this development is impossible. But as Taylor concedes, and I agree, images recur which intersect and transect various texts-images which can be traced through a matrix of changing associations and relations. (*Altarity*, p. xxx). Furthermore, as Richard Rorty submits, we cannot avoid contextualization, we can only hope for recontextualization. It is to these suppositions I would appeal as a rationale for a chapter of this nature. See Richard Rorty, *Essays On Heidegger and Others: Philosophical Papers Volume 2* (Cambridge: Cambridge University Press, 1991), p. 2.

and much experimentation.[2] One may see evidence of Bacon's iconoclasm, even indignation, from his *Novum Organum* (1620), *First Book*:

11. As the present sciences are useless for the discovery of effects, so the present system of logic is useless for the discovery of the sciences.
12. The present system of logic rather assists in confirming and rendering inveterate the errors founded on vulgar notions than in searching after truth, and is therefore more hurtful than useful.[3]

Then, near the closing of the *First Book*, he claims that if "men had at their command a proper history of nature and experience," consistently applying themselves to it, putting aside mere opinions, restraining themselves from generalization, and fully exerting their minds, then they may "fall into our way of interpretation without the aid of any art."[4]

For Bacon, the emerging Age of Reason and science would be the key to help man harness his environment. Knowledge would bring power—the power to use the external world for our personal benefit. This notion set the perfect stage for the Enlightenment project, characterizing the oncoming of modernity.[5] Bacon's conceptions were revolutionary both for their methodological implications, and their expressions of the inherent value of the scientific method itself.[6]

It is important to note that Bacon's premises were based on his theological worldview. As Bacon states in his *Advancement of Learning*: "[f]or nothing can fill, much less extend the soul of man, but God and the contemplation of God...."[7] Bacon was clearly a theist, and he was certainly not hostile to the church. Although he wished to separate the endeavors of metaphysics from those of science, and advocate man's independent ability to reason, he still linked part of man's knowledge to divine origin.[8]

---

2   Cf. Stanley J. Grenz, *A Primer On Postmodernism* (Grand Rapids: Eerdmans, 1996), pp. 58–9; Antoine Vergote, *Modernité et Christianisme: Interrogations critiques réciproques* (Paris: Les Editions du Cerf, 1999), pp. 39–40; and Kevin J. Vanhoozer, *Is There a Meaning in This Text?* (Grand Rapids: Zondervan, 1998), pp. 38–9. Vanhoozer compares Bacon's iconoclastic thinking (and considers it precursory) to that of Derrida in its eschewing of generalities for that of particulars (p. 39).

3   Francis Bacon, *Novum Organum*, Great Books of the Western World, ed. Robert Maynard Hutchins, 54 vols, vol. 30 (Chicago: Encyclopaedia Britannica, Inc., 1952), p. 107.

4   Bacon, *Novum Organum*, p. 136.

5   Grenz, *A Primer On Postmodernism*, pp. 58–9.

6   See Gilbert Hottois, *De la Renaissance à la Postmodernité*, 2e edn (Paris–Bruxelles: De Boeck Université, 1998), p. 49.

7   Francis Bacon, *Of the Proficience and Advancement of Learning: Divine and Humane*, Great Books of the Western World, ed. Robert Maynard Hutchins, 54 vols, vol. 30 (Chicago: Encyclopaedia Britannica, Inc., 1952), p. 3. Also see David West, *An Introduction to Continental Philosophy* (Cambridge, Mass.: Blackwell, 1996), p. 11.

8   Allan B. Wolter, O.F.M., "Bacon, Francis," in *Encyclopedia of Philosophy*, ed. Paul Edwards (New York: Macmillan Pub. Co. and The Free Press, 1967), p. 238.

Sir Isaac Newton (1642–1727)

One also sees a scientific revolution in the pioneering work of Sir Isaac Newton and his predecessor Galileo (1564–1642). Their use of scientific experimentation with an accompanying mechanistic view of the world, was characterisitic of the onset of modernism. Again, the goal for Newton was not merely the development of science, but of theology. Newton's belief in science was grounded in his belief that science would enhance one's understanding of God's greatness.[9] This is expressed in the well-known epitaph intended for Newton by the poet Alexander Pope (1688–1744):

> Nature and Nature's laws lay hid in night:
> God said, Let Newton be! and all was Light.

Nature became a vital and revered life-force in all human affairs, and her laws essentially became a canonized theology of sorts.[10] These factors contributed to setting the scene for the Enlightenment project and the following birth of modernity.

The Enlightenment period is often associated with the end of the Thirty Years War (1648), the Peace of Westphalia, and up to the French Revolution (1789). But the entire "intellectual" Enlightenment, one may say, stems from Francis Bacon's *Novum Organum* (1620) up to Kant's *Critique of Pure Reason* (1781). Within this "intellectual" Enlightenment, two significant "revolutions" or transformations ushered in Enlightenment principles of nature, reason, autonomy, harmony and optimism. The first was this scientific revolution I have noted in the work of men such as Bacon and Newton. The second was a major philosophical revolution in the work of René Descartes.[11]

René Descartes (1596–1650)

While Descartes was on a tour of duty in Germany in November, 1619, he sat one day in small room in a village on the Danube thinking about how he could find a unifying basis for all knowledge. He wished to provide all forms of knowledge with the same positive footing and certainty as mathematics. In a sudden moment

---

9 Grenz, *A Primer On Postmodernism*, pp. 49–50; and Stanley J. Grenz and Roger E. Olson, *Twentieth Century Theology: God and the World in a Transitional Age* (Downers Grove: InterVarsity, 1992), pp. 19–20.

10 See James C. Livingston, *Modern Christian Thought* (London: Collier, 1971), pp. 4–5.

11 Livingston, *Modern Christian Thought*, pp. 1–2; Grenz, *A Primer On Postmodernism*, pp. 60, 63. Grenz and Olson, *Twentieth Century Theology* pp. 20–22. Also see Hottois, *De la Renaissance à la Postmodernité*, pp. 64–6.

of inspiration, followed by a series of dreams that same evening, he believed he was given the key to achieve this ambitious project.[12]

Ironically, Descartes's method by which to achieve such certainty was a method of radical skepticism. He attempted to doubt everything he possibly could in order to achieve a limited confidence only in that which he found it impossible to doubt.[13] This is where Descartes came to the conclusion (influenced by Augustine)[14] of his famous *cogito*: "*Cogito ergo sum*"—"Je pense donc je suis"—"I think, therefore I am." In order to doubt, one must think. Therefore the "I" must exist in order to think to be able to doubt.[15]

Descartes proceeds to use this *cogito* as a point of support on which he may stack up more knowledge which is certain. Descartes reasons that if he can doubt the existence of his body, then his body cannot be a defining or essential characteristic of his existence. It may be the case that it is a contingent or accompanying property or characteristic. It is this developing dualism of mind and matter which revolutionized European thought. The self became a disembodied subject of experience which must find its purpose within itself.[16] With Descartes, it has been suggested, one may picture the mind as a sealed sphere, completely enclosed from the outside world. This sphere has some type of tangential relationship with another sphere, which is the body. There exists some causal relationship between the two spheres but exactly why this is the case is indeterminable. Yet, Descartes postulated that God must have made us with a substantial consciousness. Our consciousness is not referential, but our minds represent external realities.[17]

For Descartes as well, his system was built upon a theological base.[18] But Descartes's system initiated a shift in theological/philosophical thinking by placing the reasoning subject, the "self," as the starting point for philosophical thinking instead of divine revelation.[19] Robert C. Solomon, a specialist in continental

---

12 Robert Maynard Hutchins, ed., *Biographical Note: René Descartes, 1596–1650*, Great Books of the Western World, 54 vols, vol. 31 (Chicago: William Benton, 1952), p. ix; and Donald A. Cress, "Editor's Preface," in René Descartes, *Meditations on First Philosophy* (Indianapolis: Hackett Publishing Company, Inc., 1979), p. vii.

13 See René Descartes, *Meditations on First Philosophy*, trans. Donald A. Cress (Indianapolis and Cambridge: Hackett Publishing Company, Inc., 1979), pp. 17–19. Also See Vergote, *Modernité et Christianisme*, p. 55.

14 See Augustine, *The City of God*, Book XI, Chapter 26. Nicene and Post-Nicene Fathers: First Series, ed. Philip Schaff (Peabody: Hendrickson, 1994), p. 220.

15 Descartes, *Meditations*, p. 35; also see Hottois, *De la Renaissance à la Postmodernité*, pp. 68–9; and West, *An Introduction to Continental Philosophy*, p. 13.

16 West, *An Introduction to Continental Philosophy*, pp. 12–13.

17 William Barrett and Henry D. Aiken, "Introduction to Phenomenology and Existentialism,"in William Barrett and Henry D. Aiken (eds), *Philosophy in the Twentieth Century*, 4 vols, vol. 3 (New York: Random House, 1962), p. 135.

18 Gilbert Hottois notes that Descartes actually needs his notion of God for his methods to succeed. See Hottois, *De la Renaissance à la Postmodernité*, pp. 69–71.

19 Grenz and Olson, *Twentieth Century Theology*, p. 19.

philosophy, claims that Descartes was the "founder of the modern philosophical obsession with the self as the locus and arbiter of knowledge."[20] In fact, it is this transcendental self which becomes, according to Solomon, "the star performer in modern European philosophy ... whose nature and ambitions were unprecedentedly arrogant, presumptuously cosmic, and consequently mysterious."[21] Solomon submits that it is Descartes's emphasis upon a first-person objectivity of experience which drives European philosophy forward from this time on. But it is actually with Kant where the claims of the self attain even newer and greater proportions.[22]

Immanuel Kant (1724–1804)

The scientific revolution with the work of men such as Bacon and Newton, combined with the philosophical revolution of Descartes ushered in Enlightenment thought. Likewise, the second "Copernican Revolution" of Kant helped to usher it out.[23] With Kant, the self became not simply the focal point of philosophical concern, but it became its entire subject matter.[24] With Copernicus' "natural revolution," the sun became the center of the solar system. With Kant's "intellectual revolution" the mind became the epistemological center of human knowledge.[25]

Kant's revolutionary thinking was a response to the epistemological problems of empiricism. For the empiricists, such as John Locke and David Hume, the mind functions passively, without innate ideas. The mind was, according to Locke, an empty vessel or blank slate (*tabula rasa*) that receives impressions from the external world through the senses.[26]

The radical skepticism of Hume awoke Kant from his "dogmatic slumbers." Hume was greatly influenced by Newton, exalting the use of reason and appealing to that which can be known by the senses. Yet reason and experience are extremely limited for Hume—for one cannot make a necessary connection between cause and effect, either rationally or experientially.[27] So, one cannot have actual knowledge of substances or objects in the external world. Belief in the external world or even belief in the identity of the self is just a result of a habit of the mind. Since there is no objective unifying factor which necessarily links perceptions, they are only unified

---

20 Robert C. Solomon, *Continental Philosophy Since 1750: The Rise and Fall of the Self* (Oxford: Oxford University Press, 1988), p. 5.

21 Ibid., p. 4.

22 Ibid., p. 6.

23 See Immanuel Kant, *Critique of Pure Reason*, trans. Norman Kemp Smith (New York: St. Martin's Press, 1929), p. 22.

24 Solomon, *Continental Philosophy Since 1750*, p. 6.

25 See Grenz and Olson, *Twentieth Century Theology*, p. 26.

26 John Locke, *An Essay Concerning Human Understanding*, 1690. See also Grenz and Olson, *Twentieth Century Theology*, p. 26; and Livingston, *Modern Christian Thought*, p. 64.

27 Solomon, *Continental Philosophy Since 1750: The Rise and Fall of the Self*, pp. 13–14.

through the imagination. With this in mind, for Hume, metaphysics lost its firm footing, and the arguments of natural theology became uncertain.[28]

Kant took up this challenge with the publication of his *Critique of Pure Reason* (1781). Refusing to accept such a skeptical rejection of all metaphysical concepts, Kant attempted to reconcile the insights of both the rationalists and the empiricists.[29] He separated notions of *pure intuitions* (or concepts) and *empirical intuitions*: "Pure intuitions or pure concepts alone are possible *a priori*, empirical intuitions and empirical concepts only *a posteriori*."[30] Now Kant agreed that a great deal of our "knowledge" is derived from experience, as the empiricists argue, but it depends on concepts from the mind to organize those experiences.[31]

Kant's essential and critical question in the *Critique of Pure Reason* was: "How are a priori synthetic judgments possible?"[32] He believed that the reason that metaphysics had been in such a condition of "uncertainty and contradiction" was due to the failure to consider this question and to articulate the distinction between analytic and synthetic judgments.[33] Kant submitted that the mind is not passive, as the empiricists reasoned. Rather, the mind is active and imposes its cognitive forms upon the material of experience for interpretation. These forms or "categories," are a priori and unobservable. But it is through these categories of experience whereby we obtain knowledge of *phenomena*. But we cannot know the *Ding an sich*, the thing-in-itself, the noumenal or supersensible. The mind can conceive of the noumenal (i.e. a transcendent Being), but the categories are limited to the phenomenal world in terms of producing "knowledge."[34] This line of thought led Kant to his famous statement: "I have therefore found it necessary to deny *knowledge*, in order to make room for *faith*."[35]

Robert C. Solomon adeptly calls Kant's position "transcendental pretence." This "transcendental pretence" is the unsubstantiated presupposition that human experience is universal. It implies that reason dictates that one set of morals or form of government can be legislated for humankind and defended through rational argumentation. Developed to its full extent, transcendental pretence has two major characteristics: the richness and expansion of the self as all–encompassing; and, the right to project from the subjective structures of one's mind to general truth claims on the nature of humanity.[36] With this in mind it becomes apparent how Kant's work was the apex of the Enlightenment project and the gate to the modern world.

---

28 Grenz and Olson, *Twentieth Century Theology*, pp. 26–7; and Livingston, *Modern Christian Thought*, p. 64.

29 See West, *An Introduction to Continental Philosophy*, p. 18.

30 Kant, *Critique of Pure Reason*, p. 92.

31 West, *An Introduction to Continental Philosophy*, p. 18.

32 Kant, *Critique of Pure Reason*, p. 55.

33 Ibid.

34 Livingston, *Modern Christian Thought*, p. 65.

35 Kant, *Critique of Pure Reason*, p. 29.

36 Solomon, *Continental Philosophy Since 1750*, pp. 1, 2, 7.

Traits of Modernity

Defining "modernity" is somewhat less elusive than defining "postmodernity," but it is still a bit of a conundrum. As I have suggested, modernist ideals stem from philosophical revolutions (such as Descartes, Kant) that occurred in history. For the purposes of this book, I will refer to the notion of modernity less as a historic movement than an intellectual ideology or attitude.[37] Some authors distinguish *modernity* from *modernism*. However, I will use them as essentially synonymous terms, or terms which are basically reciprocative and interconnected.[38]

Modernity is characterized by humanism and reason, progress and truth. It has been defined as a "vacuous self–congratulation."[39] Jean-François Lyotard designated the term *modern* as "any science that legitimates itself with reference to a metadiscourse … making an explicit appeal to some grand narrative …."[40] Modernity may also be described as an "applied rationality."[41] It is "applied" in the sense that it created industrialism and the "modern" state—deifying the notion of progress. History was given a purpose and meaning giving direction and eschatological motivation for diligent work through time.[42]

Methodist theologian Thomas C. Oden has described modernity as an "enchantment" that is "characterized by technological messianism, enlightenment idealism, quantifying empiricism, and the smug fantasy of inevitable progress."[43] I concur with Oden and would add that the "religion" of modernity stemmed directly from the Enlightenment project. Bacon and Newton pleaded for mankind to control the environment (and know God better through it) through the advancement of knowledge and scientific experimentation. With Descartes' method of doubt, the rational self moved to center stage. Kant reconciled rationalism and empiricism and

---

37 See Thomas C. Oden, *After Modernity What?: Agenda for Theology* (Grand Rapids: Zondervan, 1990), pp. 44–7, 50; and Thomas C. Oden, "The Death of Modernity and Postmodern Evangelical Spirituality," in *The Challenge of Postmodernism: An Evangelical Engagement*, ed. David S. Dockery (Grand Rapids: Baker, 1997), p. 24.

38 See for example, Martin Henry, "God in Postmodernity," *Irish Theological Quarterly* 63/1 (1998): 3–21. Although Henry concedes that these terms are indeed interconnected he associates *modernity* with historical, social, political, and scientific facts, and *modernism* as an intellectual/cultural movement (p. 3).

39 R. Winter, "Postmodern Sociology as a Democratic Educational Practice? Some Suggestions," in Br J Soc Ed, 12/4 (1991): 471 as quoted in Paul Sampson, "The Rise of postmodernity," in *Faith and Modernity*, ed. Paul Sampson, Vinay Samuel, and Chris Sugden (Oxford: Regnum, 1994), p. 35.

40 Jean-François Lyotard, *The Postmodern Condition*, trans. Geoff Bennington and Brian Massumi (Minneapolis: University of Minnesota Press, 1984), p. xxiii.

41 See James D. Hunter, "What is Modernity? Historical Roots and Contemporary Features," in *Faith and Modernity*, ed. Paul Sampson, Vinay Samuel, and Chris Sugden (Oxford: Regnum, 1994), pp. 16–18.

42 Hunter, "What is Modernity?," pp. 20–21.

43 Oden, "The Death of Modernity," p. 24. Also note Vergote, *Modernité et Christianisme*, p. 189. Here Vergote notes a priori elements of modern rationalism.

moved the nature of the self to a transcendental, universal status. Consequently, the notions of reason and progress were possible in all spheres of life because the transcendental self structures all experience universally.[44] It is this complete development of thought often called the "project of modernity." As Martin Henry observes, this was

> the attempt to expand human power and mastery over the world in a rationally controlled fashion. In its own way, it was a quasi–religious, or at least a teleologically inspired, i.e. goal-directed, total vision of reality, for it sought through constant progress to bring about the perfection, or the maximization, of human dominance over the environment.[45]

Modernity's Impact on Christianity

The notions of modernity had a severe impact on the nature of Christian faith. Kant's revolution challenged religious assumptions of the constitution of "knowledge." Any knowledge which circumvented the scientific method could not be justifiably claimed as "knowledge" of the phenomenal world.[46] As a result, seeds were sown for the religious agnosticism characteristic of modernism.[47] Once again, I want to emphasize that the roots of this philosophical revolution were not intentionally anti-Christian. Instead, as we have seen with each of these major figures, their thinking occurred within the context of Christian theism and faith.

Following Kant, however, it was the thinking subject, the self, which defined belief content, not some external authority. Old doctrinal affirmations and creeds became anachronistic. As David Wells notes: "The whole idea of confession, in consequence, has shifted from truth with an external and objective referent to intuition which is internal and subjective."[48]

At first, it may appear as though evangelical thought would have little to accommodate from Enlightenment thinking and modernity. Yet, evangelicalism has been considered "simultaneously anti-modern and modern, a complex mosaic of both traditional beliefs and modern practices."[49] In fact, many modernist assumptions have been uncritically incorporated into the evangelical world. Reformed philosophers of the late eighteenth century advocating Enlightenment preconceptions such as "common sense realism," greatly influenced early evangelical bibliology as seen in the works of Benjamin B. Warfield and Charles Hodge. It was argued that reason and rational inquiry lead to knowledge and understanding of the significance of Scripture. Modernity is about mastery, mastery through the rational and cognitive abilities of

---

44 See Solomon, *Continental Philosophy Since 1750*, pp. 15, 29.
45 See Henry, "God in Postmodernity," p. 4.
46 See Ibid., p. 4.
47 Livingston, *Modern Christian Thought*, p. 76.
48 Wells, *No Place for Truth*, p. 118.
49 Seel, "Modernity and Evangelicals," p. 291.

man to control his world. With this model, human reason became a foundation by which to judge God's revelation.[50]

In his work *A Passion For Truth*, Alister McGrath discusses four areas where Enlightenment thinking continues to negatively influence modern evangelical thought. The first is the nature of Scripture. With its insistence on propositional revelation, evangelicals often tend to view Scripture as a textbook of doctrines, overlooking its narrative character. The second is in the understanding of spirituality. Evangelical spirituality is often simply equated with rational understanding and knowledge of Scripture while neglecting emotional, relational and imaginative traits of spirituality. The third area is that of apologetics. Frequently, a universal human rationality is erroneously assumed when laying out an evangelical defense of the Christian faith. The fourth area of influence relates to evangelism. Often evangelicals are merely concerned with proclamation of propositional truths with the purpose to persuade acceptance of these propostional truths, neglecting the essential personal aspects of truth.[51] Of course, these areas should be considered as tendencies within evangelicalism, not characteristics common to all evangelicals, or attributes of the evangelical movement as a whole. The evangelical "movement" today is too broad to be simply labeled in this manner.

Exiting Modernism and Approaching Postmodernism

Some would submit that modernism is dead, obsolete, and no longer a viable cultural force or influence.[52] They would argue that modernism has been replaced by postmodernism.[53] I am not so sympathetic to such a claim. Certainly, many changes have taken place and will continue to take place as we plunge into the twenty-first century. From my perspective, modernism is not dead or obsolete. Many ideals of modernism still remain strong forces in contemporary thinking. As Douglas Groothuis observes: "The broad lay of the land philosophically is that modernism and postmodernism both overlap and contradict one another. Modernism is not dead; ...."[54] However, I would indeed argue that the base upon which modernism was built has been severely challenged and has lost its footing. In this respect I agree with R. Albert Mohler, Jr., who puts it this way:

> It is the foundations of modernity which have crumbled, but the superstructure appears intact with regard to many of modernity's most formidable challenges to Christian truth.

---

50 McGrath, *A Passion For Truth*, pp. 167–71.

51 Ibid., pp. 173–8.

52 See David S. Dockery, "The Challenge of Postmodernism," in *The Challenge of Postmodernism*, pp. 13–14; and Wells, *No Place for Truth*, p. 60.

53 Gene Edward Veith, Jr., *Postmodern Times: A Christian Guide to Contemporary Thought and Culture* (Wheaton: Crossway, 1994), p. 19.

54 Douglas Groothuis, *Truth Decay: Defending Christianity Against the Challenges of Postmodernism* (Downers Grove: InterVarsity, 2000), p. 58.

Though the crumbling foundations are certain to doom the structure above, evangelicals will risk disaster by employing a naïveté which underestimates the extended reach of modernity's corrosive ideological solvents. The modern worldview still prevails in the mass media, the formative educational institutions, and the popular Western consciousness. Modern assumptions still frame the thinking of most North Americans and Europeans—and it is still a powerful missionary movement around the globe.[55]

Parallel with this line of thought, Marc Augé prefers the term "surmodernité" (supra-modernity) to "post-modernité" because he fails to see the disappearance of modernity (especially from an economic perspective) in Europe.[56] This does not deny, however, that various postmodern worldviews have emerged and found expression at the same time. Again, in this book I am referring primarily to intellectual postmodernism as an ideology rather than a historical period, without denying its formation through a series of historical reactions and intellectual revolutions.

In my estimation, to speak of any movement of thought from modernism to postmodernism, it is also necessary to address romanticism. The romantic reaction to modernist ideals is crucial for understanding the beginnings of postmodern thought. Robert C. Solomon declares that romanticism was "anti-Enlightenment." Although he concedes that "it was part of the same middle-class, urban mentality that made up the core of the French and English Enlightenment—without its political opportunities."[57] Solomon's assessment seems a bit over zealous. Certainly, the romanticism of the early nineteenth century radically challenged the rationalism of the Enlightenment. However, the romantics were not necessarily seeking to repudiate the Enlightenment ideals, but to enlarge them, to return to a more richly diverse tradition which included both scientific reasoning and feeling. J.H. Randall explains it this way:

> It was the voicing of the conviction that life is broader than intelligence, and that the world is more than what physics can find in it. ... Experience, in its infinite richness and color and warmth and complexity, is something greater than any intelligible formulation of it ....[58]

In a sense, romanticism was dependent on Kant. But the romantic movement took Kant's transcendental ego to a higher, universal plane. Diversity, imagination and individual expression of the self became qualities of utmost importance. Experience

---

55 R. Albert Mohler, "The Integrity of the Evangelical Tradition and the Challenge of the Postmodern Paradigm," in *The Challenge of Postmodernism: An Evangelical Engagement*, ed. David S. Dockery (Grand Rapids: Baker, 1997), p. 83.

56 Marc Augé in "La surmodernité: héritage chrétien ou récurrrence polythéiste? Entretien avec Marc Augé," in Pierre-Olivier Monteil, *La Grâce et le Désordre* (Genève: Labor et Fides, 1998), p. 97.

57 Solomon, *Continental Philosophy Since 1750*, p. 47.

58 J.H. Randall, Jr., *The Making of the Modern Mind* (New York, 1926), p. 395, quoted in Livingston, *Modern Christian Thought*, p. 81.

could not be reduced to rationalism or science.[59] It was precisely on this point of the self, the individual, the "transcendental pretence," where Solomon concedes that the "Enlightenment and romanticism turned out to be more alike than opposed."[60]

Nature ceased to be considered the vast, cosmic machine of Bacon and Newton. Instead, it became a creative life form of diverse, unrestrained potential. Contrary to the deism which came to dominate Enlightenment thought, the romantics insisted on a God who is immanent in both nature and the self. For some, this naturally led to pantheism. God became simply the term for the soul of Nature. Man and Nature, Nature and God—all comprise an organic, aesthetic Whole.[61]

It is important be cognizant of these intellectual tensions when considering the transition from modernism, romanticism, on to postmodernism—especially deconstructive postmodernism.

G. W. F. Hegel (1770–1831)

Hegel may be considered as one of the precursors of postmodern intellectual thought. He was born as Enlightenment thinking was fading, and raised in the onset of romanticism. He was influenced by both movements, but accepted neither one completely.[62] This "dual" influence is aptly noted in the fact that Hegel took key images of romanticism and labeled them "reason."[63] He was opposed to one-sided rationalism but he was also against extreme emotionalism. He desired to dialectically reconcile these experiential opposites into a higher unity. In Hegel's early theological writings he sharply distinguished between objective ('theoretical') religion of understanding and subjective ('practical') religion of the heart. He was intensely critical of Christianity for its failure to manifest true religion. True religion is the fulfillment of love, and true love must embody a religious synthesis of both objective form and subjective feeling. Christianity failed to achieve such synthesis.[64]

Yet, Hegel changed his perspective of Christianity between the years 1800 to 1807. His former scathing, negative criticism toward Christianity became replaced and transcended. His new conception of Christianity was interpreted through the method of *Aufhebung*. For Hegel, the verb form of this word, *aufheben*, provided the necessary double meaning of both "to abolish," yet also, "move to a higher level."[65]

---

59 Livingston, *Modern Christian Thought*, pp. 81–2; also see Solomon, *Continental Philosophy Since 1750*, p. 48.

60 Solomon, *Continental Philosophy Since 1750*, p. 12.

61 See Livingston, *Modern Christian Thought*, pp. 81–2; and Veith, *Postmodern Times*, pp. 35–6.

62 Livingston, *Modern Christian Thought*, p. 144.

63 Solomon, *Continental Philosophy Since 1750*, p. 48.

64 Livingston, *Modern Christian Thought*, pp. 148, 145, 149; and Robert C. Solomon, *From Rationalism to Existentialism: The Existentialists and Their Nineteenth-Century Backgrounds* (New York: Humanities Press, 1972), p. 40.

65 Livingston, *Modern Christian Thought*, pp. 149–50. See also Steve Wilkins and Alan G. Padgett, *Christianity and Western Thought: A History of Philosophers, Ideas and*

Hegel's former rejection of Christianity in a traditional sense, provided the freedom he needed to see it in a new light. It was important for Christianity to be seen philosophically. Christianity must not be seen in a merely positivistic historicity, but in "the historical actualization of the unity of the divine and human and the coming into being of the Absolute Spirit."[66] Now, I am not suggesting that it is this movement toward such an absolutizing scheme which is precursory to postmodern deconstructive thought. In fact, the notion of an all-encompassing, absolutism would instead be seen as contrary to it. Rather, what is precursory is Hegel's line of thought with regard to "abolishing" Christianity for its inadequacies and failures, in order to then take that Christianity to a higher level. It is through this "dialectical reversal" where "the creator God dies and is resurrected in the creative subject."[67] In a similar sense, it will be observed that deconstructionism is about both abolishing *and* reconstructing. It is about dissecting texts, intellectual systems, and epistemological foundations to reveal the unwritten, unexpressed, and suppressed biases with a view toward reconstructive justice. Unlike Hegel, however, deconstruction never promises a reconstruction which produces an "Absolute," but only a boundless, ever-continual process of reconstructive justice in thought and life.

We may also consider Hegel a "precursor" to postmodern thought because he may have been, as German philosopher Jürgen Habermas claims, "the first philosopher to develop a clear concept of the modern" and also the first philosopher "for whom modernity became a problem."[68] Following Hegel's line of thought (as he has been understood), such an understanding of the modern implies that the modern itself is fading away. For example, philosophy for Hegel always shows up too late to provide instruction on how the world should be. Hegel artfully elucidates this idea in a passage from his "Preface" to *The Philosophy of Right*:

> As the thought of the world, it appears only when actuality is already there cut and dried after its process of formation has been completed. The teaching of the concept, which is also history's inescapable lesson, is that it is only when actuality is mature that the ideal first appears over against the real and that the ideal apprehends this same real world in its substance and builds it up for itself into the shape of an intellectual realm. When philosophy paints its grey in grey, then has a shape of life grown old. By philosophy's grey in grey it cannot be rejuvenated but only understood. The owl of Minerva spreads its wings only with the falling of the dusk.[69]

Movements, vol. 2 (Downers Grove: InterVarsity, 2000), p. 80. Such a manner of using a word loaded with double meaning to demonstrate a dialectic, is later used as a tool characteristic of postmodern deconstructive thought, especially in the works of Jacques Derrida and Mark C. Taylor.

66 Livingston, *Modern Christian Thought*, p. 150.

67 Taylor, *Altarity*, p. xxii.

68 Habermas, *The Philosophical Discourse of Modernity*, pp. 4, 43.

69 G.W.F. Hegel, *The Philosophy of Right*, Great Books of the Western World, ed. Robert Maynard Hutchins, 54 vols, vol. 46 (Chicago: Encyclopaedia Britannica, Inc., 1952), p. 7. For further commentary on this passage see Henry, "God in Postmodernity," pp. 6–7.

Accordingly, if modernity begins to be self-aware and self-critical, it ceases to be a living, vital force and a new era of thinking begins to emerge.[70] This parallels with Hegel's perspective of consciousness and absolute knowledge as well when he states at the end of his Introduction to *Phenomenology of Spirit*: "...when consciousness itself grasps this its own essence, it will signify the nature of absolute knowledge itself."[71]

Søren Kierkegaard (1813–1855)

Although Kierkegaard is often considered "the father" of Christian existentialism, he also profoundly influenced postmodern deconstructive tendencies, including a strong influence on post-modern a/theologian Mark C. Taylor. Taylor submits that "[i]t is difficult to imagine two thinkers who have done more to shape modern and postmodern consciousness than Hegel and Kierkegaard."[72] Kierkegaard's rejection of Hegel's totalizing, systematic, and optimistic thought is perhaps at the heart of postmodern deconstructionism even today.[73] The Hegelian link between human spiritual advancement and his notion of Absolute Spirit and its self-development through history was rejected by Kierkegaard in favor of the emphasis on the subjective, the individual. Truth is not found in the abstract impersonal principles of Hegel, but in the personal subject with passionate thinking.[74] For Kierkegaard, such aspiration and possibility for the attainment of absolute "truth" is unacceptable. All rationalistic philosophy, according to Kierkegaard, has a recurrent problem of neglecting the subjective element of human existence.[75]

So Kierkegaard rejected the Hegelian dialectic in favor of his own existential version expressed in three major spheres of life: the aesthetic, the ethical and the

---

70 See Henry, "God in Postmodernity," pp. 6–7.

71 G.W.F. Hegel, *Phenomenology of Spirit*, trans. A.V. Miller (Oxford: Oxford University Press, 1977), p. 57. Habermas later gives credit to this idea as well: "Indeed it is precisely modernization research that has contributed to the currency of the expression 'postmodern' even among social scientists. For in view of an evolutionarily autonomous, self-promoting modernization, social-scientific observers can all the more easily take leave of the conceptual horizon of Western rationalism in which modernity arose." Habermas, *The Philosophical Discourse of Modernity*, p. 3.

72 Mark C. Taylor, *Deconstructing Theology* (New York: Crossroad, 1982), p. xvii. Taylor also claims: "Although Kierkegaard is notably (and probably significantly) absent from the list of authors Derrida examines, Kierkegaard's ghost haunts the project of Deconstruction and indirectly informs much of its discourse," *Deconstructing Theology*, p. xix.

73 Ibid., p. xix. Similarly, John D. Caputo and Michael J. Scanlon maintain that Kierkegaard and Nietzsche "stand as the two greatest unveilers of modernity's secret dream to be the logos of its own onto-theology." John D. Caputo and Michael J. Scanlon, "Introduction," in John D. Caputo and Michael J. Scanlon (eds), *God, The Gift, and Postmodernism* (Bloomington and Indianapolis: Indiana University Press, 1999), p. 14.

74 Grenz and Olson, *Twentieth Century Theology*, p. 64; and Colin Brown, *Philosophy and the Christian Faith* (Downers Grove: InterVarsity, 1968), p. 128.

75 Solomon, *From Rationalism to Existentialism*, p. 78.

religious. It is significant to point out that the third (the religious) must not be construed as a synthesis or logical progression of the first two (the aesthetic and ethical)—but continual possibilities of the present.[76] The existential leap from the ethical to the religious appears in three essential characteristics of what Kierkegaard calls "Religion A." The first characterisitic is that of resignation. We have often heard of the "Knight of infinite resignation" in Kierkegaard's *Fear and Trembling*. One must approach God with such fear and trembling in resignation of things past. One must sever the ties of the world and success and all it entails to have a relationship with the Absolute God.[77] These notions of repetition of spheres of religious existence and the continual severing of past ties with infinite resignation remain important concepts, as will be observed, for postmodern thinking as well.

The second characteristic of anxiety or anguish (*angst*) occurs after this separation from the ties of the world, because of one's need for personal transformation of life due Kierkegaard's third characteristic: inherent guilt. The move to "Religion B" then comes through subjective, passionate faith in the paradox of the Incarnate Jesus Christ.[78] Such faith must not be objectified. It must not be totalized and proven historically. It is not rational, it is personal and subjective. It is in fact this irrational paradox which makes true religion so powerful—for it demands a steadfast faith before the rationally unknown.[79] Colin Brown makes this observation: "For Kierkegaard the paradox of faith means that belief must be proportioned in inverse proportion to the evidence. The less evidence, the better."[80] This movement away from the grounding and availability of "objectivity" is a crucial aspect of postmodern thought.

Through Kierkegaard's recurring use of pseudonyms emphasizes the absurdity and paradoxical nature of the Christian faith, it may be argued that such a recurring emphasis and radical insistence on subjectivity may be more characteristic and precursory to existential thought than postmodern thought that denies the "self." I submit, however, that his use of pseudonyms itself demonstrates a postmodern vein. His lack of reliance on a monolithic authority base is certainly a chief characteristic of postmodern thinking. Such use of pseudonyms, humor and irony are means which Kierkegaard uses to insulate himself, as it were, from being put in a position of authority.[81] In my estimation, this, in addition to his rejection of the authoritative structure of the Lutheran church, and the absolutizing and rationality of the reigning, totalizing Hegelian philosophy of his time, all contributed to his significant influence on postmodern thought.

---

76 Livingston, *Modern Christian Thought*, p. 314.

77 See E. Herbert Nygren, "Existentialism: Kierkegaard," in *Biblical Errancy: An Analysis of its Philosophical Roots*, ed. Norman L. Geisler (Grand Rapids: Zondervan, 1981), p. 113. Despite this book's polemic title, it provides some astute background studies on various key modern philosophers. Nygren provides an excellent, concise analysis of Kierkegaard.

78 Nygren, pp. 114–15.

79 Solomon, *Continental Philosophy Since 1750*, p. 92.

80 Brown, *Philosophy and the Christian Faith*, p. 130.

81 Patrick Goold, "Reading Kierkegaard," *Faith and Philosophy* 7/3 (July 1990): 309.

Friedrich Nietzsche (1844–1900)

Nietzsche has been called "the grandfather of postmodernism."[82] Jürgen Habermas's *The Philosophical Discourse of Modernity* contains a chapter titled "The Entry into Postmodernity: Nietzsche as a Turning Point."[83] Although there were indeed fragments of opposition to Enlightenment thought prior to Nietzsche, he is the one who is most often credited with leveling the first major assault on its premise of "truth." For Nietzsche, there is nothing in the world which is identical. Consequently, we must not conceptualize univocity in a plurivocal world.[84] For Nietzsche every concept we make comes through making similar what is actually dissimilar. As Nietzsche puts it:

> No leaf ever wholly equals another, and the concept "leaf" is formed through an arbitrary abstraction from these individual differences, through forgetting the distinctions; and now it gives rise to the idea that in nature there might be something besides the leaves which would be "leaf"—some kind of original form after which all leaves have been woven, marked, copied, colored, curled, and painted, but by unskilled hands, so that no copy turned out to be a correct, reliable, and faithful image of the original form.[85]

For Nietzsche, the rationalistic enterprise of human knowledge and "truth" is completely arbitrary and illusory. Here we see the emergence of nihilism characteristic of Nietzsche's perspectivism, and as precursory to postmodern deconstructionism:

> What, then, is truth? A mobile army of metaphors, metonyms, and anthropomorphisms—in short, a sum of human relations, which have been enhanced, transposed, and embellished poetically and rhetorically, and which after long use seem firm, canonical, and obligatory to a people: truths are illusions about which one has forgotten that this is what they are; metaphors which are worn out and without sensuous power; coins which have lost their pictures and now matter only as metal, no longer as coins.[86]

Such a perspective also affects Nietzsche's view of morality:

> Truly, I say to you: Unchanging good and evil does not exist! From out of themselves they must overcome themselves again and again.
>
> You exert power with your values and doctrines of good and evil, you assessors of values; and this is your hidden love and the glittering, trembling, and overflowing of your souls.

---

82 See Lawrence Cahoone in his introduction to Nietzsche, in *From Modernism to Postmodernism*, ed. Lawrence Cahoone (Cambridge, Mass.: Blackwell, 1996), p. 102.

83 Habermas, *The Philosophical Discourse of Modernity*, p. 83.

84 See Grenz, *A Primer On Postmodernism*, pp. 88–9.

85 Friedrich Nietzsche, "On Truth and Lie in an Extra-Moral Sense," in *The Portable Nietzsche*, ed. and trans. Walter Kaufmann (New York: Penguin Books, 1976), p. 46. The title "Portable" in a sense belittles itself. This is a widely used collection including several of Nietzsche's unabridged works by one of his foremost translators into English.

86 Nietzsche, "On Truth and Lie," pp. 46–7.

But a mightier power and a new overcoming grow from out your values: egg and egg-shell break against them.

And he who has to be a creator in good and evil, truly, has first to be a destroyer and break values.[87]

Later in the same book Nietzsche even makes this bold claim: "There is an old delusion that is called good and evil."[88]

Jürgen Habermas claims that Nietzsche "renounces a renewed revision of the concepts of reason and bids farewell to the dialectic of enlightenment."[89] On the other hand, Nietzsche scholar Walter Kaufman suggests that Nietzsche actually tried to strengthen the Enlightenment by giving it a sense of the irrational through an empirical psychology. This is something that Nietzsche develops profoundly, according to Kaufman, and which Hegel neglected to develop in his *Phenomenology of Spirit*. This psychological emphasis in Nietzsche, however, should not be misconstrued as unrestrained romanticism. Instead, Nietzsche wished to harness the romantics.[90] Nietzsche may have focused on aesthetics; but romantics such as Schelling, Fichte, even Hegel, emphasized the value of aesthetic insight for the reconciliation of subject and object. Nietzsche denies this. For Nietzsche, the world is aesthetically being created and recreated continuously.[91] Nietzsche's thinking involves a complete break with religion leading to the "death of God." As Zarathustra speaks for Nietzsche: "God is dead; God has died of his pity for man."[92] Mark C. Taylor comments on the relation of Nietzsche to Hegel on this matter, effectively highlighting Neitzsche's influence on a radical postmodern theology:

> Nietzsche's "theology" of art reverses Hegel's translation of art and religion into philosophy by recasting the theological-philosophical idea as an aesthetic activity. For neither Hegel nor Nietzsche is the death of God the mere negation of the divine. To the contrary, divine creativity disappears from the heavens only to reappear on earth in a

---

87 Friedrich Nietzsche, *Thus Spake Zarathustra*, trans. R.J. Hollingdale (London: Penguin Books Ltd., 1961), p. 139.

88 Ibid., p. 219.

89 Habermas, *The Philosophical Discourse of Modernity*, p. 86.

90 Walter Kaufmann, Introduction to *The Portable Nietzsche*, ed. and trans. Walter Kaufmann (New York: Penguin Books, 1976), p. 16.

91 Grenz, *A Primer On Postmodernism*, pp. 90–92.

92 Nietzsche, *Thus Spoke Zarathustra*, p. 114. It should be noted that the death of God, for Nietzsche, was not some catastrophic event which signified the nonexistence of a once-existing Being. Nor is it an attempt to disprove the existence of such a Being. Instead, it refers to the lack of belief, or disappearance of belief in such a Being. As Nietzsche says: "The greatest recent event—that 'God is dead,' that the belief in the Christian God has become unbelievable—is already beginning to cast its first shadows over Europe." Friedrich Nietzsche, *The Gay Science: With a Prelude in Rhymes and an Appendix of Songs*, trans. Walter Kaufman (New York: Vintage Books, 1974), p. 279. Also see Robert C. Solomon, *From Rationalism to Existentialism: The Existentialists and Their Nineteenth-Century Backgrounds* (New York: Humanities Press, 1972), p. 115.

process that Hegel interprets logically and Nietzsche views aesthetically. Through this death and resurrection, the locus of creativity shifts from the transcendent Creator to the immanent web of relations in and through which everything arises and passes away.[93]

Accompanying this death of the notion of a transcendent Creator, came Nietzsche's specifically verbalized animosity against Christianity. Nietzsche says: "The very word "Christianity" is a misunderstanding: in truth, there was only *one* Christian, and he died on the cross. The "evangel" *died* on the cross."[94] Later he continues: "In the Christian world of ideas there is nothing that has the least contact with reality—and it is in the instinctive hatred of reality that we have recognized the only motivating force at the root of Christianity."[95]

For Nietzsche, we derive our metaphysical conceptions from an underlying "will to power," which is behind the existence of all persons and ideas.[96] This "will to power" (*Der Wille Zur Macht*) must be considered in view of his concept of *Übermensch* (overman). The *Übermensch* is the figure who succeeds God and also must supersede mere man. The *Übermensch* is the one with the will to power in the sense of self-mastery and self-discipline in spite of the death of God and the lack of justification for existence and morality. This will to power must not be seen as the power of dominance or oppression. In no way is this to be equated with political power or the tyrannical control asserted by the Nazis of the German Reich.[97] In fact, one author submits that Nietzsche actually advocated mixing racial groups for cultural development with the goal to develop a master race of self-controlled artists and philosophers.[98]

There is a helpful distinction which can be made between Kierkegaard and Nietzsche. In the face of such despair, in the face of this cultural "death of God," Kierkegaard suggests that we must recommit ourselves to God and Christian morality in order to escape nihilism. For Nietzsche, however, nihilism is assumed, and it is necessary to liberate oneself from this already disintegrating Christianity and its accompanying morality structure since it is irrelevant to European culture.[99]

Martin Heidegger (1884–1976)

Jürgen Habermas claims that "Heidegger wants to take over the essential motifs of Nietzsche's Dionysian messianism while avoiding the aporias of a self-enclosed

---

93 Mark C. Taylor, *Hiding* (Chicago: University of Chicago Press, 1997), p. 291.

94 Freidrich Nietzsche, *The Antichrist*, in *The Portable Nietzsche*, ed. and trans. Walter Kaufmann (New York: Penguin Books, 1976), p. 612.

95 Ibid., p. 613.

96 See Solomon, *Continental Philosophy Since 1750*, p. 116; and Grenz, *A Primer On Postmodernism*, p. 93.

97 Livingston, *Modern Christian Thought*, pp. 202–3; and Solomon, *From Rationalism to Existentialism*, pp. 125, 129.

98 West, *An Introduction to Continental Philosophy*, p. 135.

99 Solomon, *From Rationalism to Existentialism*, p. 117.

critique of reason... to reach through a destruction of Western metaphysics that proceeds immanently."[100] It is to these "deconstructive" efforts of Heidegger to which I now turn.

It would be an understatement to say that I will make no pretension to provide an adequate assessment of Heidegger's broad and complex thinking in a few short paragraphs. Yet, he has made such a profound impact on European philosophy and on postmodern deconstructionism it is essential that I attempt to convey several key elements of his thinking which have most significant implications for this study.

For Heidegger, both Descartes and Kant neglected the essential ontology of *Dasein* ("Being–there").[101] Heidegger completely discards the vestiges of Cartesian thought and turns from the notion of consciousness to that of *Being*. In Heidegger's thought, the walls of the sphere have vanished. One is no longer enclosed and separate from the outside world. Instead, we are open and outside to the world— even standing beyond ourselves in the world.[102] In Heidegger's monumental and foundational work, *Being and Time* (*Sein und Zeit*) he introduces his primary concern of Being with the notion of *Dasein*. Heidegger took this word meaning, "being there" (in terms of human existence), and expanded its significance. Heidegger says: "This entity which each of us is himself and which includes inquiring as one of the possibilities of its Being, we shall denote by the term '*Dasein*'."[103] And later he adds:

> Dasein is an entity which in its very Being, comports itself understandingly towards that Being. In saying this, we are calling attention to the formal concept of existence. Dasein exists. Furthermore, Dasein is an entity which in each case I myself am. Mineness belongs to any existent Dasein, ...
>
> But these are both ways in which Dasein's Being takes on a definite character, and they must be seen and understood *a priori* as grounded upon that state of Being which we have called "*Being-in-the-world*."[104]

It is this notion of being-in-the-world and its emphasis on a seamless holism which not only unrelentingly attacks Cartesianism, but also far surpasses the notion of Absolute in Hegel. Dasein is like the self of the idealists in that it is an activity and not a thing. However, Dasein may not be distinguished apart from the world in which it acts. Heidegger's notion of Dasein as embedded in the world is crucial for the development of postmodern deconstructionist thought because of its challenge to the western philosophical idea of "presence." Since Plato, Heidegger insists, Being has been confused with the notion of "presence." Such a notion wrongly bifurcates the self from the supposed object of knowledge: the physical world. Instead, Being

---

100 Habermas, *The Philosophical Discourse of Modernity*, p. 97.

101 Italics mine. Martin Heidegger, *Being and Time*, trans. John Macquarrie and Edward Robinson (New York: Harper and Row, 1962), p. 46.

102 Barrett and Aiken, *Introduction to Phenomenology and Existentialism*, pp. 129; 134–5.

103 Heidegger, *Being and Time*, p. 27.

104 Ibid., p. 78.

must be understood in the context of three dimensions of temporality: past, future, as well as present. Therefore Being is absence and presence, something not currently present and something which will be present.[105]

Heidegger's later writings also critique the traditional western conception of truth as correspondence.[106] We must not speak of a world external to us as if we are searching for it outside our current experience. Heidegger begins to place more emphasis on the importance of language. As he states in *An Introduction to Metaphysics*:

> Because the destiny of language is grounded in a nation's *relation* to *being*, the question of being will involve us deeply in the question of language. It is more than an outward accident that now, as we prepare to set forth, in all its implication, the fact of the evaporation of being, we find ourselves compelled to take linguistic considerations as our starting point.[107]

Ultimately, it seems, Heidegger resorts to a mysticism which is neither objective nor subjective—"an obscure picture of indeterminacy."[108] Heidegger asserts: "'Truth' is not a feature of correct propositions that are asserted of an 'object' by a human 'subject' and then 'are valid' somewhere, in what sphere we know not; rather, truth is disclosure of beings through which an openness essentially unfolds."[109]

Heidegger does make some radical moves beyond modernism. However, he still maintains the post-Enlightenment prospect of the self discovering itself as a final attempt to create some trace of totalizing unity. As we will see, Heidegger's heirs will borrow this semi-mystical, anti-metaphysical trace, in order to obliterate any sense of utopianism.[110]

Hans-Georg Gadamer (1900–2002)

It has been said that "Gadamer's philosophical hermeneutics grows directly from the philosophy of Heidegger."[111] Gadamer, a student of Heidegger, applied great effort in

---

105 Solomon, *Continental Philosophy Since 1750*, pp. 156, 160, 167; Grenz, *A Primer On Postmodernism*, pp. 105–6; and Heidegger, *Being and Time*, pp. 47, 432–7.

106 See for example, Martin Heidegger, "On the Essence of Truth," in *Basic Writings*, ed. David Farrell Krell (San Francisco: HarperCollins, 1993), pp. 115–38.

107 Martin Heidegger, The Fundamental Question of Metaphysics from *An Introduction to Metaphysics*, in *Philosophy in the Twentieth Century*, ed. William Barrett and Henry D. Aiken (New York: Random House, 1962), p. 250.

108 Solomon, *Continental Philosophy Since 1750*, p. 167. Also see Grenz, *A Primer On Postmodernism*, p. 108.

109 Heidegger, "On the Essence of Truth," p. 127.

110 Grenz, *A Primer On Postmodernism*, p. 108. James K.A. Smith points out Heidegger's influence on such thinkers as Gadamer, Ricoeur, Kuhn, and Polanyi. See James K.A. Smith, "The Art of Christian Atheism: Faith and Philosophy in Early Heidegger," *Faith and Philosophy* 14/1 (1997): 71–81.

111 West, *An Introduction to Continental Philosophy*, p. 105.

working out the hermeneutical implications of both Schleiermacher and Heidegger in his grand work, *Truth and Method* (*Wahrheit und Methode*). It is essential to highlight a few major considerations of Gadamer's thought because his influence on philosophical hermeneutical issues pertaining to postmodern deconstruction is extremely significant.[112]

One must not be confused by the title of Gadamer's magnum opus, *Truth and Method*. As David West explains: "A method, in Gadamer's terms, is a set of explicit procedures or rules designed to purge knowledge of all distorting or idiosyncratic subjective influences."[113] Although Bacon and Descartes used "method" to objectify the natural sciences, Gadamer expresses the limits of such method for the human sciences:[114]

> Hence the human sciences are connected to modes of experience that lie outside science: with the experiences of philosophy, of art, and of history itself. These are all modes of experience in which a truth is communicated that cannot be verified by the methodological means proper to science.[115]

Reminiscent of both Nietzsche and Heidegger, Gadamer turns to the value of art in order to critique the extreme rationalism of the Enlightenment project. From this starting point, Gadamer attempts to create a new understanding of both knowledge and truth—avoiding both objectivism and relativism.[116]

Gadamer believes it is impossible to ascertain authorial intent. In fact, the entire procedure of reconstructing past conditions to ascertain an original meaning or intent is questioned by Gadamer. Gadamer cogently explains his view on this notion of hermeneutics:

> Reconstructing the original circumstances, like all restoration, is a futile undertaking in view of the historicity of our being. What is reconstructed, a life brought back from the lost past, is not the original. In its continuance in an estranged state it acquires only a derivative, cultural existence. The recent tendency to take works of art out of museums and put them back in the place for which they were originally intended, or to restore achitectural monuments to their original form, merely confirms this judgment. Even a painting taken from the museum and replaced in a church or building restored to its

---

112 See Anthony C. Thiselton, *The Two Horizons* (Grand Rapids: Eerdmans, 1980), p. 25. It also must be emphasized that Gadamer's concern with hermeneutics must not be confused with detailed exegetical practice when working with particular texts. Instead, as Gadamer states: "My real concern was and is philosophic: not what we do or what we ought to do, but what happens to us over and above our wanting and doing." Hans-Georg Gadamer, *Truth and Method*, 2nd edn (New York: Continuum, 1989), p. xxviii.

113 West, *An Introduction to Continental Philosophy*, p. 106.

114 Ibid., p. 106.

115 Gadamer, *Truth and Method*, p. xxii.

116 See Grenz, *A Primer On Postmodernism*, p. 109; and Gadamer, *Truth and Method*, p. 572. Also, for Gadamer's treatment comparing Enlightenment thought and romanticism, see *Truth and Method*, pp. 273–6.

original condition are not what they once were—they become simply tourist attractions. Similarly, a hermeneutics that regarded understanding as reconstructing the original would be no more than handing on a dead meaning.[117]

The question then becomes, what is "understanding" according to Gadamer? For Gadamer, we must realize that our existence is historical, or as Heidegger affirmed, "being in the world." We are not somehow detached from history as subject and object.[118] Understanding, for Gadamer, is more than simply re-creating the meaning of others. We must gather the concepts of past history in a way which includes our current comprehension of those concepts. Gadamer calls this the "fusion of horizons."[119] The horizon of the present needs the past to help in its formation. As Gadamer clarifies: "There is no more an isolated horizon of the present in itself than there are historical horizons which have to be acquired. Rather, understanding is always the fusion of these horizons supposedly existing by themselves."[120]

Gadamer is precusory to postmodern thought by his rejection of Cartesian objectivity and acknowledgement of personal subjective influences, prejudices, and history as all important for our interpretation and understanding.[121] He also prefigures postmodern thought through his emphasis on language and interpretation and the image of play. A 'play' imagery which represents not just what we do, but something we participate in—transcending one's individual intensions. The players become absorbed into the activity. For Gadamer the hermeneutical context is much richer than even the author can comprehend.[122] This aspect of "play" with regard to postmodern deconstructive thought will become much more apparent as we later consider the work of Jacques Derrida and Mark C. Taylor.

Ludwig Wittgenstein (1889–1951)

Austrian-born philosopher Ludwig Wittgenstein has been called "the most influential western philosopher of the twentieth century."[123] His thought is also extremely significant for current postmodern discussion. He may be seen, among the others discussed as well, as somewhat of a "prophet of postmodernity." Martin Henry

---

117 Gadamer, *Truth and Method*, p. 167.

118 Grenz, *A Primer On Postmodernism*, p. 110.

119 Gadamer, *Truth and Method*, pp. 374, 375; also see 302–7 for a development of Gadamer's view of the meaning of "horizon."

120 Ibid., p. 306.

121 See C.G. Bartholomew, "Three Horizons: Hermeneutics from the Other End—An Evaluation of Anthony Thiselton's Hermeneutic Proposals," *European Journal of Theology* 5/2 (1996): 131–2.

122 See West, *An Introduction to Continental Philosophy*, p. 112; Grenz, *A Primer On Postmodernism*, p. 112. For Gadamer's analysis of "Play as the Clue to Ontological Explanation," see *Truth and Method*, pp. 101–34.

123 See Lawrence Cahoone in his introduction to Wittgenstein, in *From Modernism to Postmodernism*, ed. Lawrence Cahoone (Cambridge: Blackwell, 1996), p. 191.

submits that Wittgenstein "marks the end of an era, which we may call the era of modernity, and communicates ... the sense of a civilization in crisis."[124]

The early Wittgenstein, in the fashion of analytic logical positivism, limited philosophy exclusively to that which can be said. Language pictures reality. The name of something refers to an object. Propositions share an essential logical form.[125] However, metaphysical or ethical propositions must be recognized as nonsensical and must be transcended to see the world correctly. As Wittgenstein asserts from his early work, the *Tractatus Logico-Philosophicus*:

> My propositions serve as elucidations in the following way: anyone who understands me eventually recognizes them as nonsensical, when he has used them—as steps—to climb up beyond them. (He must, so to speak, throw away the ladder after he has climbed up it.)[126]

And, he continues, "What we cannot speak about we must pass over in silence."[127] This comment was a foreshadowing of a major development in the later Wittgenstein through his *Blue and Brown Books* (which became his *Philosophical Investigations*). In these later writings Wittgenstein denied that language has only a single purpose. Instead, for Wittgenstein language is expansive, rich and varied with many functions.[128] This is where Wittgenstein developed his famous notion of "language-game." Language does not simply hold a one-to-one correspondence to reality, as Wittgenstein previously asserted. Instead, language includes a plurality of rich and varied activities of human life—each involving a different language game. Hence, we would have religious language games and scientific language games—each working within different frameworks.[129] With some language games it is appropriate to speak of "evidence" in order to back up the concepts involved, with others it is not. One can see Wittgenstein's challenge to modernism's objectivity. Errors are based not on some all-inclusive objective, historical foundations, but are "blunders" within particular systems, particular games—language-games.[130] As a game, language

---

124 Henry, "God in Postmodernity," p. 9.

125 See John S. Feinberg, "Noncognitivism: Wittgenstein," in *Biblical Errancy*, pp. 169–73; and Grenz, *A Primer On Postmodernism*, p. 113.

126 Ludwig Wittgenstein, exerpt from his *Tractatus Logico-Philosophicus*, in *From Modernism to Postmodernism: An Anthology*, ed. Lawrence Cahoone (Cambridge, Mass: Blackwell, 1996), p. 198.

127 Wittgenstein, exerpt from his *Tractatus Logico-Philosophicus*, p. 199. Allan Megill draws an interesting contrast between Wittgenstein and Heidegger on this point: "... where Heidegger chooses language or poetry, Wittgenstein chooses silence" since the mystical cannot be put into words. (Allan Megill, *Prophets of Extremity: Nietzsche, Heidegger, Foucault, Derrida* (Berkeley and Los Angeles: University of California Press, Ltd., 1985), p. 170.

128 Solomon, *Continental Philosophy Since 1750*, p. 150.

129 Ibid.; also see Gavin Hyman, *The Predicament of Postmodern Theology: Radical Orthodoxy or Nihilist Textualism* (Louisville: Westminster John Knox Press, 2001), p. 54.

130 See Ludwig Wittgenstein, *Lectures and Conversations on Aesthetics, Psychology and Religious Belief*, ed. Cyril Barrett (Berkeley and Los Angeles: University of California Press,

is not a private affair, but a social affair requiring social interaction in particular contexts.[131]

Thomas Kuhn (1922–1996)

That which Wittgenstein did for different forms and activities of life, Kuhn applied to the form of scientific discourse itself in his famous work, *The Structure of Scientific Revolutions* (first published 1962; 2nd edn, 1970). Not only is science a different language-game than religion, but according to Kuhn, scientific discourse itself involves different language-games. Science is not some overarching control by which all activity is governed or esteemed valid for discovering the nature of reality. As Kevin Vanhoozer states: "Philosophers of science such as Thomas Kuhn argue that scientific knowledge is not a copying of reality but a construction of it."[132] We notice this in what Kuhn called "paradigm shifts" in scientific discovery. Kuhn actually uses this word "paradigm" in two senses:

> On the one hand, it stands for the entire constellation of beliefs, values, techniques, and so on shared by the members of a given community. On the other, it denotes one sort of element in that constellation, the concrete puzzle-solutions which, employed as models or examples, can replace explicit rules as a basis for the solution of the remaining puzzles of normal science.[133]

For Kuhn, paradigms are not necessarily co-extensive. By way of example, as he describes, the helium atom for a chemist was a molecule due to its action with regard to the kinetic theory of gases; however, it was not a molecule for a physicist because no molecular spectrum was displayed. Although both scientists were speaking of the same particle, they were each looking at it from their particular field and scope of research—different paradigms.[134] This plurality of perspectives along these lines is illustrated by Richard Rorty:

> The moral of Kuhnian philosophy of science is important: there is no discipline called "critique" that one can practice to get strikingly better politics, any more than there is something called "scientific method" that one can apply in order to get strikingly better physics.[135]

This type of incommensurability is noticed throughout the history of science. One criterion of evaluation that is operative in one system is not necessarily identifiable

---

1972), pp. 56–9.

131 See Grenz, *A Primer On Postmodernism*, p. 114.

132 Vanhoozer, *Is There a Meaning in This Text?*, p. 84.

133 Thomas Kuhn, *The Structure of Scientific Revolutions*, 2nd edn (Chicago: The University of Chicago Press, 1970), p. 175.

134 Kuhn, *The Structure of Scientific Revolutions*, pp. 50–51.

135 Richard Rorty, "Feminism, Ideology, and Deconstruction: A Pragmatist View" Hypatia, 8/2 Spring, 1993, http://gort.ucsd.edu/jhan/ER/rr.html (9 June 1999).

in another system. This, in a sense, exposes the objective "myth" of science. Shifts in scientific theory are not necessarily based on the addition of factual knowledge, but in radical paradigm shifts of thinking which affect the worldview of the scientific community. This change occurs socially, not through detached, neutral observation.[136] Kuhn elucidates this:

> Led by a new paradigm, scientists adopt new instruments and look in new places. Even more important, during revolutions scientists see new and different things when looking with familiar instruments in places they have looked before. It is rather as if the professional community had been suddenly transported to another planet where familiar objects are seen in a different light and are joined by unfamiliar ones as well.[137]

Kuhn's historicist model of science and paradigm shifts have themselves created a revolution in epistemological thought. Kuhn has taken into account sociological factors which influence the acceptance of theories in the scientific world. These factors have, of course, created challenges for the study of theology and the status of theological propositions which assert transparadigmatic truth claims.[138]

Some thinkers, such as Cordell Strug, dismiss the possibility of using Kuhn's thesis with respect to religious thought: "Religion, for its self-understanding, requires a conception of thought which is centered on permanent elements. (Myths have this dimension, paradigms do not. It is nonsense to conflate the two.)"[139] Strug claims that not one philosopher who has used science as its model of understanding (from Descartes to Kuhn) has ever created a description of human knowledge which has not been ultimately misunderstood and also been destructive of beliefs. As Strug insists: "If religion needs a reliable crutch, it will have to look elsewhere for one."[140] Whatever we make of Strug's conclusions, we can certainly see the tensions resulting from Kuhn's thought which have greatly influenced postmodern thought and theology.

---

136 See Lawrence Cahoone in his introduction to Kuhn, in *From Modernism to Postmodernism*, p. 309; and Grenz, *A Primer On Postmodernism*, pp. 54–5. Cf. also Jaco S. Dreyer, "The Researcher: Engaged Participant or Detached Observer," *Journal of Empirical Theology*, 11/2 (1998): 6–9.

137 Kuhn, *The Structure of Scientific Revolutions*, p. 111.

138 J. Wentzel Van Huyssteen, *Essays in Postfoundationalist Theology* (Grand Rapids: Eerdmans, 1997), p. 128.

139 Cordell Strug, "Kuhn's Paradigm Thesis: A Two-edged Sword for the Philosophy of Religion," *Religious Studies* 20 (June 1984): 279.

140 Ibid.

Structuralism: Saussure and Lévi-Strauss

Ferdinand de Saussure (1857–1913)

Although the Swiss linguist Ferdinand de Saussure predates Wittgenstein by several years, I have chosen to include him in this section due to his profound influence on the linguistic theory of structuralism, which in turn will serve as a point of departure to discuss post-structuralism and deconstructionism.

Saussure's work has been compared to that of Wittgenstein in that he sought the essential nature of language at the base of various linguistic forms.[141] However, Wittgenstein approached this task as a logician, Saussure as an empirical linguist.[142] Rather than focus on linguistic behavior and the development of phases of language (*parole*), Saussure emphasized the study of the synchronic, timeless presence of language as a systematic social institution (*langue*). This is what provides unity for language, according to Saussure.[143] However, this is not to say that diachronic linguistic study is useless. But, effective diachronic study is dependent on synchronic study—not the other way around.[144] Approached synchronically, a "linguistic sign is not a link between a thing and a name, but between a concept and a sound pattern."[145] Consequently, linguistic signs (both oral and written) are arbitrary and simply determined by social convention. However, we must understand the context of this notion of *arbitrary* according to Saussure:

> It must not be taken to imply that a signal depends on the free choice of the speaker. (We shall see later that the individual has no power to alter a sign in any respect once it has become established in a linguistic community.) The term implies simply that the signal is unmotivated: that is to say arbitrary in relation to its signification, with which it has no natural connexion in reality.[146]

Saussure effectively challenges the Enlightenment epistemological presupposition of correspondence between a sign and its signifier. He goes as far as to say: "Everything we have said so far comes down to this. In the language itself, there are only

---

141 One should note that Saussure did not publish. His views were published under the title, *Course in General Linguistics*, a compilation of his course notes in Geneva taken by various students.

142 Eric Matthews, *Twentieth-Century French Philosophy* (Oxford: Oxford University Press, 1996), p. 136. For an account of the relationship between Wittgenstein and structuralism see Thiselton, *The Two Horizons*, pp. 428–31.

143 Matthews, *Twentieth-Century French Philosophy*, pp.135–6; and Grenz, *A Primer On Postmodernism*, pp. 114–15. See Saussure, *Course in General Linguistics*, p. 9 and pp. 14–15.

144 Thiselton, *The Two Horizons*, p. 125. See Saussure, *Course in General Linguistics*, pp. 81–2.

145 Saussure, *Course in General Linguistics*, p. 66.

146 Ibid., pp. 68–9.

differences."[147] Meaning is not derived from any intrinsic or positive value of a word in and of itself, but only in relation to its differences or contrasts to other words. Consequently, with this system meaning cannot be directly attributed to a speaker, but only to the pre-existing semantic elements which are differentially related. It is the application of this structural method to the social sciences which is, in essence, structuralism.[148]

Claude Lévi-Strauss (1908–)

Claude Lévi-Strauss applied Saussure's linguistic views anthropologically.[149] Social organization is like language in that it is generationally reproduced without conscious effort. Social and cultural forms ought not to be explained in terms of their historical origins, but in their positional system in society. Lévi-Strauss sought a fundamental unity of all differing cultures from which all are basically derived.[150] Lévi-Strauss rejects the Cartesian notion of the self. We do not need to examine self-consciousness, according the Lévi-Strauss; but instead, cultural expression. We must view humans as essentially social creatures, shaped by culture, language, and ritual. The proper study is not the Enlightenment "self" but universal cultural structure.[151] Mark C. Taylor comments on this structuralism evident in Lévi-Strauss: "Structuralism's dissolution of the subject is actually an extrapolation of Saussure's insight into the differential character of identity, which ends by regarding man as essentially a structure of intersecting relations."[152]

Although Lévi-Strauss rejects the notion of transcendental pretence characteristic of philosophy throughout Europe since Descartes and Rousseau, he reforms it scientifically. In the place of the subjective self of Descartes, he imposes a universal, objective, structural theory based in the contingent structures of language and the human brain. However, these are not a priori Kantian categories, but empirical conditions which come about through human experience in the context of societal relationships.[153]

Lawrence Cahoone, a scholar of modernity, succinctly articulates the implications of structuralist thought on the self:

> Simply put, it is not the self that creates culture, but culture that creates the self. The study of abstract relations within systems or "codes" of cultural signs (words, family relations, etc.) is the key to understanding human existence. Structuralism seemed to offer the student of humanity a way of avoiding reduction to the natural sciences, while yet

---

147 Ibid., p. 118.

148 West, *An Introduction to Continental Philosophy*, p. 166.

149 See Claude Lévi-Strauss, *La pensée sauvage*, (Paris, 1962).

150 West, *An Introduction to Continental Philosophy*, pp. 166–7.

151 Grenz, *A Primer On Postmodernism*, p. 119.

152 Taylor, *Deconstructing Theology*, p. 99.

153 Solomon, *Continental Philosophy Since 1750*, p. 195; and Matthews, *Twentieth-Century French Philosophy*, pp. 138–9.

retaining objective, scientific methods, unlike the apparently subjective orientation of phenomenology, existentialsim, and psychoanalysis. At the same time, it also implied that nothing is "authentic," that there is no fundamental, originary nature of the human self against which we could judge a culture.[154]

Structuralism, however, even with its radical attack on the nature of the self, did not complete the separation from Enlightenment modernist ideals into postmodernism. Structuralists were still committed to some kind of interpretive meaning in texts and, as Lévi-Strauss submitted, a universal social structure. But a postmodern revolution followed (and one may say is continuing to occur in many contexts), that moved beyond the structuralism of Lévi-Strauss: post-structuralism/deconstructionism.[155]

Entering Postmodernism/ Post-structuralism/ Deconstructionism

To put it simply, postmodernism is a full scale challenge to modernist intellectual ideals found in the Enlightenment project. As Graham Ward states in no uncertain terms: "Postmodernism reminds modernity of its own constructed nature; the arbitrariness and instability of its constructions."[156] Gary John Percesepe echoes this thought as well when he claims that the trait of the postmodern is its search for new presentations while refusing "to cultivate a nostalgia for the unattainable."[157] The Enlightenment/modernist project rested on the false assumption of objectivity, universality, and transcendental pretense. It was driven by an irrepressible force to determine the origins and grounds for everything. Postmodernism signals the end of such grounding and those who sought to legislate it.[158] Lawrence Cahoone identifies five prominent themes in postmodernism, each of which we have seen developed at some extent by the authors we have considered in the course of this chapter: 1) the critique of *presence* (as opposed to representation); 2) the critique of *origin* (instead of phenomena); 3) the critique of *unity* (instead of plurality); 4) the critique of *transcendence* (as opposed to immanence); and 5) the predominant theme of difference or *constitutive otherness*.[159]

Cultural analyst Os Guinness also provides the following statements effectively summarizing the ideals of postmodernism:

---

154 Lawrence Cahoone in his "Introduction" to *From Modernism to Postmodernism*, p. 5.

155 Grenz, *A Primer On Postmodernism*, pp. 120–21; and Solomon, *Continental Philosophy Since 1750*, p. 195.

156 Graham Ward, "Introduction, or A Guide to Theological Thinking in Cyberspace," in *The Postmodern God: A Theological Reader*, ed. Graham Ward (Oxford: Blackwell, 1997), p. xxvi.

157 Percesepe, "The Unbearable Lightness of Being Postmodern," p. 129.

158 Ward, "Introduction," p. xxvi.

159 Cahoone in Introduction to *From Modernism to Postmodernism*, p. 14.

Where modernism was a manifesto of human self-confidence and self-congratulation, postmodernism is a confession of modesty, if not despair. There is no truth; only truths. There is no grand reason; only reasons. There is no privileged civilization (or culture, belief, norm and style); only a multiplicity of cultures, beliefs, norms and styles. There is no universal justice; only interests and the competition of interest groups. There is no grand narrative of human progress; only countless stories of where people and their cultures are now. There is no simple reality or any grand objectivity of universal, detached knowledge; only a ceaseless representation of everything in terms of everything else.[160]

This critique on objectivity by postmodern theorists is sometimes portrayed by their hostile critics as unleashed relativism. Nicholas Rescher, for example, suggests that objectivity for the postmodern theorist is the equivalent of the "non-covering of the Emperor's New Clothes." He claims, albeit too simplistically, that postmoderns simply accept whatever happens to be the "fashion of the day" where "[t]ruth and rational cogency are mere chimeras, comforting self-delusions like Santa Claus or the Tooth Fairy."[161]

Jürgen Habermas interestingly submits that the essential critique of modernity from Hegel, Nietzsche, Heidegger to Foucault and Derrida lies not, at its base, in the notion of objectivity, but in a principle of subjectivity:

Agreement also exists about the fact that the authoritarian traits of a narrow-minded enlightenment are embedded in the principle of self-consciousness or of subjectivity....

... Because this regime of a subjectivity puffed up into a false absolute transforms the means of consciousness-raising and emancipation into just so many instruments of objectification and control, it fashions for itself an uncanny immunity in the form of a thoroughly concealed domination. The opacity of the iron cage of a reason that has become positive disappears as if in the glittering brightness of a completely transparent crystal palace. All parties are united on this point: *These* glassy facades have to shatter. They are, to be sure, distinguished by the strategies they elect for overcoming the positivism of reason.[162]

Yet, I would affirm that a major characteristic of postmodern thought also includes the disappearance of the self as a subjective, autonomous, defined, central, governing presence. In structuralism, it was noted, meaning is at least in some sense preserved through an advocation of a total system including a decentered self. Yet in post-structuralism (which I designate as "deconstructionism"), neither the self nor the total system which embeds the self is considered a secure foundation for ultimate truth or meaning.[163]

---

160 Os Guinness, *Fit Bodies, Fat Minds* (London: Hodder & Stoughton, 1994), p. 105 as quoted in McGrath, *A Passion For Truth*, p. 180.

161 Nicholas Rescher, *Objectivity: The Obligations of Impersonal Reason* (Notre Dame and London: University of Notre Dame Press, 1997), p. 42.

162 Habermas, *The Philosophical Discourse of Modernity*, pp. 55–6.

163 Henry, "God in Postmodernity:" 11. Eric Matthews submits that the label "post-structuralist" is misleading, implying a separate school of thought both distinct ideologically and chronologically from the "structuralist" school. But Matthews argues, there never

Since the 1980s, Cahoone suggests, most philosophers who refer to the term "postmodernism" are more precisely meaning "poststructuralism" (or "deconstructionism")—notably in the works of the French philosophers Jean-François Lyotard, Jacques Derrida, and Michel Foucault. Such "poststructuralism" announces the end of the possibility for rational truth inquiry, the illusion of the self, the impossibility of univocity, the illegitimate nature of Occidentalism, and the oppression of modern institutions.[164] As Terrence Tilley summarizes: "In short, postmodern deconstruction, archaeology, and genealogy reveal the malignancies in the structures that present themselves as the benign face of modern, liberal individualism."[165]

What is Deconstruction?

More will be said on the nature of deconstruction specifically in a following chapter on Derrida. However, at this juncture it will be helpful to introduce some general comments, and provide citations from several relevant authors to introduce this widespread misunderstood concept.

First, it is important to realize that deconstructionism is essentially a movement which began in the context of continental philosophy. Despite its current widespread usage in American literary criticism, deconstructionism emerged from European history and thought. In terms of geography, most specifically, France. The three major French philosophers we will consider are: Jean-François Lyotard, Jacques Derrida and Michel Foucault. France has become, in a sense, "the nonempirical site of a movement."[166] I would not wish to make a major case in today's world, for a

---

was, properly, a "structuralist" school in philosophy per se. See Matthews, *Twentieth-Century French Philosophy*, p. 157. Therefore, in order to take heed of Matthews' word of caution and to avoid confusion of terms, for purposes of the discussion in this book I will primarily be referring to "post-structuralism" as "deconstructionism." It may be argued, as Stephen D. Moore suggests, "that *poststructuralism* is a more expansive umbrella term than *deconstruction*; the latter term is normally reserved for the work of Derrida, de Man, and those who draw on them,…" in Stephen D. Moore, *Poststructuralism and the New Testament* (Minneapolis: Fortress Press, 1994), p. 3. In a sense, I will be highlighting what I see to be "Derridean" style of deconstruction in the authors we are considering.

164 Cahoone in Introduction to *From Modernism to Postmodernism*, pp. 2–3, 5–6.

165 Terrence W. Tilley with Stuart Kendall in Terrence W. Tilley, *Postmodern Theologies: The Challenge of Religious Diversity* (Maryknoll: Orbis Books, 1995), p. 105.

166 Jacques Derrida, *Margins of Philosophy*, trans. Alan Bass (Chicago: University of Chicago Press, 1982), p. 114. Also see West, *An Introduction to Continental Philosophy*, pp 3–6. West cites this quotation of Derrida when discussing the differences between "analytic" and "continental" thinking. A case could be made for the inclusion of many other "continental" postmodern thinkers as well (both French and non-French), for example: Roland Barth, Julia Kristeva, Jacques Lacan, Emmanuel Lévinas, and Paul de Man. One may also include postmodern sociologist Jean Baudrillard. (See, for example, Andrew Wernick, "Post-Marx: Theological Themes in Baudrillard's America," in Philippa Berry and Andrew

clean geographical separation between Anglo-American "analytic" philosophy and continental philosophy. For example, I see an obvious continental style of thinking in the works of Mark C. Taylor, Richard Rorty, and Don Cupitt. Of course, it was the reception of several non-French thinkers (i.e. Heidegger, Nietzsche) into French philosophy which heavily influenced and shaped deconstructionist thought. One may ask: Why is France so significant for this development? As one author has put it: "More than either German or English language philosophy, French philosophy is distinguished by a strong emphasis on the relation between philosophy and religion, reason and faith."[167] Additionally, the interdisciplinary nature in the French philosophical tradition blurs the lines between philosophy and literature, as well as between reason and the imagination.[168] As a result, the French tradition makes itself more receptive to such an eclectic movement as deconstructionism. Due to its diverse, interdisciplinary influences, it is also much more difficult to "pin down" or define. In the following paragraphs I will cite several authors who have attempted to (ironically) describe deconstruction's "indescribability."

Deconstruction scholar Kevin Hart states:

> It has been endlessly quoted out of context, grafted onto various critical and political projects, become the butt of parodies, and been pronounced in so many tones, from contempt to reverence, that it cannot be formally defined without some remainder, however small. In fact the fate of the word 'deconstruction' offers one of the best indications of what deconstruction is: the demonstration that no text can be totalised without a supplement of signification. That this definition gives no hint of the wider institutional and cultural import of deconstruction points to its own need for supplementation. Yet the difficulty of pinning down 'deconstruction' is not only a consequence of the state of affairs the word describes but also a matter of polemics, politics and influence.[169]

It is, as Hart elucidates, this lack of ability to "pin down" the meaning of deconstruction which ironically helps *to* explain what it is. It does not sit tight and comfortable in our taxonomical chambers. Deconstruction constantly eludes and escapes predetermined categories. William Desmond makes the same point when he writes:

Wernick (eds), *Shadow of Spirit* (London and New York: Routledge, 1992). For example, Baudrillard's critique on mass media has had a major impact on postmodern theory. Lévinas also arguably influenced Derrida. Due to the scope and limits of this book, I have chosen not to include these authors. It was my opinion that these authors, although highly significant for postmodern studies, and perhaps postmodern theology in general, had less impact specifically on postmodern deconstructive theology as it relates to this study on apologetic methodology than the others I have included.

167 Tom Rockmore, *Heidegger and French Philosophy* (London: Routledge, 1995), p. 8, as quoted in Ward, "Introduction," p. xxxvii.

168 Ward, "Introduction," p. xxxvii–xxxviii.

169 Kevin Hart, *The Trespass of the Sign* (Cambridge: Cambridge University Press, 1989), p. ix.

Deconstruction reveals a subversive thinking that overturns, explodes, breaks down, a thinking that reverses and perverts, that inverts, that laughs. This is the laughter of thought that stiffly insists on being homeless. This is an equivocity of thought that is too busy denouncing univocity to be silent long enough to listen for any possible gesture of reconcilement, any elusive hint of home.[170]

Partially due to its elusive, at times incomprehensible, nature, some have defined deconstruction too negatively and too simplistically. It is unfortunate that Roland Hoksbergen erroneously characterizes the French deconstructionist position as an extreme relativism "which is basically the method of interpreting literature according to one's own interests and according to one's own predispositions."[171] I strongly disagree. Deconstruction is more than just a loose, hedonistic "free for all."

Postmodern theologian, Charles E. Winquist claimed that deconstruction is not simply "wild analysis," but instead a very "careful reading of texts." It points to a text "marked by its own lines of fissure and forces of disruption. What sometimes makes deconstruction seem esoteric and strange to ordinary language usage is that it attends to the unthought syntax of thinking."[172] Deconstruction involves painstaking effort and concentrated analysis. Whether or not we agree with such methodology (or lack thereof) is a different issue. One thing is certain, one must not equate deconstructionism with academic laziness or half-hearted effort. Deconstruction takes the text very seriously. This is not to say that it does not play with the text. But when it plays, it plays seriously and with great academic effort and discipline.

Deconstruction must not be confused with *destruction*. It is not simply the act of demolishing existing structures. Instead it is an intense, rigorous disassembly of various strands and layers of meaning to put the discipline of philosophy in its rightful place—simply one of many disciplines, not the ultimate guardian of all. Through this process of disassembly and careful analysis, a complete re-evaluation is made of western metaphysical assumptions.[173] Such rigorous iconoclasm results in the "cleansing" of "the hermeneutical temple of the purveyors of cheap interpretations."[174]

Often deconstruction is also viewed as a program which denies all reference, and chains one to endless links of signifiers, only leaving simply to "play vainly with linguistic strings, ..."[175] However, according to deconstructive theologian John

---

170 William Desmond, *Beyond Hegel and Dialectic: Speculation, Cult and Comedy* (Albany: State University of New York Press, 1992), pp. 290–91.

171 Roland Hoksbergen, "Is There a Christian Economics?: Some Thoughts in Light of the Rise of Postmodernism," *Christian Scholar's Review* 24/2 (1994): 128.

172 Charles E. Winquist, *Desiring Theology* (Chicago: University of Chicago Press, 1995), pp. 95–6.

173 Vanhoozer, *Is There a Meaning in This Text?*, pp. 52, 20 and Hart, *The Trespass of the Sign*, p. 19.

174 Ibid., p. 52.

175 John D. Caputo, *The Prayers and Tears of Jacques Derrida: Religion without Religion* (Bloomington & Indianapolis: Indiana University Press, 1997), p. 15.

D. Caputo, deconstruction is subject to much misunderstanding, and its intent has been widely misunderstood. Deconstruction does indeed complicate the notion of reference, but it does not intend to deny it completely. Caputo insists that this is not a retreat into total subjectivism: "This delimitation of reference is motivated not by subjectivism or skepticism but by a kind of hypersensitivity to otherness,...."[176]

But rather than attempt a scrupulous definition of "deconstruction" at this juncture, I will look to its roots in the postmodern thought of Jean-François Lyotard, followed by its most well-known context, in the work of Jacques Derrida.

---

176 Ibid., pp. 15, 17.

PART 2

Deconstruction and its Roots in Europe

Chapter 3

Jean-François Lyotard: The Dissolution of the Metanarrative

Lyotard must be considered in any discussion of the roots of deconstructive postmodernism because of his pivotal treatment on the demise of metanarratives. Although he may be less influential for the purposes of this book than other authors considered, any assessment of postmodern thought cannot ignore Lyotard. So it is my desire to simply provide several highlights of Lyotard's thinking with regard to postmodernism as it relates to this book, and mention some specific influences his thinking has had on other scholars entering the postmodern scene.

Jean-François Lyotard (d. 1998), was professor emeritus at the University of Paris–Vincennes, and is perhaps most known for his famous definition of the term postmodern as "incredulity toward metanarratives."[1] Lyotard has been rightfully considered a pioneer of philosophical postmodernism in France.[2] In the 1950s to early 1960s Lyotard had associations with a left-wing Marxist group known as *Socialisme ou barbarie*, and he was an active participant in the French political uprisings in May, 1968. Such oppositional sympathies, along with studies in phenomenology, the Frankfurt school, and the language philosophy of Wittgenstein, all motivated Lyotard's critique of the intellectual and social modernism which eventually succeeded his Marxist tendencies.[3]

---

1   Jean-François Lyotard, *The Postmodern Condition*, trans. Geoff Bennington and Brian Massumi (Minneapolis: University of Minnesota Press, 1984), p. xxiv. Fr: "l'incredulité à l'égard des métarécits." Jean-François Lyotard, *La Condition Postmoderne*, Collection Critique (Paris: Les Editions de Minuit, 1979), p. 7.

2   See Gilbert Hottois, *De la Renaissance à la Postmodernité*, 2e edn (Paris–Bruxelles: De Boeck Université, 1998), p. 448. One may also note Lyotard's influence in the United States. He taught at University of California at Irvine and at Emory University.

3   Eric Matthews, *Twentieth-Century French Philosophy* (Oxford: Oxford University Press, 1996), p. 180; and Hottois, *De la Renaissance à la Postmodernité*, p. 448. It is interesting to note that Lyotard was also influenced by Anglo-American thought. Consequently, his French or European distinctives need to be viewed with this in mind. See William A. Beardslee, "Christ in the Postmodern Age: Reflections Inspired by Jean-François Lyotard," in David Ray Griffin, William A. Beardslee, and Joe Holland, *Varieties of Postmodern Theology* (Albany: State University of New York Press, 1989), p. 66. Beardslee points out that Lyotard was especially influenced by the work of American sociologists. This truly illustrates, as previously noted in the words of Derrida, that the continental formation of postmodern deconstructive thought is the "non-empirical site of a movement."

Rejection of the Metanarrative

For Lyotard, modernity is characterized by metanarratives used by western societies in order to legitimate science and the state. A metanarrative and a philosophy of history are one and the same according to Lyotard. The modern view sees history as a meaningful, directed process—an all-inclusive, encapsulating narrative. For Lyotard, these narratives may take different forms, but the two major ones he identifies as the "narrative of emancipation" (as seen in modern science and the politics of the French Revolution) and the "speculative narrative" seen in Hegelianism and Marxism. Both of these grand narratives imply the notion of guaranteed progress through the application of reason to capitalist ventures as well as to politics and morality. Both have also been important in modern philosophy and have contributed toward the self-consciousness of the West's complete identification with modernity.[4]

According to Lyotard, the postmodern mood or condition has lost its faith in these metanarratives. History is no longer seen as a directed, goal-oriented process. Nietzsche's announcement of the cultural "death of God" is followed by the death of history and progress as well.[5] Lyotard elucidates this notion of postmodernity in relation to modernity:

> It is not the case of "abandoning" the project of modernity, as Habermas has said with regard to postmodernity, but of the "liquidation" of that project. With this annihilation, an irreparable suspicion is engraved in European, if not Western, consciousness: that universal history does not move inevitably "toward the better", as Kant thought, or rather, that history does not necessarily have a universal finality.[6]

Consequently, grand political ideologies and plans to unify society must be rejected. Modernity has witnessed the demise of such plans with the residue of world wars, fascism, totalitarianism, and genocide. Any attempts at unity and institutional order are totalizing modernist theories based on mistaken Enlightenment assumptions which can no longer be trusted.[7] This rejection of the metanarratives in modernity stems from their failure: they have not kept their promises. They promised freedom but failed to provide it. The market did not free humanity from poverty. Nor were such proclamations of liberty universal enough for all humanity. Human rights and freedom were too encased in particular social identities. Yet, in another sense, the universality of the metanarratives is the primary reason for their demise. The

---

4   David West, *An Introduction to Continental Philosophy* (Cambridge, Mass.: Blackwell, 1996), pp. 197–8. See Lyotard, *The Postmodern Condition*, pp. 8, xxiii, 31–7.

5   West, *An Introduction to Continental Philosophy*, pp. 198–9.

6   Jean-François Lyotard, *The Postmodern Explained* (Minneapolis: University of Minnesota Press, 1992), p. 51.

7   West, *An Introduction to Continental Philosophy*, p. 199. Also see Hottois, *De la Renaissance à la Postmodernité*, p. 449.

metanarratives of modernity, in effect, suppress the rich diversity of language–games, the small narratives, and attempt instead to squeeze them into a totalizing mold.[8]

The loss of faith in the metanarrative is also due to many new technological developments. From the pervasive use of the internet and email, increased television programming, to the widespread use of cellular phones—to name but a few—it is impossible to maintain any semblance of rational control. Social interaction in today's postmodern world is beyond the sphere of rational maintenance. Such changes may result in even more decentralization of political power structures.[9] As Lyotard comments:

> Knowledge in the form of an informational commodity indispensable to productive power is already, and will continue to be, a major—perhaps the major—stake in the worldwide competition for power. It is conceivable that the nation-states will one day fight for control of information, just as they battled in the past for control over territory, and afterwards for control of access to and exploitation of raw materials and cheap labor.[10]

But, if an attempt is made to speculate on the outcome, and give some kind of systematic explanatory system one would be regressing to totalizing metanarratives which are simply passé and inadequate to the postmodern condition.[11]

The metanarratives, that is, those narratives which hold a legitimizing function, no longer retain credibility for Lyotard. Whether one is speaking of Hegelian dialecticism or Christianity and the narrative of "martyred love," they are a "distillation of speculative modernity."[12] This does not mean for Lyotard, however, that we are left without any credible narratives at all. For the decline of metanarratives "does not stop countless other stories (minor and not so minor) from continuing to weave the fabric of everyday life."[13]

Postmodernism and Science

This rejection of the metanarratives of modernity is especially seen in Lyotard's discussion regarding a postmodern philosophy of science. Reminiscent of both Wittgenstein and Kuhn, Lyotard regards modern science as an example of a particular language game absent of universal foundations:

---

8 Miroslav Volf, *Exclusion and Embrace: A Theological Exploration of Identity, Otherness, and Reconciliation* (Nashville: Abingdon, 1996), pp. 106–7.

9 Christopher Norris, *Derrida* (London: Fontana, 1987), p. 154.

10 Lyotard, *The Postmodern Condition*, p. 5.

11 Norris, *Derrida* (London: Fontana, 1987), p. 154. See Lyotard, *The Postmodern Condition*, p. 7.

12 Lyotard, *The Postmodern Explained*, p. 18. Also see R. Albert Mohler, "The Integrity of the Evangelical Tradition and the Challenge of the Postmodern Paradigm," in *The Challenge of Postmodernism: An Evangelical Engagement*, ed. David S. Dockery (Grand Rapids: Baker, 1997), p. 70.

13 Lyotard, *The Postmodern Explained*, p. 19.

Scientific knowledge requires that one language game, denotation, be retained and all others excluded. A statement's truth-value is the criterion determining its acceptability.... A statement of science gains no validity from the fact of being reported.... The game of science thus implies a diachronic temporality, that is, a memory and a project. The current sender of a scientific statement is supposed to be acquainted with previous statements concerning its referent (bibliography) and only proposes a new statement on the subject if it differs from the previous ones. Here, what I have called the "accent" of each performance, and by that token the polemical function of the game, takes precedence over the "meter." This diachrony, which assumes memory and a search for the new, represents in principle a cumulative process. Its "rhythm," or the relationship between accent and meter, is variable.[14]

The Enlightenment perspective of science was a paradigm of rational objectivity. Lyotard calls this entire notion into question by dethroning science to become only one "language-game" among many.[15] The postmodern scientist is not committed to an overarching method or grand narrative, but she is one committed to telling stories.[16] A postmodern philosophy of science challenges the modernist notion of ubiquitous progress through demonstrating respect to local scientific contextual narratives and rejecting grand narratives that attempt to explain the entire scientific enterprise as some unified essence. Instead, science must be viewed in a dynamic fashion throughout history.[17]

However, for Lyotard, the "stories" told by the scientist still require verification. It is this verification that Lyotard calls "legitimation by parology" (*la légitimation par la paralogie*).[18] This parology, for Lyotard, provides freedom of knowledge and the possibility of new discovery through breaking the rules of a particular language game within science. In terms of traditional logic, parology refers to unconscious false reasoning. Parology is a term used in contrast to sophism, which is the deliberate use of false reasoning with intent to deceive. Lyotard uses the term parology with a slightly altered nuance of breaking the rules of a language game and hence, reasoning falsely. Yet, it is by this breaking of rules where one renews the language game with human creativity, thus guarding it from mere repetition.[19] As Lyotard puts it:

Rules are not denotative but prescriptive utterances, which we are better off calling metaprescriptive utterances to avoid confusion (they prescribe what the moves of language games must be in order to be admissible). The function of the differential or imaginative or paralogical activity of the current pragmatics of science is to point out these metaprescriptives (science's "presuppositions") and to petition the players to accept

---

14 Lyotard, *The Postmodern Condition*, pp. 25–6.

15 Matthews, *Twentieth-Century French Philosophy*, p. 183.

16 Lyotard, *The Postmodern Condition*, p. 60.

17 J. Wentzel van Huyssteen, *Essays in Postfoundationalist Theology* (Grand Rapids: Eerdmans, 1997), p. 268.

18 Lyotard, *The Postmodern Condition*, p. 60. Cf. Lyotard, *La Condition Postmoderne*, p. 98.

19 Beardslee, "Christ in the Postmodern Age," p. 67.

different ones. The only legitimation that can make this kind of request admissible is that it will generate ideas, in other words, new statements.[20]

This rejection of the appeal to science as the ultimate unifying category is a positive move for Lyotard, fostering creativity and invention. Each shifting area of inquiry has its own language-game, incompatible with others. Lyotard disagrees with Habermas who suggests that legitimacy can reside in consensus. But if legitimacy was ascribed to consensus, violence would be committed to the "heterogeneity of language games." Instead, postmodern knowledge enhances our awareness of differences and helps us "tolerate the incommensurable."[21] It is precisely this notion of heterogeneity that leads us to the cultural pluralism and notion of a decentered self inherent in Lyotard's thought.

Lyotard's Postmodern Decentered Self

Although significantly more will be said later on the idea of the loss of the self in the postmodern milieu in the work of Mark C. Taylor, I see markings of this declared loss in the thinking of Lyotard. The postmodern, decentered self that one notices in Lyotard is not a self which yields to God, but to an endless multiplicity.[22] Through the playing of a myriad of language games with a variety of rules, the idea of a centered self has been lost. The centered, creative self of romanticism and modernism is now a mere point on a complex pattern and network of exchange. The isolated, consistent self is passé. To live is to move in a web of language games which are unrelated, and significant creativity is found in the breaking of rules and established conventions.[23] Lyotard states it this way:

> A *self* does not amount to much, but no self is an island; each exists in a fabric of relations that is now more complex and mobile than ever before. Young or old, man or woman, rich or poor, a person is always located at "nodal points" of specific communication circuits, however tiny these may be. Or better: one is always located at a post through which various kinds of messages pass.[24]

Ethic

Based on his radical skepticism, one may suspect the absence of any notion of ethics or morality in Lyotard's postmodern thinking. But Lyotard is not espousing ethical or political nihilism. He submits that the value of "justice" remains. In fact he does

---

20 Lyotard, *The Postmodern Condition*, p. 65.

21 See Stanley J. Grenz, *A Primer On Postmodernism* (Grand Rapids: Eerdmans, 1996), pp. 47–9; and Lyotard, *The Postmodern Condition*, p. xxv.

22 Martin Henry, "God in Postmodernity," *Irish Theological Quarterly* 63/1 (1998): 20.

23 Beardslee, "Christ in the Postmodern Age," pp. 65, 66.

24 Lyotard, *The Postmodern Condition*, p. 15.

have a sense of ethics; he simply denies their normative value for all peoples at all times.[25] Consensus is no longer a legitimate value. But the value of justice itself is "neither outmoded nor suspect" so one must therefore "arrive at an idea and practice of justice that is not linked to that of consensus."[26]

Perhaps Lyotard is highly motivated by idealistic notions of maximum freedom and creativity. Knowledge must not be reserved for systems, but it must be available to all people. People are different, so it is important for us to guard differences and cultural diversity, otherwise universal norms will threaten those differences.[27]

Critique and Theological Implications

Lyotard has made some pertinent challenges to our times that are worthy of theological consideration. I would certainly affirm his rejection of the myth of the progress of knowledge as the overall answer for humanity. Lyotard most rightly denies the grand narrative of science as the ultimate paradigm of objectivity. The "Grand Idea of Emancipation" and its inherent promise of freedom has indeed failed. Simply leaving the market free from the influence of social reformers with mistaken notions does not guarantee freedom from poverty. The Marxist "grand narrative" in the socialization of work was also a failure.[28]

However, in my estimation, the denial of certain totalizing and abusive metanarratives does not necessarily imply the need to reject all metanarratives. As a discipline of inquiry, Christian theology, intrinsically asserts a metanarrative.[29] From such a theological perspective, contrary to the central tenets of Lyotard, Christians affirm that history is a directed process with expressed goals for human beings—both spiritually and physically. If Christian theology was simply relegated to one language

---

25 West, *An Introduction to Continental Philosophy*, p. 200; and Glenn Ward, *Teach Yourself Postmodernism* (London: Hodder Headline Plc, 1997), p. 168.

26 Lyotard, *The Postmodern Condition*, p. 66. Also see West, *An Introduction to Continental Philosophy*, p. 200. We will see the "indeconstructibility" of justice as a recurring theme in postmodern deconstructive thinkers.

27 Ward, *Teach Yourself Postmodernism*, p. 168.

28 Volf, *Exclusion and Embrace*, pp. 105–6; and Grenz, *A Primer On Postmodernism*, p. 164.

29 James K.A. Smith argues against this in "A Little Story about Metanarratives: Lyotard, Religion, and Postmodernism Revisited," in Myron B. Penner (ed.), *Christianity and the Postmodern Turn: Six Views* (Grand Rapids: Brazos Press, 2005), pp. 123–40. Smith states that "the biblical story is not a metanarrative in Lyotard's sense" since a Lyotardian metanarrative is a system that claims to be legitimated by universal Reason (p. 125). I am not completely convinced, although I agree that Lyotard's claims have been exaggerated. Lyotard himself seems clearly to include the Christian biblical narrative of "redemption of original sin through love" as a grand narrative in his *The Postmodern Explained*, especially note p. 25. Further, the Christian narrative is at the least, often taken as a grand narrative by scholars and theologians and often put to the test of "universal Reason" as if it were so within the conditions of modernism.

game, or small narrative among others, it would, by nature of its own definition, not be "Christian" theology at all. Christian theology insists on the uniqueness of Jesus Christ with universal, cosmic claims: the Word that became flesh, the Son, the Creator, the redeemer and the ultimate Judge of all mankind.

There are various and sometimes conflicting mini-narratives in the world, which Lyotard rightly challenges us to appreciate by nature of their differences. Elements of truth will be found in many non-totalizing, multi-faceted mini-narratives. However, this recognition of plurality does not negate the Christian insistence on the grand narrative of the gospel that transcends them all.[30] But I would say the Christian grand narrative must not be defined as totalizing in the sense of *violent* exclusion. It is based in a God who loves and cares and offers His gift of grace to all. The doors of the gospel are open to all and they enter into the arms of a loving God.[31]

I recognize that this point of departure still presents a radical contrast to the Lyotardian postmodern vow to wage war on totality.[32] For Lyotard, as we have seen, it is the universal nature *of* a grand narrative which results in its failure. Grand narratives cannot reconcile the myriad of heterogeneous language-games.[33] As mentioned previously, the one overarching exception to this is the notion of justice. In his critique of such exception, Alister McGrath asks the following: "Yet how can justice be a universal value, given the presuppositions of postmodernity? Lyotard is silent in this respect, probably aware that pursuit of this question would do little to advance his theoretical cause."[34] Croatian theologian, Miroslav Volf, also provides a helpful critique of Lyotard at this key point: "But does not justice overarch heterogeneous language games? we may protest. What happened to their principled incommensurability? Does not each language game have its own account of justice?"[35] Of course, as Volf points out, Lyotard is searching for a non-totalizing, nonconsensual idea with which to apply his notion of justice. Volf submits:

As we listen to the call to recognize the autonomy of heterogeneity we hear the back door squeaking open and what Lyotard has driven out through the front door rushing back in. Is he not peddling something that looks very much like the Enlightenment's grand narrative of freedom under the label of nonuniversal justice?[36]

Volf also wisely questions the intentions behind the need to rid ourselves of the grand narratives. We remove the grand narratives because they commit violence to small narratives. But it seems that Lyotard failed to provide the necessary resources

---

30 Grenz, *A Primer On Postmodernism*, pp. 164–5.

31 See Volf, *Exclusion and Embrace*, p. 110.

32 Lyotard in appendix of Lyotard, *The Postmodern Condition*, p. 82. Appendix translated by Régis Durand.

33 See Volf, *Exclusion and Embrace*, p. 106.

34 Alister McGrath, *A Passion For Truth: The Intellectual Coherence of Evangelicalism* (Downers Grove: InterVarsity, 1996), pp. 197–8.

35 Volf, *Exclusion and Embrace*, p. 107.

36 Ibid.

to still prevent the bigger despots among the small from taking over those who are weaker. The ones suffering injustices will have difficulty continuing a peaceful struggle. Will not those having significant differences end up with the stronger position of power taking over the weaker position? Surely aspirations of perfect and complete information will not remedy this situation either. Information is so rapidly changing, it remains unattainable. Without any overarching criteria by which we can apply to a struggle among differences, the weak will continue to lose and the strong will continue to win.[37]

I agree with Volf in his positive assessment of Lyotard's rejection of the grand narratives of emancipation. Christians must insist that the problem of the messianic must rest with God. In this sense, as Volf suggests, and I concur, Lyotard has helped us to ask the correct question of how to live in a state of peace without the possibility of complete reconciliation. Volf puts it this way:

> Both the modern project of emancipation and its postmodern critique suggest that a nonfinal reconciliation in the midst of the struggle against oppression is what a responsible theology must be designed to facilitate. Anything else would amount to a seductive theology of a false liberation that would prove most unhelpful precisely for those in whose name it has been promulgated and who need it the most.[38]

It is this idea of "nonfinal" reconciliation that I find most promising in application for apologetic proposals in view of deconstructive theology. I will make an effort to develop these further in subsequent chapters.

---

37 Ibid., pp. 108–9.
38 Ibid., pp. 109–10.

Chapter 4

The Deconstructionism of
Jacques Derrida

The postmodern perspectives of Lyotard attempted to take the problem of meaning away from a totalizing structure and place it locally. However, with the deconstructive postmodernism of Derrida and Foucault, it is fundamentally impossible to make meaning present at all, regardless of where it is situated.[1] As such, these poststructuralist, deconstructionist notions are often considered "elusive, slippery, and ungraspable."[2] It is to these notions, as we will see in the figure of Jacques Derrida, that I now turn.

Introduction and Biographical Background

Jacques Derrida (1930–2004) is perhaps one of the most baffling, controversial and misunderstood philosophers of today. He is often viewed as a Nietzschean nihilist in favor of anarchistic relativism. Derrida received outlandish personal attacks due to his complex perspectives. He was accused of ruining philosophy departments, for destroying academic standards, and even for ruining the university itself.[3]

I offer the following example to illustrate one such vociferous attack against Derrida. In 1992, Derrida was nominated to receive an honorary degree from Cambridge University. However, on 9 May 1992, a letter appeared in the London Times by certain "anti-deconstruction" signatories. It attempted to persuade the Cambridge faculty to vote against granting this degree to Derrida based on the supposition that Derrida's "style defies comprehension." The letter stated that "[A]ttacks upon the values of reason, truth, and scholarship is not, we submit, sufficient grounds for the awarding of an honorary degree in a distinguished university." The vote was taken, Derrida winning, 336 in his favor to 204 in opposition.[4] This example among many others illustrates how much this man is widely misunderstood and often disliked, especially among those in the Anglo-American tradition of philosophical analysis.

---

1   Wentzel van Huyssteen, *Essays in Postfoundationalist Theology* (Grand Rapids: Eerdmans, 1997), p. 271.

2   Ibid.

3   John D. Caputo, ed., *Deconstruction in a Nutshell: A Conversation with Jacques Derrida* (New York: Fordham University Press, 1997), p. 41. See also, Eric Matthews, *Twentieth-Century French Philosophy* (Oxford: Oxford University Press, 1996), pp. 165–7.

4   Caputo, *Deconstruction in a Nutshell*, p. 39.

Derrida himself may not have approved of this analysis of himself nor of my analysis of deconstruction. Derrida's works are too vast and diverse to summarize. He would insist on a full reading and re–reading of his texts as well as the texts he "deconstructs" in order to discover the substance of his complex arguments. In this brief chapter, I may even be approaching these topics with, as Derrida would say, a "logocentric" bias. Nonetheless, I will proceed. For support on this meager effort, I cite Derrida scholar John D. Caputo:

> If I were more responsible, like Derrida, I would not try to put deconstruction in a nutshell. But alas, nobody's perfect, and besides Derrida himself has said that we can be flexible on this point and occasionally interrupt or transgress the absolute prohibition against nutshells with occasional exceptions.[5]

I trust that, in spite of these expressed inadequacies, this chapter will provide the reader with some "traces" of Derrida's background and thinking. In order to do this I will provide some biographical and academic background on Derrida which appears to have influenced his thinking. Then I will examine several major themes in Derrida that have greatly influenced radical postmodern theology, beginning with "deconstructionism." Finally, I will consider several implications of deconstruction with respect to theology with a brief critique and response.

Jewish Background

I do not wish to minimize nor overly emphasize the Jewishness of Derrida's thought. Derrida was born in 1930 to Sephardic Jewish parents in El Biar, Algiers, but Derrida is not what one would consider a "Jewish" writer like Buber or Levinas. Not only was he not religiously devoted to Judaism, he was raised in an Arab nation, and his language, education and culture were French.[6] Caputo submits that Derrida was "Jewish without being Jewish, Jewish *sans* Judaism, married outside Judaism, his sons uncircumcised, he an atheist."[7] In describing his broken alliance with Judaism, Derrida declared himself as "the last of the Jews."[8] Ironically, we still note a Jewish

---

5   Ibid., p. 201.

6   John D. Caputo, *The Prayers and Tears of Jacques Derrida: Religion Without Religion* (Bloomington & Indianapolis: Indiana University Press, 1997), p. 230. Cf. also p. 304. This work is perhaps the most extensive on the influence of Judaism, or at least the broken alliance with Judaism, in Derrida's works. As Caputo notes, such influences are clearly seen in Derrida's work "Circonfession: cinquante–neuf périodes et periphrases," in Geoffrey Bennington and Jacques Derrida, *Jacques Derrida* (Paris: Editions du Seuil, 1991). Published in English as: "Circumfession: Fifty–nine Periods and Periphrases," in Geoffrey Bennington and Jacques Derrida, *Jacques Derrida* (Chicago: University of Chicago Press, 1993).

7   Ibid., p. xvii.

8   Derrida, "Circumfession," p. 154. (Fr): "*le dernier des Juifs*" ("Circonfession," p. 145). Cf. also, "Circumfession," p. 122, and (Fr): "Circonfession," p. 117.

passion in his writing, even if it is a passion to break his alliances with Judaism itself. In this sense perhaps Derrida is "haunted by the figure of the Jew."[9]

One sees such "haunting" demonstrably in Derrida's work, "Circumfession: Fifty–nine Periods and Periphrases."[10] He clearly uses a play on words in the title to exhibit his "in-between" state: Jewish yet non-Jewish, affected by "confessional" Christianity, yet non-Christian. Derrida was circumcised a Jew, but the cut of circumcision signifies more than just a wound in the flesh, it represents both his union with and separation from Judaism.[11] As Caputo puts it: "Derrida uses circumcision constantly to circle around his own Jewishness, his own circumscription within Judaism by this ancient rite, his own inside/outside relation to the circle of Judaism."[12]

It is beyond the scope and purpose of this work to provide a thorough analysis of how Derrida's Jewish background has affected his writings. Nevertheless, as I consider several of Derrida's themes, I will briefly mention some parallels with Judaism related to Talmudic thought and structure. Additionally, I will show that Derrida's notion of the messianic equally provides a Jewish flavor to his work.

Academic Formation

Derrida attained his baccalaureate in 1948. While he was a lycée student, Derrida read Maurice Merleau-Ponty and Jean Paul Sartre. At the age of nineteen, he moved to France. After hearing, by chance, a radio broadcast about Camus, he was motivated to continue his studies in philosophy at the École Normale Supérieure (ENS), where he became greatly attracted to the phenomenology of Edmund Husserl.

Like Michel Foucault, Derrida studied under the Hegel scholar and French translator of the works of Husserl, Jean Hyppolite. He completed his mémoire on meaning, structure and genesis in Husserl. Derrida critiqued Husserl's reasoning and began to form his own styles of reading and writing.[13] As he discovered problems

---

9   Caputo, *The Prayers and Tears of Jacques Derrida*, p. 230. Caputo even surmises that deconstruction itself may be the product of a "Jewish mind." p. 263.

10   As noted above, this is found in Geoffrey Bennington and Jacques Derrida, *Jacques Derrida* (Chicago: University of Chicago Press, 1993).

11   However, we are not saying that Derrida's playful usage of the word "circumfession" is only limited to these representations. His intentions with this word are greatly layered and diverse. See Derrida, "Circumfession," pp. 14, 70–74, 93–5, 224–9. Also see Caputo, *The Prayers and Tears of Jacques Derrida*, pp. 283, 304.

12   Caputo, *The Prayers and Tears of Jacques Derrida*, p. 283.

13   As Derrida explains: "Husserl, thus ceaselessly attempts to reconcile the *structuralist* demand (which leads to the comprehensive description of a totality, of a form or a function organized according to an internal legality in which elements have meaning only in the solidarity of their correlation or their opposition), with the *genetic* demand (that is the search for the origin and foundation of the structure). One could show, perhaps, that the phenomenological project itself is born of an initial failure of this attempt," in *Writing and Difference* (Chicago: University of Chicago Press, 1978), p. 157.

in phenomenology and in the entire philosophical tradition, he began to distance himself from traditional philosophical inquiry. During the sixties, Derrida helped in writing the avant–garde journal, *Tel Quel*. This journal marked a new French criticism of positivism in literary studies by drawing upon the influence of semiology, structuralism, psychoanalysis, and Marxism.[14] During this time, Derrida focused on the topic of the "linguistic sign," as did the structuralists, although he never became a structuralist himself. Derrida gave a paper at a conference organized by Johns Hopkins University in 1966 titled, "Structure, Sign and Play in the Discourse of the Human Sciences," which marked the beginning of the "literary" deconstruction movement in the United States.[15] The following year, 1967, was Derrida's most influential year of publishing. A few years later, he began dividing his time between teaching in Paris and the United States.

In 1977 Derrida participated in an exchange with John R. Searle regarding the philosopher J.L. Austin and speech-act philosophy. This exchange marked a deepening rift between Derrida's work and that of Anglo-American philosophers. However, three English texts on Derrida were published in 1986 which addressed his philosophical concerns. These publications marked a positive change in the Anglo-American criticisms of Derrida's works.[16]

Major themes in Derrida

As previously noted, the dominant idea or theme when considering Derrida is "deconstructionism." To attempt any understanding of deconstruction, especially as it relates to the discussion of apologetic theology, it is also necessary to examine several parallel themes that emerge in Derrida's discussions such as "writing and speech," the concept of *"différance,"*, "presence and violence" in writing, and his notion of the "messianic." Often these parallel themes are inter-connected, and ought not to be considered apart from the general theme of deconstruction as a whole. Each theme will be unveiled in the context of a previously mentioned theme, moving toward a larger picture of the whole. Before I begin, however, it will be helpful take a glimpse at the idea of "deconstructionism" in the broadest sense.

Deconstructionism and Defining the Indefinable

Derrida resisted any attempts to define "deconstructionism." After a brief analysis of the various issues surrounding this complex theme, one may agree that the term

---

14　Christopher Norris, *Derrida* (London: Fontana Press, 1987), p. 241.

15　Ibid., p. 13; and pp. 241–2.

16　Ibid., p. 245 and note also the bibliography on pp. 260–61. These works are: Rodolphe Gasché, *The Tain of the Mirror: Derrida and the Philosophy of Reflection* (Cambridge, Mass.: Harvard Univ. Press, 1986); Irene E. Harvey, *Derrida and the Economy of Différance* (Bloomington: Indiana Univ. Press, 1986); and John Llewelyn, *Derrida on the Threshold of Sense* (London: Macmillan, 1986).

is indeed "indefinable." In Derrida's "Letter to a Japanese Friend," Derrida gives a response to the question of attempting an approximate definition of deconstruction. He states:

> All sentences of the type "deconstruction is X or deconstruction is not X," *a priori* miss the point, which is to say that they are at least false. As you know, one of the principal things at stake in what is called in my texts "deconstruction," is precisely the delimiting of ontology and above all of the third–person present indicative S is P.[17]

So, a major purpose of deconstruction is to demonstrate that texts and traditions do not have direct definable meanings. For Derrida, it would be scandalous to even suggest some kind of restrictive textual definition of something that is intended to exceed boundaries and be indeterminable. Someone once asked Derrida if he could describe what deconstruction is "in a nutshell." Derrida responded: "Sometimes, of course, I confess, I am not able to do that. But sometimes it may be useful to try nutshells."[18] Working from this modest proposal from Derrida himself, I will attempt to offer a few helpful "nutshells" on deconstruction, admittedly biased and colored from my limited knowledge, preoccupations, and interpretations.

The philosopher who had the deepest impact on Derrida was no doubt, Martin Heidegger.[19] In fact, it is from Heidegger that Derrida derives the word "deconstruction" (from the German *Destruktion*)—a word that Heidegger used to "indicate the task of loosening up the Western philosophical tradition in order to expose how being has been variously determined as presence."[20] I will proceed by saying what deconstruction *is not* and what it *does not*, before addressing what it *is* and what it *does*, in order to help us understand some of its essential characteristics.

What Deconstruction is not and What it does not:

First of all, deconstruction is not a method, a style, a technique or a hermeneutic for interpretation.[21] Deconstruction is not simply a matter of providing a negative critique of any certain philosopher's or theologian's statements and denying their objective truth content. It is not a procedure. It is not parasitic and ultimately negative as its verbal image may seem to suggest. Nor is it simply a matter of an "anything

---

17　Jacques Derrida as quoted in Norris, *Derrida*, p. 19–20.

18　Caputo, *Deconstruction in a Nutshell*, p. 31.

19　See Norris, *Derrida*, pp. 160–61. Norris explains that Derrida "demand[s] a reason for reasonableness itself." Like Heidegger, Derrida considers rationality a historical formation. He, like Heidegger, insists on re-thinking the origin of reason itself. But Heidegger wishes to return to some "primordial state of Being when language was in touch with the ultimate truths of experience." (p. 160). For Derrida this was not possible because of too many logocentric assumptions ingrained in the Western philosophical enterprise.

20　Hart, "Jacques Derrida," p. 160.

21　Norris, *Derrida*, p. 18. Also see Jean Greisch, "Déconstruction et/ou Herméneutique," in Pierre Gisel and Patrick Evrard (eds), *La Théologie en Postmodernité* (Genève: Labor et Fides, 1996), p. 356.

goes" and "to each his own" interpretation.[22] It is unfortunate that the image evoked by the word "deconstruction" is often that of destroying or "destructing" an existing structure. This image neglects to suggest that such a dismantling of a structure may reveal something new about that building itself which was previously concealed. In a similar fashion, if one were to understand "deconstruction" as a way of reading a text in order to bring to light something previously concealed, it may create a much more positive image.[23]

Derrida himself provides us with some helpful insights on what deconstruction is *not*:

> Deconstruction cannot limit itself or proceed immediately to a neutralization; it must, by means of a double gesture, a double science, a double writing, practice an overturning of the classical opposition and a general displacement of the system.... Deconstruction does not consist in passing from one concept to another, but in overturning and displacing a conceptual order, as well as the nonconceptual order with which the conceptual order is articulated.[24]

Derrida does not see texts as meaningless; he sees them as having a superfluity of meaning. So, deconstruction analyzes a text so thoroughly as to discover the many ways the text itself did not communicate upon initial reading. It is important to remember that "[d]econstruction shows how meaning overflows limits; it does not erase limits."[25] Deconstruction is not hermeneutical, nihilistic, anarchistic relativism. Such a mistaken notion rests on the failure to understand what deconstruction affirms. Deconstruction ought to be valued as critical affirmation, an affirmation which is the "*différance*" of being and meaning.[26] This word, *différance* (with an intentional "a" in place of the "e") is a word coined by Derrida (on which I will say more later) that "produces both the discourse of metaphysics and the means of ungrounding it."[27]

Deconstruction is not "destruction" or "demolition," but it is a way of opening up and responding. Derrida is not arguing for an "anything goes" philosophy; instead, he is promoting a "democratic open–endedness." But it is this "open-endedness" which "makes those who have appointed themselves the Guardians of Truth nervous."[28]

---

22 Nicholas Rescher, *Objectivity: The Obligations of Impersonal Reason* (Notre Dame and London: University of Notre Dame Press, 1997), p. 198. Cf. also p. 209.

23 Matthews, *Twentieth-Century French Philosophy*, p. 173.

24 Jacques Derrida, *Margins of Philosophy*, trans. Alan Bass (Chicago: University of Chicago Press, 1982), p. 329.

25 Hart, "Jacques Derrida," p. 161.

26 See Caputo, *Deconstruction in a Nutshell*, p. 128; and also Hart, "Jacques Derrida," pp. 159–67.

27 Hart, "Jacques Derrida," p. 161.

28 Caputo, *Deconstruction in a Nutshell*, pp. 57, 58.

What Deconstruction is and What it does:

According to Derrida himself, deconstruction is the "experience of the impossible."[29] It is going to the limit of that which is and can be never present. It moves beyond all boundaries, limits, and confines. As Caputo puts it: "One might even say that cracking nutshells is what deconstruction *is*. In a nutshell."[30] Deconstruction interrupts, disjoins, and disturbs the tranquility of limits and relentlessly pursues the impossible.[31] Deconstruction desires to transgress, it "is a passion for trespassing the horizons of possibility ... a passion for the impossible...."[32] It "insistently attempts to show us that what is claimed to be present is really absent and that the given is itself a construction of human discourse."[33] In essence, it claims that we cannot claim to have grasped ultimate reality as it purely is.[34]

Derrida scholar Christopher Norris elucidates and helpfully summarizes deconstruction as the following:

> [D]econstruction is the vigilant seeking-out of those 'aporias', blindspots or moments of self-contradiction where a text involuntarily betrays the tension between rhetoric and logic, between what it manifestly *means to say* and what it is nonetheless *constrained to mean*. To 'deconstruct' a piece of writing is therefore to operate a kind of strategic reversal, seizing on precisely those unregarded details (causal metaphors, footnotes, incidental turns of argument) which are always, and necessarily, passed over by interpreters of a more orthodox persuasion.[35]

Deconstruction at base seeks to question and dismantle the entire western philosophical enterprise that is commonly viewed as unbiased, pure foundational inquiry. Deconstruction also seeks to makes us more aware of the needs, values, and oppressions of the other. Philosophy, as a discipline, is often seen as the overarching method, regulating tool, or encompassing umbrella for governing and systematizing all truth claims. Deconstruction overthrows this whole assumption.[36]

---

29 Jacques Derrida as quoted in Caputo, *Deconstruction in a Nutshell*, pp. 32.

30 Caputo, *Deconstruction in a Nutshell*, p. 32.

31 Ibid., pp. 32, 33.

32 John D. Caputo, *The Prayers and Tears of Jacques Derrida: Religion Without Religion* (Bloomington & Indianapolis: Indiana University Press, 1997), p. xix.

33 J. Richard Middleton and Brian Walsh, *Truth is Stranger Than It Used to Be: Biblical Faith in a Postmodern Age* (Downers Grove: InterVarsity, 1995), p. 33.

34 Ibid., p. 34.

35 Norris, *Derrida*, p. 19.

36 One should note the parallel here with the perpetual skepticism and rejection of gullibility characteristic of Talmudic thinking. According to Judaic studies scholar, Jacob Neusner, Talmudic skepticism only produces limited insight. The Talmudic approach is to have humility in one's learning, understanding that truth-claims "of putative authorities, ancient or modern" are "no more than mortal." Jacob Neusner, *Invitation to the Talmud: A Teaching Book*, revised and expanded edition (San Francisco: Harper and Row, Publishers, 1973), pp. 279, 278.

Univocal textual meaning is undone and the logocentrist and objectivist nature of typical western philosophical thinking is rejected. Yet, as Graham Ward cautions, it is not that Derrida is "some maverick conquistador of logocentrism," but there is "the recognition that it is continually fissured."[37] It also seeks to repudiate the commonly accepted correspondence theory of truth which assumes an immediate connection between language and the external world. Deconstruction demonstrates the clear bifurcation between reality and the linguistic representations we give it.[38] On the other hand, deconstruction is not simply a prison in which we are locked into the futility of playing with linguistic strings. Such a notion is "a particularly perverse one, given the dynamics and motivations of deconstruction."[39]

Simply put, Derrida's deconstruction differs from traditional philosophical inquiry in the following three aspects: 1) By his style of questioning;[40] 2) By questioning philosophy itself; and 3) By refusing the traditional distinction between philosophy proper and other areas of the liberal arts or intellectual pursuit.[41] Deconstruction is by no means a simple, loose reading of texts, but a rigorous inquiry, an engaged, extremely careful analysis of texts and philosophical systems to bring to light that which is typically suppressed. In this sense, deconstruction parallels the meticulous nature of Talmudic dialectic: "argument and counterargument, thesis and refutation," and reflection upon "old issues in new ways" with unrelenting, highly disciplined, careful reading of texts.[42]

Derrida's rejection of "logocentrism" is key to understanding the deconstructionist project. Philosophy is not some overarching umbrella, grid, or tool by which to make objective judgments on other systems of thought, itself being exempt from criticism. Instead, philosophy itself, for Derrida, is more like a particular literary genre itself which includes texts which must be analyzed and studied as other types of literature. This "situatedness" of philosophy is key to understanding the deconstructionist agenda. Derrida makes this clear in an essay titled, "Qual Quelle" that is included in his work, *Margins of Philosophy.* In this essay Derrida interacts with the French writer, Valéry, who reminds us that philosophy is "written." This being the case, the following task is given:

> [T]o study the philosophical text in its formal structure, in its rhetorical organization, in the specificity and diversity of its textual types, in its models of exposition and production—

---

37   Graham Ward, *Barth, Derrida and the Language of Theology* (Cambridge: Cambridge University Press, 1995), p. 182.

38   Grenz, *A Primer On Postmodernism*, p. 148.

39   Caputo, *The Prayers and Tears of Jacques Derrida*, p. 15.

40   Derrida often uses juxtaposed prose with overlapping styles or tones in one work, or he may display two texts by running them together; idem., chapter one, "Tympan" in *Margins of Philosophy* (Chicago: University of Chicago Press, 1982). One may argue that Derrida was influenced by the juxtaposed literary structure of the folios of the Babylonian Talmud. See Jacob Neusner, *Invitation to the Talmud: A Teaching Book*, pp. 171–3.

41   Matthews, *Twentieth-Century French Philosophy*, p. 168.

42   Neusner, *Invitation to the Talmud*, pp. 168–9, 273.

beyond what previously were called genres—and also in the space of its mises en scène, in a syntax which would be not only the articulation of its signifieds, its references to Being or to truth, but also the handling of its proceedings, and of everything invested in them. In a word, the task is to consider philosophy also as a "particular literary genre," drawing upon the reserves of a language, cultivating, forcing, or making deviate a set of tropic resources older than philosophy itself.[43]

Norris observes that deconstruction begins by finding the "stress-points where writing resists any attempt to reduce it to an order of univocal (*single-voiced*) truth." This is why Derrida pays meticulous attention to the *letter* of the text and the seemingly insignificant details which many philosophers have ignored "in the interests of preserving a conceptual status quo."[44] However, in order to understand more of what this entails I must proceed with the Derridean themes of "Writing and Speech" and "*Différance*."

Writing and Speech

Derrida distinguishes between "speech" and "writing" in order to elucidate his critique of logocentrism and what he calls the "transcendental signified." Naturally, speaking is closer to its source than writing. When one speaks, the words are broadcast into the air, then they vanish. Writing, however, is not dependent upon one's presence "at the scene" for it to remain in existence. Speech has an immediate "sense" connotation, writing does not. The idea of "speech" implies presence, whereas "writing" implies absence. Speech allows direct connection with "truth" which writing does not allow. For Derrida, this all rests upon the mistaken western notion of logocentrism—looking to the "*logos*," the word, or language, as the carrier of meaning.[45] Derrida describes this:

Yet if reading must not be content with doubling the text, it cannot legitimately transgress the text toward something other than it, toward a referent (a reality that is metaphysical, historical, psychobiographical, etc.) or toward a signified outside the text whose content could take place, could have taken place outside of language, that is to say, in the sense that we give here to that word, outside of writing in general. That is why the methodological considerations that we risk applying here to an example are closely dependent on general propositions that we have elaborated above; as regards the absence of the referent or the transcendental signified. *There is nothing outside of the text.* [there is no outside-text; *il n'y a pas de hors-texte*].[46]

---

43 Derrida, *Margins of Philosophy*, p. 293.

44 Norris, *Derrida*, p. 86.

45 Grenz, *A Primer On Postmodernism*, p. 141.

46 Jacques Derrida, *Of Grammatology* (Baltimore: Johns Hopkins University Press, 1976), p. 158.

Derrida esteems the written word above the oral word.[47] Western philosophy tends to avoid writing to pursue speech, assuming that there exists some "presence" of being which we may come to know. Derrida criticizes such "realist" perspective of language which links statements to fixed reality or objective truth. Language cannot signify or represent the essential nature of reality through a "transcendental signified" such as God, consciousness, truth, the Idea, or the Self. For Derrida, "the original, or transcendental signified, is never absolutely present outside a system of differences. The absence of the transcendental signified extends the domain and the play of signification infinitely."[48] Deconstruction is used to remind us that the origin of language does not lie in the correspondence between thoughts and objects, but with writing.[49] Derrida claims:

> There has to be a transcendental signified for the difference between signifier and signified to be somewhere absolute and irreducible. It is not by chance that the thought of being, as the thought of this transcendental signified, is manifested above all in the voice: in a language of words [mots].[50]

It is certainly the case that western philosophy has been transmitted in the form of words, that is, written texts. Once this is accepted, one can see a separation between what the philosopher perceives himself to be saying and what is actually contained in the text. The text will inevitably contain various assumptions of which the author is not aware. This is where deconstruction steps in.[51]

Différance vs. Presence/Violence in Writing

Derrida coined a new French word "*différance*" (with an "a" following the "r") to express his contrary views to logocentrism.[52] As Derrida puts it:

> In the delineation of *différance* everything is strategic and adventurous. Strategic because no transcendent truth present outside the field of writing can govern theologically the totality of the field. Adventurous because this strategy is not a simple strategy in the sense that strategy orients tactics according to a final goal, a *telos* or theme of domination, a mastery and ultimate reappropriation of the development of the field.[53]

---

47 See John M. Ellis' critique of Derrida on this point in *Against Deconstruction* (Princeton: Princeton University Press, 1989), pp. 18–19.

48 Derrida, *Writing and Difference*, p. 280.

49 See Carson, *The Gagging of God*, p. 109 and Grenz, *A Primer On Postmodernism*, pp. 142, 150. See also Derrida, *Of Grammatology*, pp. 20, 49.

50 Derrida, *Of Grammatology* (Baltimore: Johns Hopkins University Press, 1976), p. 20.

51 Matthews, *Twentieth-Century French Philosophy*, p. 170.

52 See Derrida, *Margins of Philosophy*, pp. 1–27 for his essay on "Différance."

53 Ibid., p.7.

This word, *différance*, combines the meanings of two words *différer* and *différence*. Of course the joining of these two meanings into one word is exactly Derrida's intention. Derrida views reality in terms of differences (as opposed to self–identity) and also in terms of perpetual deferment (as opposed to that which is eternally present).[54] *Différance* has exactly the same pronunciation as the French word *différence*. This word play itself expresses Derrida's criticism of western logocentrism. Writing is not, according to Derrida, simply representative of human speech which is *present* and immediate.[55] Derrida quotes Saussure to explain this:

> [I]n language there are only differences. Even more important: a difference generally implies positive terms between which the difference is set up; but in language there are only differences *without positive terms*. Whether we take the signified or the signifier, language has neither ideas nor sounds that existed before the linguistic system, but only conceptual and phonic differences that have issued from the system.[56]

Derrida makes a distinction between a word in itself, a phonic signifier, and that to which it signifies, the concept or idea that the word conveys. The words we use arise from their particular context, which in turn refer to other contexts. Language is essentially a long chain of signifiers that refer to other signifiers. As Graham Ward notes: "Derrida proposes that Western metaphysics has been dominated by the desire to reappropriate the sign's deferred presence...."[57] Signs always refer to other signs, so it is necessary to "defer" our assumptions to provide meaning. This does not eradicate meaning, however, because "traces" of meaning continue to be found through the chain of signifiers.[58]

The spelling of the word *différance* is to remind us that the word *différence* is not "present" in the text "literally;" nevertheless, the meaning of the word *is* still present. Gayatri Chakravorty Spivak, the translator of Derrida's, *Of Grammatology* into English, comments on this:

> For differance, producing the differential structure of our hold on "presence," never produces presence as such.... The structure of "presence" is thus constituted by difference

---

54 Matthews, *Twentieth-Century French Philosophy*, p. 168.

55 Derrida, *Margins of Philosophy* (Chicago: University of Chicago Press, 1982) p. 7 and see Grenz, *A Primer On Postmodernism*, pp. 142–5.

56 Ferdinand de Saussure, *Course in General Linguistics*, trans. Wade Baskin (New York: Philosophical Library, 1959), pp. 117–18, 120 as quoted in Derrida, *Margins of Philosophy*, pp. 10–11. Derrida himself notes: "*Différance* is the systematic play of differences, of the traces of differences, of the *spacing* by means of which elements are related to each other." Jacques Derrida, *Positions*, trans. Alan Bass (Chicago: The University of Chicago Press, 1981), p. 27.

57 Graham Ward, *Barth, Derrida and the Language of Theology*, p. 214.

58 See Derrida, *Margins of Philosophy*, pp. 23–5; Jacques Derrida, *Positions*, pp. 26ff; and Grenz, *A Primer On Postmodernism*, pp. 143–4. For a discussion comparing the notion of "trace" in both Levinas and Derrida, see Graham Ward, *Barth, Derrida and the Language of Theology*, p. 184ff.

and deferment. But since the "subject" that "perceives" presence is also constituted similarly, differance is neither active nor passive. The "–ance" ending is the mark of that suspended status. Since the difference between "difference" and "differance" is inaudible, this "neographism" reminds us of the importance of writing as a structure. The "a" serves to remind us that, even within the graphic structure, the perfectly spelled word is always absent, constituted through an endless series of spelling mistakes.[59]

For Derrida, "there is nothing outside the text" (*il n'y a pas de hors-texte*).[60] We have the text itself, not a transcendental signified to which the text refers. This is not to say that history does not exist, or that there is no reality outside the written text. But, it does question that "which assimilates all forms of history and knowledge to the unfolding of a teleological scheme whose end-point is self-present truth."[61] In the western intellectual tradition there is a metaphysics of presence, or a mimetic theory of truth which assumes a basic connection between reality and our description of reality.

Deconstruction attacks this perspective of "presence" and attempts to show us that what is often assumed to be present is actually absent. For Derrida, meaning cannot be final—if it was, it would be a form of "presence." For finality implies mastery, and mastery, control. The traditional and typical rhetoric of scientific objectivity and nonbiased observation often discloses a desire for mastery and control. In this sense, a realist metaphysics of presence is also a metaphysics of violence. This violence is expressed by trying to place the various complexities of the world into a unified, thematic, whole through language. It is this very thing, according to deconstructionists such as Derrida, that western intellectuals have violently used to justify conquest and superiority in the political world.[62]

Again, this deconstructive process is intended not to be "destructive" nihilism, but "constructive" therapy to overcome such tendencies of violence. Therapy, however, is often difficult, it often "cuts" through to one's innermost being, thoughts, and emotions in order to bring healing. Deconstruction seeks to bring to light these underlying modernist tendencies of presence and metaphysics of violence so that constructive healing may begin.[63]

59　Gayartri Chakravorty Spivak as quoted in the preface of Derrida, *Of Grammatology*, p. xliii.

60　Derrida, *Of Grammatology*, p.158.

61　Norris, *Derrida*, p. 71.

62　Middleton and Walsh, *Truth is Stranger Than It Used to Be*, pp. 33–4. See also James K.A. Smith, "How to Avoid Not Speaking," in James H. Olthuis (ed.), *Knowing Other-Wise: Philosophy at the Threshold of Spirituality* (New York: Fordham University Press, 1997), note 4, p. 231. For some additional helpful comments along this line see Henry H. Knight III, *A Future For Truth* (Nashville: Abingdon Press, 1997) p. 59.

63　Middleton Walsh, *Truth is Stranger Than It Used to Be*, p. 34.

The Messianic

Perhaps the first and last word in deconstruction is the word "come" (*viens*). It is this notion of "come" which leads us to the messianic theme of deconstruction according to Derrida:

> This universal structure of the promise, of the expectation of the coming has to do with justice—that is what I call the messianic structure. This messianic structure is not limited to what one calls messianisms, that is, Jewish, Christian, or Islamic messianism, to these determinate figures and forms of the Messiah. As soon as you reduce the messianic structure to messianism, then you are reducing the universality and this has important political consequences. Then you are accrediting one tradition among others and a notion of an elected people, of a given literal language, a given fundamentalism.[64]

This is how Derrida distinguishes between a "messianism" and the "messianic." A messianism determines the specific identification of a Messiah within a particular people group, hence provoking violence and war in the name of "God." However, the "messianic" pertains to the nature of promise—a future always to come. This messianic coming must not be confused with an actual presence of a messiah located in historical records. If this were the case, it would not truly be "messianic." The true "messianic," or the true Messiah, is that to which we may *always* say "come." If a Messiah ever *actually* came in real space and time it would close off all possibility of hope and promise and expectation.[65] Maurice Blanchot would call this messianic notion of deconstruction the "*le pas au delà*" (the beyond that is never reached but always pursued).[66]

Deconstruction stops closure. It desires to keep things open, to keep the dialogue going, to keep on reading without settling the issues. Deconstruction keeps religion open to "constant reinvention, encouraging religion to reread ancient texts in new ways, to reinvent ancient traditions in new contexts."[67] In this way, deconstruction does not destroy religion, it rather reimagines and reconceives it. It chastises religion for its tendency to confuse faith with knowledge. In this perspective, religion becomes dangerous and ultimately violent when it sees itself as the supreme knowledge only granted to a chosen few. Clearly, this notion of the messianic is perhaps Derrida's closest link with, while remaining his clearest separation from, Judaism. Derrida's *messianic* does sustain the open-ended, and endlessly progressive nature of Talmudic inquiry, where nothing is affirmed as the final answer or completed solution.[68] Derrida's messianic is always open to the future, never determined and never specifically obtained. Derrida's messianic is clearly not Jewish or Christian

---

64 Jacques Derrida as quoted in Caputo, *Deconstruction in a Nutshell*, p. 23.
65 Ibid., pp. 159–63.
66 Maurice Blanchot as quoted in Caputo, *Deconstruction in a Nutshell*, p. 163.
67 Caputo, *Deconstruction in a Nutshell*, p. 159.
68 Neusner, *Invitation to the Talmud*, p. 279.

in any eschatological sense. For Derrida's Messiah never comes, never arrives, but always comes and always will endlessly come.[69]

Implications for Theology: Critique and Response

General Theological Considerations

Although Derrida claims that deconstruction "blocks every relationship to theology."[70] it ought not be construed as the *destruction* of theology.[71] In fact, deconstruction has many theological implications. As with deconstruction, theology certainly involves carefully thinking through texts and carefully considering Scripture and its expression in society through the texts of others. Due to these factors alone, deconstruction merits serious attention by students of theology.

Derrida is in fact concerned with metaphysics in theology. Of course, this concern may be entirely for the sake of dismantling metaphysics *from* theology. A contemporary deconstructive theology according to Derrida

> would seem to be to liberate theology from what has been grafted on to it, to free it from its metaphysical-philosophical super ego, so as to uncover an authenticity of the "gospel," of the evangelical message. And thus, from the perspective of faith, deconstruction can at least be a very useful technique when Aristotelianism or Thomism are to be criticized or, even from an institutional perspective, when what needs to be criticized is a whole theological institution which supposedly has covered over, dissimulated an authentic Christian message. And [the point would seem to be] a real possibility for faith both at the margins and very close to Scripture, a faith lived in a venturous, dangerous, free way.[72]

Derrida certainly attempts to unsettle traditional metaphysics, but his deconstructionism should not be construed as a negative theology as such. Derrida does not speak of deconstruction in the context of negative theology, but he does concede that it will often bear a likeness *to* negative theology with similar expressions, sidetracks, and wording. He admits that on occasion it may not even

---

69 Martin Kavka draws a parallel between Derrida's notion of messianic, and the radically interior Messiah of Levinas, where the self is appropriated as Messiah. "This type of messianism—like Derrida's 'messianic,' both bracketed from determinable messianism yet founded in the Jewish tradition—is a corollary of Levinisian phenomenology." Martin Kavka, "The Rationality of Derrida's 'Religion without Religion': A Phenomenological Gift for John D. Caputo," 18 November 1999, http://www.jcrt.org/archives/01.1/kavka.html (4 Oct. 2005).

70 Jacques Derrida as quoted in Mark C. Taylor, *Erring* (Chicago: The University of Chicago Press, 1984), p. 219.

71 François Nault affirms this in *Derrida et la théologie: Dire Dieu après la déconstruction* (Paris: Les éditions du Cerf, 2000), p. 37. Cf. also p. 260.

72 Jacques Derrida in James Creech, Peggy Kamuf, and Jane Todd, "Deconstruction in America: an interview with Jacques Derrida," *Critical Exchange* 17 (1985): 12 as quoted in Hart, "Jacques Derrida," p. 162.

be distinguishable from negative theology. Yet the aspects of différance that are "thereby delineated are not theological" for Derrida. Negative theologies are concerned with disengaging God's superessential nature from our finite categories of presence, namely essence and existence. These categories cannot do justice to a God who is beyond such finite descriptions. Yet, the negative theologian's end desire is to still acknowledge an ineffable superior mode of Being that is beyond our predicates of existence.[73] So negative theologies move from talk about God to God's immediate unknowable presence. Of course, to accomplish this one must mentally obliterate any preconceived predications of this God derived from revelatory events.[74] Negative theology uses language void of ontological predicates of God, but still desires to approach the revealed God of positive theology. Deconstruction takes this a step further by consistently challenging the whole enterprise of assuming language can be used without equivocation or corruption. For Derrida, there is always the possibility of textual grafting and contamination. Wherever there is différance, positive description is not possible. But neither is silence. Approaching the revealed God remains the hidden promise of negative theology. Silence also bears the markings of différance.[75]

We enter the dilemma. Language is by nature contextual. If we say that God cannot be affirmed, denied or revealed in the present, we should avoid speaking of God altogether. Otherwise, we do violence to the nature of language. But we cannot escape language. As basic communication theory suggests, one cannot *not* communicate. Applied hermeneutically, I would submit that one cannot *not* interpret. By implication, even silence communicates and interprets. Derrida would suggest that a non-contextual silence would not be possible. Similarly, in my understanding, silence about God is also not possible. As negative theologies and Christian mystics attempt to honor "God" through silence, they must presuppose first the "God" of which they determine to be silent about. In this sense, and according to this perspective, silence itself commits metaphysical violence.

When we speak of God, our discourse will necessarily use a system of signifiers. We cannot speak of God outside the text. When we speak, we inevitably use generalities and particularities. Scripture itself is contextualized historically and linguistically. One may agree with Derrida and claim that language always presents barriers. But the question is whether or not these barriers may be overcome to any degree. For the deconstructionist, the metaphysical "letter," so to speak, cannot be delivered because of a fallible postal system due to contextuality, ruptures in communication, and misunderstandings.[76] James K.A. Smith comments on this:

---

73 Derrida, *Margins of Philosophy*, p.6.

74 Hart, "Jacques Derrida," p. 163.

75 Ibid., pp. 163–4.

76 See Smith, "How to Avoid Not Speaking," pp. 219–32. Cf. James K.A. Smith, *The Fall of Interpretation: Philosophical Foundations For a Creational Hermeneutic* (Downers Grove: InterVarsity, 2000), pp. 119–20.

> For Western metaphysics, and for fundamentalist theology (which is very modern), the letter is not able to arrive; that is, the letter *always* arrives. Metaphysics and fundamentalism have an extremely reliable—I should say "infallible"—postal system.... It is this impeccable postal service that frightens Derrida. Such a (theological) system, built on a flawless telecommunications network, knows God and speaks for God *without mediation.*[77]

Smith claims that, for Derrida the "letter" is *non posse advenire* (not able to arrive) because all discourse is conditioned linguistically, culturally and historically. The position of "fundamentalist" type of theologies (whether Protestant, Catholic, or otherwise) is *non posse non advenire* (not able not to arrive) which is simply a delusion due to the chain of endless signifiers of all text and discourse. The letter is simply not able to arrive because of the reality of a flawed postal system in which we live.

Although I share Smith's disdain with those holding biblicist delusions of infallible accuracy, I would question Smith's seemingly hasty generalization of the position of "fundamentalist theology." Perspectives on the impact of cultural, historical and linguistic distanciation are too numerous and varied to impose such a sweeping statement as the fundamentalist "position" that "the letter always arrives." For example, the evangelical supposition that the Bible is the authoritative, inspired Word of God does not contend, at the same time, that man can infallibly interpret or apply that Word. Nor would it contend that our translations are perfect renditions of the original absent of any cultural baggage whatsoever.

If one concurs with Derrida, that the letter is not able to arrive at all, or that language presents a complete barrier, would be reductionistic. For this presupposes the impossibility of supernatural divine intervention—even if through fallible language. To continue with Smith's metaphor, when Derrida claims that the postal *system* is fallible, he assumes that the postal *service* is man-created and not God-created. To push the metaphor, what if God were the founder and chief executive officer of the postal service, and also the one in charge of insuring that the postal carriers effectively carried out their responsibilities? Would language still be an insurmountable barrier? If this were the case, would I necessarily be obliged to say that the letter *never* arrives? It seems as though Derrida presupposes that God could not act supernaturally through fallible human agents. He seems to assume the impossibility of a God who could choose to reveal himself in such a revelatory way. Smith does offer a creative, valuable option avoiding the violence of metaphysical and negative theology. He claims that we want to avoid not speaking because we have a message to tell, a gospel to proclaim. This occurs by telling *our* story. We must recognize that certainty is an illusion and tell our own healing, helping "good news" (*eu–angelion*) story. Smith supports his perspective by the example of the disciples:

---

77 Smith, "How to Avoid Not Speaking," p. 221.

The disciples were committed to a theology (and a Christology) from below: they attested to that which they had seen, telling their stories to any who would listen. In the ev–angelistic theology that I am proposing, we too simply point others to the One whom we have embraced. We take them to see him, show them who he is. We do not come with postal/metaphysical backups, nor are we silent in the face of their trials and burdens; rather, we simply say, "Come and see" (John 1:46). Come and see the One who has healed us and helped us and fed us. We can point to the Lamb (John 1:29) and lead others to him (John 1:42). As such, we are only imitating the early Christian community, who were sent as witnesses—attestors—to testify concerning that which they had seen and heard and experienced (Matthew 28:19–20; Acts 1:8)... In telling stories we can avoid speaking violently and also avoid not speaking.[78]

Story telling avoids violence, Smith tells us, because it involves praise instead of predication.[79]

Although Smith's option is not fully developed in this short paragraph, his admonition is quite relevant. We have indeed lost the art of story telling due to many of our western logocentric biases. We need to learn to tell of the gospel and its healing in our lives through imaginative and creative, non-violent discourse. However, Smith does not address the issue of conflicting personal stories. In challenging others to tell "good" stories he does not address the nature of the "good." He suggests that these stories should offer the hope of healing, but he does not acknowledge that the scalpel of the healer is often sharp and painful. He claims that story telling avoids violence since it is a discourse of praise. Yet we should also ask about the relevance of story telling with the purpose of "non-violent" confrontation in order to stimulate positive, healing change in others.

Deconstruction and the Christian Ethic

Deconstruction may help us in our consideration of a Christian ethic. Caputo claims that deconstruction "refocuses Christian ethics on the ethics of the other, the lame and the leper, the widow, the orphan and the stranger."[80] Derrida is to be appreciated for exposing sources of distortion and coercion in communicative structures.[81] Certainly, the institutional power of Christianity must be guarded and delimited in order to protect those who have suffered from abuses of its power.

Does deconstruction always genuinely protect the "other" as Caputo claims? If the deconstruction of texts necessarily implies that one ought never consider authorial intentionality to any degree, then deconstruction is committing that which it seeks to avoid at all cost: interpretive violence to both the author and the text. I

---

78 Ibid., p. 230.

79 Ibid.

80 John D. Caputo, "The Good News About Alterity: Derrida and Theology," *Faith and Philosophy*, 10/4 (1993): 467.

81 Kevin J. Vanhoozer, "The Spirit of Understanding: Special Revelation and General Hermeneutics," in *Disciplining Hermeneutics*, ed. Roger Lundin (Grand Rapids: Eerdmans, 1997), p. 161.

would not argue against the need to seek out a "repressed otherness" of culturally conditioned, contextualized language. In my estimation, deconstruction must be ethically responsible in this regard. If deconstruction becomes an excuse for licensing interpretive violence, then it fails to achieve the "hermeneutic humility" it seeks.[82] However, we should give credit to deconstructive initiatives that provide a renewed sense of the multiplicity of the Christian tradition.[83] We must be aware of the repressed, oppressed other in our midst. Being sensitive to the other may involve the deconstruction of normal denominational, ecclesiological, anglo-centric, euro-centric "comfort zones," lest by our silence and lack of involvement with "others," we commit nonverbal violence in the name of Christianity.

Deconstruction and the Messianic

One may argue that Derrida's notion of the messianic is based on a realized eschatology. According to Graham Ward, a "realized eschatology is continually postponed," yet, he argues, Derrida cannot make such a claim. Instead, Ward submits, Derrida can only claim "that the chain of substituting signifiers will, as far as one can judge, continue indefinitely. The economy of *différance*, therefore, questions but can never erase eschatology."[84]

Certainly, if Derrida's conception of the messianic is true, the notion of a Christian or Jewish Messiah is not true. Christians believe that the Messiah Jesus did indeed enter history as God incarnate. This view speaks of promise and continued expectation as the self and others discover a reconstituted identity through what evangelical theology would call "sanctification." Simply the fact that the Messiah Jesus did enter history does not close off promise and future expectation. Indeed, prophecy was fulfilled, yet continued expectation remains in that of the Second Advent. The eager expectation of the future Messiah, coming again in the flesh, opens up many possibilities of hope and promise. This Messiah was realized in space and time, and will be again in the future. This belief continues to open up unlimited expectations of hope and promise on a transcendent scale of existence; which, in evangelical theology may be termed the "glorified state."[85]

I believe that Derrida begs the question when he claims that we must not reduce the Messiah to a determinate figure within a historical context (which he terms a messianism) thereby accrediting one tradition among others. This presupposes that man created the notion of such a Messiah, and assumes that such a Messiah did not

---

82 Ibid., pp. 158–61. Also see Anthony C. Thiselton, "Communicative Action and Promise in Interdisciplinary, Biblical, and Theological Hermeneutics," in Roger Lundin, Clarence Walhout, and Anthony C. Thiselton, *The Promise of Hermeneutics* (Grand Rapids and Cambridge, U.K.: Eerdmans-Paternoster, 1999), p. 181.

83 Caputo, "The Good News About Alterity," p. 467. Although I would not agree with all of Caputo's pluralistic affirmations here, he helps us think through several positive aspects of forming a "Christian deconstruction" of sorts.

84 Ward, *Barth, Derrida and the Language of Theology*, p. 215.

85 I will address this theme more extensively in a later chapter.

nor could not actually enter history in time and space. If indeed the Messiah Jesus entered history, it does not necessarily imply an ethnocentric elitist "messianism." Instead, it serves as the ultimate example for understanding both God and self. Jesus willingly chose to accept violence and hostility upon himself. Anthony Thiselton provides some helpful insights on this issue especially with respect to the book of Hebrews:

> Betrayal, arrest, torture and crucifixion carried this role of self-as-victim to the ultimate. But while this resonates with postmodern perceptions of selfhood, it is not the whole story. Being 'on the receiving end' of hostile power-interests (12:3), constituted for Jesus an episode within the larger narrative which only in its wholeness defined his selfhood.[86]

Thiselton continues to say that the epistle of Hebrews affirms that the example of Jesus Christ provides a definitive interpretation of true humanness. Unfortunately, in the present, self–interest (both individually and institutionally) and manipulation both deface true selfhood. Yet, as the future promise begins to unveil, "interpreting God and human selfhood will come to display ever-closer affinities, even if God will always be God, and human self, a human self."[87]

Deconstruction and the Metanarrative

I would credit Derrida with bringing to our attention the fact that many of our ideologies expressed even in the name of "Christianity" may often be used as oppressive devices. The fact is, we do often see reality simply from our own perspectives, ideals, and presuppositions. We must challenge ourselves to break free from those systems of thought which do not allow an exchange of thoughts from others. Yet, a distinctively Christian theology cannot wholeheartedly endorse Derrida's criticism against "metaphysics of presence" or that which Jean-François Lyotard would term the "metanarrative."[88] As noted before, I believe it is possible to reject many of the rationalistic Enlightenment excesses such as the assumptions of the progress of knowledge, and the total objective nature of the scientific enterprise, while still affirming an overarching, historical metanarrative from the Bible.[89]

In Derrida's well-known essay, "Plato's Pharmacy," he undertakes a deconstructive commentary on Plato's *Phaedrus*. Here Derrida discusses the recurring term *pharmakon* ("drug") which Socrates relates to "writing" as opposed to "speech." This word can actually mean either "poison" or "cure." On one hand it threatens the presence of speech, and on the other it is the means for communicating that presence.

---

86 Anthony C. Thiselton, *Interpreting God and the Postmodern Self* (Edinburgh: T&T Clark, 1995) p. 163.

87 Ibid.

88 See above section on Lyotard, and Jean-François Lyotard, *La Condition Postmoderne*, Collection Critique (Paris: Les Editions De Minuit, 1979) especially note pp. 7–9.

89 See Grenz, *A Primer On Postmodernism*, pp. 163–4. This is not to say that there may be many "mini-narrative" strands within the larger metanarrative.

These antithetical meanings consequently defeat attempts by "logocentric" scholars to simply choose one term or the other on the basis of context.[90]

Derrida does not simply apply this term *pharmakon* to writing, but he uses it also to symbolize the ambiguity of life. In view of this, I would pose the following question: May we not also apply Derrida's usage of this term to the idea of a metanarrative itself? Perhaps one could say that a metanarrative is both a cure or a medicine, as well as a poison. It may be used for good will or evil. Ultimately, one cannot simply reject the idea of a metanarrative based on an assumption of its inherent violent nature. It should be noted that "the claims made for deconstruction depend on the very questionable assumption that the 'logocentrism' which Derrida criticizes has been shown to be flawed."[91] I submit that the problem with a perniciously based metanarrative is rooted in the violence of the human heart instead of the inherent violence of the notion of metanarrative itself.[92]

I am suggesting that the biblical metanarrative does address the issues of concern to the deconstructionist, free from accusations of totalization and violence. Instead, Scripture may free one from violence, and help one see "shalom" and justice (the one term Derrida would say is not "deconstructible").[93] J. Richard Middleton and Brian J. Walsh summarize this well:

> Such transformation is, of course, never guaranteed. It is not a mechanical function of the text but depends on our response, we who claim this text as canonical. This means that we must be willing for the biblical text to judge our constructions, to call us into question, to convert us. In one sense, then the charge of totalization addressed to Christianity can only be answered by the concrete, nontotalizing life of actual Christians, the body of Christ who as living epistles (as Paul calls the church in 2 Cor 3:1–3) take up and continue the ministry of Jesus to a suffering and broken world. That is ultimately the only answer that counts.... so that the Scriptures might be a living resource, contributing to the genuine empowerment of the church in the exercise of its mission in a postmodern world.[94]

If we are indeed to practice or attempt a "Christian" deconstruction we must not dilute nor "destruct" the essential nature of the Christian message. Christians may effectively engage latent deconstructionist concerns while maintaining their allegiances to Jesus, "Who did not hesitate to deconstruct the law of the sabbath in name of divine justice, or to sit down to dinner with sinners and the outcast.... who was, to the scandal of all, a teacher of alterity, who to everyone's consternation kept spreading the good news about alterity."[95]

---

90 See Norris, *Derrida*, p. 37. See also Middleton and Walsh, *Truth is Stranger Than It Used to Be*, p. 79.

91 Matthews, *Twentieth-Century French Philosophy*, p. 177.

92 Middleton and Walsh, *Truth is Stranger Than It Used to Be*, p. 79. Cf. also the previous critique of Lyotard.

93 See Caputo, *Deconstruction in a Nutshell*, pp. 125–9. Cf. also with Lyotard's exception (above) in the notion of justice.

94 Middleton and Walsh, *Truth is Stranger Than It Used to Be*, p. 107.

95 Caputo, "The Good News About Alterity," 468.

However one views deconstructionism, I believe it is important to respond to Derrida seriously and respectfully. Caputo reminds us that a "deconstructive reading is exceedingly close, fine-grained, meticulous, scholarly, serious, and, above all, 'responsible,' both in the sense of being able to give an account of itself in scholarly terms and in the sense of 'responding' to something in the text that tends to drop out of view."[96] With this in mind, I now turn in the following chapter to another, who it has been said, "shared with Derrida the leadership of 'post–structuralism," the French thinker, Michel Foucault.[97]

---

96 Caputo, *Deconstruction in a Nutshell*, p. 77.
97 J.G. Merquior, *Foucault* (London: Fontana Press, 1991), p. 13.

Chapter 5

Michel Foucault:
The End of Man?

Introduction and Background

In various works charting the development of postmodernism, Michel Foucault is often examined prior to Jacques Derrida. This is perhaps for two major reasons. First, he died in 1984 and Derrida in 2004. Second, Foucault is often seen more closely connected with French structuralist thought than with the post-structuralist thought typical of Derrida.[1] However, I am purposefully considering Foucault's position subsequent to Derrida for the following reasons: First, despite the significant differences between the two thinkers, I am attempting to show how Foucault fits into my reading of a 'Derridean' flavour of deconstruction as it relates to theology. In this sense, then, I wish to present Foucault in light of my reading of Derrida to show how he "deconstructs" dominating systems of thought which greatly shape our theological thinking.[2] Although Foucault does not directly refer to Derrida, his notion of power in social relations has been said to be "no less differential or relational" than Derrida's notion of *différance* in his critique of the western metaphysical tradition.[3]

"Paul-Michel Foucault" was born in Poitiers, France on October 15, 1926. (He later rejected the name "Paul" because it was the same name as his father whom he despised as a young man). His father was a surgeon, as were both of his grandfathers, and his mother was a woman of independent wealth. Foucault was raised Roman Catholic, although his parents were not devout. Holding a pessimistic outlook on the public school system following the Second World War, Foucault's mother enrolled him in a Catholic (Jesuit) school in 1940. Evidently this was not a positive experience for Foucault because he left his Catholic education with a hatred of religion. He became a boarder at the Lycée Henri IV in Paris in 1945, to read philosophy in preparation for entrance to the acclaimed Ecole Normale Supérieure.

---

1   However, Foucault strongly objected to being designated a "structuralist." As Foucault states in his "Foreword to the English Edition" of *The Order of Things: An Archaeology of the Human Sciences* (London: Routledge, 1970), p. xiv: "In France, certain half-witted 'commentators' persist in labelling me a 'structuralist'. I have been unable to get it into their tiny minds that I have used none of the methods, concepts, or key terms that characterize structural analysis."

2   See Terrence W. Tilley, *Postmodern Theologies: The Challenge of Religious Diversity* (Maryknoll: Orbis Books, 1995), p. viii. Cf. James M. Byrne, "Foucault On Continuity: The Postmodern Challenge To Tradition," *Faith and Philosophy* 9/3 (1992): 344.

3   Stephen D. Moore, *Poststructuralism and the New Testament* (Minneapolis: Fortress Press, 1994), p. 90.

Foucault studied with such thinkers as Maurice Merleau–Ponty, Jean Hyppolite, and Louis Althusser; and he received subsequent education at the Sorbonne. He received the *license de philosophie* in 1948, the *license de psychologie* in 1949, and the *agrégation de philosophie* in 1952. Foucault had also joined the communist party during this time, but broke his ties with it in 1951. In 1952, while employed in the Faculty of Letters at the University of Lille, he also received the *diplôme de psycho-pathologie* from the Institut de psychologie at Paris.[4]

For four years, from 1955–1958, Foucault taught in the French department at the University of Uppsala, Sweden. He then became director of the French institutes of both Warsaw and Hamburg. Afterward, he returned to France in 1960 to become the director of the Institut de Philosophie at the Faculté des Lettres in Clermont-Ferrand. Foucault became well known both academically and politically through his alignments, his writings and his travels. He taught, wrote and campaigned for leftist political causes, including gay rights. In San Francisco, he became especially engrossed in the gay community. While back in Paris, on June 25, 1984, Foucault died of AIDS.[5]

Foucault, although quite diverse in his intellectual pursuits, was certainly not a theologian. In fact, Foucault and Derrida were in agreement that theology must be avoided and separated from postmodern thought.[6] Stephen D. Moore points out ironically, that Foucault twice made a comparison of his own to work to negative theology. Foucault saw humanism as a displaced theology, and the "birth of man" coinciding with the "death of God."[7] Foucault scholar, Jeremy Carrette, claims that the creative association of Foucault with negative theology, even though it may be "interesting and valid in its own right," is a "secondary theological redaction." Carrette forthrightly maintains that "Foucault was an atheist" and "his work on religion does

---

4 Stanley J. Grenz, *A Primer On Postmodernism* (Grand Rapids: Eerdmans, 1996), pp. 124–5; Eric Matthews, *Twentieth-Century French Philosophy* (Oxford: Oxford University Press, 1996), pp. 147–8; Gary Gutting (ed.), *The Cambridge Companion to Foucault* (Cambridge: Cambridge University Press), pp. xi–xii in Jan Niemeier, "Paul, Liberty, and Foucault—An Assessment of Postmodern Ethics in the Light of Paul's Concept of Freedom" (B.A. thesis in theology, Livets Ord University, Uppsala, Sweden, 1999), p. 49. Also see J. G. Merquior, *Foucault* (London: Fontana Press, 1991), p. 14; and Mary McClintock Fulkerson and Susan J. Dunlap, "Michel Foucault (1926–1984): Introduction," in *The Postmodern God: A Theological Reader*, ed. Graham Ward (Oxford: Blackwell, 1997), p. 116.

5 Grenz, *A Primer On Postmodernism*, pp. 125–6; Matthews, *Twentieth-Century French Philosophy*, p. 148; Merquior, *Foucault*, pp. 14–15; Gutting, *The Cambridge Companion to Foucault* in "Paul, Liberty, and Foucault," pp. 49–50. Also, Jeremy R. Carrette devotes the first chapter (pp. 7–24) of his book, *Foucault and Religion: Spiritual Corporality and Political Spirituality* (London and New York: Routledge, 2000), to an outline of Foucault's work.

6 Brian Ingraffia notes, ironically, that Foucault even criticized Derrida's program for its subconcious theology. See Brian D. Ingraffia, *Postmodern Theory and Biblical Theology* (Cambridge: Cambridge University Press, 1995), pp. 6–7.

7 Moore, *Poststructuralism and the New Testament*, p. 93, note 38.

not sustain a traditional theological worldview."[8] Of course, one could certainly ask in what manner "negative theology" would be a "traditional theological worldview." It is said that Foucault even at times denied that he was a philosopher.[9] Throughout most of his life, Foucault evidently preferred to refer to himself as an "archaeologist of knowledge."[10] All in all, Foucault has greatly influenced philosophical and theological studies alike, especially in the area of postmodernism.

One writer remarks: "In Foucault, the Enlightenment project reaches its dead-end." With him we see the "shift from the radical subjectivism of the Enlightenment's left wing to the absolute deconstruction of meaning when radical subjectivism reaches its conclusion."[11] Foucault was profoundly influenced by Nietzsche. He, like Nietzsche, assumed the death of God as well as the prevalent Nietzschian notion of the pervasiveness of "power" at the base of history, tradition, and culture.[12] In view of Foucault's personal and academic background, I will now consider several themes which have influenced theological thinking with respect to postmodern deconstruction.

Major Themes Influencing Theology

Rejection of the Enlightenment Self : The End of Man

A strong (anti-) theological, postmodern deconstructionist theme which we see in Foucault is a conscious anti-humanism—the crumbling of the Enlightenment "man" as a self–conscious center.[13] As J.C. Merquior writes:

> Foucault invites us to awake from the "anthropological slumber" which is the oxygen of modern knowledge. For we are haunted by history and humanism; and we are a prey to history as a form of thinking because of our humanist obsession—our man besotted way of looking at reality.[14]

---

8 Carrette, *Foucault and Religion*, p. xi.

9 Allan Megill, *Prophets of Extremity: Nietzsche, Heidegger, Foucault, Derrida* (Berkeley and Los Angeles: University of California Press, Ltd., 1985), p. 187. Yet, as Megill points out, Foucault's more accurate statement on this is found in *Power/Knowledge: Selected Interviews and Other Writings, 1972–1977*, ed. Colin Gordon, trans. Colin Gordon, Leo Marshall, John Mepham, and Kate Soper (New York: Pantheon Books, 1980), p. 66: "And for all that I may like to say that I am not a philosopher, nonetheless if my concern is with truth I am still a philosopher." Cf. Megill, Ibid. p. 366, note 7.

10 Grenz, *A Primer On Postmodernism*, p. 124.

11 R. Albert Mohler, "The Integrity of the Evangelical Tradition and the Challenge of the Postmodern Paradigm," in *The Challenge of Postmodernism: An Evangelical Engagement*, ed. David S. Dockery (Grand Rapids: Baker, 1997), p. 72.

12 Fulkerson and Dunlap, "Michel Foucault (1926–1984): Introduction," p. 122; and Byrne, "Foucault On Continuity:" 338.

13 Cf. Byrne, "Foucault On Continuity," 336.

14 Merquior, *Foucault*, p. 51.

One may recall the dictum of Lévi-Strauss, "the ultimate goal of the human sciences is not to constitute, but to dissolve man."[15] Was Lévi-Strauss's task turned into a destiny by Foucault? Byrne shows this is clearly evident in Foucault's concluding words in *The Order of Things*: "As the archaeology of our thought easily shows, man is an invention of recent date. And one perhaps nearing its end."[16] Foucault claims that we cannot remember a time when man did not exist, nor even imagine him not existing because of our blindness from the "recent manifestation of man." Foucault admits the influence of Nietzsche on this:

> It is easy to see why Nietzsche's thought should have had, and still has for us, such a disturbing power when it introduced in the form of an imminent event, the Promise–Threat, the notion that man would soon be no more—but would be replaced by the superman; in a philosophy of the Return, this meant that man had long since disappeared and would continue to disappear, and that our modern thought about man, our concern for him, our humanism, were all sleeping serenely over the threatening rumble of his non-existence.[17]

It is significant to point out that this Foucauldian death of man, like Nietzsche, implies also the death of God. Carrette notes: "In [Foucault's] work there was no need to demolish religious thinking. Rather his work builds on the assumptions of a deceased religious order. It assumes the death of God."[18] Foucault submits that, for Nietzsche, the death of God is actually "synonymous" with the death of man. The promise of the Nietzschean "superman" or "overman"[19] (Übermensch), signifies the imminent death of man. According to Foucault, this is the way that Nietzsche is offering both a promise and a task, marking a threshold by which philosophy may rightly think again. So, the end of man is a return to a beginning for philosophy. Foucault expresses this "nihilist optimism:"[20]

> It is no longer possible to think in our day other than in the void left by man's disappearance. For this void does not create a deficiency; it does not constitute a lacuna that must be filled. It is nothing more, and nothing less, than the unfolding of a space in which it is once more possible to think.[21]

---

15 Claude Lévi-Strauss, *The Savage Mind* (London: Wiedenfeld and Nicolson, 1972), p. 245 as quoted in Byrne, "Foucault On Continuity," 336.

16 Foucault, *The Order of Things*, p. 387. Cf. Byrne, "Foucault On Continuity," 336.

17 Foucault, *The Order of Things*, p. 322.

18 Carrette, *Foucault and Religion*, p. 55; also cf. pp. 79–80.

19 As James C. Livingston rightly points out, the English word "superman" is unduly ambiguous since it has been identified with Nazism, and is also associated with a comic book character. Although still a bit awkward, the better literal English translation of Nietzsche's term Übermensch would be "Overman." See James C. Livingston, *Modern Christian Thought* (London: Collier, 1971), p. 195 (note).

20 Such "nihilistic optimism" is later developed, as we will see, in the a/theology of Mark C. Taylor.

21 Foucault, *The Order of Things*, p. 342.

We must keep in mind that by these assertions Foucault is not denying the existence of human beings. Rather, he is using "man" as a metaphorical representation to describe the discourse which has given rise to the current description of "man" as a product of socio-cultural factors and relations of power.[22] We may equate this Foucauldian erasure of the notion of "man," in this context, to the postmodern denial of the Enlightenment self. In this respect, the "self" or "man" is made through the use of language, it is not the foundational ground for language.[23] So, the death of "man" also implies the death of the author—an author whose speech is no longer his own. The author is no longer the main subject at hand. The author only becomes a subject "when he or she is 'subjected' to a system of differences and distinctions—in short, when subjugated to a language."[24] As Foucault writes: "The author function is therefore characteristic of the mode of existence, circulation, and functioning of certain discourses within a society."[25]

This is akin to the Lyotardian rejection of the grand narrative. The Enlightenment anthropology of an a priori "human nature" ("Man") is an over-arching scheme which was produced by a "particular historical situation."[26] In other words, the self has fallen "victim to a regime."[27] Foucault's postmodern deconstructionism is certainly seen in this anti-foundational perspective of the independent self. This corresponds with the Derridean notion of the absence of a transcendental signified to which signifiers may refer.[28]

Hence, this "self," "human nature," "man," or "subject" has been subjected to socially produced divisions and manipulations which have denied it internal substance.[29] In fact, Foucault would insist that the notion of the modern "self" is

---

22 Byrne, "Foucault On Continuity," p. 336.

23 See Grenz, *A Primer On Postmodernism*, p. 130.

24 Kevin J. Vanhoozer, *Is There a Meaning in This Text?* (Grand Rapids: Zondervan, 1998), pp. 70–71.

25 Michel Foucault, "What Is An Author?," in *The Foucault Reader*, ed. Paul Rabinow (New York: Pantheon Books, 1984), p. 108.

26 Eric Matthews, *Twentieth-Century French Philosophy* (Oxford: Oxford University Press, 1996), p. 149.

27 Anthony C. Thiselton, *Interpreting God and the Postmodern Self* (Edinburgh: T&T Clark, 1995), p. 134.

28 See Grenz, *A Primer On Postmodernism*, p. 128; and Megill, *Prophets of Extremity*, p. 211.

29 Perhaps the best examples of this are found in Foucault's earliest works, such as *Madness and Civilization: A History of Insanity in the Age of Reason* (Cambridge, U.K.: Cambridge University Press, 1965). This is illustrated in the following quote from his chapter on "The Birth of the Asylum:" "It is thought that Tuke and Pinel opened the asylum to medical knowledge. They did not introduce science, but a personality, whose powers borrowed from science only their disguise, or at most their justification. These powers, by their nature, were of a moral and social order; they took root in the madman's minority status, in the insanity of his person, not of his mind. If the medical personage could isolate madness, it was not because he knew it, but because he mastered it; and what for positivism would be an image of objectivity was only the other side of this domination." (pp. 271–2).

indirectly brought about by excluding the other.[30] One cannot reduce the notion of "man" to simple human consciousness; it must be examined in the context of social relations.[31] For Foucault social relations are "power" relations—another major theme to which I now turn.

Power, Truth, and Discourse

The notion of "power" is perhaps the most common characteristic associated with Foucault, especially in terms of looking at his work in dialogue with theology.[32] For Foucault, power is fundamental to human culture, knowledge, tradition and discourse. Knowledge is linked to both power and discourse. Discourse identifies and defines and establishes the basis of knowledge claims. Such claims are then arbitrarily established as truths which systems and institutions find helpful.[33] Such "institutions" are "those in which power wears a white coat and a professional smile."[34] Foucault describes this relationship between power, truth, and discourse in the following:

> Truth is a thing of this world: it is produced only by virtue of multiple forms of constraint. And it induces regular effects of power. Each society has its régime of truth, its "general politics'" of truth: that is, the types of discourse which it accepts and makes function as true; the mechanisms and instances which enable one to distinguish true and false statements, the means by which each is sanctioned; the techniques and procedures accorded value in the acquisition of truth; the status of those who are charged with saying what counts as true. ...
>
> "Truth" is linked in a circular relation with systems of power which produce and sustain it, and to effects of power which it induces and which extend it.[35]

For Foucault, truth is made by those who broker the power. As may be seen in Foucault's *Madness and Civilization*, the notion of "madness" does not depend upon some objective scientific criterion, but on the power and interests of those in

---

30 Miroslav Volf, *Exclusion and Embrace: A Theological Exploration of Identity, Otherness, and Reconciliation* (Nashville: Abingdon, 1996), p. 62. Volf cites Foucault in "The Political Technology of Individuals," in *Technologies of the Self*, ed. Luther H. Martin et al. (Amherst, The University of Massachusetts Press, 1988), pp. 145–62.

31 Glenn Ward, *Teach Yourself Postmodernism* (London: Hodder Headline Plc, 1997), p. 129. See also Paul Rabinow, Introduction, in *The Foucault Reader*, ed. Paul Rabinow (New York, Pantheon Books, 1984), pp. 7–8.

32 See Carrette, *Foucault and Religion*, pp. 36, 148.

33 Byrne, "Foucault On Continuity:" 338; Grenz, *A Primer On Postmodernism*, p. 132.

34 Moore, *Poststructuralism and the New Testament*, p. 112. Cf. Thiselton, *Interpreting God and the Postmodern Self*, p. 140.

35 Foucault, *Power/Knowledge*, pp. 131, 133.

authority.[36] But power is not a "thing," it is a complex web or mode of interaction.[37] The boundaries which have become social "truths" must be deconstructed. The challenge for philosophy, then, is essentially to critically challenge domination at all levels, whether political, institutional, economic or sexual.[38]

Miroslav Volf points out that Foucault speaks of truth as "produced." Whether statements are inherently true or false is not a concern of Foucault; but how they function as either true or false. He is concerned with the effects of these produced truths. In other words, what is significant is not an independent reality, but the "why and how" discourse which produced the given "truth."[39] Foucault writes:

> Now I believe that the problem does not consist in drawing the line between that in a discourse which falls under the category of scientificity or truth, and that which comes under some other category, but in seeing historically how effects of truth are produced within discourses which in themselves are neither true nor false.[40]

However, one should not too hastily assume that all manifestation of power is wrong for Foucault. Power denotes not only negative relations of dominance and control but positive ones of creativity and reasoning."[41] Although the notion of repression comes through quite strongly in *Madness and Civilization*, Foucault later states that "the notion of repression is quite inadequate for capturing what is precisely the productive aspect of power."[42] Power must not simply be equated with a prohibition. This is too negative. One would not be brought to obey power if this were the case. As Foucault continues: "What makes power hold good, what makes it accepted, is simply the fact that it doesn't only weigh on us as a force that says no, but that

---

36 Alister McGrath, *A Passion For Truth: The Intellectual Coherence of Evangelicalism* (Downers Grove: InterVarsity, 1996), p. 193. Cf. Grenz, *A Primer On Postmodernism* (Grand Rapids: Eerdmans, 1996), p. 132. As Catherine Keller notes, it is significant to remember that Foucault is not localizing power itself in a some top-down hierarchy. Foucault has shown how "epistemic imperialism" has worked itself out in both the "bourgeois establishments of knowledge/power" and also in the "revolutionary reactions."(Catherine Keller, "Power Lines," in *Power, Powerlessness, and the Divine: New Inquiries in Bible and Theology*, ed. Cynthia L. Rigby (Atlanta: Scholars Press, 1997), p. 67. Cf. Foucault, *Power/Knowledge*, p. 98.

37 David West, *An Introduction to Continental Philosophy* (Cambridge, Mass: Blackwell, 1996), p. 172. Cf. Foucault, *Power/Knowledge*, p. 98.

38 See Michel Foucault, "The Ethic of Care for the Self as a Practice of Freedom," in James Bernauer and David Rasmussen (eds), *The Final Foucault* (Cambridge, Mass.: Massachussets Institute of Technology Press, 1988), p. 20 as quoted in McGrath, *A Passion For Truth*, p. 193.

39 Volf, *Exclusion and Embrace*, p. 245. Cf. also p. 249.

40 Foucault, *Power/Knowledge*, p. 118.

41 Thomas R. Flynn, "Partially Desacralized Spaces: The Religious Availability of Foucault's Thought," *Faith and Philosophy* 10/4 (October 1993), p. 476.

42 Foucault, *Power/Knowledge*, p. 119. Cf. Megill, *Prophets of Extremity*, p. 241.

it traverses and produces things, it induces pleasure, forms knowledge, produces discourse."[43]

This is not to say, however, that these "discourses" are not violent. For Foucault, knowledge is indeed violence, and the expression of "truth" is an imposition.[44] As Foucault states: "We must conceive discourse as a violence which we do to things, or, in any case as a practice which we impose on them."[45] Theology would be no exception. The philosopher's critical task is that of examining how effects of truth compete with each other, not to assert what is or is not true.[46] For Foucault, the intellectual's job is not to change the consciousness of others, but display the various regimes which produce "truth." Hence, truth is not emancipated from all systems of power, for truth *is* power. But we must detach the power of truth from its various hegemonic forms in which it functions.[47]

Power, Sex, and Confession

Foucault's interests in penology, the asylum and sexuality resonate with his task of investigating the ways that western discourse has marginalized the other through the effects of the use of power—especially as it relates to the human body.[48] It is the totalizing structures of western discourse that have socially programmed one's own bodily identity and its relationship with other bodies.[49] It is not my intention to digress into a complex discussion of Foucault's notions of sexuality, which is certainly beyond the scope of this book. Nonetheless, I cannot altogether avoid his sexual discourse because of its key significance to his views on the pernicious totalizing and subjugating effects of religion. Foucault's perspectives on the power of religious discourse and the postmodern deconstructionist rejection of absolutizing schemes is a key idea in my development of apologetic insights in this regard.

In Foucault's *History of Sexuality*, he attempts to discredit the hypothesis that sex became repressed as the West entered the Victorian era. Instead, Foucault argues, sex and talk of sex was multiplied. This especially occurred in the context of confession, where sex became discourse.[50] Such discourse of disclosure of

---

43 Foucault, *Power/Knowledge*, p. 119.

44 Volf, *Exclusion and Embrace*, p. 247. Cf. Megill, *Prophets of Extremity*, p. 250.

45 Foucault, *The Order of Things*, p. 316 quoted in Volf, *Exclusion and Embrace*, p. 247.

46 Volf, *Exclusion and Embrace*, p. 249. We may compare Foucault with Kuhn, *The Structure of Scientific Revolutions*, on this concept. See J. G. Merquior, *Foucault* (London: Fontana Press, 1991), pp. 36–8. Merquior describes the differences and similarities between Foucault's epistemes and Kuhn's notion of paradigms.

47 Foucault, *Power/Knowledge*, p. 133.

48 Byrne, "Foucault On Continuity," 339; and Fulkerson and Dunlap, "Michel Foucault (1926–1984): Introduction," p. 118.

49 Vanhoozer, *Is There a Meaning in This Text?*, p. 181.

50 See Carrette, *Foucault and Religion*, p. 28. Carrette notes that "Foucault's discussion of Christianity is therefore diminished by his over-dependency on confession as the central

"repressed" desires between priest and parishioner was the truth of oneself revealed in a "power relationship." The words of the confessor are given authenticity and definition by the priest, the "expert." Yet, such confession, for Foucault, gives a false sense of liberation. It actually extends the hegemonic domain of power instead.[51] It is this intrusive, individually based, "pastoral" conception of power, inspired by the Catholic Church, which helped direct one's conscience. Modern states apply a similar pastoral power in relation to the health and welfare of their people.[52]

For Foucault, discourse on sexuality turned sex into an absolute yet abstract area of study. It was discourse about sex which actually produced sexuality.[53] Foucault states: "What the discourse of sexuality was initially applied to wasn't sex but the body, the sexual organs, pleasures, kinship relations, interpersonal relations, and so forth."[54] Since we have marginalized sex and sexual practices, and made it a "sin," we have turned it into a problem and a burden.[55] So, it was the developing religious discourse about sex which marginalized, excluded, and defined our notions of sex, and in so doing, it produced the abstraction of "sexuality." Once defined and contained as such, for Foucault, it became subject to imposed limitations, and it became "sin." Eventually *scientia sexualis* merged the confession with scientific discourse. In this way, acts of "confession" moved from an act of religious penance, into the judicial system, medicine, and psychiatry.[56] As Foucault explains:

> The confession was, and still remains, the general standard governing the production of the true discourse on sex. It has undergone a considerable transformation, however. For a long time, it remained firmly entrenched in the practice of penance. But with the rise of Protestantism, the Counter Reformation, eighteenth–century pedagogy, and nineteenth-century medicine, it gradually lost its ritualistic and exclusive localization; it spread; it has been employed in a whole series of relationships: children and parents, students and educators, patients and psychiatrists, delinquents and experts.[57]

Foucault believed the contemporary obsessions with sexual identity and acts of "normalization" were forms of subjugation, an extension of the effects of *scientia sexualis*. From this standpoint, religious communities asserting the normality of

---

and most important tenet of the religion."

51 Fulkerson and Dunlap, "Michel Foucault (1926–1984): Introduction," pp. 119–20. Cf. West, *An Introduction to Continental Philosophy*, p. 176.

52 West, *An Introduction to Continental Philosophy*, p. 174. West cites Michel Foucault, "Afterword: The Subject and Power," in H.L. Dreyfus and P. Rabinow, *Michel Foucault: Beyond Structuralism and Hermeneutics* (Brighton: Harvester, 1982), pp. 214–15.

53 Ward, *Teach Yourself Postmodernism*, p. 131; Megill, *Prophets of Extremity*, p. 253.

54 Foucault, *Power/Knowledge*, p. 210.

55 Ward, *Teach Yourself Postmodernism*, p. 132; Michel Foucault, "We 'Other' Victorians," in *The Foucault Reader*, p. 297.

56 Fulkerson and Dunlap, "Michel Foucault," p. 120. Cf. Michel Foucault, "The Repressive Hypothesis," in *The Foucault Reader*, pp. 314–15.

57 Foucault, excerpt from *The History of Sexuality*, vol. 1, in *The Postmodern God: A Theological Reader*, ed. Graham Ward (Oxford: Blackwell, 1997), p. 127.

heterosexual relationships, for example, are simply caught up in "modern bio-power," not in faithfulness or some kind of true "morality."[58] In my estimation, Foucault is saying that we have marginalized and oppressed the other due to our discourse, due to our desire for harnessing, managing, and controlling our affairs. Through our discourse on sexuality and the subjugative effects of our religion, and its subsequent totalizing discourse on sexuality, we have oppressed and marginalized areas of potential creative development.

History and Tradition: A Genealogical Reading

Foucault's understanding of history and tradition stems from his views of knowledge and power. History cannot make disinterested, objective claims.[59] Greatly influenced by Nietzsche, Foucault writes:

> In appearance, or rather, according to the mask it bears, historical consciousness is neutral, devoid of passions, and committed solely to truth. But if it examines itself and if, more generally, it interrogates the various forms of scientific consciousness in history, it finds that all these forms and transformations are aspects of the will to knowledge: instinct, passion, the inquisitor's devotion, cruel subtlety, and malice.[60]

I believe it is important to distinguish between Foucault's earlier stress on "archaeology" and his later emphasis on Nietzschean "genealogy."[61] Foucault's archaeology of knowledge was concerned with the analysis of rules of discourse, or the uncovering of the "truth constitutive rules of exclusion in any discourse...."[62] His emphasis on genealogy, a term borrowed from Nietzsche, gives more attention to the position of power as it relates to the "fabric(ation) of truth and knowledge."[63] It emphasizes, as I have suggested, that knowledge is something which is generated within social institutions. Genealogy helps "unearth" those unconscious rules which the members of those social institutions accept in order to deem some things as true

---

58 Fulkerson and Dunlap, "Michel Foucault (1926–1984): Introduction," p. 121.

59 Grenz, *A Primer On Postmodernism*, p. 133.

60 Foucault, "Nietzsche, Genealogy, History," in *The Foucault Reader*, p. 95. See Grenz's comments in *A Primer On Postmodernism*, p. 133.

61 See Matthews, *Twentieth-Century French Philosophy*, p. 153. Some scholars point out that Foucault borrowed the term "archaeology" from Kant. See for example, Moore, *Poststructuralism and the New Testament*, p. 129; also see Jeremy R. Carrette, *Foucault and Religion: Spiritual Corporality and Political Spirituality* (London and New York: Routledge, 2000), p. 10.

62 Jürgen Habermas, *The Philosophical Discourse of Modernity*, trans. Frederick Lawrence (Cambridge, Mass.: The MIT press, 1987), p. 248. Also see Matthews, *Twentieth-Century French Philosophy*, p. 151.

63 Moore, *Poststructuralism and the New Testament*, p. 130.

and others as false. In this sense, he is attempting to liberate us from the notion of "objective truth" in order to look at new perspectives in all aspects of life.[64]

Foucault challenges the assumption of history as a teleological, progressive movement. David West affirms that Foucault's Nietzschean genealogy "renounces the credulous faith in history as progress and traces specific institutions and forms of discourse to 'naked struggles of power' instead."[65] Foucault claims that a genealogical reading of history is "the inverse of the Christian world, spun entirely by a divine spider." Instead, "[t]he forces operating in history are not controlled by destiny," but they are "a profusion of entangled events."[66] History and tradition are not things which we can ontologically presume. Instead, we create our "historical" understandings from ambiguous and disjointed phenomena.[67] Habermas submits that Foucault wishes to get rid of the notion of the macroconsciousness of history. One can see how this again echoes the Lyotardian notion of "incredulity" toward the metanarrative. Such an idea of a global historiography must "be dissolved, not indeed into a manifold of narrative histories, but into a plurality of irregularity emerging and disappearing islands of discourse."[68]

Traditional, linear models of history tend to provide legitimization to current structures and to obscure past struggles. Foucault's genealogy, although not a traditional "theory" of history, seeks to point out historical directions which were not followed and events which often do not mesh with a traditional linear historical narrative. This is not, however, to come up with another theory of order. Foucault does not express concern for an Enlightenment utopian ideal for the betterment of society. He is more concerned with simply "unearthing" subjugated knowledges.[69]

Implications for Theology: Critique and Response

Truth and Power

The notion of truth continues to be one of the foremost challenges to the theologian when addressing deconstructive postmodern issues. Foucault's thought is no exception. As we recall, Foucault inherited from Nietzsche the notion that truth is something produced in the context of power relationships, not a function of verifiable

---

64 Matthews, *Twentieth-Century French Philosophy*, p. 152–4. See also Habermas, *The Philosophical Discourse of Modernity*, p. 248. Cf. Foucault, "What is Enlightenment," in *The Foucault Reader*, p. 46.

65 West, *An Introduction to Continental Philosophy*, p. 171.

66 Foucault, "Nietzsche, Genealogy, History," in *The Foucault Reader*, pp. 88–9. Cf. Byrne, "Foucault On Continuity," 343.

67 Byrne, "Foucault On Continuity," 343.

68 Habermas, *The Philosophical Discourse of Modernity*, p. 251.

69 Grenz, *A Primer On Postmodernism*, pp. 136–7. Cf. Foucault, "Two Lectures," in *The Foucault Reader*, pp. 81–2.

evidence or logical propositions. What is "true" is not the question, but rather, *how* and *why* something is true.[70]

But what obligates us to accept Foucault's proposal of the worthiness of the effort to pursue his significant question (i.e. examining the effects of "truth" as opposed to whether something is "true" or "false")? Is not Foucault, in some sense, succumbing to some hidden "regime" of truth in telling us what *the* significant question is? If we legitimate the correctness of Foucault's suggestion are we not, in effect, affirming the "truth" of his analysis? Is this itself another "regime" of power that we are succumbing to? If we do accept Foucault's submission of what the central question of truth is, is this not itself the result of a power relationship asserted by Foucault (from his writing) upon us? D.A. Carson affirms that "it is important to recognize that on Foucault's view even Foucault's view is manipulative and controlling, so we should not take it too seriously, less we find ourselves enslaved by it!"[71] I agree with Carson on this apparent inconsistency in Foucault, but at the same time I believe one must take the points Foucault is making very seriously.

I would applaud the connection that Foucault has drawn between truth and power. With Foucault we have power then we have truth. Yet truth itself may give increasing power to those in power. This is a needed reminder that as human beings we are indeed limited and finite in our knowledge, and in our morality. Our culture and limitations taint the things we claim to know. As Miroslav Volf submits: "The little knowledge we have is skewed because we suppress truth through desire to overcome others and protect ourselves. As we seek to know we are caught in the field of powers that distort our vision. Michel Foucault was right to remind us of this."[72] But Foucault is giving us much more than a helpful reminder, he seems to be redefining the entire traditional notion of truth. Truth is that which *passes* for the truth. In this sense, all cultural systems and all "truth" claims must be equally valid—that of both victims and perpetrators. At the least, one ought to admit the risk of holding such an egalitarian position.[73]

As Volf suggests, if truth is simply that which "passes" or that which is imposed upon people, then we cannot properly speak of a gain in knowledge, but only a gain in power. We define our own truth and we assert it before those who oppose us. We choose our weapons carefully, and we strategically use compelling logic. But will

---

70 Douglas Groothuis, *Truth Decay: Defending Christianity Against the Challenges of Postmodernism* (Downers Grove: InterVarsity, 2000), p. 30; and Volf, *Exclusion and Embrace*, p. 245.

71 D.A. Carson, *The Gagging of God: Christianity Confronts Pluralism* (Grand Rapids: Zondervan, 1996), p. 102.

72 Volf, *Exclusion and Embrace*, p. 247; Also see pp. 246–7. Cf. Foucault, *Power/ Knowledge*, p. 131.

73 Volf, *Exclusion and Embrace*, p. 248. For these thoughts Volf cites Barry Allen, *Truth in Philosophy* (Cambridge: Harvard University Press, 1993), and Bernard-Henri Lévy, *Gefährliche Reinheit* (Fr. *La pureté dangereuse*), trans. by Maribel Königer (Wien: Passagen Verlag, 1995), p. 210.

we use violence?[74] Of course, Foucault's thinking reminds us that we can easily commit verbal and written violence with the intellect alone. Through manipulation of truth and applying it coercively, we are using forms of oppression to assert our claims to knowledge and impose them on others. This is unquestionably something we must guard against.

Volf proposes an alternative to Foucault that preserves his keen insight on the relation between power and knowledge. At the same time, Volf attempts to avoid the problems which arise from Foucault's notions of truth being "produced" and "imposed." Volf argues that if we are to *know truly we need to want to exercise power rightly.*[75] Volf submits that God's truth, contrary to Foucault's perspective, is *the* truth, not simply one truth among many. God is omnipresently seeking the good, through His truth, for all creation. According to Volf, we need to try to "emulate God's way of knowing" with our "creaturely" limitations. This does not mean that we can obtain God's mind. "But we can try to see the other concretely rather than abstractly, from within rather than simply from without."[76] This is done through a purposeful and proactive identification with the other's perspectives both socially and historically; at the same time, keeping in mind that we will, no matter how hard we try, still be enmeshed in our own predispositions and assumptions.[77] It is this stimulation to dialogue which will be a theme of major importance as I develop my later argument for apologetic methodology in view of postmodern deconstructionist concerns.

Volf advances a "theology of embrace" as a means to reach out to the other. Volf states: "There can be no truth between people without the will to embrace the other .... If truth cannot do without the will to embrace, neither can embrace do without the will to truth."[78] With such a proactive will to identify with the other, we are following and modeling the example of Jesus. Jesus renounced the power of violence and championed the power of truth. But the "truth" of Jesus is more than simply uttering factual statements; it involves one's entire character. "Truth" defined the very being of Jesus. Hence, to defeat truth is to defeat life.[79] If power is used correctly it will champion truth and promote life.

Power does not necessarily cause suffering and oppression. Power may be used rightly to alleviate it, especially in the context of community.[80] We see examples of this today in various humanitarian projects supporting downtrodden people in third world countries. The ones with the financial backing, the time, and the mental fortitude to face such challenges may be seen as the "powerful." Nevertheless, these efforts are used to deliver and liberate. Such means or uses of power are not

---

74 Volf, *Exclusion and Embrace*, p. 249.

75 Ibid., p. 249. Italics are Volf's.

76 Ibid., p. 251.

77 Ibid., pp. 251–3.

78 Ibid., pp. 258.

79 Ibid., pp. 267–8. Cf. Jn. 14: 6a: "I am the way and the truth and the life."

80 I will explore this further in a subsequent chapter where I explore the early Christian community development in the book of Acts.

necessarily imperialistic or used as a means to oppress—in fact, just the opposite. The Christian's proper sense of power and its relation to knowledge can be used, in a case such as this, as a tool of compassion to meet the suffering other. Yet, such knowledge of available "power" in some situations, may in turn cause great grief in situations of powerlessness. I may be aware of the other's suffering, yet unable to do anything about it. I am powerless to effect a change with my will.[81] William Desmond provides some pertinent statements in this regard:

> Indeed, the will to power is crushed by the suffering of the other, and yet one goes with eyes open towards this crushing negativity. There is no reason for this, if we think in terms of self-interest and self-preservation. Quite the opposite, there is every reason why one ought not to expose oneself. Yet one is exposed, one does expose oneself. I can do nothing for the other. This is beyond my will. And still the pained going out of compassion solicits in me a different willingness. This is not will to power, but a willingness beyond power; a *willingness that renounces will*, that sacrifices its own self insistence in breach of the rationality of self-preservation.[82]

In my estimation, it is this "willingness beyond power" that both exerts the will to compassion yet renounces the will to self-interest, which is promising for the pastoral power of Christianity.

Pastoral Power and Confession

Stephen Moore highlights Foucault's notion of Christianity's "pastoral power." Such pastoral power, spread by Christianity in the ancient world, is a sacrificial type of power, not simply a commanding type of royal power that a king demands of his subjects. Instead, this pastoral power, modeled by the apostle Paul, must explore the innermost being, soul, and consciousness of people.[83] This pastoral disrobing of one's outward being to reach one's inner secrets comes to full expression in Paul's "ecclesiastical descendents" in the religious act of confession.

Foucault submits that the act of confession became a significant ritual used to produce truth. It also became an imperative. It was even demanded by threat and force.[84] But is such an abuse really following in the vein of the apostle Paul? Instead, the notion of confession by Paul, seems to be more in context with public attestation

---

81 William Desmond, *Perplexity and Ultimacy: Metaphysical thoughts from the Middle* (Albany: State University of New York Press, 1995), p. 151.

82 Desmond, *Perplexity and Ultimacy*, p. 153.

83 Moore, *Poststructuralism and the New Testament*, pp. 110–11. Moore cites Michel Foucault, "The Subject and Power," in Herbert L. Dreyfus and Paul Rabinow, *Michel Foucault: Beyond Structuralism and Hermeneutics* (2nd edition; Chicago: University of Chicago Press, 1983), p. 214. Cf. Thiselton, *Interpreting God*, pp. 140–41.

84 Foucault, *The History of Sexuality*, trans. Robert Hurley (New York: Pantheon Books); vol. 1: An Introduction, 1978, pp. 58–9, in Moore, *Poststructuralism and the New Testament*, p. 111.

of belief in Christ, rather than some personal display of all known personal sins.[85] I will later suggest how the foundations of the spread of Christianity as charted in the book of Acts demonstrate not some kind of ecclesiastical, imperialist power-play; but instead display a loving, suffering tolerance.[86] I agree with Anthony Thiselton when he claims that Paul's call for humility and servanthood for the community is not for the purpose of control, but to "protect those who might otherwise be despised or considered socially inferior; in other words, precisely to protect the 'social deviants' for whom Foucault shows concern."[87]

Even if we we agree that confession is a pernicious ecclesiastical desecendent, as Foucault would suggest, Mary McClintock Fulkerson and Susan J. Dunlap wonder if Foucault has "simply missed some of the liberating effects of confessional practices that include self-identification, submission, repentance, and forgiveness?"[88] Although Foucault's context is certainly a reaction to Catholicism (or we should say, "anti-Catholicism") it also relates to the development of Protestantism. Perhaps this is even more relevant for Foucault. For, it is through Protestantism where confession "lost its ritualistic and exclusive localization" and spread throughout a number of relationships from "children and parents, students and educators, patients and psychiatrists, delinquents and experts."[89]

Granted, one may cite many abuses in the power structures and discursive practices of these types of relationships. However, to submit that a non-ritualistic spread of confession in the context of "power-plays" came through Protestantism is greatly overstated. Although, the entire notion of confession is turned upside down with Protestant ideals. Confession is no longer made to the authority figure of the priest in the confines of ecclesiastical structure. Instead, confession is made directly to God for the absolution of sins. Fulkerson and Dunlap rightly observe that to approach the study of religion in the context of Foucault "requires that a religion be analyzed as a formation of discursive practices."[90] Certainly religion, and even Protestantism, includes "discursive practices." But, to limit confession, especially Protestant confession, to discursive practices is omitting a major idea in Protestantism. The major Protestant principle of "justification by grace through faith" rests on an assumption of personal relationship with a forgiving, personal God.

---

85 Cf. Rom. 10:9–10; Phil. 2:11; 1 Tim. 6:12; 2 Tim. 2:19.

86 Cf. Thiselton, *Interpreting God*, p. 142.

87 Ibid., p. 142.

88 Fulkerson and Dunlap, "Michel Foucault (1926–1984): Introduction," p. 121.

89 Foucault, excerpt from *The History of Sexuality*, in *The Postmodern God*, p. 127.

90 Fulkerson and Dunlap, "Michel Foucault (1926–1984): Introduction," p. 121. It is significant to keep in mind that Foucault largely has sexual issues in mind. As he states: "The confession was, and still remains, the general standard governing the production of the true discourse on sex." This is based in Foucault's submission that "[f]rom the Christian penance to the present day, sex was a privileged theme of confession." In Michel Foucault, excerpt from *The History of Sexuality*, in *The Postmodern God*, pp. 127, 126. Although there is much more that can be said regarding Foucault's views of sexuality and their implications to theological thought, we must limit ourselves at this juncture to the broader notion of confession.

This surely implies much more than discourse. In my estimation, this Foucauldian approach mistakenly presupposes an objectification of "confession" and presupposes the absence of a personal God. It fails to see the intensely subjective nature of making confession as an acknowledgement of wrongdoing in the context of restoration of personal relationship. Confession then becomes something which continually frees, heals and restores relationship. In this sense, it would be the absence of confession which binds, oppresses and separates, not that which causes it.

History and Genealogical Methodology

James M. Byrne claims that Foucault's historical methodology presents an "intense challenge" to Christian theological history as the "unbroken handing-on of the gospel by means of the scriptures and the life and teaching of the church."[91] I would certainly agree. It is perhaps here where I notice the most distinctive Derridean vein to Foucault's work. To read history in a Foucauldian fashion, as Byrne points out, demands close attention to discontinuities and breaks which are ordinarily suppressed by tradition in order to promote strong continuity. Of course, the Foucauldian tradition also denies a transcendental authority and a "metaphysics of history." So the question becomes: What sense do we make of a theology taking these notions into consideration?[92]

I would credit Foucault for bidding us to consider the ambiguous nature of all traditions and cultures and the systems of power and thought by which these traditions and cultures communicate and pass on their thinking. Power mechanisms certainly reside in our own traditions, and we need to be aware of these and how they influence our discourse and behavior.[93] As Foucault challenges us, history ought to be deconstructed with the intent to find the oppressed other, to find those "truths" which were, and are culturally and socially subjugated. Power mechanisms have indeed produced various claims to truth. However, I would not wish to go so far as to affirm with Foucault, the "fabrication" of truth. Historical discourse cannot claim objectivity; however, this does not negate that certain events *actually* occurred. Historical events often appear as a collection of many "entangled" events. But to categorically deny the absence of any macroconscious direction is to make a metaphysical leap which has gone too far. Such denial itself, ironically makes a sweeping truth statement—a statement that Christians are not willing to concede.

Nevertheless, Foucault's underlying concerns regarding networks of power exchanges are significant for our theologizing.[94] By way of response, I will attempt, in subsequent chapters, to analyze and re-consider our own methodologies with regard to evangelical apologetics in view of these concerns.

---

91 Byrne, "Foucault On Continuity:" 343.

92 Ibid., p. 344.

93 Ibid., p. 343.

94 Ibid., p. 344.

Ethics

As I pointed out above, it seems that Foucault's challenge to the idea of objectivity in history is itself a presupposed notion of some sort of truth. The same would go for Foucault's ethic. Although not explicitly stated as such, I still gather from Foucault's "genealogical" writing that oppression and repression is wrong and freedom is good. Alister McGrath points out that Foucault's critique betrays presupposed moral values, and Foucault certainly seems to expect his readers to intuitively share these social and moral values.[95] McGrath poses several questions pertinent to Foucault's implicit assumptions:

> Yet why is struggle preferable to submission? Why is freedom to be chosen, rather than repression? And what moral frameworks or criteria are proposed, by which this implicit assumption may be defended? ... That many shared his intuitive dislike of repression ensured he was well received—but the fundamental question remains unanswered. Why is repression wrong?[96]

However, one must not presume that since Foucault does not justify his ethical position, nor defend a position on moral absolutism, that he was without moral conviction. He was not simply a moral relativist. The issue in question, however, was whether or not Foucault's Nietzschean skeptical assumptions "entitled" him to such convictions.[97] Any sense of Foucault's "moral" convictions stemmed from the autonomous subject within the relativity of truth games. Beyond the games that we play in the name of "truth," there is no absolute ethical imperative.[98] In fact, what Foucault desires is ultimate freedom from an absolutist morality for the purpose of self-transformation by encountering ultimate pleasure.[99] Jan Niemeier points out this key weakness in Foucault's ethic. Such a notion of freedom or justice which is concerned with the other, but only in the sense of self-transformative, self–realization, "does not solve the problem of human freedom, since it does not harmonize individual interests with the totality of other interests."[100] Our theology and apologetic methodology must take Foucault's concerns seriously by examining the connections among mechanisms of power, tradition, ethics and our own expressed theological propositions.[101]

I will now turn to deconstructive thought in America and its relation to postmodern theology. Many of the postmodern deconstructive themes began in the context of European thought, although I do not want to over-emphasize the

---

95 McGrath, *A Passion For Truth*, p. 194. See also Groothuis, *Truth Decay*, pp. 202–4.

96 McGrath, *A Passion For Truth*, p. 194. Cf. Alister McGrath, *Intellectuals Don't Need God & Other Modern Myths* (Grand Rapids: Zondervan, 1993), pp. 179–80. Cf. Groothuis, *Truth Decay*, pp. 202–3.

97 West, *An Introduction to Continental Philosophy*, p. 177.

98 Niemeier, "Paul, Liberty, and Foucault," p. 16.

99 Ibid., p. 19.

100 Ibid., pp. 46–7.

101 Byrne, "Foucault On Continuity:" 348.

geographical "centeredness" of these themes. Nonetheless, I will observe some nuanced differences representative of American thinking. I will limit the discussion to Mark C. Taylor and Richard Rorty.

PART 3

Deconstruction in America

Chapter 6

Mark C. Taylor:
Embracing Nihilism

Introduction and Background

This chapter will attempt to present a basic introduction to the deconstructive theology of Mark C. Taylor. Although Taylor's breadth of research in the humanities spans from philosophy and religion to the arts and media, I will concentrate on Taylor's postmodern deconstructive theological views, while providing a brief critical analysis of his perspectives as they relate to postmodern evangelical methodology.

Mark C. Taylor (b. 1945) is Cluett Professor of Humanities at Williams College, Williamstown, Massachusetts and visiting professor at Columbia University. In 1995 the Carnegie Foundation of Princeton, New Jersey, named Taylor the "Liberal Arts Professor of the Year for the Advancement of Teaching." Taylor may be one of the most enigmatic professors of religion in America today. As one author has put it, "[i]n tone, Taylor is masked ironic, transgressive and extravagant …."[1] Taylor's advocates would say that he has made profound contributions in philosophy, art, architecture, and virtual culture. Others would say that he is too eclectic and obscure for his own good.[2] Theologian Terrence Tilley suggests the following for understanding Taylor:

> Perhaps the best clue is that his writing represents a twentieth-century radicalization of the writing of apophatic mysticism. The way of many mystics is to write interminably to say that God can neither be what they say nor what they omit. Like those mystics, perhaps Taylor writes incessantly and playfully about that of which no one can write in an effort to open a place for a way beyond.[3]

Taylor began teaching at Williams College in 1973 and has remained there to this day, holding a number of chairs and teaching in several departments. Taylor uses many creative means when teaching. For example, Taylor went to Las Vegas

---

1   Gillian Rose, "New Jerusalem, Old Athens From *The Broken Middle*," in *The Postmodern God: A Theological Reader*, ed. Graham Ward (Oxford: Blackwell, 1997), p. 323.

2   See Scott Heller, "From Kant to Las Vegas to Cyberspace: A Philosopher on the Edge of Postmodernism," *The Chronicle of Higher Education*, May 29, 1998, http://www.williams.edu/mtaylor/interviews/pages/980529_chronicle_001.html (26 Sept. 2005).

3   Terrence W. Tilley with Tami England, "The A/theology of Mark C. Taylor," in Terrence W. Tilley, *Postmodern Theologies: The Challenge of Religious Diversity* (Maryknoll: Orbis Books, 1995), pp. 58–69.

with a class to experience first hand the reality of American culture.[4] As Taylor says: "The world and academia are changing at an extraordinarily rapid pace, and it is incumbent on us to find ways to be creatively and constructively involved in the process."[5]

In 1992 Taylor taught a course and a "global seminar" which used electronic communication (e-mail, teleconferencing) and linked students at Williams College to the University of Helsinki, Finland.[6] Taylor developed this course with Finnish professor Esa Saarinen and titled it "Cyberscapes." In this course, students examined the political, social and philosophical implications of new electronic technologies.[7]

Since the writing of his book, *Erring: A Postmodern A/theology* (1984), Taylor has produced a variety of works on culture and art, religion and virtual culture, and philosophical reflections on death.[8] Earlier, however, Taylor was a more traditional scholar working with Kierkegaard, Hegel, and Nietzsche.[9] According to Taylor, "To go from Kant and Hegel to Las Vegas and cyberspace looks like a stretch, but there's a logic to it."[10] Taylor contends that Las Vegas should be understood as a religious experience—where image is everything and loss is part of everyday life.[11] Taylor contends that "Las Vegas is the realization of the Kingdom of God on Earth. ... [r]eligion is the most interesting where it is least obvious."[12]

Taylor affirms that communications technology continues to layer images on a culture dominated by symbols, therefore something is being lost. Taylor challenges his students to understand how culture seeks meaning up to this time. If the students

---

4   Seth Rogovoy, "Mark Taylor: Cyberprofessor from Hell or Visionary Educator," *Berkshire Eagle*, February 3, 1996, http://www.berkshireweb.com/rogovoy/interviews/taylor. html (26 Sept. 2005).

Elsewhere Taylor claims that Las Vegas is perhaps "the most important religious phenomena in the United States...where the death of God is staged as the spectacle of the Kingdom of God on earth." Mark C. Taylor, "Betting On Vegas," in *God, The Gift and Postmodernism*, John D. Caputo and Michael J. Scanlon (eds) (Bloomington and Indianapolis: Indiana University Press, 1999), p. 230.

5   Sara Helberger,"Bringing the Academy into the Electronic Era," *Harvard Alumni Review*, February, 1998, http://www.williams.edu/mtaylor/interviews/pages/980201_ harvardalumni_001.html (26 Sept. 2005)

6   It was through his efforts in this course which, in part, contributed toward his Carnegie Foundation award as the college professor of the year in the U.S. in 1995, see Heller, "From Kant to Las Vegas."

7   Helberger, "Bringing the Academy."

8   For example, to name a few: *Hiding*, University of Chicago Press, 1997; *About Religion: Economies of Faith in Virtual Culture*, University of Chicago Press, 1999; *The Moment of Complexity: Emerging Network Culture*, University of Chicago Press, 2002; and *Grave Matters* (with Dietrich Christian Lammerts), Reaktion Books, 2002.

9   Heller, "From Kant to Las Vegas."

10   Ibid.

11   Ibid.

12   Helberger, "Bringing the Academy."

understand what is lost they may view future opportunities to be gained.[13] Taylor relates this perspective in commenting on his Carnegie teaching award in 1995, and claims:

> Part of what captured the Carnegie Foundation's imagination was the technological stuff, but it's all grounded in the philosophy of religion. I don't want to be seen as just hype for this brave new world we're moving into, but as an effort to understand the losses and gains of it all. I see human experience as a lifelong process of attempting to negotiate the inevitability of loss, and I think that's what religion involves, wrestling with loss.[14]

Taylor may be considered the first American "post-ecclesiastical systematic or philosophic theologian" who is "free of the scars or perhaps even the memory of Church theology, and the first theologian to address himself solely to the purely theoretical or cognitive problems of theology."[15] Taylor began his professional work studying Kierkegaard from a modern theological perspective, where theology is free from the influence of the church and "thereby free of the very power and ground which theological thinking itself negated in realizing its modern epiphany."[16]

Taylor enjoys delivering a "five-minute history of Western philosophy" which sets the background for his theological views. He moves from Plato's forms and earthly matter to the Enlightenment, on to the introduction of the individual, the collective unconscious, and archetypes as given by Freud and Jung. Taylor suggests that these thoughts provided the turn for a cultural transformation of belief from that of divine creation of humanity to human creation of the idea of the divine. He then brings post-structuralism and deconstructionism of Derrida into the equation along with ideas of the redeeming value of art.[17]

Formation of Taylor's "Theology"

Having examined some basic background and formative issues regarding Taylor, we will now attempt to describe the basic framework of Taylor's *a/theology*. Although Taylor has published numerous books and articles which refer to his theological views, it is in his book *Erring* where he most thoroughly develops his deconstructive theological manifesto.[18]

---

13 George Judson, "Education Life: Bridging the Gap Between Religion and Technology," *The New York Times*, Section 4A (Jan. 7, 1996).
    http://www.williams.edu/mtaylor/interviewstimes.html (8 Feb. 2006).

14 Mark C. Taylor in Judson, "Education Life."

15 Thomas J.J. Altizer in foreword of Mark C. Taylor, *Deconstructing Theology* (New York: Crossroad, 1982), p. xii.

16 Ibid.

17 Helberger, "Bringing the Academy."

18 Some of his ideas were previously articulated in his book *Deconstructing Theology* (1982), and in a chapter he wrote titled, "Text as Victim," in *Deconstruction and Theology*, ed. Thomas J.J. Altizer (New York: Crossroad, 1982), pp. 58–78. Since then, Taylor has

Taylor has been greatly influenced by the work of Jacques Derrida and deconstructionism, and actually uses deconstructionism to do theology.[19] Taylor believes that "[d]espite its overt atheism, postmodernism remains profoundly religious, and this atheistic religiosity offers a promising point of departure for a truly postmodern theology."[20] Taylor calls this an "a/theology." In his prelude, Taylor lays the foundation for his theological deconstructionism:

> Postmodernism opens with the sense of *irrevocable* loss and *incurable* fault. This wound is inflicted by the overwhelming awareness of death—a death that "begins" with the death of God and "ends" with the death of our selves. We are in a time between times and a place which is no place. Here our reflection must "begin." In this liminal time and space, deconstructive philosophy and criticism offer rich, though still largely untapped, resources for religious reflection. One of the distinctive features of deconstruction is its willingness to confront the problem of the death of God squarely even if not always directly ... *deconstruction is the "hermeneutic" of the death of God.* As such, it provides a possible point of departure for a postmodern a/theology.[21]

For Taylor, the world is radically different to what it was, so the way we approach theology must be radically different as well. We have been wounded with an overwhelming sense of death, beginning with the death of God, then moving to the death of the self. The death of God was anticipated in Hegel, Kierkegaard and Nietzsche but only became completely realized in this century.[22]

In Taylor's view many contemporary philosophers of religion and theologians are unaware of the death of God and are relating as if he were still alive and well and relevant for our lives. For Taylor, this mistaken notion is what prevents most western theologians from embracing postmodernism. Western theology rests on a polar or

---

written additional theologically significant works, including *Altarity* (1987), *Tears* (1990), *Disfiguring: Art, Architecture, Religion* (1992), "Reframing Postmodernisms" included in Philippa Berry and Andrew Wernick (eds), *Shadow of Spirit* (1992), among other journal articles and books.

19 William A. Beardslee has also related Taylor's work to Lyotard: "Taylor, like Lyotard, rejects conventional narrative and replaces it, as the title of his book suggests, with "erring," which means both wandering and, like Lyotard's parology, transgressing-breaking the established patterns in the directionless movement of life." William A. Beardslee, "Christ in the Postmodern Age: Reflections Inspired By Jean-François Lyotard," in David Ray Griffin, William A. Beardslee, and Joe Holland, *Varieties of Postmodern Theology* (Albany: State University of New York Press, 1989), p. 67.

20 Mark C. Taylor, *Deconstructing Theology* (New York: Crossroad, 1982), p. xx.

21 Mark C. Taylor, *Erring* (Chicago: The University of Chicago Press, 1984), p. 6.

22 However, as Taylor himself concedes: "For neither Hegel nor Nietzsche is the death of God the mere negation of the divine. To the contrary, divine creativity disappears from the heavens only to reappear on earth in a process that Hegel interprets logically and Nietzsche views aesthetically. Through this death and resurrection, the locus of creativity shifts from the transcendent Creator to the immanent web of relations in and through which everything arises and passes away." Mark C. Taylor, *Hiding* (Chicago: University of Chicago Press, 1997), p. 291.

"dyadic" foundation seen with various opposing concepts such as: God/world, life/death, etc.[23] For example, Barth's negation of immanence becomes an affirmation of transcendence. Altizer's negation of transcendence becomes a negation of Barth's negation and also "an affirmation of coincidence of opposites. For Barth, the kingdom of God is elsewhere, and for Altizer, the kingdom of God is already here."[24] As Taylor says, "What *neither* Barth *nor* Altizer confronts is the possibility of the impossibility of the presence of the Kingdom—here or elsewhere, now or then. Consequently, neither thinks the negative radically enough."[25]

Instead, Taylor desires to begin where we are today, and invert the entire system. We must do our theology with a sense of dislocation.[26] Taylor submits that western philosophy and theology must be totally un-done and re-made by deconstructive criticism. The intellectual die that both joined and separated opposites must now be completely recast and reformulated. So what we have left is not simply an opposite from a previous way of thought, but a totally new way of thought arising from a new identity.[27]

Deconstruction takes apart (from within) the entire structure of traditional western theology. If theological thought rests traditional, deconstruction will challenge, oppose, and exclude theology.[28] As Taylor admits:

> In many ways, deconstruction might seem an unlikely partner for religious reflection. As a form of thought it appears avowedly atheistic. Derrida speaks for others as well as himself when he adamantly maintains that deconstruction "blocks every relationship to theology." Paradoxically, it is just this antithetical association with theology that lends deconstruction its "religious" significance for marginal thinkers ... deconstruction expresses greater appreciation for the significance of the death of God than most contemporary philosophers of religion and theologians.[29]

The modern era is repressive for Taylor because of its boundaries, whereas his postmodern a/theology is free and unbounded and "allows the rethinking and unthinking of all modern concepts. By opening oneself to and embracing the absence of foundations, one combats repression."[30]

Taylor moves back and forth between the "both/and" of Hegel and the "either/or" of Kierkegaard. By adapting Derrida, Taylor submits a theology summarized in the words "neither/nor." The key theme to Taylor's work is that of "margin." Taylor

---

23 Millard J. Erickson, *The Word Became Flesh* (Grand Rapids: Baker, 1991), pp. 316, 318.

24 Tilley with England, "The A/theology,"p. 63.

25 Taylor, *Disfiguring*, p. 316–17 as quoted in Tilley with England, "The A/theology," p. 63.

26 Erickson, *The Word Became Flesh*, pp. 316–18.

27 Taylor, *Erring*, p. 10.

28 Erickson, *The Word Became Flesh*, pp. 318–19. See also Taylor, *Deconstructing Theology*, p. xix.

29 Taylor, *Erring*, p. 6.

30 Tilley with England, "The A/theology," pp. 65, 66.

encourages embracing the in between, the marginal space in a world of opposites.[31] Terrence Tilley observes similarities between Taylor's theme of "margin" and the notion of "nothing" from Heidegger. Both are illustrating the need for people to deny those things which tie them down as well as to accept and even find fulfillment in negation.[32]

Taylor does not provide analytical theological argumentation, typical of modern methodology. Instead, in the fashion of Derrida, Taylor uses wordplay and associations to make his connections. He follows Derrida in holding that language refers not to external objects, but to other signs and meanings.[33] The essentials of Taylor's theology are based in the deconstruction of four basic elements throughout traditional western theology: God, self, history and the book. For Taylor, these traditional notions are not stable or certain as many believe. I will briefly address each of these four deconstructed topics in Taylor's theology which provide the backdrop to his "negative" affirmations.

Death of God

Taylor submits that we must abandon all previous conceptions that we have had regarding "God:" "To think the unthinkable Other, erroneously named altarity, it is necessary to unthink all we have thought with the name "God"….[34] In fact, Taylor argues that "[t]he return to, and of the sacred is impossible apart from the death of God, i.e., the personal God of Christianity. A fully developed heterology, therefore, is an 'atheology' (*athéologie*)."[35] Elsewhere however, Taylor does attempt to clarify that the "death of the transcendent Father need not be the complete disappearance of God, but can be seen as the birth of the divine, which now is grasped as an immanent and eternal process of dialectical development."[36]

Taylor suggests that there are four predictable responses to the death of God, or as Taylor terms, "the disappearance of the divine Author." The first group is indifferent to religious questions. This is the typical unreflective person who is completely engaged in his/her everyday activities without thinking much about life and experience. The second group is troubled by modern and postmodern implications for traditional religious beliefs. Usually this group manifests defiance if foundational beliefs are

---

31 Ibid., pp. 59, 61.

32 Ibid., p. 60.

33 Erickson, *The Word Became Flesh*, p. 319.

34 Taylor, *Disfiguring*, pp. 318–19 as quoted in Tilley with England, "The A/theology," p. 65. Taylor uses this coined word "altarity" to illustrate undecidability. He claims it is a "slippery word whose meaning can be neither stated clearly nor fixed firmly." Although the actual difference between this word and the English word "alterity" is simply the replacement of an "a" for the original "e," "it evokes dimensions of difference and aspects of otherness overlooked, excluded, or repressed by the notion of *différance*. Mark C. Taylor, *Altarity* (Chicago: The University of Chicago Press, 1987), pp. xxviii–xxix.

35 Taylor, *Altarity*, p. 136.

36 Taylor, *Deconstructing Theology*, p. 102.

challenged. A third group warmly embraces and accepts such news of the death of God—in fact, they feel a sense of liberation from an authoritarian structure of a constricting, domineering father. There is also a fourth group that Taylor believes is growing. This group finds themselves on the border between belief and unbelief—in the middle of extremes. They keep looking without finding, yet they continue their quest, remaining on the margin.[37]

Taylor claims that humanistic atheism is a modern form of the Death of God belief. He charts Death of God theology from its origins in Reformation thought with Luther's *pro nobis* (Christ lived and died "for us")—stressing the significance of the subjective self. This emphasis was further developed with Descartes' *cogito*— the autonomous human self is central, and God is simply another object of the self's thought. The autonomous self displaces the previous master and transfers the divine attributes to the human self. But, this does not resolve the problem of master and slave for Taylor, it only relocates it. For the sovereign God is simply replaced by a new sovereign self.[38] We must affirm with Nietzsche that we have culturally killed God by our secular materialism, and accept that God is irrelevant to everyday life. No longer are there divine foundations for society. Since the foundation for everything in God is lost, the self is also lost in the temporal nature of history.[39]

Death of the Self

By mastering an external object, namely "God," we internalize this object. By putting it to death and "possessing" this object (the other) we in turn become possessed by it. This external object now inside us (internalized) is both repressive (externally) and seductive (internally).[40] As Taylor claims: "The repressive master and the seductive demon join forces to split the subject. Suffering the victimization it has sought to inflict, the subject becomes 'un corps morcelé' rather than an integral self."[41] This is the end of the self. As Taylor says, "the a/theologian welcomes the death of God and embraces the disappearance of the self."[42]

---

37 Taylor, *Erring*, pp. 4–5. Also see comments in Erickson, *The Word Became Flesh*, pp. 316–17.

38 Ibid., pp. 20–22, 25; also see Erickson, *The Word Became Flesh*, p. 320.

39 Tilley with England, "The A/theology," p. 61.

40 Erickson, *The Word Became Flesh*, p. 320.

41 Taylor, *Erring*, p. 31.

42 Ibid., p. 104. The notion of "self" to which Taylor is referring is the "narcissistic" subject of modernism, the independent center of consciousness and identity—unique and autonomous. Again, see *Erring*, pp. 32–3, 86. James H. Olthuis describes this de-throned self as the "self as the child of enlightenment, fully present to itself, self–conscious, sovereign, absolute agent, given power over the world as object ... a production of this very world and processes it was said to master." James Olthuis, "Crossing the Threshold: Sojourning Together in the Wild Spaces of Love," in *Knowing Other-Wise: Philosophy at the Threshold of Spirituality*, ed. James H. Olthuis (New York: Fordham University Press, 1997), p. 238.

The humanist of modernism resists the death of the self, failing to see it is an outworking of the death of God. However, the postmodern deconstructionist sees this connection. For Taylor, nihilism can be seen positively if this total loss of the self is accepted: favorably if one simply accepts the loss of the self. The error of the modern humanistic atheist, is an inability to accept loss, with anxiety about death. This type of nihilism is a sign of weakness, rather than strength. Instead one must accept the total loss of the self, the crucified self. Taylor says that "nihilism is the mark of the cross. On Golgotha, not only God dies, the self also disappears."[43]

Perhaps a clear way to present this position using traditional theological terminology would be to say if God disappears, then the *imago dei*, the self created in that God's image, also disappears.[44] Taylor affirms this elsewhere:

> God and self are always made in each other's image. The disappearance of one eventually entails the disappearance of the other ... God doesn't simply disappear, he goes underground. ... God doesn't simply die, God becomes man....That's what happens in the Enlightenment and the nineteenth century. The creative God is displaced onto the creative subject.[45]

Taylor goes as far as to say that the "birth of universal humanity is impossible apart from the death of the individual self."[46]

Denial of History as Directed Process

Along with a hermeneutic of the death of God comes the elimination of history as a directed process. There is no pre-determined beginning, middle and end. There is no "ideal" to which we are headed.[47] History is not a guided tour given by a transcendent God leading us to some kind of predestined outcome. History does not end in apocalypse, but with "deferral."[48] The end of history presupposes the death of a transcendent God and the notion of a sovereign self. Taylor submits that "[t]he death of the Alpha and the Omega, the disappearance of the self, and the overcoming of unhappy consciousness combine to fray the fabric of history."[49] Taylor concedes, however, that it is important to remember prominent historical events "[i]n order to

---

43 Taylor, *Erring*, p. 33. Also see Erickson, *The Word Became Flesh*, pp. 320–21.

44 David Ray Griffin, "Postmodern Theology and A/theology: A Response to Mark C. Taylor," in David Ray Griffin, William A. Beardslee, and Joe Holland, *Varieties of Postmodern Theology* (Albany: State University of New York Press, 1989), p. 33.

45 Mark C. Taylor in "Imagologies and Other Philosophical Conversations with Mark C. Taylor," Interview by David Lionel Smith, January 1997, http://www.williams.edu/ mtaylor/ interviews/pages/970101_masshumanities_001.html (29 Sept. 2005).

46 Mark C. Taylor, *Tears* (Albany: State University of New York Press, 1990), p. 62.

47 See Griffin, "Postmodern Theology and A/theology," p. 34.

48 Charles E. Winquist, *Desiring Theology* (Chicago: University of Chicago Press, 1995), p. 116.

49 Taylor, *Erring*, p. 73.

grasp the relationship of the closure of history and opening of erring.... The drama of history stages the flight from death."[50]

The Closed Book

The notion of the "closed book" is a natural outworking of Taylor's analyses. As Charles E. Winquist notes: "[Taylor] sees that the death of God proclaimed by Nietzsche follows the proclamation of *absolute knowledge* by Hegel. It is Hegel's proclamation of absolute knowledge that is both the end of history and the closure of the book."[51] In view of Taylor's deconstruction of God, self, and history, it follows that there cannot be an authoritative "book" which is prescriptive for all of life. As Taylor writes, "a text is not a finished product, but is an ongoing production which continuously emerges in and through the activity of interpretation."[52] Taylor affirms that Christianity is a religion of the book, and the West is a book culture. But, the closure of the book is being repeatedly rewritten since it is part of an unfolding theological network. But if the book is regulative, the tendency of theology will be systematic and scientific—the direction to which western theology consistently leans. The systematic theologian will do his work as a book—with a beginning, middle and end. The notion of an omnipresent, incarnate logos, Taylor submits, is the center of the book for the Christian.[53] It is the logos that situates our theology by pointing backward to creation and directing us forward to the kingdom at the end of time. This is the omnipresent logos of the incarnation and redemption, the foundation of systematic theology. The book of the logos is now closed and we are standing outside its closure. Hence, the former systematic theologian who realizes the implications of this closure, must become a "writer."[54]

But writing cannot be fully past or present for Taylor—it is always an endless series of traces. Writing is a wound which uses cuts to expose the fact that traditional limits cannot stand.[55] Taylor, following the lead of Derrida, affirms the elimination of any translinguistic referent for linguistic signs, because signs only refer to other signs—there is no "real thing" beyond language. For Taylor this completely undermines the grounding of the western ontological tradition. The anchor is gone.[56] Taylor says: "The sacrifice of God is the death of the transcendental signified, which marks the closure of the classical regime of re-presentation."[57] In this classical sense,

---

50 Ibid., p. 151.

51 Winquist, *Desiring Theology*, p. 115.

52 Taylor, "Text as Victim," p. 66.

53 Taylor, *Erring*, p. 79.

54 Ibid.

55 Tilley with England, "The A/theology," p. 64. See Taylor, *Tears*, p. 231: "To write after the death of God ... to write beyond the end of theology is to betray nothing .... Write to betray nothing. An end "beyond" the end of theology. An end that never arrives but always betrays."

56 Taylor, *Erring*, p. 172.

57 Taylor, *Hiding*, p. 233.

then, for Taylor, the book is closed and theology is at an end. Yet, following this "end," Taylor affirms a new beginning:

> The task of thinking at the end of theology is to think nothing otherwise than by not thinking. The nothing remaining after (the) all has been thought marks the end of theology by inscribing an end that does not belong to theology. This end implies the closure of theology, which at the same time is the opening of a previously unimaginable a/theology.[58]

Taylor's Optimistic Nihilism: An "Erring" A/theology

As one can imagine, Taylor's elimination of these crucial areas of theological thought leave a certain emptiness in western thought. To fill this emptiness, Taylor proposes what he terms an "a/theology" in which God becomes writing, self becomes trace (or as Taylor terms it, "Markings"), history becomes erring for "mazing grace," and book becomes text—with "erring scripture."[59] Taylor's a/theology is an attempt at affirmative nihilism: "rather than suffering these losses passively, it actively and willingly embraces nihilism and thereby overcomes it."[60] He says "it might be defined as something like a non-negative negative theology that nonetheless is not positive. A/theology pursues or, more precisely, is pursued by an alterity that neither exists nor does not exist but is beyond both Being and Nonbeing."[61] Yet, ironically, Taylor likens death of God theology to Christian redemption in that death leads to rebirth. Taylor adds: "When negation is doubled, it yields affirmation. By negating transcendence, the death of God leads to the total presence of Being here and now."[62] Taylor summarizes the ironic optimism of his eschatology in the following words:

> the denial of utopia can become utopian and the loss of the dream of salvation can become a salvation. The impossibility of reconciliation means that there is no resurrexit here or elsewhere, nor in the future. The door is closed, closed tightly; there is no upper room.[63]

---

58 Taylor, *Tears*, p. 206.

59 Tilley with England, "The A/theology," pp. 61–2. See also the chapter headings for part two of Taylor, *Erring*.

60 Griffin, "Postmodern Theology and A/theology," p. 34. See also Taylor, *Erring*, p. 140.

61 Taylor, *Disfiguring*, p. 316 as quoted in Tilley with England, "The A/theology," p. 62. Taylor's approach should not be confused with pure "negative theology." Elsewhere, Taylor succinctly articulates the difference: "While negative theologians tend to regard nothing as the binary or dialectical opposite of being, the a/theologian interprets nothing as neither being nor nonbeing." Taylor, *Tears*, p. 225.

62 Mark C. Taylor, "Reframing Postmodernisms," p. 19.

63 Taylor, *Disfiguring*, p. 317 as quoted in Tilley with England, "The A/theology," p. 69.

Erring

"Erring," according to Taylor, is a wandering, a deviation from the intended course.[64] Consequently, the erring thinker is not necessarily theological or nontheological, theistic or atheistic. An a/theology is for those in the margin. This "/" of Taylor's a/theology (which can be written, yet is not spoken) signifies both closeness and distance, likeness and difference, interior and exterior.[65] The symbol between the "a" and "theology" is like a "permeable membrane" forming a border where "fixed boundaries disintegrate." Of course, this completely subverts western theology. Theology, for Taylor remains ambiguous, errant and erratic. The theologian is wandering and even heretical—one who does not look to the past, nor to the eschaton.[66]

Taylor believes that through the tool of deconstruction, and by staying in this position of the "middle," it will reveal a brand new way of reading and writing scripture. Yet, this "endless spinning" and this "vertiginous wordplay" is not an easy path. Taylor relates this to the path of Golgotha and asserts that at "the threshold of absolute passage, the cross marks the intersection of ascent and descent that is the 'marriage of heaven and hell.'"[67] But Taylor does not want to leave people in a world completely nihilistic, without religious reflection at all. He is actually attempting to form some "constructive" perspectives by his deconstruction methods in his a/theology.[68] As may be observed, Taylor depends a great deal on the thoughts of Hegel. With Hegel, there is an organic character to all reality. Hegel asserts that thesis and antithesis become synthesized, each is "lifted up" into a new entity. Yet, with Taylor, differences continue to exist in tension with each other, always interchanging.[69] Consequently, the search is never-ending for Taylor, but it is this search that keeps us alive and going so that we don't end in despair.[70]

Christology and Incarnation

Taylor's views of christology and incarnation are extremely significant for the main contours of his deconstructive a/theology. In fact, there is a necessary relationship

---

64 This term does not originate with Taylor. For example we may note Heidegger's usage of this term in his essay, "On the Essence of Truth," in *Basic Writings*, ed. David Farrell Krell (San Francisco: HarperCollins, 1993), pp. 132–5. Heidegger states: "Man's flight from the mystery toward what is readily available, onward from one current thing to the next, passing the mystery by—this is *erring*." (p. 133)

65 Taylor, *Erring*, p. 12. François Nault points out a similar ambiguity in the French, see François Nault, *Derrida et la théologie: Dire Dieu après la déconstruction* (Paris: Les éditions du Cerf, 2000), p. 119.

66 Taylor, *Erring*, pp. 12–13.

67 Ibid., p.13.

68 Tilley with England, "The A/theology," p. 68.

69 Erickson, *The Word Became Flesh*, pp. 324–5.

70 Tilley with England, "The A/theology," p. 69.

between the death of God and Taylor's "radical christology" which is *"thoroughly* incarnational." For Taylor, the divine *"is"* the incarnate word and the "embodiment of the divine is the death of God."[71] The incarnation is not a one-time event in history, limited to one individual at one particular place. The divine is *"forever* embodied" in this radical christology. As Taylor claims:

> inscription is a continual (though not necessarily a continuous) process ... God is what word means, and word is what "God" means. To interpret God as word is to understand the divine as scripture or writing.[72]

Taylor says that a death of God a/theology is really a "radical Christology" which "finds its completion in the crucifixion of the individual self and the resurrection of universal humanity.[73] Taylor's Hegelian background emerges here—the antithesis of a transcendent and the immanent (God and the world) become synthesized. As Erickson comments on Taylor: "Thus, Jesus was not a once-for-all incarnation of God, but an example of God's continual relating to the world.... Particularity gives way to universality, and transcendence gives way to immanence."[74] For Taylor the incarnation appears to essentially be the activity of writing, which is a "diffused presence of God." Not only does Taylor rarely use the term "Christ," he also takes "the traditional functions of Christ–revealing God, sustaining reality, delivering humans from their predicament" and reassigns them "to the free play of words and ideas."[75]

Mazing Grace

Another important concept for Taylor is the idea of what he terms "mazing" grace. Taylor implores us to wander, to err and move about, to deviate, free from the false security of modernism. Instead we are to wander, to err and move about, to deviate. It is through this erring which leads us to grace. As Taylor puts it: "Erring is serpentine wandering that comes, if at all, by grace—grace that is mazing."[76]

A "maze" is a labyrinth of winding, interconnecting, passages. To "be mazed" is to be perplexed, to wander about in one's mind either through delusion or deception. Taylor says: "Behind the mask of the player there is always another mask. Mazing grace situates one in the midst of a labyrinth from which there is no exit." Taylor applies this concept to his view of grace in his a/theology: "The maze through which the erring trace wanders is neverending."[77] He claims that this is a "second innocence"

---

71 Taylor, *Erring*, p. 103.
72 Ibid., p. 104.
73 Taylor, "Text as Victim," p. 73.
74 Erickson, *The Word Became Flesh*, p. 323.
75 Ibid., pp. 324; 325–6. Cf. Taylor, *Erring*, pp. 103–106.
76 Taylor, *Erring*, pp. 150–51.
77 Ibid., p. 168.

which presupposes the death of God. To accept the death of the transcendent God and to accept this loss straightforwardly, is grace.

Critique and Theological Implications

Positive Aspects For Consideration

Can we learn anything at all from Taylor if he radically transgresses everything we cling to? I believe that we can indeed glean some helpful insights from Taylor's a/theological concerns.

Serious Contextualization Millard Erickson, in *The Word Became Flesh*, contends that Taylor's book, *Erring*, is intended to be read as an apologetic work. Although I am not so inclined to agree, Erickson does point out that Taylor is attempting to cling to some type of belief network while drawing upon elements in historic Christianity. In order to address people who are struggling in the "margin" of belief and unbelief, Taylor uses the insights of contemporary philosophical innovations in deconstructive thought to address their struggle.[78] In this age, many simply ignore all aspects of Christianity, yet Taylor actively takes many Christian ideas and thoughts and interacts with them in view of contemporary culture.[79] I would also credit Taylor for taking recent intellectual developments seriously as Erickson suggests, but it is difficult to understand Taylor's proposals as an "apologetic" in any typical sense of the term. Although he clings to fragments of Christian vocabulary, the fragments become only truncated specimens of a lost Christianity. In my estimation, this has little or nothing to do with either positive or negative apologetics in the broadest sense of the word.

"Mazing" I would suggest a drawing a parallel between Taylor's notion of "mazing grace" and Derrida's notion of the messianic. Both involve a continual wandering and "hoping" of sorts. Both are seeking—endlessly seeking in earnest expectation of that which is to come yet never will arrive. Both offer the continual *viens—viens toujours*. As I noted with Derrida, there are positive aspects of such notions. It does challenge us to think again of the unlimited expectations of hope and promise even as applied to Christian eschatology. Taylor does, through his notion of "mazing," affirm a perpetual state characteristic of humanity. We do walk or "wander" through life not knowing or understanding the beginning or end. We are extremely limited in our knowledge of outcomes. Qoheleth certainly instructs us in this in Ecclesiastes 3:11. Here we find that God has "set eternity in the hearts of men; yet they cannot fathom what God has done from beginning to end." Life is indeed an enigma we must live with, as difficult as it may be. We do wander and "maze" through life

---

78 Erickson, *The Word Became Flesh*, p. 317.

79 Ibid., p. 327.

unaware of what it may bring—either in forms of happiness or extreme grief and suffering. But for Qoheleth, this "mystery" or "mazing" through life, being unaware of the outcome, is not some sort of "blessing" as Taylor construes it, but a burden we must endure.[80]

Nevertheless, Taylor has surely made a poignant observation and provides a needed reminder of our limitations. We are extremely limited in our knowledge of outcomes. Donald Bloesch supports this affirmation as well:

> Evangelical theology is a *theologia viatorum* (a theology of wayfarers), not a *theologia comprehensorum* (a theology of those who have arrived conceptually). It sees itself on a pilgrimage to a heavenly city where faith will be supplanted by direct vision, but at present it is content simply to walk by faith.[81]

We do wander, we do err. But is this wandering always to be embraced as joy and freedom in the sense that Taylor seems to characterize it? Undoubtedly not, from my perspective. We should keep in mind the context of this aforementioned passage in Qoheleth. Such unawareness and lack of knowledge in life may indeed be a burden on man (Eccles. 3:10). However, Qoheleth affirms that God "has made everything beautiful in its time" and also "set eternity in the hearts of men." No, the mystery and wandering may not always be joy-filled, but one may be assured that those who follow God can have the confidence that God will bring all things to completion for the greatest good. It is this confidence, in the midst of the enigma of life, which motivates us to keep pushing forward.

The Closed Book and Open Story   Although Taylor does not develop an ethic (as will be argued later) I would submit that Taylor's notion of the closed book may stimulate some positive theological thinking with regard to Christian doctrine and practice of the Christian story. When we think of the development of Christianity in the Acts narrative (which I will also examine in a later chapter) we do find an "end" to the book as such. But it is an "open-ended" end. The Acts narrative discontinues, but the story of Christianity continues—and we live out that story as interpreters. The written narrative upon which the Christian movement was based stops in Acts with Paul under Roman guard. From this "closed book" forward, the Acts narrative must be lived out, not simply put into doctrinal propositions. I am not denying the value of doctrinal propositions, I am simply saying that one must not make propositional content *the* only content and sum of Christianity. Now I realize that Taylor is not saying this. I am simply listening and interacting "apologetically" to Taylor's challenges, concerns, notions, and reactions to Enlightenment excesses and re-baptizing them for this context. In this, sense, Taylor's concerns do stimulate us and remind us that in some senses, the book is closed and now we need to live out its truths as an open story in the narrative context of Christian community. Often,

80 See Gerhard Von Rad, *Wisdom In Israel* (Nashville: Abingdon Press, 1972), p. 234.

81 Donald G. Bloesch, *Essentials of Evangelical Theology: God, Authority, & Salvation*, vol. 1 (San Francisco: Harper & Row, 1978), p. 19.

when Christian theology is too propositionally emphasized, doctrines become dry, stale truths, with supposed "objective" content. Instead, we must remember that the Christian narrative must be lived out as our personal story as a chapter in the history of the Christian church.

Image of God I would not affirm nor warmly embrace the death of God as Taylor would implore us to do. However, he certainly helps one understand how the death of God would necessitate a death of the self. In Christian theology we would affirm the imago dei in its broadest sense (imago essentialis) as the defining characteristic of humanity both in terms of homo creatus and homo peccator.[82] As such, the essence of humanity is defined in terms of its relation and dependence upon God. If God is dead, then so is humanity. In terms of theological anthropology, if God is no longer a part of the "picture," then the image of God "fades away, leaving behind an unidentified, and perhaps unidentifiable, 'humanity.'"[83]

In this regard, Taylor awakens us to the great importance of the *imago dei* in theological thought. With both Foucault's and Taylor's deconstructive assault on the notion of man—one is challenged with the importance of developing a rigorous theological anthropology. Taylor's "death of self" reminds us of the critical necessity for fresh theological research on the *imago dei*. How is the *imago dei* related to the cultural mandate of dominion? What sense can we make of such a notion of "dominion" in a postmodern theological context? What is the significance of "likeness" and "image" in relation to Christology and sanctification? What is the relationship between "body" and the *imago dei*? These questions, among others, are questions which may surface due to Taylor's challenges. Although such questions will remain rhetorical due to the limitations and focus of this book, they certainly help point us forward to further inquiry.

Problematic Aspects For Our Consideration

In spite of these promising notions stimulating positive theological inquiry, in my estimation there are several significant problems with Taylor's postmodern deconstructive a/theology. Charles E. Winquist submits that "[t]he task that Taylor has defined is to think and live the disaster of nothing."[84] But, practically speaking, it is difficult to see how one can live life in view of such a disaster. Can the loss of these modern foundations of God, Self, History, and Book actually be turned into any sort of gain? Is Taylor's a/theological deconstruction really an affirmation, as he

---

82 See G.C. Berkhouwer, *Man: The Image of God*, trans. Dirk W. Jellema, Studies in Dogmatics (Grand Rapids: Eerdmans, 1962), pp. 37–66, 119. I am simply drawing a general observation here. Due to space and the limitations of this book, I will not attempt to develop the theology of the *imago dei* in terms of *dominium, analogia relationis, theosis*, and other related aspects. See Berkhouwer, *Man: The Image of God*, pp. 67–75ff.

83 Martin Henry, "God in Postmodernity," *Irish Theological Quarterly* 63/1 (1998): 20.

84 Winquist, *Desiring Theology*, p. 122.

claims it is, or does he end up denying some things that are simply undeniable? Is there any world remaining when Taylor has finished his program of deconstruction where it is even possible to "err?"[85] I will attempt to address these questions and concerns more specifically.

Absence of Grief Theologian Kevin J. Vanhoozer suggests that Taylor's work is "permeated with a manic-depressive tension between grief and relief at the deaths of God, the author, and meaning." Taylor is like Nietzsche in that he attempts "to turn the loss of meaning into a net gain for humanity. For it is only when we abandon the hope of a higher life and of recovering the hidden meaning of life that we can abandon ourselves to this life."[86] Taylor claims that the postmodern person must not accept nihilism passively, but actively—and must willingly embrace it.[87] But we should rightly ask with Vanhoozer: Is nihilism truly freedom, or are Taylor's celebrations premature? Is it really possible to have joy and freedom following the death of God?[88]

However, I am not disqualifying Taylor's perspectives simply because they may be painful to many. Certainly, many truthful beliefs may be *painfully* true. But a truthful *theological* perspective, I would argue, must provide more than apparent internal consistency. A theology must respond effectively to the human condition and *true* human needs. Taylor does not seem to acknowledge the deep, emotional, element of grief that should characterize the loss that he is advocating. He is contemplating no less than eliminating the entire base of beliefs from which all who usually consider themselves "Christian" are framing their emotional, religious, and family identity. Although he certainly refers many times to a sense of loss and awareness of death that one embraces in postmodern thought, his "theology" lacks the practical wisdom to help one work through such emotional grief as human beings. Instead, Taylor abruptly moves forward with an abstruse intellectualism seemingly unaware of such a desperate human condition he is placing others in.[89]

On the other hand, Tilley suggests that

---

85 Tilley with England, "The A/theology," pp. 59; 69; 68. Of course I am aware that Taylor may say that his deconstructive program is never finished, and he may also deny the use of the word "program" for his agenda.

86 Kevin J. Vanhoozer, *Is There a Meaning in This Text?* (Grand Rapids: Zondervan, 1998), pp. 72, 73.

87 See Taylor, *Erring*, p. 140.

88 Vanhoozer, *Is There a Meaning in This Text?*, p. 73.

89 See Erickson, *The Word Became Flesh*, p. 325. Don Cupitt, although not specifically referring to Mark C. Taylor, also submits that such a departure from past traditional notions, will be extremely difficult for theology. Cupitt states: "A religious tradition finds it even more difficult to admit that it is in terminal crisis and needs to make a break with the past than does a philosophical. And would not a *complete* break require an entirely new language, which nobody would be able to understand?" Don Cupitt, *The Long-legged Fly* (London: SCM Press Ltd., 1987), p. 120.

Taylor does recognize our relationships and our erring as part of being human. He also knows that there are no answers and that the journey is what *living* is all about. But if the door *is* shut, then we are not wandering and erring, we are lost and hopeless.[90]

Perhaps one can say that Taylor "recognizes our relationships and our erring as part of being human" yet does not adequately address the emotional impact and consequential outworking of that "erring." As I asked before, does Taylor recognize the suffering and grief that often accompanies such wandering and "erring?" Wandering is not often joyful, as Taylor seems to characterize it. Panic and pain often accompany wandering because of lack of direction, and the brute fact of suffering in the journey of life. By rendering this wandering in such an optimistic manner it seems like Taylor truly minimizes the plight of mankind.

Critique of "Mazing Grace" As we have seen, the wandering that we have the "opportunity" to face in the midst of such loss, Taylor terms "mazing grace." Scott Cowdell provides a pertinent, yet modest critique of Taylor's notion of grace:

> Yet while the notion of grace is often naïvely interpreted in what amounts to escapist terms, involving preservation of the self against forces of dissolution, here however it is shorn of any such dubious doctrine of providence. Here grace is simply the capacity to live loose-limbed and open-eyed. It is the 'steep and rugged pathway', and as in Luther it is the *via crucis*. Yet it is also the yellow brick road! There is much in this therefore that I would heartily affirm....
>
> ... Ideally, all of this heralds the end of monarchial selfhood and the birth of a non-possessive delight in things that can cope with anguish and disappointment. There is courage to be garnished too, as when the members of collectives face individual death in the name of a noble cause.
>
> Yet in all this I have misgivings. Serious though this life might be, is it necessarily so?[91]

On a different level, Tilley also believes that Taylor has given in to modernity by losing touch with apophatic theology. If the door is shut, and the room beyond it is denied, as Taylor claims, then this is indeed despair.[92]

Derrida scholar John D. Caputo also provides a pertinent critique of Taylor's a/theological proposal. Caputo believes that Taylor has essentially taken Derrida too far, and has too closely associated Derrida with "Death of God" theology. Taylor attempts to write to those in the margin between theism and atheism, as if these two positions were stable. Like Derrida, he appreciates the quality of "undecidability" and the trouble we are faced with if we attempt to make judgment claims about the truth of God or other things as well. However, Caputo believes that Taylor does not in actuality remain "on the slash of undecidability" but in fact "makes a reductionistic

---

90 Tilley with England, "The A/theology," p. 69.

91 Scott Cowdell, "Radical Theology, Postmodernity and the Christian Life in the Void," *The Heythrop Journal* 32/1 (1991), p. 66.

92 Tilley with England, "The A/theology," p. 69.

decision against God."[93] Caputo is saying that Taylor's deconstructive a/theology inevitably turns against itself. Taylor is so careful to obliterate every ground of religious belief that he ends up even annihilating his own system.

The Violence of Despair   Once again, it is necessary to consider whether or not Taylor has adequately handled the human condition of despair if he pulls out all the plugs. If we are indeed trapped in a maze of endless wandering and "erring" all of our days without any hope of escape or finality, then we are "placed not in joyous disempowerment but in panoptic dominion."[94]

Although he precedes Taylor, Heidegger himself acknowledged the inherent oppression in this notion of errancy:

> Because man's in-sistent ek-sistence proceeds in errancy, and because errancy as leading astray always oppresses in some manner or other and is formidable on the basis of this oppression of the mystery, specifically as something forgotten, in the ek-sistence of his Dasein man is *especially* subjected to the rule of the mystery and the oppression of errancy.[95]

Gillian Rose specifically addresses the "erring" a/theology of Taylor in the following insight:

> If the beginning and the end are abolished so that all is (divine) middle—*Mitte ist überall*—joyful erring would not be achieved nor would pure virtue "without resistance"; one would be left helpless in the total domination of the maze, every point equally beginning and end. This is to encounter not pure freedom but pure power and to become its perfect victim.
>
> Violence lurks in the labyrinth.[96]

Rose provides a criticism genuinely worthy of our consideration. She submits that there is violence in nihilism itself. It is so difficult to imagine how we can warmly embrace nihilism when it violates all that we understand to be true. It appears that Taylor's a/theological wandering only "lives parasitically on a theological host."[97] It is important to consider the implicit violence of essentially destroying all historical Christian understandings committed by Taylor's a/theological proposal. Human beings need some understanding of history and destiny. The making of landmarks is simply a device people use to measure their lives in order to live their lives to the fullest on a daily basis. Furthermore, if one accepts such a/theological, deconstructive,

---

93   John D. Caputo, *The Prayers and Tears of Jacques Derrida: Religion Without Religion* (Bloomington & Indianapolis: Indiana University Press, 1997), p. 14.

94   Rose, "New Jerusalem, Old Athens, " p. 329.

95   Martin Heidegger, "On the Essence of Truth," in *Basic Writings*, ed. David Farrell Krell (San Francisco: HarperCollins, 1993), p. 134.

96   Rose, "New Jerusalem, Old Athens," p. 329.

97   See Winquist, *Desiring Theology*, p. 123.

nihilistic violence, is such a belief system really Christian at all? Such a theology seems to be ultimately self-destructive and unworkable in real life.[98]

Ironically, we may even ask this: Is Taylor's a/theology radical enough? He attempts to be extremely radical by eliminating all that is thought about God, whether positive or negative. But, I believe his nihilism is still a nihilism operating in the shadow of the non-existent God of Christian theology. In this sense, such nihilism is "intrinsically, even if parasitically" a "Judeo-Christian religious concept."[99] Taylor's notions are derived within the context of the denial of the monotheism of Christian theology. That is, he assumes the negation of the "Christian" God. If Taylor truly wants to emphasize the death of God, then should he not be more complete in nihilism by eliminating "God" in a pantheistic context as well?

Ethics A Christian theology (or a/theology?) will demonstrate ethical concerns based in some manner on the lifestyle of Jesus Christ.[100] Taylor's a/theology rarely refers to Christ, and also seems to be lacking any serious immediate ethical concern other than freedom from oppressive, transcendent religious structures which people have put upon themselves.[101] Erickson provides some severe criticism on this point with which I concur:

> Responsible theology, however, should be translatable into religion....What does one who holds a deconstructive a/theology have to say, for example, to the parents of a teenager who is addicted to cocaine, or to a wife whose husband has just left her for another woman, or to a man who has just been informed that he has a fast-growing terminal malignancy? ...Without minimizing Taylor's personal angst, we must recognize that he does not touch the problems of the major segments of society.[102]

In addition to the emotional, personal, and ethical shortcomings of Taylor's a/theology, there are also legitimate logical concerns. Now, I must be careful with my words here. Taylor of course is radically questioning the entire enterprise of both "legitimation" and "logical." So how can I proceed with such a criticisim? We must ask ourselves what Taylor is essentially arguing for in his works. If he is not attempting himself to make any significant claims to what is indeed real in some sense, how can I accept or reject what he is purporting? With all of Taylor's linguistic word plays, is it possible to make any decision on what is right and what

---

98 See Erickson, *The Word Became Flesh*, p. 331: "It is difficult to assess in what sense deconstructive a/theology is to be called Christian. In particular, so little is made of the historical person of Jesus of Nazareth that one wonders whether there is any justification for calling the movement Christian. Perhaps it is not intended to be Christian. At times, in fact, the movement shows resemblance to Buddhism."

99 Henry, "God in Postmodernity," p. 20.

100 Again, see Erickson, *The Word Became Flesh*, pp. 329, 330.

101 See Griffin, "Postmodern Theology and A/theology," p. 39: "The moral goal of this form of postmodernism is to strike a blow against all totalitarianisms, present and potential, by undermining every possible form of totality thinking."

102 Erickson, *The Word Became Flesh* (Grand Rapids: Baker, 1991), p. 330.

is wrong? Is it truly possible to have an effective exchange of communication with Taylor's suppositions?[103] Is any form of meaningful evaluative judgment from other perspectives possible with Taylor? Is Taylor indeed denying what postmodern theologian David Ray Griffin calls, "hard-core commonsense notions?" Such things are those which "cannot be denied without contradicting one's own practice."[104]

According to Taylor, the human subject has no power of self-determination, yet, as Griffin points out, Taylor describes the self as "a cipher for forces that play through it."[105] Taylor's claim that an author originates nothing (cf. Derrida) is contrasted by Taylor's consistent use of the pronoun "I," and by the fact that he uses an index of the authors he cites. Griffin submits that Taylor could not engage in writing without a presupposition of responsible actions for what we do indeed say as a basis of credit or blame. Consequently, as Griffin points out, Taylor is inconsistent in the way he portrays the nature of the self.[106]

Secondly, Griffin claims that although Taylor explicitly denies the correspondence theory of truth, he implicitly affirms it since his book contains truth claims. For Taylor does believe his claims are at least in some sense true—in that they correspond to reality.[107] Taylor indeed uses forms of argumentation in order to demolish traditional objective approaches. There is a sense in which Taylor is attempting to persuade his readers into adhering to his perspective. This is an element which should be considered when evaluating Taylor's method. After all, Taylor also uses traditional chapters, numbers, and organizing principles in most of his books. Taylor also explains the process by which things have occurred in the past, and how things are now, and how things should be.[108]

Finally, Griffin also submits that Taylor denies that, as humans, we may act with intention for matters of good or evil, better or worse. As Taylor says, "the understanding of history as a directed process remains bound to a view of the self as an intentional agent."[109] Yet, Griffin claims that "[e]liminative postmodernism arises out of a deep moral passion to overcome evil ... based on the conviction

---

103 Ibid., pp. 327–8ff.

104 Griffin, "Postmodern Theology and A/theology," p. 35-6. There are four "hard-core commonsense notions" that Griffin claims are common to all persons which cannot be denied. These are: 1) the freedom of power of self-determination; 2) the fact that an actual world exists independently of one's perception of it; 3) one's interpretative ideas are true if they correspond with that independent existing world (correspondence theory of truth) and, 4) a distinction is possible, for some events, between what actually happened and what could have happened for either better or worse.

105 Taylor, *Erring*, p. 106 as quoted in Griffin, Beardslee, and Holland, *Varieties of Postmodern Theology*, p. 36.

106 Griffin, Beardslee, and Holland, *Varieties of Postmodern Theology*, p. 36.

107 Ibid., pp. 37–8.

108 Erickson, *The Word Became Flesh*, p. 329. Erickson cites Walter Lowe, "A Deconstructionist Manifesto: Mark C. Taylor's *Erring*," *Journal of Religion*, 66/3 (July 1986). See pp. 324–5 on this particular criticism.

109 Taylor, *Erring*, p. 154.

that the dominant western systems of thought have had extremely destructive consequences."[110] Of course, Taylor's theology is full of ideas related to how a deconstructive approach may help overcome such negative notions of modernity. If Taylor had nothing "good" or "better" to say, why else would he need to write the book?[111] So, it seems as though Taylor in some sense maintains intentional agency while at the same time negating its use.

Although I largely agree with Griffin's appraisal of Taylor's internal inconsistencies, I question whether he may be pushing too far in his critique of Taylor's denial of the correspondence theory of truth. Does such a negative critique square with the genre of Taylor's writing? I believe it may not. The broader concerns of radical deconstructionists like Taylor are not to demonstrate the absence (or "reality"?) of things like houses, people, toothbrushes, and chickens. Taylor puts on his jeans in the morning and rides a real motorcycle. Denying such things is not what his work is about. Instead in his own "Dionysian" way, he is pointing out the conflation of the realities we perceive and the images we make of those realities. When it comes to doing theology these images have been expressed in texts. All images and texts then are inaccurate renderings, traces and fabrications. What Taylor seems to be doing in this a/theological endeavor is a sportive iconoclasm of language and theology stemming from the egoism of modernist ideology.[112] With this "sportive" genre in mind, the statements, style, and vocabulary will certainly be marked by extremes and radical irony.

If it were at all possible to summarize a major concern which emerges from Taylor's theological (or a/theological) position, it would be that of mastery and domination causing repression of difference among humanity.[113] It is fitting and relevant to address these postmodern concerns, and I believe Taylor is a significant dialogue partner in this regard. But in my estimation Taylor's a/theological nihilism still falls short of providing a theological appeal to the concerns of man as an entire person—emotionally and historically, but also to some common principles of logic which form the basis of everyday conversation and human development.

---

110 Griffin, Beardslee, and Holland, *Varieties of Postmodern Theology*, pp. 38–9.

111 Ibid.

112 See Carl Raschke, *The Next Reformation: Why Evangelicals Must Embrace Postmodernity* (Grand Rapids: Baker, 2004), pp. 86–8.

113 Taylor, *Erring*, p. 15. As Taylor puts it: "The deconstruction of the Western theological network discloses the recurrent effort of human beings to achieve a position of domination. This struggle appears to grow out of the conviction that mastery results from the ability to secure presence and establish identity by overcoming absence and repressing difference. The battle for mastery, however, is always self-defeating."

Chapter 7

Richard Rorty:
Pragmatic Postmodernism

Introduction and Background

The American pragmatist Richard Rorty is not a theologian. In fact, he rarely speaks of theology or of theologians. He is not even in favor of Taylor's a/theology:

> If we are going to have theologians at all, it will be nice to have theologians with a sense of humor, a faculty in which Heidegger was notably deficient. But, as the old-fashioned kind, the kind without the slash, I keep wishing that we didn't have any theologians. I wish we would stop running together the needs of religious believers with the needs of the philosophers.[1]

Nevertheless, Rorty is well known by many theologians, and is often quoted and discussed in contemporary thought especially in relationship to postmodern hermeneutical issues. His works have not only prompted much debate concerning the role of philosophy and epistemological foundations, but he himself has achieved a high level of popularity across university campuses in North America.[2]

Rorty was born in 1931 in New York City. He received a bachelor's degree in 1949, and a master's degree in 1952, both from the University of Chicago. He went on to Yale University for his Ph.D., which he completed in 1956. He taught at Wellesley College from 1958–1961, before teaching at Princeton University from 1961–1982. From 1982–1998 he was professor at the University of Virginia, becoming professor Emeritus in 1998. Currently, he is Professor of Comparative Literature and, by courtesy, of Philosophy at Stanford University in California.

Rorty began his academic career as an analytic philosopher, characteristic of Anglo-American thought, believing that tools of logic and scrupulous analysis of language could form answers to complex philosophical questions. In 1967, he published a major anthology in this vein of linguistic philosophy titled *The Linguistic Turn*. Several years later, however, he began questioning traditional

---

1   Richard Rorty, "Comments on Taylor's 'Paralectics'," in R.P. Scharlemann (ed.), *On the Other: Dialogue and/or Dialectics* (Landham, University Press of America, 1991), p. 74 as quoted in François Nault, *Derrida et la théologie: Dire Dieu après la déconstruction* (Paris: Les éditions du Cerf, 2000), p. 261 note 9.

2   See Stanley J. Grenz, *A Primer on Postmodernism* (Grand Rapids: Eerdmans, 1996), p. 151.

modern philosophy. He developed an interest in continental philosophy such as French poststructuralism and Nietzsche's perspectivism. He published *Philosophy and the Mirror of Nature* (1979), in which he criticized the perspective that the mind reflects the representation of external reality, that is, the correspondence theory of truth.[3] Rorty claimed that the aim of this book was

> to undermine the reader's confidence in "the mind" as something about which one should have a "philosophical" view, in "knowledge" as something about which there ought to be a "theory" and which has "foundations," and in "philosophy" as it has been conceived since Kant.[4]

By 1982, Rorty was ready to abandon foundationalism in favor of pragmatism. Later, he further developed his liberal pragmatic views in affirmation of individual liberty as seen in *Contingency, Irony, and Solidarity* (1989), and in *Objectivity, Relativism, and Truth: Philosophical Papers, Vol. 1* (1991).[5]

In this chapter I will attempt to provide a brief introduction to the neo–pragmatic, postmodern philosophy of Rorty and its implications/relationships with theology. This will be followed by a critique of his perspectives for theological thought and practice. I will first broadly examine Rorty's pragmatism, perhaps better termed "neo–pragmatism." Then, I will discuss similarities and differences between Rorty and Derrida. I will try to show how Rorty's pragmatic postmodernism is indebted to Derrida's deconstructionism.[6]

---

3   See Roger Lundin, *The Culture of Interpretation: Christian Faith and the Postmodern World* (Grand Rapids: Eerdmans, 1993), p. 35.

4   Richard Rorty, *Philosophy and the Mirror of Nature* (Princeton: Princeton University Press, 1979), p. 7.

5   See Gilbert Hottois, *De la Renaissance à la Postmodernité*, 2e édition (Paris-Bruxelles: De Boeck Université, 1998), p. 452. Hottois distinguishes two significant periods in Rorty's works. The first period is Rorty's critique of Anglo-Saxon philosophy (i.e. analytic and linguistic) which includes *The Linguistic Turn* (1967) and his questioning of modern epistemology and ontology in *Philosophy and the Mirror of Nature* (1979). The second period is Rorty's development of a postmodern pragmatist philosophy as found in *Consequences of Pragmatism* (1982) and *Contingency, Irony, and Solidarity* (1989).

The following sources were helpful in obtaining the above brief biographical information: "Rorty, Richard," in *Microsoft(R) Encarta(R) 98 Encyclopedia*, 1993–1997 Microsoft Corporation and "Rorty, Richard," in *Columbia Encyclopedia*, 1995.

6   Although, Rorty's thinking has also been related to both Nietzsche and Foucault. Alister McGrath claims that Rorty is "perhaps the most distinguished American philosopher to develop Foucault's dislike of general principles and normative standards ...." Alister McGrath, *Intellectuals Don't Need God & Other Modern Myths* (Grand Rapids: Zondervan, 1993), p. 180.

Rorty's (*anti*)-Philosophy: Postmodern Neo-Pragmatism

Rorty, like Derrida, attempts to displace the modernist exaltation of philosophy as the discipline which provides a specialized insight on the nature of truth. Rorty even says that the pragmatist (himself included) "tries to defend himself by saying that one can be a philosopher precisely by being anti-Philosophical."[7] He suggests instead that philosophy is more like literary or cultural criticism. Rorty also denies a realist view of language. He advocates what he calls an "antirepresentational" account, which does not render "knowledge," as that which necessarily "fits" with reality. Instead, it is to be seen as a series of habitual actions that we acquire to cope with reality. Concepts are tools which we use for a purpose, they do not echo reality.[8]

Rorty explains the reasoning behind naming his book *Philosophy and the Mirror of Nature*:

> It is pictures rather than propositions, metaphors rather than statements, which determine most of our philosophical convictions. The picture which holds traditional philosophy captive is that of the mind as a great mirror, containing various representations—some accurate, some not—and capable of being studied by pure, nonempirical methods. Without the notion of the mind as mirror, the notion of knowledge as accuracy of representation would not have suggested itself.[9]

For the pragmatist, Rorty affirms, sentences are not simply true because they correspond to reality. Consequently, there is no need of concern regarding what would "make" a sentence true.[10] Since Rorty works from an assumption of nonrealism, he purports a notion of truth as a human convention mediated by language. This is obviously contrary to the modernist epistemological assumptions which are grounded in the correspondence theory of truth. Rorty's pragmatist view purports coherence as opposed to correspondence. The goal is to make our beliefs and our desires coherent.[11]

Rorty is not making a positive claim, but a negative claim. He says that we should not hold the traditional distinction between knowledge and opinion. The realist criticizes Rorty for denying the intrinsic nature of truth. But Rorty refutes

---

7   Richard Rorty, *Consequences of Pragmatism* (Minneapolis: University of Minnnesota Press, 1982), p. xvii. Douglas Groothuis discusses Nietzsche and Rorty in terms of "value creation" and states that "Nietzsche's thundering pronouncements and Rorty's relaxed but radical ruminations share the same essential philosophical defect." Douglas Groothuis, *Truth Decay: Defending Christianity Against the Challenges of Postmodernism* (Downers Grove: InterVarsity, 2000), p. 200.

8   Kevin J. Vanhoozer, *Is There Meaning in This Text?* (Grand Rapids: Zondervan, 1998), p. 55, and Richard Rorty, *Objectivity, Relativism, and Truth: Philosophical Papers Vol 1* (Cambridge: Cambridge University Press, 1991), p. 1.

9   Richard Rorty, *Philosophy and the Mirror of Nature*, p. 12.

10   Rorty, *Consequences of Pragmatism*, p. xvi.

11   Grenz, *A Primer on Postmodernism*, pp. 152–4.

the claims that his pragmatism is relativistic, because he denies *any* epistemological system or theory of truth.[12] As he explains:

> So when the pragmatist says that there is nothing to be said about truth save that each of us will commend as true those beliefs which he or she finds good to believe, the realist is inclined to interpret this as one more positive theory about the nature of truth: a theory according to which truth is simply the contemporary opinion of a chosen individual or group. Such a theory would, of course, be self-refuting. But the pragmatist does not have a theory of truth, much less a relativistic one. As a partisan of solidarity, his account of the value of cooperative human inquiry has only an ethical base, not an epistemological or metaphysical one. Not having *any* epistemology, *a fortiori* he does not have a relativistic one.[13]

Consequently, "knowledge" for Rorty, is simply like "truth," it is merely a "compliment paid to the beliefs" for which we think no further justification is needed at a particular moment.[14] In other words truth claims, for Rorty, are only justified in the sense of their efficiency in persuasion in the context of currently existing systems of belief.[15]

Rorty appreciates linguistic philosophers such as de Saussure and Wittgenstein, and Derrida, for their rejection of essentialism in language. These philosophers rightly point out that meaning in sentences is derived from their place in the context of a web of relations with other beliefs and desires. However, Rorty would take this a step further and claim that nonessentialism ought to be applied to all elements of philosophical theory: truth, knowledge, morality and language.[16]

Rorty suggests that there are three basic characterizations of pragmatism. First of all, pragmatism is anti-essentialism (nonessentialism) as applied to notions of "truth" and "knowledge."[17] Essentialists would claim that objects would have intrinsic "essences" or properties—the "essential" characteristics of that object. On the other hand, nonessentialists, or as Rorty terms "antiessentialists," concentrate on relational properties.[18] He does not make a distinction between objects prior to the belief formation process and objects that are made during the belief formation process. He adds that "[a]ntiessentialists think of objects as what we find it useful to talk about in order to cope with the stimulations.[19]

Rorty's second characterization of pragmatism denies any difference between facts and values, between that which *is* and that which *ought* to be. His third and final characterization of pragmatism advocates unlimited inquiry without constraints

---

12 Rorty, *Objectivity, Relativism, and Truth*, pp. 23–4.

13 Ibid., p. 24.

14 Ibid.

15 Christopher Norris, *Derrida* (London: Fontana, 1987), p. 155.

16 Grenz, *A Primer on Postmodernism*, p. 152.

17 Rorty, *Consequences of Pragmatism*, p. 162. The three characterizations of pragmatism are provided on pp. 162–6.

18 Grenz, *A Primer on Postmodernism*, p. 152.

19 Rorty, *Objectivity, Relativism, and Truth*, pp. 106–7.

(except conversational ones). Of course, conversational constraints cannot be anticipated—"[t]here is no method for knowing *when* one has reached the truth, or when one is closer to it than before."[20]

The way in which Rorty shapes his version of pragmatism makes it distinctively postmodern. In typical postmodern fashion, he rejects Cartesian dualism and the idea of the self as an independent thinking substance. As Rorty says, "Think of human minds as webs of beliefs and desires, of sentimental attitudes—webs which continually reweave themselves so as to accommodate new sentimental attitudes."[21] He would, however, ask us to forget about the origin of these beliefs and attitudes. We ought to view our lives as parts of a large social and cultural context in community. Anything we say about "truth" comes from concepts particular to the society and social context in which we live.[22] As Rorty says of pragmatists: "…what matters is our loyalty to other human beings clinging together against the dark, not our hope of getting things right."[23]

Rorty and Derrida

It is important to note that the non-realist, in the Rortian sense, is not denying the existence of a physical reality that we see, hear, and touch. Instead, the non-realist claims that all meaningful distinctions which we observe and classify with words are linguistic creations. Such non-realism reminds us both of Derrida and Nietzsche. Ultimately, such non-realism is in opposition to Platonism. Plato believed in a transcendent reality which provided the metaphysical stability for language. Nietzsche, Derrida and Rorty all reject translinguistic referents or extra-linguistic realities.[24]

Rorty would say that the history of philosophy since Plato has not been useful. Like Derrida, he believes that philosophy has been too preoccupied with theory. Instead of being concerned about right language, we should learn to appreciate the plurality of human vocabulary and its various purposes. Instead of trying to convince others of correct perspectives, we should try to solve actual problems. Instead of constantly searching for Truth, we should move forward and do something which is useful.[25]

Rorty appreciates Derrida for demonstrating the "bankruptcy" of epistemology and coming up with useful deconstructive tools which remind us that "philosophy" is simply a form of writing and not a privileged discipline which dispenses Truth. Rorty comments on this agreement:

---

20 Rorty, *Consequences of Pragmatism*, pp. 165–6.
21 Rorty, *Objectivity, Relativism, and Truth*, p. 93.
22 See Grenz, *A Primer on Postmodernism*, pp. 156–7.
23 Rorty, *Consequences of Pragmatism*, p. 166.
24 Vanhoozer, *Is There Meaning in This Text?*, pp. 57–8.
25 Ibid., pp. 100–101.

Pragmatists and deconstructionists agree that everything is a social construct and that there is no point in trying to distinguish between the "natural" and the "merely" cultural. They agree that the question is which social constructs to discard and which to keep, and that there is no point in appealing to "the way things really are" in the course of struggles over who gets to construct what.[26]

On the other hand, Rorty does not appreciate Derrida's long, drawn-out arguments. These arguments represent lapses into pointless philosophy which assumes that truth claims may either be asserted or criticized.[27] Instead, Rorty attempts, through his postmodern neo-pragmatism, to turn philosophy in a direction which is ethically responsible rather than completely disintegrating it as with Derrida's deconstruction.[28] Rorty appears to read Derrida as heading toward similar pragmatist conclusions, although, he is "held up along the way by some unfortunate tangles with Kant, Husserl and other old-fashioned seekers after truth."[29]

Rorty says that in order for one to understand Derrida it is essential to see his work as a development of a non-Kantian tradition. The Kantian tradition does not really believe that "writing" itself is truth—but points us to truth. One may see the truth through the representation of written words. Philosophy, for the Kantian, is an attempt to put an end to writing. However, Rorty asserts that for Derrida, writing simply leads to more and more writing. In a similar fashion, history does not lead to absolute truth either, but simply to more and more history.[30]

Rorty considers Derrida's "shadowy, deconstructive" side to be the "good side" of his work. But he also believes Derrida has a "luminous, constructive, bad side" as well.[31] Derrida attempts to say something about language, according to Rorty, which will not imply a sense of "sign" or "representation." Instead, Derrida uses the notion of "trace" as an alternative. With this alternative, however, Rorty says that Derrida "comes perilously close to giving us a philosophy of language, and thereby perilously close to slipping back into what he and Heidegger call 'the tradition of onto-theology.'"[32]

Perhaps the broad difference between Rorty and Derrida is that Rorty does not agree that "the ethical call of the singular comes to us in the form of a quasi-transcendental 'imperative'... we are not called to justice by anything exterior, transcendental, or trace-like."[33] Derrida emphasizes such "trace" or residue to the

26 Richard Rorty, "Feminism, Ideology, and Deconstruction: a Pragmatist View" (Special Issue: Feminism and Pragmatism) *Hypatia* 8/2 (Spring 1993), http://gort.ucsd.edu/jhan/ER/rr.html (29 Sept. 2005).

27 Norris, *Derrida*, pp. 150–51.

28 Matthews, *Twentieth-Century French Philosophy*, pp. 174–5.

29 Norris, *Derrida*, p. 155.

30 Rorty, *Consequences of Pragmatism*, pp. 93–4.

31 Ibid., p. 99.

32 Ibid., p. 100.

33 Ronald A. Kuipers, "Singular Interruptions: Rortian Liberalism and the Ethics of Deconstruction," *Knowing Other-Wise: Philosophy at the Threshold of Spirituality*, ed. James

themes we create. He is not saying that there is nothing antecedently real, but he is simply emphasizing its exteriority. Once something is thematized, then it has disappeared because it becomes interior to the system which was thematized.[34]

I believe Ronald A. Kuipers rightly suggests that we ought not to consider thinkers like Rorty and Derrida as simply advocating an "everything is permissible" attitude. Both thinkers seem to be very serious about advocating something which is more edifying for theoretical activity than current modernist paradigms. Although they admittedly use a radically ironic tone, Rorty and Derrida are not giving up on reality, nor are they saying that we create the world simply by describing it. However, if it were not for our descriptions, they would say, we would not have a "world" understanding. They both are attempting to show the impact of culture, language, and history on one's perception of the world. Both philosophers are challenging us to become acutely aware of the limits and biases of our thinking and the impossibility of neutrality.[35]

Rorty, however, is not as concerned as Derrida to demonstrate the process of deconstruction on particulars. Rorty's emphasis is on protecting the freedom of the individual for private efforts and preventing suffering. Consequently, Rorty advocates a strict bifurcation between the public and private spheres of human life. Public justice should interfere very little with private concerns. Derrida, however, would not advocate such a separation because ethics must be as much a private doing as it is public.[36] More must be said on such differences between Rorty and Derrida before the theological implications of Rorty's thought are considered.

Theological Implications and Critique: God/Ethics/Utopia

As I previously stated, Richard Rorty is not a theologian. In fact, he says quite little regarding the subject of theology or of anything religious. Nevertheless, several theological themes emerge as we examine Rorty's thinking. Perhaps two areas of greatest concern for Rorty with very pertinent theological implications are his ethics and his notion of utopia. We may also note several crucial implications for the field of hermeneutics. Before I discuss these areas, however, I will first examine a statement Rorty has made about belief in God.

God

In his essay, "Philosophy as a Kind of Writing," Rorty suggests why it is the case that Derrida does not explicitly and clearly state his view about reality and language. Rorty claims:

H. Olthuis (New York: Fordham University Press, 1997), pp. 106–7.

    34 Ibid., p. 109.

    35 Ibid.

    36 Ibid., pp. 110–11. See Richard Rorty, *Contingency, Irony, and Solidarity* (Cambridge: Cambridge University Press, 1989), p. 63.

To this one can only reiterate that Derrida is in the same situation in regard to language that many of us secularists are in in regard to God. It isn't that we believe in God, or don't believe in God, or have suspended judgment about God, or consider that the God of theism is an inadequate symbol of our ultimate concern; it is just that we wish we didn't have to have a view about God. It isn't that we know that "God" is a cognitively meaningless expression, or that it has its role in a language game other than the fact-stating, or whatever. We just regret the fact that the word is used so much.[37]

It seems as though Rorty places "God" in the same category as other items and pieces of information or opinion. Although his statement is, in a sense, "asserting" various denials about his notion of God, or the absence of his notion of God, he still seems to assume that "God" is some impersonal "thing" in which one has the capacity to "suspend judgment" about, or may use as an "inadequate symbol."[38] It appears that Rorty mistakes "God" for simply a word, a concept, or a form of language. If we are indeed to take Rorty's comments seriously on this written page as a mode of interpersonal communication, why are we not to assume that "God" as a personal Being has not in some manner communicated with us interpersonally and at some time? He claims that he wishes he did not have to have a view about God— and so refuses to take a stand either way. But in what sense is this fundamentally different to suspending judgment about God—which Rorty says he does not do? If indeed God thinks, creates, exists and communicates just as Rorty himself (but not necessarily in the same fashion or with the same intelligence), then is it not essential that one make some kind of judgment or response to this God?

Rorty's postmodern pragmatic philosophy is very politically motivated on the liberal side.[39] When asked how the "Cultural Left," with esoteric intellectual pursuits, can respond to the problems in America today, Rorty says past pragmatist philosophers should be used as models, for example, John Dewey and the poet Walt Whitman. According to Rorty, a fair and classless society should be pursued in America. Such a society is one which looks for its ultimate authority in democratic consensus, not to God, not to a monarchy, and not to some abstract idea of Nationhood. Rorty, in

---

37 Rorty, *Consequences of Pragmatism*, pp. 97–8.

38 Furthermore, as Douglas Groothuis observes, Rorty elsewhere claims to be a "freeloading atheist"—which is a "very telling admission of metaphysical guilt." As a "freeloader" Rorty would be depending for life on "another entity without contributing anything positive to that entity" (Groothuis, *Truth Decay*, pp. 190-91).

39 It should be noted that the word "liberal" as associated with Rorty is used in the distinctively American sense, associated with leftist, socialistic tendencies. Perhaps the better word to use in a European context would be "socialist." Nonetheless, I will continue to use the word "liberal" because Rorty himself uses it and relates it to his way of thinking. As Christopher Norris notes (in the context of discussing Rorty): "'Post-modern' liberalism conceives itself more on the American model, as a generalized consensus of ideas and interests that works to guarantee the flourishing and continuance of a certain communal self-image." Norris, *Derrida*, p. 153.

accord with Dewey and Whitman, would agree that there is no God, or reality, or anything else which takes priority over the consensus of a free people.[40]

Rorty wishes to replace any notions of religious or philosophical accounts of a "suprahistorical ground" or "end of history convergence," with the narratives in history of liberal institutions which diminished cruelty and allowed free and equal communication. A liberal society, for Rorty, is not served by having philosophical foundations.[41]

Once again, the Christian theologian may rightly submit that there is a fundamental difference between a "philosophical foundation" and a theistic, personal Being, with whom communication or even revelation is possible. If such a Being, God, indeed exists and does interact with man, then such a Being is not simply an intellectual assent to some "suprahistorical ground." If this Being has communicated and revealed himself, he cannot simply be replaced with some kind of post-religious liberal utopia.

Ethics

Private/Public Split Perhaps the area where Rorty expresses his greatest passion is again in his extremely left wing, politically based ethic.[42] J.S. Mill expressed two of Rorty's primary concerns: Governments must balance between leaving the private lives of people alone on the one hand, and preventing suffering on the other.[43] As a result of these concerns, we see an emphasis of a public/private split in Rorty's thinking. Although, for Rorty, we are not called to justice in our ethic by any transcendental, metaphysical imperative, or even anything "trace-like," we may still pursue the liberal ethical goals of minimizing cruelty and valuing other perspectives. For Rorty, justice has a better chance if it is simply pursued because it is valued, not because it is based on something transcendental.[44] Rorty's ethic, then, is very much centered on community; it is contextual. Ethical "standards" and human rights are not based or anchored in some independent ground of truth of human nature. There is no universal standard of "human nature;" therefore, there are no universal human rights, nor universal moral truth.[45] Any strong disagreement with particular lifestyles, religion, or belief–systems is seen as judgmental and exclusionary. Instead of being judgmental, one must be a "liberal ironist" and face "up to the contingency

---

40 Scott Stossel, "A Conversation with Richard Rorty," *The Atlantic Monthly Company*, April 23, 1998), http:// www.theatlantic.com/unbound/bookauth/ba980423.htm This interview is no longer available without an online subscription. However, a pertinent excerpt is found on http://www.erraticimpact.com/~20thcentury/html/rorty_richard.htm (27 Jan. 2006).

41 Rorty, *Contingency, Irony, and Solidarity*, pp. 68, 52.

42 See Gilbert Hottois, *De la Renaissance à la Postmodernité*, p. 458.

43 Rorty, *Contingency, Irony, and Solidarity*, p. 63.

44 Kuipers, "Singular Interruptions," pp. 107, 116.

45 Eduardo J. Echeverria, "Do Human Rights Spring from our Nature as Human Beings? Reflections on Richard Rorty," *Philosophia Christi*, 20/1 (Spring 1997): 41.

of his or her own most central beliefs and desires." There are no "well-grounded theoretical answers" to moral questions or dilemmas.[46]

Miroslav Volf's criticism on this point of Rorty's is relevant here. Volf submits that he himself does not reject exclusion due to a contingent preference for a certain society, as Rorty would affirm; but he rejects exclusion because it "names an objective evil." As Volf submits: "A judgment that names exclusion as an evil and differentiation as a positive good, then, is itself not an act of exclusion. To the contrary, such judgment is the beginning of the struggle against exclusion."[47] Volf readily admits that "we do make exclusionary judgments, and we make them far too often .... But the remedy for exclusionary judgments are certainly not 'ironic stances.'"[48] Instead, Volf adds, we need to adequately differentiate between what is truly "exclusion" and what is "differentiation." Such differentiation, of course, must be made in humility due to our inclination to "misperceive and misjudge because we desire to exclude."[49] In order to implement social change for equality of all persons, Rorty also denies the relevance of divine intervention or decree. He says:

> It just doesn't matter whether God ordains, or "the mass of productive forces" dialectically unfolds, or difference plays, beyond the control of any of us. All that matters is what we can do to persuade people to act differently than in the past.[50]

For Rorty, it simply does not matter what determines whether social structures change. Instead, what is important is that we free up our imaginations from the past so they can be re-oriented toward the changes to be made so that future practices will be different than the past. We must visualize new practices, not simply criticize and harbor the old ones. We must not, according to Rorty, use philosophy as some sort of indispensable tool with which to break new ground.[51]

For example, when Rorty speaks to the issue of feminism and the need to correct historical injustices to women, Rorty does not pursue the reasons or bases for these injustices. Instead he simply claims that pragmatists and deconstructionists can do no more than help "rebut attempts to ground these practices on something deeper than a contingent historical fact"—namely, the fact that men have oppressed women for many years. Consequently, the imagination must be freed from simply criticizing the past and envision the future where social practices are better.[52] Not all would agree, of course, with Rorty's assessment. I would certainly agree, as others would,

---

46 Rorty, *Contingency, Irony, and Solidarity*, p. xv. Also see Miroslav Volf, *Exclusion and Embrace: A Theological Exploration of Identity, Otherness, and Reconciliation* (Nashville: Abingdon, 1996), pp. 67–8.

47 Volf, *Exclusion and Embrace*, p. 68.

48 Ibid., p. 68.

49 Ibid.

50 Rorty, "Feminism, Ideology, and Deconstruction."

51 Ibid.

52 Ibid.

that there are societal and contextual grids which accompany ethical understanding.[53] However, does this negate any notion of ethical objectivity? Simply because we make affirmations of a fact within a particular historical-cultural context, does not mean we are completely restricted to that context. As Nicholas Rescher states: "The fact that we make our assertions within time does not prevent us from asserting timeless truths."[54]

Projects Before Principles Rorty advocates putting projects before principles. He insists that we need liberal groups to join together to pass laws that will help with socio-economic equality. He says that when he first began studying philosophy he looked for "first principles." He thought that if he had the right principles, the rest would fall into place. However, he admits that he was wrong. Instead, he argues, we can only figure out which principles we want to use once the projects are put into place.[55]

Although Rorty may deny "first principles," he does indeed have some "first assumptions." His idea of the politically Left joining together to accomplish such political endeavors is certainly built on an understanding of unity, agreement, and mutual respect. Are these not indeed "principles?" If "principles" are not first, as Rorty argues, then why should any projects be started at all? Is not the alleviation of inequality based on a "first principle" of the sort that "equality" of persons and opportunities is better than "inequality" and unjust treatment? The answers to these questions appear self-evident, based on assumed first principles. Ultimately, I would submit, there will be some type of principles, articulated or non-articulated, before projects.[56]

Moral Principles? Does it make sense to speak of something such as a "moral principle" if there is nothing exterior from which to draw the "principle?" Rorty suggests that we should follow Michael Oakeshott's thinking on this (who follows Hegel). As Rorty summarizes:

> We can keep the notion of "morality" just insofar as we can cease to think of morality as the voice of the divine part of ourselves and instead think of it as the voice of ourselves

---

53 Groothuis, *Truth Decay*, p. 191; and Nicholas Rescher, *Objectivity: The Obligations of Impersonal Reason* (Notre Dame and London: University of Notre Dame Press, 1997), p. 61.

54 Rescher, *Objectivity*, p. 61. Also see Groothuis, *Truth Decay*, pp. 191–2.

55 Richard Rorty, "First Projects, Then Principles," *The Nation* (22 December 1997), http://www.physicsforums.com/archive/t-2693_%22First_Projects,_Then_Principles%22_ by_Richard_Rorty.html (29 Sept. 2005). Three of the most important projects Rorty claims should be addressed are 1) an end to political campaign bribes; 2) universal health insurance; and, 3) equal opportunity education.

56 Jean-Marc Ferry lends support to this in Jean-Marc Ferry, "Les Idéalisations de la Pratique Communicationnelle Sont-Elles 'Métaphysiques?'," *La Théologie en postmodernité*, eds Pierre Gisel and Patrick Evrard. (Genève: Labor et Fides, 1996), p. 174.

as members of a community, speakers of a common language. We can keep the morality-prudence distinction if we think of it not as the difference between an appeal to the unconditioned and an appeal to the conditioned but as the difference between an appeal to the interests of our community and the appeal to our own, possibly conflicting, private interests.[57]

Rorty would not believe that moral quandaries are resolved by repentance and change of heart in the individual, but by "radical relocation" or "redescription." Rorty, with a preferential perspective of morality, would deny any real transforming power or influence of a supernatural Being.[58]

The Other, the Stranger The idea of identifying with the other, the stranger, those different from himself, is extremely important for Rorty's ethic. Rorty says that the "process of coming to see other human beings as 'one of us' rather than 'them' is a matter of detailed description of what unfamiliar people are like and of redescription of what we ourselves are like."[59] We must recognize the stranger as a human being as we are ourselves, and we must make the stranger's face our own. We must identify with the stranger's experience pain and humiliation.[60] Here Rorty "invokes" Christian elements, while rejecting the relevance of the existence of God:

> For it is part of the tradition of *our* community that the human stranger from whom all dignity has been stripped is to be taken in, to be reclothed with dignity. This Jewish and Christian element in our tradition is gratefully invoked by freeloading atheists like myself, who would like to let differences like that between the Kantian and the Hegelian remain "merely philosophical." The existence of human rights, in the sense in which it is at issue in this meta-ethical debate, has as much or as little relevance to our treatment of such a child as the question of the existence of God. I think both have equally little relevance.[61]

There is nothing transcendent to justify or guarantee our sensitivity to others on ethical matters. However, Rorty does believe that literature may help us to reconcile the "private" and "public." Rorty says that "novels and ethnographies which sensitize one to the pain of those who do not speak our language must do the job which demonstrations of a common human nature were supposed to do." Rorty continues by saying these novelists perform a task that is socially useful by helping us "attend

---

57 Rorty, *Contingency, Irony, and Solidarity*, p. 59. Rorty refers to Michael Oakeshott, *Of Human Conduct* (Oxford: Oxford University Press, 1975), pp. 78–9.

58 As Roger Lundin comments: "By holding out the promise of temporary, temporal renewal through the power of radical redescription, it denies the transforming power of the Word and closes off the eternity to which the entire drama of the life, death and resurrection of Christ points the way." Roger Lundin, "The Pragmatics of Postmodernity," *Christian Apologetics in the Postmodern World*, eds Timothy R. Phillips, and Dennis L. Okholm. (Downers Grove: InterVarsity, 1995), p. 34.

59 Rorty, *Contingency, Irony, and Solidarity*, p. xvi.

60 See Kuipers, "Singular Interruptions," p. 117.

61 Rorty, *Objectivity, Relativism, and Truth*, p. 202.

to the springs of cruelty in ourselves, as well as to the fact of its occurrence in areas where we had not noticed it."[62]

I agree with Rorty on the value of profound literary texts which break in to our lives and attune us to the suffering of others. Powerful literature can help us learn lessons for social change.[63] This is where I suggest that the biblical narratives are quite powerful. In this, I would offer a theologically "Christian" interpretation, or "re–working" so to speak, of Rorty's challenge. The Bible narratives paint a clear picture of a God who identifies and cares for the poor and the unjustly treated. The New Testament account of the foundation and growth of the Christian church shows a suffering and scattered people doing the will of God. Stephen was martyred, and many Christians suffered. In Acts 11:21 it says, "The Lord's hand was with them and a great number of people believed and turned to the Lord." Jesus continually addressed the poor, and the value of caring for one's neighbor is seen particularly in the parable of the Good Samaritan documented in Luke, chapter 10. The New Testament account shows sensitivity to the other through its own multi-cultural beginnings. This is particularly noted in the first "Christian" church at Antioch. For instance, we note the multi-racial names given of the prophets and teachers in Acts 13:1. Paul, a Jew, spent much of his time working with Gentiles from the beginning of his apostolic work. Philip baptized the Ethiopian eunuch in Acts 8. Paul's letter to the Galatians (3:28) testifies that there "is neither Jew nor Greek, slave nor free, male nor female, for you are all one in Christ Jesus." I would call for a return to these narrative accounts, to immerse ourselves in their stories, background, and histories. If we seek to become attuned to the early Christians and their lives, seeking to identify with their suffering through the power of the story, we will become more attuned and sensitive to the injustices done to others.[64]

General Criticisms of Rorty's Ethic Are we compelled to follow Rorty's postmodern ethic? If we choose not to accept it because of the fact that it is not based on anything substantive, then we are simply doing that which Rorty says we cannot do. We cannot, according to Rorty, "base" our ethic—because the "substantive" does not exist, whether it be in the notion of truth, or in the concept of a Being such as God. In this regard it appears that Rorty has isolated himself from criticism. Is it actually possible that the lofty moral ideals that Rorty imagines cannot be based on anything transcendental? Can Rorty use Christian notions of justice without assuming any of its "transcendental baggage?"[65]

Douglas Groothuis submits that Rorty's notion of moral redescription for the liberal ironist is simply an "agreement with Christian conscience" which is "intrinsically whimsical, haphazard, arbitrary and contingent." Groothuis adds that

---

62 Rorty, *Contingency, Irony, and Solidarity*, pp. 94–5. See also, Kuipers, "Singular Interruptions," pp.112-13.

63 See Rorty, *Contingency, Irony, and Solidarity*, pp. 141ff.

64 I will develop this further in a subsequent chapter.

65 Kuipers, "Singular Interruptions," p. 119.

Rorty seems to admit this on the one hand; however, "on the other hand he wants to live off the borrowed moral capital of a Judeo-Christian civilization despite the fact that he denies objective moral and spiritual truth, divine revelation and a determinate human nature possessing intrinsic moral and spiritual value."[66]

As we saw with Rorty's response to feminism, his view of morality is simply that of conformity to historical facts. With a progressive transformation of general feelings in the community of a human rights culture, for Rorty, concrete political changes must be implemented for the betterment of human beings. One may ask, however, how does this provide a necessary and persuasive reason for social change? Without showing some reasons or purposes for moral change it is doubtful whether or not any change will occur. Also, who determines if a particular community is better than another community with morally conflicting or even morally threatening values?[67]

Eduardo J. Echeverria critiques Rorty's rejection of the existence of the substantive, integrated self.[68] Since he denies the existence of such a self, he also argues against such a self as possessing universal human rights. Echeverria says that Rorty's position "cannot supply any notion of transcendent dignity, in fact, it explicitly denies humans such inherent dignity."[69] I believe Echeverria begs the question here with respect to Rorty. Is this not Rorty's point? We do not have something transcendent in which to base our rights according to Rorty; they come simply because of our community relationship. On the other hand, I heartily agree with Echeverria in his questioning of whether Rorty's community-based ethic provides any real value or dignity for the individual person, which seems to be fundamental for human nature and life. In response to Rorty, we should embrace Echeverria's challenge to affirm, in our theology, an ontological basis for the dignity of the human person, or human dignity will be simply "conferred" on the individual by his/her community. We must further investigate how to fully realize our personhood in both our relationship to God and to others.[70]

Utopia

I have been alluding throughout this chapter to Rorty's broad notions of utopia: the elimination of suffering, and the guarantee of free expression.[71] Rorty would echo Dewey's ideal society where "culture is no longer dominated by the ideal of

---

66 Groothuis, *Truth Decay*," p. 189. For a further analysis of Rorty's ethic also see Groothuis, *Truth Decay*, pp. 187–202.

67 See Echeverria, "Do Human Rights" 44–5.

68 Ibid., 47–9. Rorty's denial of an integrated, substantive self is a typical postmodern, deconstructive notion. I have noted this especially in the work of Michel Foucault and Mark C. Taylor.

69 Ibid., 49.

70 Ibid., 52.

71 For a helpful commentary on Rorty's utopia in this regard, see Hottois, *De la Renaissance à la Postmodernité*, pp. 460–62.

objective cognition but by that of aesthetic enhancement."[72] In Rorty's postmodern pragmatism he imagines a post-metaphysical culture, which in his mind, is no more impossible than a post-religious culture. Rorty summarizes his liberal "utopia:"

> In my utopia, human solidarity would be seen not as a fact to be recognized by clearing away "prejudice" or burrowing down to previously hidden depths but, rather, as a goal to be achieved. It is to be achieved not by inquiry but by imagination, the imaginative ability to see strange people as fellow sufferers. Solidarity is not discovered by reflection but created. It is created by increasing our sensitivity to the particular details of the pain and humiliation of other, unfamiliar sorts of people. ...
>
> This process of coming to see other human beings as "one of us" rather than as "them" is a matter of detailed description of what unfamiliar people are like and of redescription of what we ourselves are like.[73]

Rorty's utopia is politically based and locally centered. His utopia is not a vision for some apocalyptic breakthrough or grand political upheaval. Instead, through local reform and constant political change we must make the change.[74] Although we must begin with the social networks and communities in which we live, he does not believe this implies relativism. To be "relativistic" implies the belief in a metanarrative which Rorty denies. Consequently, he believes that he isolates himself from an unjust accusaton of being a relativist. As Rorty says: "To accuse postmodernism of relativism is to try to put a metanarrative in the postmodernist's mouth."[75]

To criticize Rorty, it is begging the question to reproach his lack of worldview or metanarrative. This is exactly Rorty's point, as with Lyotard and Derrida—that we must reject any notion of a totalizing metanarrative. Instead, I would challenge the basic assumptions behind this notion. Is not the absolute claim of the absence of something as grand as any possible worldview, in itself making some kind of absolute claim? If we are indeed to read and evaluate Rorty's challenges as his readers, are we not compelled to use some criteria external to ourselves and our community?

Several areas of common ground have been suggested with Rorty's postmodern pragmatism. I would readily acknowledge sympathy for the elimination of suffering, and freedom of dialogue and expression of humankind. However, from my perspective, the rejection of all grand narratives must be denied. Instead I propose a re-examination of the biblical narratives, based on a grand narrative, as a partial response to stimulate a reawakening to the afflictions of human beings as well as the creation in which they live and participate. As discussed above, I believe that these accounts identify with the "marginalized others" of society: the poor, the suffering, and the oppressed. But a strictly human focused call to emancipation suppresses the needs of the larger order of creation. I agree with J. Richard Middleton and Brian

---

72 Rorty, *Philosophy and the Mirror of Nature*, p. 13.
73 Rorty, *Contingency, Irony, and Solidarity*, p. xvi.
74 See Hottois, *De la Renaissance à la Postmodernité*, p. 461.
75 Rorty, *Objectivity, Relativism, and Truth*, p. 202.

J. Walsh who insist that we renew ourselves to a biblical account of the nonhuman creation which has also been violently marginalized in our postmodern society:

> We offer this biblical vision of a covenantal creation, wrought by the overwhelming generosity of God's love and eloquent in its songs of praise and groans of sorrow, in critique of the mechanistic worldview of modernity, in opposition to any anthropocentric mastery and exploitation of the world (whether that be in the industrialization of modernity or the hyperreality of postmodernity), and in fulfillment of the important postmodern sentiment of wanting to hear the voice of the marginalized other.[76]

Walsh and Middleton emphasize that such a worldview of creation is not simply an invitation to oppress the other with a "metaphysics of presence" or an "ontology of violence." Creation is given for "covenantal responsibility," not our mastery.[77]

The biblical narratives do not simply help us identify with the suffering other, and the other of creation. They do help us with our individual struggles. But we must not simply leave it at that. These same narratives also "speak of the creative, judging, and redeeming power of God in nature and human affairs."[78] Rorty, however, insinuates that all languages of truth will become obsolete. Interpretation will only shape one's world to whatever end it may be. Is this really all there is to Christian claims to truthful reality? I will continue to challenge and interact with this notion in subsequent chapters.

---

76 J. Richard Middleton, and Brian Walsh, *Truth is Stranger Than It Used to Be: Biblical Faith in a Postmodern Age* (Downers Grove: InterVarsity, 1995), p. 152.

77 Ibid.

78 Lundin, *The Culture of Interpretation*, p. 245.

PART 4

Deconstruction in Britain

Chapter 8

Don Cupitt: Theological Necrophilia

Introduction and Background

I have previously considered representatives of theological deconstructionist thought from continental Europe and America. I now turn to a representative from the United Kingdom: Don Cupitt. In my estimation, Cupitt writes in the least academically obscure language compared with other writers in the same genre of postmodern deconstructive theology considered in this book. Although his knowledge and research is obviously broad, he cites fewer references than others, yet offers honest personal insights into his theological and intellectual pilgrimage. Cupitt may also be less well known than other "makers of theology" in the postmodern deconstructive vein I have discussed. Nonetheless, he has certainly made his mark and contribution both through his prolific writing, and through a BBC television series, "Sea of Faith," broadcast in 1984.[1]

Don Cupitt was born in 1934 in Lancashire, England. In 1955 he graduated from Cambridge University after studying biology and the history and philosophy of science. Cupitt was influenced by the thinking of Karl Popper, and eventually adopted an anti-realist position with regard to the philosophy of science. Although he was influenced by "religious" Anglicanism, Cupitt also brought his philosophical anti-realism to his theological perspectives—which greatly affected his later work.[2]

Cupitt's "religion" was certainly not traditional. Cupitt states that he "never looked for or believed in miracles, answers to prayer, particular providences or the 'supernatural' in the popular sense."[3] He vehemently opposed the "psychological tyranny" of an institutional "conservative and pietistic" Protestantism.[4] Instead, Cupitt turned to British empiricism and moral philosophy while beginning theological

---

1   See Anthony C. Thiselton, *Interpreting God and the Postmodern Self* (Edinburgh: T&T Clark, 1995), p. 81. Thiselton notes that Cupitt wrote twenty books from 1976–1994 (p. 88).

2   Scott Cowdell, *Atheist Priest?: Don Cupitt and Christianity* (London: SCM Press Ltd, 1988), pp. xv–xvi. The anti-realism to which I am referring, for Cupitt, would be the denial of the possibility of "objective" reality, and the denial of an objective Being, God, who is external to us. In postmodern theological discourse this would be the denial of onto-theology.

3   Don Cupitt, *Explorations in Theology 6*, SCM Press, 1979 in Cowdell, *Atheist Priest?*, p. xvi.

4   Ibid.

studies at Wescott House, Cambridge in 1957. It was during this time that he began reading Kierkegaard.[5]

Cupitt earned the M.A. degree and became ordained deacon to the Diocese of Manchester in 1959. Later, he began working as an assistant chaplain at Salford Royal Hospital. Cupitt refused to see God as the reason behind the causes of the various maladies he observed. One morning, after giving last rites to a dying patient, Cupitt experienced an "enlightenment" of disillusionment. He came to believe that his religious act of giving such last rites would not actually alter this patient's real eternal destiny. Nevertheless, in his estimation it was still a good act to do in and of itself, and he hoped that someone would do the same thing for him when the time came.[6]

After serving as Vice-Principal of his theological college *alma mater*, Cupitt became Fellow and Dean of Emmanuel College at Cambridge, and a lecturer in philosophy of religion, in 1966, where he remained until his recent retirement.[7] His first two books were *Christ and Hiddenness of God* (1971), and *Crisis of Moral Authority* (1972). As Anthony Thiselton points out, Cupitt's *Christ and Hiddenness of God* (1971) was an apophatic attack on "objectifying theology."[8] Cupitt may have been opposed to theological reification, yet he admits that he was still clinging to a "will-to-realism" in these earlier works—which, in his estimation was mistaken. As Scott Cowdell claims, in Cupitt's later period, since *Taking Leave of God* (1980), Cupitt has pulled away from such "realist" tendencies, "reckoning with Nietzsche," Wittgenstein, and modern French thinking.[9] Cupitt himself expresses his philosophical/theological movement:

> I started from a position of super-high orthodoxy which gradually turned into a non-objective belief in God at the end of the seventies. Since then I've moved away from Christian existentialism towards a more social, linguistic Christian humanism.[10]

I will primarily direct my efforts to the thinking of this later Cupitt for the study at hand. As with the other thinkers we have discussed, my purpose is not to fully and exhaustively present Cupitt's work. Instead, I will consider several theologically related themes which have, in my estimation, made a significant contribution to postmodern deconstructive theological tendencies. Cupitt, as with the others I have

---

5   Cowdell, *Atheist Priest?*, p. xvi.

6   Ibid., pp. xvii–xviii. Also see Thiselton, *Interpreting God*, p. 87.

7   Cupitt retains his current title as "Life Fellow and Former Dean of Emmanuel College," Cambridge, England.

8   Thiselton, *Interpreting God*, p. 89.

9   Cowdell, *Atheist Priest?*, p. xviii. However, we not only see the influence of French postmodern writers such as Derrida, Foucault, but also American writers operating in a similar vein as we have discussed, Mark C. Taylor and Richard Rorty.

10   Cupitt as quoted in Walter Schwarz, "Our Father Who Art on Earth," *The Guardian* (21 Sept. 1987): 21 in Cowdell, *Atheist Priest?*, p. xix.

considered, also has made his "mark" on postmodern deconstructive theological thought.[11]

In his pivotal work, *Taking Leave of God*, Cupitt claims that "religion is dying" and "fading away from the world." Why? Cupitt sees this as the result of the church attempting to maintain its "social authority" and "emulate the new sciences" which were the result of intellectual growth occurring since the late middle ages. Some have tried to reconnect this ever-widening gap without success. Now the church is simply a museum of past tradition. Those who remain faithful, "love the museum." Also, Cupitt adds, "most theologians love being scholarly museum curators." Yet, there are a few "dissidents or heretics" who "still hope it might be possible to reconnect religion with modernity."[12] Cupitt claims to be one such "dissident." In view of this, I will highlight several of these "reconnections" that Cupitt is offering. For the purpose of this chapter, I will attempt to "condense" several postmodern deconstructive theological themes emphasized in Cupitt's theology concisely expressed in one of his works, *After God: The Future of Religion* (1997): the "Eye of God," the "Blissful Void," "Solar Living," "Poetical Theology," and "World Religion."[13] These themes will serve as the point headings in the following outline of Cupitt's "Major Theological Themes."

Major theological themes

Eye of God

For Cupitt, not only is religion dying, but "[m]ost of Christianity has already been lost ...."[14] Christianity manifested itself temporally in human culture, but now its time has been spent. The efforts of theologians to demythologize Christianity in order to prevent its inevitable decay into superstition, have had little success, according to Cupitt, because most find value in understanding the "myth" in a literal fashion, even when the authority of that myth is deteriorating.[15] For Cupitt,

---

11 Again, my efforts in this book are primarily dedicated to evaluating some of these themes and discussing their implications for Christian apologetic methodology today. One possible objection to my perspective may be that I have failed to take into account where the author's position may have changed since the writing of the particular works discussed. This objection, however, neglects to understand my larger purpose. Regardless of whether the author's position has changed, in my estimation, the previous writing and thinking of the author in question has still affected the development of postmodern deconstructive theological thought and tendencies. It is precisely these tendencies, not simply the author's exact current position, which I am seeking to highlight for the development of this book.

12 Don Cupitt, *Taking Leave of God* (London: XPress Prints, SCM Prints Ltd, 1980), pp. 154–5.

13 Don Cupitt, *After God: The Future of Religion* (London: Basic Books, 1997).

14 Ibid., p. 81.

15 Don Cupitt, *Sea of Faith* (London: British Broadcasting Company, 1984), p. 10.

Christian theology "should dismantle its objects, change its rules and abolish its long entrenched methods of representation,…"[16]

Cupitt still wishes to salvage certain forms of Christian religion for postmodern expression. However, "God," for Cupitt, cannot be salvaged, because "God has long been dead." Cupitt adds: "The old metaphysics of God was destroyed by Hume and Kant, and will not be revived."[17] Instead, Cupitt unabashedly proposes a non-realist view of God. Cupitt goes as far as to say: "In short, only the person who thinks that God does not exist can really know how to praise God, worship God, love God, and thank God aright."[18] But if God does not exist, what of the notion of "God" may be recovered following his death? Cupitt would suggest that what is to be recovered is not God himself, but a type of belief in God. But this retrieval of "belief in God" must be re-interpreted "and seen as involving a certain form of consciousness and practice of selfhood." This recovered, nonrealist notion of God is an "attempt to salvage at least something of a God's eye view of oneself and of our life, *after* the death of God." Hence, to believe in God is to live as if one is really under the watchful eye of God and to regard oneself from the "standpoint of eternity."[19]

Unlike the obligatory God of Kant's Categorical Imperative, Cupitt's nonrealist God is a voluntary "form of consciousness, worth preserving and cultivating." He defines his postmodern "after God" religion as that which "makes you smarter than your god." The idea is to look at oneself as if you were looking from the universal eye of God, hence providing one with a more distinct and clear perspective and "moral vision."[20] As a Christian nonrealist, Cupitt admits, he actually loves this voluntary, nonetheless dead God more now than before. As Cupitt says: "I still pray and love God, even though I fully acknowledge that no God actually exists. Perhaps God had to die in order to purify our love for him."[21] He insists that love for this "dead" God is a pure, religious love, akin to Kierkegaard's notion of the unselfish love we feel for dead loved ones.[22] He draws a parallel with the omnipresent attribute of this God with that of a dead person:

> The omnipresence of the dead is exactly like that of God in that although we take the thought of them along with us wherever we go, we also need a place where there is a

---

16 Daniel Bulzan, "Apophaticism, Postmodernism and Language: Two Similar Cases of Theological Imbalance," *Scottish Journal of Theology* 50/3 (1997): 277. Cf. Don Cupitt, *The Long-legged Fly* (London: SCM Press Ltd., 1987), pp. 1–2.

17 Don Cupitt, *After God*, pp. 82, 83.

18 Don Cupitt, *The Religion of Being* (London: SCM Press, 1998), p. 124.

19 Cupitt, *After God*, pp. 82, 83.

20 Ibid., pp. 83–5.

21 Ibid., pp. 85. See also Cupitt, *Taking Leave of God*, p. 166: "I continue to speak of God and to pray to God. God is the mythical embodiment of all that one is concerned with in the spiritual life."

22 Cupitt, *After God*, pp. 86.

special marker of their absent presence, or present absence. The marker—gravestone, altar, or whatever—makes us talk, and thereby acts as a midwife of truth.[23]

We continue living and praying *coram Deo*, as if God were still alive, just as we would continue to talk with and think of a dead loved one. It is this voluntary consciousness, a self—consciousness even, of the "Eye of God" which is a "trick" which helps us to love life in a morally fulfilling fashion. For Cupitt, this is the preserved "remnant" or possible "reconnection" to the idea of God—the God who is dead.[24]

Blissful Void

In my view, Cupitt's notion of the "Blissful Void" is reminiscent of Mark C. Taylor's notion of "optimistic nihilism." For Cupitt this is a therapeutic discipline of "cool sublime" which he equates with Buddhist meditation and Christian "contemplative prayer." This "Blissful Void" is not a rational, Kantian sublime resulting in pride through some sort of personal, rational contemplation of the vastness of Nature. Instead, it is just the opposite. The self disappears "into immanence," an "empty void bliss" of "absolute nothingness"—where nothing at all matters.[25] As Scott Cowdell observes, "Cupitt leads the way into the 'passive nihilism' which frightened even Nietzsche."[26] We certainly see the absence of the ego in Cupitt's following statement:

> When the self and the world become completely deconstructed, egoism is uprooted. Only pure, undifferentiated and objectless awareness remains: the ego has lost internal structure. There is no longer anything *there* that is anxious for itself or that might attempt to assert itself by domination or by projecting and imposing its own ordered self-expression upon the world.[27]

What possible use is such "Discipline of the Void" for Cupitt? Cupitt submits that this notion is crucial in view of the lack of objective foundations in our postmodern culture. Since there is nothing fixed, and all is fleeting and contingent, we can easily be "overcome with vertigo." Therefore, we need a discipline of meditation on the "underlying universal emptiness and nothingness" which replaces the "old metaphysical God." This, Cupitt claims, will help us give perspective to our lives.[28] Does this mean we do away with religion? No, not according to Cupitt. People often equate religion with metaphysical theism and optimism. But religion "has more than one face." Cupitt adds: "One of its faces shows us an optimistic vision of cosmic

---

23 Ibid., p. 87.

24 Ibid., pp. 125, 104.

25 Ibid., pp. 87–8; 125.

26 Cowdell, *Atheist Priest?*, p. 28.

27 Don Cupitt, *The World to Come* (London, SCM Press, 1985), p. 136f. as quoted in Cowdell, *Atheist Priest*, p. 29.

28 Cupitt, *After God*, pp. 88–9.

order, but another, equally important, is a face of otherness, darkness, exile, loss and martyrdom."[29]

How is such nihilism "therapeutic" for living a happy life? Cupitt illustrates this by posing the following question: "If nihilism is a Bad Thing, why is it that the Dalai Lama is such a happy man and the Pope is such an unhappy man?" Cupitt's basic answer lies in the fact that the Pope himself, has no Pope, no other person to look up to, to "sustain his faith." So, he is unhappy. On the other hand, since the Dalai Lama believes in Nothing, the emptiness consumes him. He is completely free of institutional obligation. If the Tibetan people desire his position to continue, it will continue. If not, it will not. As Cupitt exclaims: "O lucky man, sceptical saint, holy nihilist, true un/believer! Why isn't a Christian allowed to be like that?"[30]

Solar Living

Cupitt uses the notion of "Solar Living" as he makes a transition from the subject of meditation to that of active living. This notion describes "an expressivist ethic of self-outing, self-outpouring, self-shedding....We pour ourselves out recklessly into symbolic expression and then pass on, pass on, and pass away, without regret."[31] There is no objective reality. There are no absolutes. We are our own makers of meaning. Personal perceptions such as colors and feelings are only our own, which are projected outward. In this sense, we "pour ourselves out as the sun," so we identify "ourselves completely with the outpouring flux of all existence." For Cupitt personally, this means that his life keeps moving on, even though he must leave behind the "expressed self" he continues to produce.[32] The whole notion of Being is that of pure transience. Since nothing is fixed, we should not attempt "to *capture* the fleeting moment," instead, "we should kiss it as it flies." For in order to really "let Being be we must let it go."[33] Solar "loving" then, is also "free from all clinging and calculation." Solar loving, like a burning sun, fervently burns, but then fades away. It is simply "given over to its own utter transience."[34] This is what Cupitt terms "solarity"—"to live by dying all the time, heedless, like the sun ... Solar ethics is a radically emotivist and expressionist reading of the ethics of Jesus."[35]

Cupitt's thinking with respect to the incarnation of Jesus and the "eternal Word" is certainly related to this notion of "Solar Living." As Cupitt writes in *The Long-Legged Fly*:[36]

---

29 Don Cupitt, "Unsystematic ethics and politics," in *Shadow of Spirit*, ed. Philippa Berry and Andrew Wernick (London and New York: Routledge, 1992), p. 154.

30 Cupitt, *The Religion of Being*, pp. 61–2.

31 Cupitt, *After God*, p. 125.

32 Ibid., pp. 89–90.

33 Cupitt, *The Religion of Being*, p. 68.

34 Don Cupitt, *The Last Philosophy* (London: SCM Press, Ltd., 1995), pp. 81–2.

35 Cupitt, *After God*, p. 90.

36 Cupitt derives this curious title from some lines of W.B. Yeats' *Last Poems*, which read "Like a long-legged fly upon the stream/ His mind moves upon silence." This insect skates

We have to say Yes to what is before us, in all its contingency. Such is, I believe, the final message of an incarnational religion. The Eternal descends into the contingent world and is diffused through it. There aren't now two worlds but just one, in which the Word has become flesh and body has become language. In terms of knowledge, the world becomes a communications network, a dance of signs. In terms of vision, the world is seen as it was seen by the Paris school of painters from Monet to Matisse. We do not accept that this world is grey and shadowy in contrast with an eternal world elsewhere. On the contrary, the artist sets out to invest the most everyday things with the radiance of Paradise.[37]

Cupitt agrees that in Christian thought, God's eternal Word actually does become a true, human person. This person is sent into the world to live and die among other human beings. However, the Word Incarnate is turned back into words and becomes the "Word of God Written." Cupitt claims that Christian ritual affirms that the "gospel book" is Christ himself. The progression is as follows: "So a message became an eternal Spirit, who became a human being, who became a text, which in turn is symbolically a person again."[38]

In my estimation, Cupitt's Christology is vague. As Scott Cowdell observes: "One cannot help but conclude that Jesus and the Christ remain something of a surd in Cupitt's arithmetic."[39] Although Cupitt's *The Last Philosophy* may shed some light. In my estimation, Cupitt appears to be saying that the "incarnation" symbolically demonstrates the move from God as objective "Spirit"—somewhere "out there"—back into the realm of human persons. God's "kingdom" is moved from an objective, visible, eschatological notion, to a hidden, subjective non-reality in the "human heart." When God is absent (prior to the incarnation), God is some objective being up in heaven. When "God" is present, he is "the power of life and of the Word in one's subjectivity."[40] It is such daily creativity and freedom, linked with Cupitt's notion of "incarnation," that is characteristic of Cupitt's Solar Living.

Poetical Theology

Poetical theology, for Cupitt, is a theology infused with the ideals of romanticism. It is the art of telling "old stories in new ways."[41] It is dramatic and theatrical. Poetical theology takes place among poets and dramatists who infuse old myths with fresh perspectives. Of course, to do "poetical theology," one needs to feel freedom from

---

upon the surface of a pond, darting this way and that, extremely sensitive to both food and danger. Cupitt takes this pond-skating insect as an image of religious thought today. In this reductionistic age we must, like this insect, make our world out of the minimal "horizontal" materials available to us. That is, we work with what we have before us, not from what we attempt to bring down to us from a false notion of a transcendent Being. See Don Cupitt, *The Long-legged Fly* (London: SCM Press Ltd., 1987), introductory author's note.

37 Cupitt, *The Long-legged Fly*, p. 8.
38 Cupitt, *After God*, p. 17.
39 Cowdell, *Atheist Priest?*, p. 68.
40 Cupitt, *The Last Philosophy*, pp. 125–6.
41 Cupitt, *After God*, p. 125.

traditional totalitarian constraints and the absence of fear from accusations of blasphemy.

Cupitt credits Augustine, who quotes the Roman writer, Varro, in *The City of God*, as the source of this idea. As Cupitt explains, Varro distinguished among philosophical theology (theology taught by philosophers); civil theology (state religion practices in the temples); and poetical theology (the poets reworking old myths about the gods in the context of the theater). Cupitt claims that Augustine desired to suppress such a notion of poetical theology so that his own narrative theology would have no rivals. Augustine's system was totalitarian, according to Cupitt; it had to have complete and dogmatic control. Therefore, poetical theology could only reenter Christianity indirectly through the Renaissance revival accompanied by the nonrealistic treatment of the classical mythological gods of Greece and Rome. Within any totalitarian system, art and creativity is suspect. However, if such elements enter by effectively mocking and exploiting that which is considered the rival and vain, why should the Church object?[42] As Cupitt puts it: "Such a playful type of poetical theology was tolerable and tolerated precisely because it does not undermine but rather confirms the authority of the normality that it mocks."[43]

Since Christianity has truly died as a dogma today, Cupitt suggests that it may perhaps be "reborn as and in art"—that is, a complete transformation through a poetical theology. Creativity of this sort is threatening to overarching dogmatic systems. Yet if we set ourselves free of such threatening systems, blasphemy cannot take place. Our religious traditions are still important, but we must acknowledge their similarities with traditions of art, for their particular importance may fade through the centuries. Hence, for Cupitt, it is important that we lose our inhibitions in order to create and develop new meanings and new narratives derived from the old traditions. This will create a contemporary theology full of moral vision for ardent living.[44] He suggests that the historic progression of art may be equated with theology. In the past, art was the visible celebration by the artist of an external objective thing or person independent of the artist. The artist was not attempting to provide a personal expression, but simply depict the truth of an "external public mythic reality." Today, art is personal creative expression. For Cupitt, so it is for theology as well.[45]

World Religion

Cupitt understands that we now live in an increasingly trans-national, trans-cultural world. As a result of this globalization and "postphilosophical" postmodern environment, comes the end of a realist metaphysic and objective morality.[46] Instead

---

42　Ibid., pp. 114–15.

43　Ibid., p. 116.

44　Ibid., pp. 115–16, 119–20, 125.

45　Cupitt, *Sea of Faith*, p. 246.

46　By "realist metaphysic and objective morality" I am referring to the possibility of objective knowledge of reality, and the grounding of ethics within that reality. The view of an

we are moving toward a "thoroughgoing permissive pluralism."[47] This is a good thing for Cupitt. Belief systems which demonstrate pragmatic results become "true" for those concerned. Freedom and diversity of expression are the keys for building our world today. The more religious groups the better. We must "build our worlds in the ways that seem best to us" and "we have no basis for calling other people's worlds irrational. Let a hundred flowers bloom!"[48]

But how do we prevent radical religious fundamentalism while at the same time guarding those traditions which seem best to us? For Cupitt, the answer lies in practicing one's local faith "on a *strictly* nonrealistic or consistently demythologized basis."[49] This will guide us and move us to a world religion where each piece of modern art can "peacefully coexist" in one global art gallery.[50] This would include the "three thousand or so New Religious Movements" and the "thousand or so New Age groups" as well as the "various major faiths that are all flourishing, teeming, in Western countries today."[51]

Critique and Evaluation

It is not my intention in this section to contend with Cupitt's bold assertion of the nonrealism of God, in a traditional negative apologetic fashion. That is, I will not react to Cupitt by providing a barrage of evidences for the existence of a self-existent, actual Being, God. Such argumentation is beyond the scope and focus of this interactionist apologetic project. Furthermore, such arguments are quickly dismissed by the postmodern deconstructive theologian such as Cupitt.[52] Traditional arguments bolstered in favor of a theist position are based upon modernist assumptions of rational inquiry and the correspondence theory of truth, which is, of course, why they are considered irrelevant to that which is considered "postmodern" and "deconstructionist." Instead, as I have attempted to do with previous thinkers considered, I will provide some critical comments on the consistency and theological viability of the aforementioned aspects of Cupitt's thought.

"objective" or "realist" metaphysic would be a direct contrast with what Cupitt critic, Brian Hebblethwaite, would call a voluntarisitic, expressivistic and pragmatic view of Christianity. See Brian Hebblethwaite, *The Ocean of Truth: A Defence of Objective Theism* (Cambridge: Cambridge University Press, 1988), pp. 14, 16.

47 Cupitt, *After God*, pp. 121–3.
48 Ibid., p. 123.
49 Ibid., p. 127.
50 Ibid., pp. 123–4.
51 Ibid., p. 123.
52 Cupitt, *Taking Leave of God*, pp. 15–21

Theological Necrophilia

Cupitt does make an effort to maintain the notion of God for his postmodern deconstructive theology. Cupitt's nonrealist option of living "as if" under the eye of God does acknowledge the need for some type of human, voluntary, unselfish movement toward something beyond our immediacy. For Cupitt, this is the kind of love we are to have for this non-existent God. In my view, it is difficult to see his suggestion as more than a bizarre sort of "theological" necrophilia. What sense can we really make out of "purely" loving a God who is dead? If we define love as some form of sacrificial giving and acceptance of another, is Cupitt's suggestion really a viable and optional form of conscious loving? One thing love certainly involves, no matter how one specifically defines it, is relationship. If "God" is simply a useful concept, how can we apply a term that is clearly relational? Cupitt relates this love for a dead God to that of the loss of a loved one.[53] Certainly, one would affirm certain feelings, memories, and associations of genuine love with that of a lost loved one. Yet, this love is based on the fact that this person actually existed, actually lived, and was actually in relationship with us. However, Cupitt's supposition of the death of God is not making a truth claim about the nonexistence of a real, actual Deity or Being. Cupitt's dead God *never* actually existed as a being in reality. As Cupitt states: "[God] is not a being, but the universal sign—of relation, a principle of otherness and difference that divides the Void to form the field of meanings and gradations of value."[54] When he speaks of the "death of God," as with other "death of God" theologies, the word "death" simply functions as a metaphor to describe the lack of current cultural–historical necessity or relevance to affirm the notion of God. It seems difficult, therefore, to reconcile his notion of pure love to that of a God who was in actuality never present in reality, without regressing to an endless series of abstractions. Ironically, Cupitt affirms this himself: "All thought is transacted in signs and is hermeneutical or interpretive. The movement is not from one level to another, from sign to an independent signified, but always horizontal, from sign to sign."[55] Yet, the question remains as to whether Cupitt's description of the pure, voluntary love he claims for God can understandably be applied to such a differential view of thought, signs, and language.

Cupitt claims that the "Eye of God" is one among several "tricks" which help us to love life in a morally fulfilling fashion.[56] However, it does not seem clear on how such a "trick" can be that essential to our morality. When we think of tricks, we think of deceptions. It seems that what Cupitt is advocating is a series of self-imposed deceptions for the sake of moral living, the first of which is the Eye of God. These "tricks" are clearly expressed as options for living, not as notions which ought to be

---

53   Cupitt, *After God*, pp. 86–7.

54   Cupitt, *The Long-legged Fly*, p. 106.

55   Ibid., p. 100. See also Bulzan, "Apophaticism, Postmodernism and Language," p. 278.

56   Cupitt, *After God*, p. 104.

imposed on others. But what sense can we make of such "tricks" being self-imposed? As we have seen, Cupitt has forthrightly expressed that he knows that God does not in reality exist. So, how can such a "trick" effectively work to change his moral vision in life? Certainly some people may be deceived with regard to their religious beliefs—and such a deception may actually contribute to their moral living. But the key to their moral change and development was that they genuinely supposed their belief to be true. Cupitt seems to be saying that he knows belief in God is not true, but it still can be used as a self-imposed "trick" for moral development. I believe this is difficult to reconcile.

Nevertheless, in my estimation, Cupitt's notion of the Eye of God may stimulate "reality" theists to reflection with regard to their own beliefs and their own possible self-hypocrisy. Keith Ward, even as a critical respondent to Cupitt, adds credence to this: "What Cupitt has done is to identify clearly and bring into the open the main problems confronting the believer today. He voices the inner doubts and hesitations of many believers, and forces them to greater honesty and clarity."[57] If one truly believes in the continued existence of an actual personal God, does he or she actually live in the world as if under the "eye" of this God? Does intellectual and verbal assent to a belief without corresponding actions still count as genuine belief? If we are convinced (for whatever reasons) that God actually exists, does our lifestyle truly reflect that belief in action?

Cupitt is arguing that such a God does not, in reality, exist; however, it may still be quite helpful for us to live *as if* God does exist. But what does such a life look like? Would such a life be characterized by acts of charity and goodness? Does living *as if* under the eye of God when one affirms God does not exist, result in a similar lifestyle pattern as living under the eye of God as one fully convinced he does exist? A main concern of deconstructionists is the use of theological manipulation resulting from the oppressive authoritarian structure of the notion of such a conceived God. Would not the same sort of theological manipulation result if one was living as if this same God existed in reality? Furthermore, would this not be a grand theological hypocrisy? In my view, it does not seem existentially viable to "playact" or pretend a life as if the Christian God exists, when such a life would demand active, emotional participation with others in Christian community, and even beckoning others to join in such participation.[58]

---

57 Keith Ward, *Holding Fast to God: A Reply to Don Cupitt* (London: SPCK, 1982), p. x.

58 See Kevin J. Vanhoozer, "The Voice and the Actor: A Dramatic Proposal about the Ministry and Minstrelsy of Theology," in *Evangelical Futures: A Conversation on Theological Method*, ed. John G. Stackhouse (Grand Rapids; Leicester, England; and Vancouver, B.C.: Baker, InterVarsity, and Regent College Publishing, 2000), pp. 96–7.

Constructive Nihilism

Cupitt has been likened to both Nietzsche and Mark C. Taylor in his attempt to turn nihilism into a constructive notion to provide a "net gain for humanity."[59] We observe such an embrace of nihilism most explicitly in Cupitt's notions of Blissful Void and Solar Living. I would offer a similar criticism to the issue addressed in response to Mark C. Taylor. What sense can we make out of nihilism offering us something which we can optimistically embrace? Scott Cowdell, a moderately favorable critic of Cupitt, acknowledges such lack of reassurance from Cupitt's view:

> ... Cupitt remains confident for the future survival of Christianity. He describes it as being like the amoeba: 'immortal', well able to ingest its own death and thus to draw life from its dissolution. One realizes, however, that such arduous images are no comfort for those who seek the quiet life theologically, preferring the 'green pastures' to the steep and rugged pathway'.[60]

Cupitt's "therapy" of complete and unlimited emptiness is indeed reminiscent of Taylor's a/theological optimistic nihilism. I would also note similarities between Taylor's notions of erring and "mazing grace" with Cupitt's idea of Solar Living. Cupitt, however, seemingly places much less emphasis on the idea of aimless and directionless wandering in his scheme. It seems that much of Taylor's thinking seems to remain in highly theoretical abstractions and cognitive play. On the other hand, Cupitt is making a genuine attempt to apply concrete and practical thinking to the existence of mankind in day to day affairs. I would critique him, as I did with Taylor, for the lack of a developed moral vision; however, he is certainly advocating that we embrace "real" life, and invest ourselves enthusiastically and wholeheartedly in the practical events of the day.

Cupitt has associated his own views with that of Buddhism. Certainly, one's mind may be drawn to Buddhist values when thinking of Cupitt's notion of a nihilistic Blissful Void. But is the void truly "blissful" for the Buddhist, when the goal is a total renunciation of desire? Keith Ward has pointed out that the Buddhist teachings are quite different from those of Cupitt.[61] Cupitt's Void is optimistic—full of promise and hope. The hope lies in the fullness of life lived in immediacy—Solar Living. There is not a renunciation of desire as with the Buddhist—but a reaching out and grasping of desire at the moment of opportunity.

---

59 Kevin J. Vanhoozer, *Is There a Meaning in This Text?* (Grand Rapids: Zondervan, 1998), pp. 72–3. Cf. also Thiselton, *Interpreting God*, p. 107. Thiselton also brings out the "positive evaluation" of Buddhism offered by both Nietzsche and Cupitt.

60 Cowdell, *Atheist Priest?*, p. 26.

61 Ward, *Holding Fast to God*, p. 79. However, Cupitt may disagree. Cupitt states in a later work (perhaps in response to Ward's critique?) that "the cessation of desire in early Buddhism was more a matter of getting rid of an intellectual error than a matter of extinguishing the biological drives." *The Long-legged Fly*, p. 122.

I commend Cupitt for awakening us to see and embrace the here and now—to live life to the fullest in the present. Our minds may be drawn to the challenge of Qoheleth to live our daily lives "under the sun" in the fear of the Lord. This biblical theme eloquently expounded in the teaching of Ecclesiastes is often neglected especially by those caught up in fundamentialist, theologically dispensational eschatological themes. Cupitt's thinking can motivate us to remember to "stop and smell the roses"—realizing and appreciating the simple things in life—all as gifts from God.[62] Unlike Buddhism, Keith Ward notes, in the teaching of Qoheleth, "[t]here is no tendency to renounce all desire; the meaning of life must be found in it even for the despairing Teacher of Wisdom."[63] If we move in this direction, embracing life for what it is, we do justice to both the other of humanity and the other of creation.

Theology and Myth

Before Cupitt put forward the notion of poetical theology as found in *After God*, he had previously acknowledged the need to go beyond our old religious myths to a new, "fully conscious" faith. However, such a new faith still uses and re-works myth. For Cupitt, myth "is the best, clearest, and most effective way of communicating religious truth," and "religious belief-systems are works of human art and the vehicles of cherished spiritual values and intuitions."[64]

In my estimation, it is this aspect of Cupitt's thought which holds the most promise for a positive contribution for engaging postmodern deconstructive theology. The value of myth and imagination does provide fresh religious perspective and freedom from perceived totalitarian or ecclesiologically related constraints. Telling an old story in a new way can be an extremely helpful way to get back to the essential ingredients of the old story itself which has been lost in modern cultural trappings. Such "poetical theology" is what C.S. Lewis did in his profound "Christian" reworking of the myth of Cupid and Psyche in *Till We Have Faces*.[65] However, Lewis took the use of myth even beyond this level. He used "myth" to re-tell an older myth to express an even higher order myth—to convey what he perceived to be divine truth. Hence his work is profound myth, but it is also profoundly Christian.

But Cupitt assumes that a poetical theology must stem from a nonrealist view of God. I would disagree. I suggest that a poetical theology may well be used (in the vein of C.S. Lewis) to express Christian realism using mythical and archetypical elements. Such efforts may renew and refresh the vitality of the Christian message

---

62 I will develop this further in a later chapter dealing with hope and promise in apologetic dialogue.

63 Ward, *Holding Fast to God*, p. 80.

64 Cupitt, *Taking Leave of God*, p. 166.

65 See C.S. Lewis, *Till We Have Faces: A Myth Retold* (San Diego, New York, and London: Harcourt Brace Jovanovich, 1956). I will discuss this work further in a subsequent chapter.

which has often been trapped in authoritarian verbiage and static, fundamentalistic expression.[66]

Global Theology

Although I do not agree with Cupitt's global theological proposal, it does challenge us with the need to recognize various strengths in differing religious traditions as the cultures behind them. Evangelical theologian, Gerald R. McDermott notes that if Christians simply view non-Christian relgions "as netherworlds of unmixed darkness" the gospel message will be seen as "arrogant obscurantism." Perhaps others will see the beauty of Christ, if they sense that their religious traditions are respected as containing elements of religious truth.[67] Of course, this assumes that a genuine effort is made for critical, interactive dialogue. Keith Ward correctly notes that observing strengths in other religious traditions may serve as a corrective for our own tradition:

> The possible mistakes are many, as in every field of human endeavor, and with every form of religion: and one valuable way of correcting one's most natural mistakes is to look to other forms of sincere and intellectually subtle and spiritually fruitful religion. There we may find prompts to lead us to see treasures in our own tradition we have missed.[68]

Not only will observing positive insights (and weaknesses for that matter) help to serve as a corrective for our own tradition, such insights may also help illuminate truths which our own tradition has neglected. Ward observes that no great religion will be entirely wrong, but each may have something to contribute, if even in a partial sense, to our understanding of God and "broaden and deepen" our own views. Making observations of positive insights from various religious traditions does not imply blind acceptance, nor blind rejection. Instead, I am advocating the practice of sincere listening to the differing perspectives and views of others, hence maintaining respect for the persons holding these views.[69] Stanley J. Grenz, expressing similar sympathies to Ward, rightly submits:

---

66 I will also develop these thoughts further in a subsequent chapter devoted to "Apologetic Imagination."

67 Gerald R. McDermott, *Can Evangelicals Learn From World Religions?: Jesus, Revelation and Religious Traditions* (Downers Grove: InterVarsity, 2000), pp. 10, 217. Cf. also Anne Marie Reijnen, "Variété des vérités," *Analecta Bruxellensia*, 4 (1999): 49–61. Reijnen submits: "La vérité qui guide nos pas doit au moins avoir un 'interface' avec la vérité de nos frères et soeurs en humanité. (p. 61) (trans. "The truth that guides our steps must at least have an 'interface' with the truth of our brothers and sisters in humanity.") Of course, the extent and nature of this "interface" would be crucial to our understanding of interactive dialogue and respect.

68 Ward, *Holding Fast to God*, p. 154.

69 Ibid., pp. 154, 157.

The process of critical appraisal provides the context for determining the value of interreligious dialogue. Because we must assume that all human religions are mixtures of truth and error, the study of other religious traditions and discussions with devotees can be mutually enriching, even for Christians who often shun such exercises.[70]

Cupitt's proposal for "World Religion" may remind us of the conciliatory parent intervening between disputing siblings and saying, "If we would just all get along, then everything would be fine." As noble and utopian as such thinking may be, we must ask ourselves if this is in any way a viable proposal. Does Cupitt effectively take into account the emotional importance of the outworking of religious beliefs? One may grant that Cupitt acknowledges this through his proposal of practicing our faith(s) on a "demythologized" basis—living as separate pieces of art, peacefully hanging side by side in the same global museum. But, if each one is still practicing his or her religious beliefs "as if" under the eye of his or her own "god," Cupitt's proposal will not result in the absence of religious conflict. If religious beliefs are consciously absent of ontological claims to reality, then people are simply playing symbolic games to provide guidance to their lives. Even if I did grant the possibility of this (which I would not), it is still the case that people play their own games in a very serious, often emotionally charged fashion which easily leads down the path to conflict.

Certainly the use of symbolism is very important in religion. Yet, as Ward points out, Cupitt's view neglects to take into account the real nature of religious beliefs. Religious beliefs do, in fact, make ontological "truth" claims to reality and the ultimate destiny of humankind. Cupitt may sincerely desire to follow his self-perceived false mythologies about a non-existent God, but as soon as he attempts to tell others what they mean when following their own notions of "God" or "gods," then he is making a truth claim as well. If some submit that God truly does exist as a self-existent Being, and Cupitt responds that God may be useful to believe in, but does not in exist in objective reality, then there is a genuine factual dispute about the nature of reality which must be addressed.[71]

In view of these genuine disputes on the possibility of objective religious knowledge, along with other postmodern deconstructionist claims I have examined, I will now turn in the next chapter toward some proposals for an apologetic methodology.

---

70 Stanley J. Grenz, *Renewing the Center* (Grand Rapids: Baker, 2000), p. 278.
71 See Ward, *Holding Fast to God*, p. 156.

PART 5

Apologetic Methodology in View of Deconstructionist Concerns

Chapter 9

Preliminary Methodological Considerations

Restatement of Purpose

Again, the intention of this book is not to provide an elaborate treatment or critique of postmodernism as such, nor even of postmodern theology. The purpose is to provide sufficient analysis of the roots and concepts in postmodern deconstructive theology by way of the selected "case studies," in order to reevaluate and rethink evangelical apologetic methodologies in view of these developments. It is to this aspect which I will turn shortly. However, I must first say a brief word regarding the overall methodology. Many studies often use a more "logical" approach moving from theory to application. It may appear to the reader that I have completely reversed this by moving from application to theory. In one sense this is true. I have sought to use an interactionist, dialogically centered apologetic approach while engaging these "case study" thinkers. In another sense, however, it is through the process of active engagement with these thinkers that has allowed me to identify the crucial points of conversational contact by which one *can* develop an apologetic dialogue. This is admittedly circular in its approach, but not ultimately so. I would prefer to describe such methodology as "conversational." After cursory research, I made various proposals for positive apologetic dialogue with these thinkers addressed. I began applying and testing these ideas in the course of theological engagement and critical appropriation with the ideas proposed in the case studies which stimulated the notions for an apologetic process in view of postmodern deconstructive concerns.

In the course of these apologetic considerations, my reading of these authors is different from other several current discussions in that I have deliberately avoided detailed analyses of hermeneutical issues. Such issues have been competently addressed by others.[1] Such hermeneutical issues are extremely important and must be considered. Certainly, deconstruction is primarily about the "deconstruction" of texts—so it is primarily, perhaps, a hermeneutical issue. Yet, as Kevin Vanhoozer has argued, deconstruction is the "death of God put into hermeneutics," which is essentially a theological mistake resulting from an improper view of God.[2]

---

1   As noted, for example, in the fine work of Anthony Thiselton and Kevin Vanhoozer, among others.

2   Kevin J. Vanhoozer, *Is There a Meaning in This Text?* (Grand Rapids: Zondervan, 1998), p. 456.

Consequently, there are additional issues which are also worthy of consideration that are both implications of, and results of the hermeneutical issues; issues which greatly affect apologetic methodology and application. Of course, the hermeneutical issues are not completely isolated from apologetic discussion, but I am simply saying that it will not remain my primary concern here. Instead, my reading is an attempt to focus on apologetic insights one may glean from several primary themes found in deconstructive theology.

Inadequacies of Current Methodologies

Traditionally speaking, apologetics is considered both negative and positive. *Negative* apologetics is defensive in nature. *Negative* in the apologetic context is not to be misconstrued as misdirected or improper. Instead, *negative* apologetics seeks to defend Christianity from its non-Christian assaults and objections and demonstrate such attacks as epistemologically unwarranted. *Positive* apologetics is offensive. It is not "offensive" in that it seeks to offend, but in terms of strategy or approach. It seeks to advance persuasive arguments and reasons for belief in Christianity, even seeking to demonstrate epistemological obligation to accept Christianity.[3] I will submit a perspective which is somewhere between these two perspectives. It will use aspects of each form, but will not be pertinacious on either.

In terms of apologetic methodologies, some are so presuppositionalistic that they really could not engage the postmodern deconstructionist at all. Other evidential apologetic methodologies exclusively concentrate on historical evidences and philosophical proofs for the existence of God. What we may call "existentio–phobia" often plagues our modernist-based apologetic thinking and practice. Often, the past is stressed to such a great extent that current existential experiences and the hope of the future are neglected in forming an apologetic. On the other hand, I do not want to advocate such an extreme anti-objectivism that abandons the use of all natural theology and historical evidences with the intent to herald religious relativism and pluralism.[4] A balance must be sought. Nevertheless, an apologetic which relies exclusively on Enlightenment, modernist ideals in view of postmodern concerns must be reconsidered. Alister McGrath insists that evangelicalism must "purge itself of the remaining foundational influences of the Enlightenment" otherwise we are "allowing ideas whose origins and legitimation lie outside the Christian gospel to exercise a decisive influence on that gospel." Consequently, he adds, evangelicalism

---

3   See Harold A. Netland, "Truth, Authority and Modernity: Shopping for Truth in a Supermarket of Worldviews," in *Faith and Modernity*, ed. Paul Sampson, Vinay Samuel, and Chris Sugden (Oxford: Regnum, 1994), p. 101; and Steven B. Cowan (ed.), *Five Views on Apologetics*, (Grand Rapids: Zondervan, 2000), p. 8.

4   See William Lane Craig's word of caution in "A Classical Apologist's Response" in *Five Views*, p. 290.

must "complete the apologetic and theological adjustment to the decline of modernity; this task remains a priority for the movement." [5]

Many current apologetic methodologies are simply inadequate to effectively interact with postmodern deconstructive thought. But, as D.A. Carson puts it:

> This does not mean that evidentialism has nothing useful to say, or that a Reformed apologetic is invalid.... What is reasonably clear, however, is that "standard" approaches to apologetics simply do not touch the committed deconstructionist. [6]

Carson is right. Many apologetic systems may effectively respond and defend themselves from postmodern deconstructive assaults, but they neglect to actively engage and interact with such thinking. I propose that this interactive aspect needs to be an expressed part of one's apologetic methodology in view of postmodern influences. I am suggesting interaction not simply as a detached observer, but as an *engaged* participant. [7] I am seeking to identify, sympathize, and think carefully and critically with postmodern deconstructive thought. As Andrew Gustafson appropriately notes: "The often overlooked responsibility of being a good apologist is to be a good listener." [8] However, to say we are a listening, engaged participant is not to imply that we completely affirm all such perspectives. We may be engaged, whether or not we are in disagreement or agreement.

The Possibility of Constructive Deconstruction in Apologetics

If apologetics is concerned with evidences and truth claims—how can one rightly borrow anything from postmodern deconstructive thought which seems to run counter to all truth claims? What does the Christian apologist have to say to those who seem to have devalued the notion of truth? If all claims to "truth" are equally valid, how can Christian claims be taken seriously? Amidst such disadvantages, however, Alister McGrath suggests that deconstructionism actually creates advantages as well for the Christian apologist:

> ... apologetics no longer labours under the tedious limitations of the intensely restrictive Enlightenment worldview, fettered by the illusions and pretensions of pure reason. Christianity can no longer be dismissed as a degenerate form of rational religion. The

---

5   Alister McGrath, *A Passion For Truth: The Intellectual Coherence of Evangelicalism* (Downers Grove: InterVarsity, 1996), p. 200.

6   D.A. Carson, *The Gagging of God: Christianity Confronts Pluralism* (Grand Rapids: Zondervan, 1996), p. 96.

7   See Jaco S. Dreyer, "The Researcher: Engaged Participant of Detached Observer," *Journal of Empirical Theology* 11/2 (1998): 7–9.

8   Andrew Gustafson, "Apologetically Listening to Derrida," *Philosophia Christi*, 20/2 (1997): 17.

severe limitations of the modern mentality are intellectually passé, and need no longer be a serious difficulty for the apologist.[9]

Stanley J. Grenz said that postmodernism requires a new embodiment of the gospel. According to Grenz, a postmodern gospel is expressed in four areas: 1) it is post-individualistic; 2) post-rationalistic; 3) post-dualistic; and 4) post-noeticentric.[10] I will briefly comment on all four of these and apply them to a postmodern (deconstructive) apologetic.

A postmodern apologetic must be post-individualistic. Modernism extols the importance of the individual. The rational, autonomous self is seated on the throne. With a postmodern apologetic the shackles of such a radical individualism must be broken. Instead, we must seek and affirm the value of community. The human subject does not stand alone, it is part of a tradition, a heritage. We should not abandon the importance of the individual, but we must realize that Christian individuals are part of a community of believers, the Church, the body of Christ—the primary organism through which God works his purposes today. For Christians, community is essential for the life of the person as well as in the process of knowing God.[11]

A postmodern apologetic must also be post-rationalistic. Where modernism elevated the sovereign power of reason and rational thinking, postmodernism has de-throned such notions. A postmodern apologetic must not jettison all notions of logic and reason, but it must insist on avenues of understanding which lie beyond simply the cognitive level, embracing the concept of mystery and personal encounter. We are more than logical humanoids, we are relational beings with feelings and emotions which help shape our worldviews.[12]

Third, a postmodern apologetic needs to be post-dualistic. As we recall, the modern mindset was built upon Descartes' division of mind and matter. This was a fundamental Enlightenment principle which affected the entire modernist project. A postmodern apologetic must be more "wholistic" and speak to the entire human person. We see the relation between this point and the previous one. A post-rationalistic apologetic essentially implies a post-dualistic apologetic. The human person involves intellectual, emotional, bodily aspects which are interdependent. As Christians we must remember the theological emphasis placed not only on the "soul" as an immaterial thinking substance, but also the "soul" as representative of people as entire beings. This is not to deny the immaterial aspect of our humanness, but it is to emphasize human wholeness. The biblical emphasis on "body" must not be neglected. For example, we have "bodily" resurrection from the dead, the church as the "body" of Christ, the body as the temple of the Holy Spirit, and many other positive characteristics that must not be dismissed.[13]

---

9   McGrath, *A Passion For Truth*, p. 188.

10   Stanley J. Grenz, *A Primer On Postmodernism* (Grand Rapids: Eerdmans, 1996), pp. 167–74.

11   Ibid., pp. 167–9.

12   Ibid., pp. 169–71.

13   Ibid., pp. 171–2.

Grenz also pointed out another characteristic of this post-dualistic aspect which is essentially implied in his post-individualistic emphasis. A post-dualism is more than simply uniting that which Descartes separated. It is also placing the whole human person back into a "social and environmental context that forms and nourishes us."[14] Ted Peters provides some helpful thoughts relevant to this regarding how postmodern thinking attempts to overcome the fragmentation of modernism:

> By giving priority to the whole, postmodernists believe we can reintegrate thought with feeling, objectivity with participation. This means that we need to get beyond the machine model of the world. The model of the living organism appears better because it integrates things around the dynamic movement of life....
>
> ... Because the whole is both creative and synthetic, it has the potential for uniting what has been fragmented, for healing what has been broken.[15]

Fourth, a postmodern (deconstructive) apologetic must be post-noeticentric. From Bacon and Newton onwards into the Enlightenment, the value of knowledge was heralded as supreme. Knowledge became that which is good by its inherent nature. The more knowledge one has, the better one is. A postmodern apologetic will not be so optimistic with respect to such claims. Christians ought to stress biblical wisdom (as we read in the book of Ecclesiastes) over the accumulation of knowledge. Knowledge often does breed a sense of power, and power does often corrupt. A postmodern apologetic will stress the value of faith, of a pure heart, and that of correspondence between right thinking and behavior. Christianity must be seen as more than intellectual adherence to a set of statements. It must breathe life and grace into a broken empty world.[16]

Rob Faesen, S.J., citing the work of Jean Gerson, the chancellor of the Sorbonne in the beginning of the fifteenth century, claims there are two ways that we speak of God: deductive and inductive. The deductive is the way of philosophy, the way of reason and logic. Applied to this study, this is the way of modernity and the Enlightenment project. The inductive way is that of direct experience, characteristic of mystical experience and the reading of mystical texts. The mystical writer, says Faesen, is not saying things which are irrational—he or she is not eliminating reason; but he or she is describing a direct experience with God. Both aspects are valid and both complement each other.[17]

---

14 Ibid., p. 172.

15 Ted Peters, *God—The World's Future: Systematic Theology for a Postmodern Era* (Minneapolis: Fortress, 1992), pp. 17–18. It should be noted that Peters' postmodern approach is not akin to a/theological deconstructionism, but to process theology. Nevertheless, I believe Peters' comments are still pertinent here. I would not apply Peters' call for "creativity" and "synthesis" in the sense of process theology to my methodology, but I would affirm that creativity and synthesis themselves are significant for thinking post-dualistically toward a more biblically centered whole-person mentality.

16 Cf. Grenz, *A Primer On Postmodernism*, pp. 172–3.

17 Rob Faesen, S.J., "What is a Mystical Experience? History and Interpretation," *Louvain Studies*, 23/3 (1998): 231.

Although it is beyond the scope of this book to discuss the nature of mystical experience, I do submit that there are helpful aspects of personal experience, inductive ways in which we may speak about God or Christianity, which have been neglected in modernist apologetic methodologies; and which, if considered, may greatly aid us in our current efforts. It is these aspects of complementarity including the inductive/ deductive, negative and positive, rational-evidential and experiential aspects of apologetics that are worthy of reflection. In view of these, I favor a whole-person, relationally centered, dialogue-based apologetic which appeals to reason, human sensibility, emotion, and imagination in order to help "taste" Divine reality.[18]

Reformed Epistemological Apologetic

Each of these reflections for a postmodern deconstructive apologetic methodology are not uniquely my own. In light of current apologetic methodological studies, I would adhere to a variation of Kelly James Clark's reformed epistemological approach as defended in Steven B. Cowan's, *Five Views on Apologetics*, (Zondervan, 2000).[19] I use the words "loose variation" because I will find divergences, adaptations and different emphases in my approach as it relates to postmodern deconstructive apologetics. Again, it is not my attempt to lay out a fully complete apologetic methodology, but I would offer some reflections that I trust will greatly benefit an apologetic methodology in view of notions presented *by* postmodern deconstructive theology.

It may be helpful if I briefly summarize the reformed epistemological apologetic approach as summarized by Clark, followed by my submission of several points of departure from this approach. Clark suggests that belief in God, as with belief in other persons, does not require evidential support in order for it to be a rational belief.

---

18 Peter J. Schakel uses this metaphor to discuss the later apologetic approach of C.S. Lewis. See Peter J. Schakel, *Reason and Imagination in C.S. Lewis* (Grand Rapids: Eerdmans, 1984), p. 150. I will discuss this approach further in a later chapter.

19 See especially pp. 266–84. Cowan's book is one of the most recent and well-balanced books on varieties of apologetic methodologies. This book includes defenders of the Classical Method, the Evidential Method, the Cumulative Case Method, the Presuppositional Method, and the Reformed Epistemological Method. In past years, other evangelical attempts have been made to articulate apologetic methodologies, such as Bernard Ramm's *Varieties of Christian Apologetics* (Grand Rapids: Baker, 1962); and Gordon R. Lewis's, *Testing Christianity's Truth Claims* (Chicago: Moody, 1976). Ramm distinguishes three basic apologetic families (which then, would include various sub-systems): 1) subjective immediacy (i.e. Christian experience); 2) natural theology; and 3) revelation. Ramm was certainly a competent apologist and analyst of religious epistemology. Yet, as Cowan points out, however, Ramm's taxonomy is too general and falls short of effectively distinguishing methods in apologetics. Gordon Lewis, on the other hand, emphasized six religious epistemologies: 1) pure empiricism; 2) rational empiricism; 3) rationalism; 4) biblical authoritarianism; 5) mysticism; and 6) verificationism (*Testing Christianity's Truth Claims*, p. 7). Cowan equally points out that Lewis's categories do not necessarily imply different apologetic methodologies (Cowan, *Five Views*, pp. 9–12).

Of course, this is not a view unique to Kelly. The esteemed American philosopher of religion, Alvin Plantinga, is considered the first and most contemporary defender of this position.[20] As finite beings, we cannot meet the strict and endless demands to provide evidence for all of our beliefs. In fact, most of our beliefs, including most of those asserted in academic research such as this, are simply based on the testimonial evidence of others. We believe that Australia exists, for example, not because we have personally been there, but because others testify to its reality through travel literature, history books, and personal testimony. The reformed epistemological model takes seriously the limitations of human knowledge and realizes that we cannot attain a godlike grasp of all relevant evidence. Humans do not possess the cognitive tools necessary to provide proof for all beliefs through evidence.[21]

Of course, it is one thing to assert that we do not and cannot provide evidence for all of our beliefs, but it is quite another thing to say that we do not need evidence for such an ultimately significant belief as belief in God. Clark claims there are three reasons to submit why it is proper to believe in God without the need for evidential argument. First, most people do not have the access or ability to assess complex theistic arguments. Also, even if the theistic arguments are seen as valid and sound, they still cannot prove this theistic being's knowledge or character. Furthermore, the use of evidences is not unbiased and presuppositionless. One's personal capacities of reason sift available evidences and determine which is and is not useful. Second, God has given each of us an internal awareness of Himself—a *sensus divinitatis*, but most have suppressed this awareness. Third, belief in God is more akin to belief in a person rather than a scientific theory. Scientific methodology cannot be the guide for all human awareness and endeavor.[22] Clark's reformed epistemological apologetic does not preclude the use of any evidence; however, he simply wants to emphasize its shortcomings. Clark, affirming the view of C. Stephen Evans, does claim that evidences play an important role in defeating the defeaters of naturalism in critical biblical scholarship. When the critical scholar poses threats to solid Christian claims, evidences may be used to defeat such oppositions.[23]

Clark is resistant to making a "coercive" case from Scripture to support his apologetic methodology. He claims there is simply a lack of sufficient Scriptural evidence to support such a case.[24] But may Clark be succumbing to his own critique of

---

20 Others included would be Nicholas Wolterstorff, William Alston, and George Mavrodes. See Kelly James Clark, "Reformed Epistemological Apologetics," in *Five Views*, pp. 267–8. For Plantinga's thorough articulation of the "proper basicality" of God see Alvin Plantinga, "Reason and Belief in God," in Alvin Plantinga and Nicholas Wolterstorff, eds, *Faith and Rationality: Reason and Belief in God* (Notre Dame: University of Notre Dame Press, 1983), pp. 16–93.

21 Clark, "A Reformed Epistemologist's Response," in *Five Views*, p. 88; and "Reformed Epistemological Apologetics," Ibid., pp. 268–70.

22 Clark, "A Reformed Epistemologist's Response," p. 86; "Reformed Epistemological Apologetics," pp. 271–3; "A Reformed Epistemologist's Closing Remarks," pp. 365–6.

23 Clark, "A Reformed Epistemologist's Response," pp. 144–5.

24 Clark, "Reformed Epistemological Apologetics," pp. 274–5.

the demand for such "evidence?" May it not be possible to submit a "soft" evidential case from Scripture by way of apologetic example—not necessarily as evidential conclusive "proof" per se, but for the purpose of our reflection and practice? In the following chapter I will suggest this is clearly possible with the example of the apostle Paul at Athens in Acts 17.

I appreciate Kelly Clark's critique of the Enlightenment project's demand for conclusive evidence which has plagued modern apologetics in many respects. Moreover, I appreciate his affirmation of the value of evidences in view of critical objections to the Christian faith by the suppositions of naturalistic biblical scholarship. Clark also admits that in some cases belief in God may be based on noncoercive evidences or arguments.[25]

Clark's first reason for a non-evidentially based apologetic lies in his view of the limitations of man. I applaud Clark for his emphasis on the noetic effects of sin impairing the judgment of man. But I believe he overstates his case on this issue. Simply due to the fact that many do not have access or ability to assess complex theistic arguments, does not necessarily negate their truth or relevance. If man's reasoning ability is impaired, this may simply be the consequence of sin, even of original sin. Furthermore, I believe that many of the complex theistic arguments have been articulated and published in simplified forms and varieties, and are more accessible than Clark seems to indicate. Nevertheless, I agree with his assessment of the ultimate value of theistic arguments, and readily concur with his estimation of Craig's persuasive and brilliant defense of the kalam cosmological argument.[26] However, the theistic arguments, even at their best, cannot prove the necessary existence of the Christian Tri–une God, with all of his attributes.

Clark's second reason is based on the *sensus divinitatis*. I believe Clark has made us aware of something which is often neglected in our apologetics. The use of the imagination and story often reflect God's creative attributes in a very realistic and persuasive manner. As Clark affirms:

> But the scales can fall from the mind's eye in a wide variety of means: on a mountaintop, while listening to a sermon, through a humbling experience, or by reading The Chronicles of Narnia ... . In all these cases, the scales slide off the mind's eye when the overweening

---

25 Ibid., p. 273.

26 See Clark, "A Reformed Epistemologist's Response," p. 86. William Lane Craig is perhaps the most avid proponent of the kalam cosmological argument today. Craig submits that the argument itself was first developed by Christian thinkers to rebut Aristotle, but became widely used by Islamic theologians in the late Middle Ages as an argument for the existence of God. It is basically a *reductio ad absurdum* argument which argues that anything which has come to exist must have a cause. The universe did come to exist at some point in time—otherwise there would be an infinite series of past events. Since an actual infinite series of past events is impossible, the universe must have a beginning or first cause—which is God. See William Lane Craig, *Apologetics: An Introduction* (Chicago: Moody, 1984), pp. 62–3. Also see J.P. Moreland, *Scaling the Secular City* (Grand Rapids: Baker, 1987), pp. 18–42 for an excellent statement and defense of the argument.

self is dethroned (not to mix too many metaphors!). Humility, not proofs, seems more appropriate to the realization of belief in God.[27]

I agree that often a variety of approaches are helpful in our apologetic practice. How we balance this aspect with the use of reason remains the challenge. I will pursue this fascinating line of thought further in upcoming chapters.

Clark's third reason for a non-evidentially based apologetic lies in the fact that God is a person; therefore, belief in God is belief in a person, not simply a scientific theory. Of course, this confuses the belief *in* God with belief *that* God exists. As Craig rightly points out, Clark's third reason "assumes that there is such a personal being as God to be known—which is precisely the question."[28] Nevertheless, Clark's distinction is significant. The way we go about showing that a person both exists and believing in that person's character is different than the demonstration or proof of a scientific theory. Any attempts to show the reasonableness of belief in God must keep this in mind.

I have identified divergences and have made several caveats to the reformed epistemological apologetic methodology as purported by Kelly James Clark. Nevertheless, I still believe, among major apologetic methodologies today, it best responds to, while allowing interaction with, the challenges of postmodern deconstructive theology.[29] Clark even acknowledges the value of a hermeneutics of suspicion which "provides a much needed corrective to our natural tendency toward spiritual pride...."[30] However, Paul Feinberg notes an objection that deserves comment: "If any form of postmodernism like deconstructionism is true, then there can be no task for apologetics, and discussions about methods for defending the faith are meaningless."[31] I would readily agree with Feinberg if one accepted deconstructionism *in toto*, but this surely is not my intention. Instead I have offered a recontextualized appropriation of the writers considered, without necessarily holding to their particular assumptions or agendas. This idea is summarized well by Merold Westphal:

> There is a negative side to this activity, for the need to recontextualize stems from not sharing the same assumptions or the same agenda. Thus, to appropriate is to say, "No. In this respect and in that respect I do not share your vision and find it necessary to locate myself at a different site from yours." But appropriation is affirmation and acceptance as well; and it is this which distinguishes it from simple refutation. It says, "Yes. I think

---

27 Clark, "Reformed Epistemological Apologetics," p. 273.

28 William Lane Craig, "A Classical Apologists Response," in *Five Views*, p. 285 note 1.

29 As Cowan notes in *Five Views*, he does not presume to provide the exhaustive list of apologetic methodologies. It is his hope with the other contributors that "this work promotes additional fruitful discussion of apologetic methodology ...." It is my desire to promote such discussion through this book as well.

30 Clark, "Reformed Epistemological Apologetics," p. 280.

31 Paul D. Feinberg, "Cumulative Case Apologetics," in *Five Views*, p. 169.

you are right about that, though it will come out a bit differently in the context of my assumptions and agenda."[32]

I simply want to keep the conversation going, to keep listening, while acknowledging strengths and rejecting weaknesses of particular perspectives. I am suggesting that a dialogue-based approach, whether in the context of theories of deconstructionist theology or interreligious dialogue, provides the mutual respect necessary for keeping such conversation going.[33] I believe a modified approach to a reformed epistemological apologetic best accomplishes this. Clark puts it well when he says: "Our success as apologists depends on our willingness to recognize our own shortcomings and also our willingness to listen to the other and to begin with our shared beliefs and commitments."[34] Of course it must be said that listening to the other, respecting the other, and engaging in dialogue with the other does not imply a mutual compliance and adaptation of beliefs. Alister McGrath aptly says: "... dialogue cannot be conducted on the basis of the deeply patronizing assumption that 'everyone is saying the same thing.' Dialogue implies respect, but it does not presuppose agreement."[35]

With these observations in mind, in the following chapters I will offer several aspects of prolegomena for apologetic consideration in view of postmodern deconstructive theology. These will be built on our previous critical-interactive observations (from Lyotard, Derrida, Foucault, Taylor, Rorty, Cupitt) while keeping in mind the postmodern gospel "contours" as suggested by Grenz. First of all, I will consider helpful lessons from the book of Acts in the consideration of apologetics in view of postmodern deconstructive thought. Second, I will consider an open-dialogue approach of engagement *with* these postmodern deconstructive masters of suspicion.[36] Third, I will will consider the use of imagination and myth in apologetic dialogue and its relation to hope and promise. Next, I will submit a plea for a "soft foundationalism"[37] for our apologetic groundwork. Finally, I will attempt to bring together some concluding reflections on a person-centered, dialogue-based apologetic in view of postmodern deconstructive thought.

---

32 Merold Westphal, "Appropriating Postmodernism," in Merold Westphal (ed.), *Postmodern Philosophy and Christian Thought* (Bloomington: Indiana University Press, 1999), p. 2.

33 See Alister E. McGrath, "A Particularist View: A Post-Enlightenment Approach," in Dennis L Okholm and Timothy R. Phillips (eds), *More Than One Way?: Four Views on Salvation in a Pluralistic World* (Grand Rapids: Zondervan, 1995), pp. 156–7.

34 Clark, "A Reformed Epistemologist's Response," p. 89.

35 McGrath, "A Particularist View," p. 156.

36 I have essentially attempted to model this in the previous chapters.

37 I acknowledge the oxymoron of a "soft foundation." But this baffling combination is a common expression for a moderate philosophical foundationalism. I will address this more extensively in chapter 13.

Chapter 10

Christian Appeals to Deconstructionist Concerns: Two Lessons from the Book of Acts

J. Richard Middleton and Brian J. Walsh claim that the biblical metanarrative "addresses our postmodern situation with both compassion and power" and it also does significantly more than just escaping the postmodern deconstructive charge of totalization and violence.[1] In fact, as they submit, "the story the Scriptures tell contains the resources to shatter totalizing readings, to convert the reader, to align us with God's purposes of shalom, compassion and justice." But this is not a mere apologetic "ploy." The story of Scripture must be told so that it "might be a living resource" to the world today.[2] I would express agreement with Middleton and Walsh on this, but it is beyond the scope of this book to develop an account of how I believe the story of Scripture as a whole may be used to address the postmodern context. Nonetheless, I would like to consider several features from the book of Acts which I believe are critical to the discussion at hand.

In this chapter I will consider the context of the gospel metanarrative of Christian "beginnings" that I see in the book of Acts, with postmodern deconstructionist "sensitivities," and demonstrate what I believe to be positive "antitotalizing dimensions" to enable further apologetic dialogue in view of postmodern deconstructionism.[3] First, I will consider the emphasis in Acts on multi-cultural

---

1   As noticed in Lyotard and Derrida in particular.

2   J. Richard Middleton and Brian Walsh, *Truth is Stranger Than It Used to Be: Biblical Faith in a Postmodern Age* (Downers Grove: InterVarsity, 1995), p. 107. Middleton and Walsh develop the biblical metanarrative into six "Acts," which they adapt from N.T. Wright's, "How Can the Bible Be Authoritative," *Vox Evangelica*, 21 (1991): 7–32: Act I is creation; Act II is the fall of man; Act III is the story of Israel; Act IV is the story of Jesus; Act V is the story of the church; and Act VI is the eschaton or consummation (*Truth is Stranger Than It Used to Be*, p. 182).

3   See Timothy R. Phillips and Dennis L. Okholm, "Introduction," in Timothy R. Phillips and Dennis L. Okholm (eds), *Christian Apologetics in the Postmodern World* (Downers Grove: InterVarsity, 1995), p. 20. Here Phillips and Okholm are referring to the chapter by J. Richard Middleton and Brian J. Walsh in the same book, "Facing the Postmodern Scalpel: Can the Christian Faith Withstand Deconstruction?" pp. 131–54. I am indebted to William J. Larkin, Jr., for the idea of using the book of Acts to create postmodern dialogue along these lines from his paper, "The Recovery of Acts as 'Grand Narrative' for the Church's Evangelistic Task in

community through the local church and its shared sufferings and marginalization at the hand of oppressors. Second, I will look to the apostle Paul at Athens in Acts 17 as an effective example and springboard for engaging the postmodern "masters of suspicion" as seen in deconstructive theology.

The Book of Acts: The Story of Christian Community

Although the book of Acts only covers a period of approximately 30 years, it is crucially important in terms of Christian beginnings. A key theme which emerges from this narrative that spans the commissioning of the disciples to the time of Paul's imprisonment, is that of community in the context of the church. These first "Christians" ate together, prayed together, and shared each other's possessions.[4] Certainly it takes the transformation of the individual to affect the community, but the emphasis in the book of Acts is clearly upon the community of the church, rather than the individual. This coming together was theologically based on the result of the Spirit's coming at Pentecost. Stanley J. Grenz states it well:

> In addition to being an objective event, the Spirit's coming at Pentecost was also subjectively experienced. Each person present was "filled with the Spirit" (vs. 4). This resulted in the inauguration of a new corporate reality, a fellowship of all who were given "the one Spirit to drink" (1 Cor. 12:13). The sense of community resulting from the inward experience of the Spirit formed the basis for the subsequent sharing of the goods within the Jerusalem church. Because they all participated in the same spiritual reality, they wanted to share with one another the material goods they possessed (Acts 2: 44-45).[5]

However, the formation of this new community was much more than simply a subjective response to this objective occurrence. Middleton and Walsh observe that this new "ingathering" and formation of community was brought about through hearing again the wonders of God and His redemptive action in Jesus (see Acts 2:11; 22-36). The curses of Babel, they submit, were "redressed at Pentecost" where the "Spirit began to work a new creation and form a new people." This scattered people now became a community. Hearing anew this story of God "breaks down old barriers" and "empowers those who enter this story through repentance (vv. 37-47) to begin to live out of the story."[6]

---

a Post-Modern Age," presented at the *Evangelical Theological Society* (Orlando: November 19, 1998).

    4   See Acts 2:42–47; 4:32–37.

    5   Stanley J. Grenz, *Theology For the Community of God* (Carlisle: Paternoster, 1994), p. 479.

    6   Middleton and Walsh, *Truth is Stranger Than It Used to Be*, p. 189.

Heterogeneous Community

Development and Characteristics This community did not remain local or homogeneous. I see the summary of the expansion of this community in Acts 1:8: "…you will be my witnesses in Jerusalem, and in all Judea and Samaria, and to the ends of the earth." Accordingly, the book unfolds with this same progression. The first portion of the narrative pertains to early church beginnings in Jerusalem with Peter and Stephen. The next section moves to work in Samaria, the coastal plain, and into Caesarea with Philip and Peter. Beginning with chapter 13, the apostle Paul becomes the dominant figure in carrying the gospel message to the "ends of the earth." But the point was not political imperialism. The point was to carry the gospel message of openness and reconciliation to form a community, the church. This community formation was bi-directional: First, God reconciling men and women to Himself, then man (generic) being reconciled to his fellow man.

The expansion of the church was certainly not a homogeneous assertion of power and knowledge. It became a multi-national, multi-cultural community. Even the first "prophets and teachers" at the first church in Antioch in Acts 13 were socially and culturally diverse. Barnabas, a Levite, was from Cyprus. Simeon called Niger ("black" or "dark complexioned) was probably from Africa. He may have been the Simon of Cyrene who carried the cross of Jesus to Golgotha in Luke 23:26 (cf. Mark 15:21). Also included is Lucius of Cyrene (a Roman), Manaen (who had been raised with Herod Antipas), and Saul (Paul), who was from Cilicia. The church was (and is or should be) the movement of God embracing both Gentiles and Jews and bringing them together in community.[7] As Stephen A. Rhodes reminds us:

> God's intention has always been that the church be a multicultural, multinational community—a church of all languages, ethnicities, nationalities and peoples. And yet for all of this diversity, this church proclaims it unity through common faith in Jesus Christ.[8]

The process by which this early community, the church, developed, was by no means through acts of political power and conquest.[9] Instead, it grew through the strength

---

7   I. Howard Marshall, *The Acts of the Apostles*, Tyndale New Testament Commentaries, 20 vols., vol. 5 (Leicester: InterVarsity, 1980), p. 214; Richard N. Longenecker, *The Acts of the Apostles*, ed. Frank E. Gaebelein, 12 vols;, *The Expositor's Bible Commentary*, vol. 9 (Grand Rapids: Zondervan, 1981), p. 416; and William J. Larkin, *Acts* (ed.) Grant R. Osborne, The IVP New Testament Commentary Series (Downers Grove: InterVarsity, 1995), p. 190.

8   Stephen A. Rhodes, *Where Nations Meet: The Church in Multicultural World* (Downers Grove: InterVarsity, 1998), p. 20.

9   By "early church" I am referring to the pre–Constantinian expansion of Christianity. Regrettably, the Christian gospel has obviously been used with an "imperialist" agenda at various periods throughout history. In view of this, Lesslie Newbigin reminds us that "[w]hen coercion of any kind is used in the interests of the Christian message, the message itself is corrupted….we negate the gospel if we deny the freedom in which alone it can be truly believed." *The Gospel in a Pluralist Society* (Grand Rapids: Eerdmans, 1989), p. 10. Cf. also, pp. 223–4.

of diversity *in* community. The early church community was both *communal* and *multicultural* in its practice. This is not to say that the church did not utter a proclamation of truth in a metanarrative. The message of the gospel is indeed a metanarrative. But it is not a metanarrative which is intrinsically oppressive simply because it makes universal truth claims. Its claims are seen as true, they are received and given as good news, "motivated by a love that has been graciously given."[10] It is not a metanarrative of exclusion of the other, but of embrace and acceptance.[11] In this sense, it is an "antitotalizing" metanarrative. As Middleton and Walsh add: "This is a vision of life that will replace the decentered, multiphrenic self of postmodernity with a biblical understanding of the self as empowered and responsible agent in community."[12] I concur with Middleton and Walsh when they claim that it is precisely this that we see at Pentecost in Acts chapter two.

In affirming a postmodern apologetic with deconstructive postmodern "sensitivities," we must break loose from the radical individualism which characterizes modernist thinking. I am suggesting that the book of Acts reminds us of this. The process of "knowing" is not simply the process of discovery of the detached, objective self. One must affirm the value of knowledge mediated through the community of the church. It is important to remember we are within a community of diverse, reconciled people, who are reaching out to embrace others into this community. It is through this "Spirit-formed community" where we may actively live out a "covenantal alternative to both the worn-out worldview of modernity and the fragmentation of postmodern times."[13]

Negative and Positive Apologetics   As David Dockery notes: "In order for the new postmodern generations to consider the plausibility of Christianity they must be convinced of its authenticity, as well as its community-building characteristics, before they will hear its truth claims."[14] The "objective" apologetic implications of this are extremely significant. The discipline of apologetics is often seen as strictly verbal argumentation or presentation. Yet, if the church concretely manifests the value of community and multicultural diversity it will provide a substantial negative and positive apologetic. It will provide a visual *negative* apologetic in response to the postmodern deconstructive accusation of Christianity's cultural oppression

---

10 Henry H. Knight III, *A Future For Truth* (Nashville: Abingdon Press, 1997), p. 77. Of course I am not suggesting, as mentioned before, that the Christian metanarrative cannot be or has not been used to oppress and dominate. But simply because it can be and has been used improperly does not mean that the metanarrative itself is, as Knight says, "essentially oppressive" (p. 77).

11 See Miroslav Volf, *Exclusion and Embrace: A Theological Exploration of Identity, Otherness, and Reconciliation* (Nashville: Abingdon, 1996).

12 Middleton and Walsh, *Truth is Stranger Than It Used to*, p. 191.

13 Ibid., p. 192.

14 David S. Dockery, "The Challenge of Postmodernism," in *The Challenge of Postmodernism: An Evangelical Engagement*, ed. David S. Dockery (Grand Rapids: Baker, 1997), p. 17.

through totalization and exclusion. It will also provide a *positive* apologetic through its persuasive demonstration of the fruits of Christian community.

However, Christians do not pursue a racially and culturally diverse community simply for the purpose of apologetic dialogue, or due to its political correctness. Christians pursue multicultural communities because this pursuit is a part of the essential nature of the gospel message (to "make disciples of all nations"—Mt. 28:19), and because it is a normative value for the Christian community. It has the apologetic advantage of exemplifying the meaning of living in unity with diversity.[15]

A Heterogeneous Ecclesiology: Evangelical Pluralism? There is a certain sense in which I am arguing for an *evangelical pluralism* by acknowledging our individual limitations and promoting the value of community (with diversity). However, this is not to say that I am not promoting any particularist claims whatsoever. By simply stating the word "evangelical" I am indeed making particular claims.[16] Such *particularism* is often prejudicially viewed as *exclusivism*, a term that elicits thoughts of arrogance, superiority, imperialism, violence, intolerance, and closed-mindedness.[17] But even this term is subject to the following disclaimer:

> Exclusivism should be understood in terms of theological and not social exclusivism.... It should not be understood as restricting association with adherents of other faiths, nor as encouraging intolerance or disrespectful behavior toward those of other faiths.[18]

I would indeed acknowledge respect for the concerns raised by religious pluralists,[19]

---

15 Rhodes, *Where Nations Meet*, pp. 17, 20. This "normative" view of the gospel is what, in part, distinguishes my position as "evangelical." Paul Lakeland suggests that "[w]ithin the apologetic moment of theology, ... theological statements are not claims about the way the world is or should be, but rather about the ways in which we are as individuals and as faithful communities within a wider world of which we are inescapably a part." [Paul Lakeland, *Postmodernity: Christian Identity in a fragmented age* (Minneapolis: Fortress, 1997), p. 91.] In my view, apologetic moments in theology are more than descriptive, as Lakeland suggests. I am favoring descriptive and prescriptive statements in doing apologetic work. It is my contention that normative or prescriptive theological statements are necessary to make warranted relgious and ethical decisions.

16 See chapter 1 on the definition of *evangelical*.

17 Dennis L Okholm and Timothy R. Phillips, "Introduction," in Dennis L Okholm and Timothy R. Phillips (eds), *More Than One Way?: Four Views on Salvation in a Pluralistic World* (Grand Rapids: Zondervan, 1995), pp. 15–16.

18 Harold Netland, "The Uniqueness of Jesus in a Pluralistic World," *Religious and Theological Studies Fellowship Bulletin* 5 (November/December 1994): 8, 20 as quoted in *More Than One Way?*, eds Okholm and Phillips, p. 16.

19 In this context I am defining "pluralist" as one who maintains that all religions may "provide independent salvific access to the divine Reality." (Okholm and Phillips, "Introduction," in Okholm and Phillips (eds), *More Than One Way?*, p. 17.)

but it is not my intent to provide such treatment here.[20] What I am suggesting is emulating the value of community and embracing an *evangelical* plurality within the community of the Christian church at large as a means of bearing a multi-cultural, anti-totalizing witness to the world.

D.A. Carson states these intentions well:

> Indeed, in certain respects believers can embrace pluralism more lavishly than the secularists can. Our heavenly Father created a wonderfully diverse world: let us adore him for it. He makes each snowflake different; we make ice cubes. Quite clearly, God likes diversity in the color of human skin—he has made people wonderfully diverse. Similarly, apart from the wretched sinfulness endemic to all cultures, one must assume that God likes cultural diversity as well. In the realm of knowing, we join the experts of deconstruction and of the new hermeneutic in insisting on human finiteness: more, we go further and insist on human sinfulness. The noetic effects of sin are so severe that we culpably distort the data brought to us by our senses to make it fit into self-serving grids. We are not only finite, on many fronts we are blind.[21]

I am suggesting an apologetic methodology that is influenced by a heterogeneous ecclesiology. We must transcend barriers of countries, race, culture, and gender. But to apply this, it is necessary to actively initiate and engage in cross-cultural relationships. The key is consistent cultural and intellectual humility in academic dialogue and proactively seeking correction and clarification in community.[22] This is not to say that an appeal to community provides a guarantee of truth or objectivity. It is important to stand against the tyranny of a totalitarian collective. But this is not the issue here. I am simply saying that to create an effective apologetic in view of postmodern deconstructionist challenges, we must proactively generate community interaction.[23] We must acknowledge that our own perspectives are quite limited, so it will greatly benefit us and others to interact with a broad range of backgrounds. I concur with Millard Erickson when he suggests that this will work itself out in different dimensions. Through the study of the history and theology of the church, we may interact with believers from the past. Horizontally, we can dialogue with those from different cultures, nations, and ecclesiastical traditions. Additionally, we should converse with those working at different intellectual or theoretical levels—

---

20 For a good analysis of salvation and pluralism see Okholm and Phillips (eds), *More Than One Way*. Such views as normative pluralism, inclusivism, salvation in Christ, and salvation in Christ alone are discussed and debated by different authors holding to each position.

21 D.A. Carson, *The Gagging of God: Christianity Confronts Pluralism* (Grand Rapids: Zondervan, 1996), pp. 97–8.

22 See Joel B. Green (ed.), *Hearing the New Testament* (Carlisle: The Paternoster Press, 1995), p. 408.

23 Millard J. Erickson, *Christian Theology*, 2nd edn (Grand Rapids: Baker, 1998), p. 173; and Stanley J. Grenz, *A Primer On Postmodernism* (Grand Rapids: Eerdmans, 1996), p. 168.

both higher and lower levels.[24] This can provide us with a broader perspective of humanity that will not only prove enriching to us and those with whom we communicate, but it will act as an ongoing corrective against intellectual tyranny.

The Problem of Incommensurability One of problems that arises in this challenge to a heterogeneous ecclesiological model for an apologetic is that of incommensurability. This is where we may learn from hermeneuticists such as Gadamer. Gadamer's process of the "fusion of horizons," as we recall from the previous chapter on historical context, challenges us to look beyond our own traditions. Although Gadamer seemed to be primarily making an historical distinction (i.e. the horizon of the present and the horizon of the past) the challenge is certainly applicable to the task at hand.[25] The key to this problematic issue is, as I have suggested, to keep the dialogue going. The mere act of seeking to understand other perspectives from those of our own helps continue the conversation, and leads us to reflect on and at times revise our own perspectives.

Missiologist Paul G. Hiebert advocates a critical realist position along with community hermeneutics as a helpful model pertinent to my affirmation of a heterogeneous ecclesiology. Hiebert claims that community hermeneutics first involves choosing the domain of study, setting the standards and methods for the research, providing the conceptual problems, and acknowledging various assumptions and biases. Next, the members of the community must verify their findings through critical interaction with each other. This helps to correct biases and helps move toward agreement. Then their results are tested against the history of interpretation, and current research relevant to their field. This manner of research helps "decentralize" the conquest of truth and also prevents its misuse by those desiring to control "knowledge" for their own ends.[26] Hiebert applies this notion of "community hermeneutics" theologically:

> … community hermeneutics guards us against the privatization of faith and from our personal misinterpretations of Scripture. Just as others see our sins more clearly than we see our (personal and cultural) own, so they see our theological biases and errors more clearly that we do. Similarly, the cultural biases of local churches must be checked by the international community of believers in all cultures and ages. Furthermore, we must remember that God is continually at work in his church, shaping and reshaping it into his likeness.[27]

---

24 Erickson, *Christian Theology*, pp. 173–4.

25 Roland Hoksbergen, "Is There a Christian Economics?: Some Thoughts in Light of the Rise of Postmodernism," *Christian Scholar's Review* 24/2 (1994): 132. Cf. Hans-Georg Gadamer, *Truth and Method*, 2nd edn (New York: Continuum, 1989), pp. 302–7.

26 Paul G. Hiebert, *Missiological Implications of Epistemological Shifts: Affirming Truth in a Modern/Postmodern World* (Harrisburg: Trinity Press International, 1999), pp. 94–5.

27 Ibid., p. 102.

How does Hiebert deal with the nature of disagreement using a critical realist model? He claims that with this model, disagreements are less confrontive and more harmonious in their resolution. Changing or rejecting a theory or a model carries less emotional content than rejecting truth itself. But he agrees that critical realists certainly hold their theories firmly. There is still a desire to let the theories reflect a commitment to truth. At the same time, they understand the limitations of human knowledge.[28]

In relation to this, Stephen A. Rhodes submits that a key passage for the consideration of cross-cultural conflict resolution is found in Acts 15. As the church was coming to grips with its growing multicultural identity, dialogue was essential. All those involved took their task seriously and worked together with common respect to seek a solution. Eventually, James proposed a compromise which was commonly affirmed as the direction of the Spirit of God. Everyone shared in making the decision, taking responsibility for it, and sharing it with others.[29]

The Value of Personal Story Entrusted in Community

Although I am placing an emphasis upon the limitations of the individual and the value of community, I am certainly not rejecting the value of the self, or one's personal story. In fact, I would affirm the value of one's personal redemptive story within the community context. Henry H. Knight's analysis of evangelical theology in view of postmodernism also lends support to this:

> In postmodernism the autonomous individual of the Enlightenment is being supplanted by a more holistic vision of humanity, emphasizing relationality and cooperation. Instead of the individual being prior to the community, the community is prior to the individual; participation in the community with its network of practices and relationships is what constitutes the personhood of the individual.[30]

The metanarrative of Acts must theologically become our personal story as well. There will certainly be skepticism or even hostility from those holding a strong anti-metanarrative position, but as one writer insists, this position is not ultimately viable: "Human beings cannot live without the meaning and purpose that such stories

---

28 Ibid., pp. 95–6. I would agree with Hiebert's application of "critical realism" by way of application to my suggestion of a heterogeneous ecclesiology as an effective model in view of postmodern deconstructive criticisms. But I am not necessarily endorsing a complete "critical realist" epistemology. Middleton and Walsh express the following caution: "Our problem with critical realism is that such an epistemological framework still carries too many overtones of a realism that has proven to be bankrupt and has legitimately been deconstructed by postmodern thought.... 'If only we are sufficiently self–critical,' the critical realist seems implicitly to be saying, 'then we will finally get to the thing itself.'" (*Truth is Stranger Than It Used to Be*, p. 168). Although, I don't fully endorse Walsh and Middleton's extreme pessimism with regard to the complete bankruptcy of reason, I believe their caution is worthy of notation.

29 Rhodes, *Where Nations Meet*, p. 178.

30 Knight, *A Future For Truth*, p. 53.

give."[31] Grand narratives, I would argue, give us an interpretive scheme by which to live out our hopes, dreams and convictions (or lack therof). This is a common characteristic of humanity. Christians must know their story, and must live in the community of the story where their identity is to be found. In the gospel story, the deepest human needs will be met, and the most profound resources will be found for facing failure and defeat.[32] This happens through Christians appropriating the biblical narrative as their personal salvation history. Now I am not referring to some kind of existential mind-jockeying here. Theologically, within the Reformed tradition, we speak of guilt and justification being "legally" imputed to man before and after regeneration, respectively. As guilt is part of our real, legal inheritance with Adam, so justification is part of our real, legal, inheritance with Christ. I am suggesting that we are also realistically connected in community with all those redeemed to whom God's gracious, sanctifying works are imparted (cf. Rom. 5; Eph. 2). Through this realistic connection in the community, the church itself becomes a visible, tangible and corporate apologetic expression. With this "community" or church as apologetic paradigm, I am not trying to minimize the importance of theological truth. Instead, I am emphasizing that truth may be derived through the dimension of community as well.[33]

This community is entrusted with a story to be told through both word and through conducting one's life as an embodiment of that story. It is not a story which is imposed for imperialistic purposes. Nor is it the Christian's job to insure the conversion of others.[34] As Lesslie Newbigin puts it:

> She tells it simply as one who has been chosen and called by God to be part of the company which is entrusted with the story. It is not her business to convert the others. She will indeed—out of love for them—long that they may come to share the joy that she knows and pray that they may indeed do so. But it is only the Holy Spirit of God who can so touch the hearts and consciences of the others that they are brought to accept the story as true and to put their trust in Jesus.[35]

Suffering Community

As I have noted, the expansion of the church was not an imperialistic "power play." At the heart of the Christian gospel is

---

31 Bill Kynes, "Postmodernism: A Primer For Pastors," *The Ministerial Forum: Evangelical Free Church Ministerial Forum* (1997): 6. I readily acknowledge that this statement expresses my underlying Christian presupposition.

32 Ibid., p. 6; and Newbigin, *The Gospel in a Pluralist Society*, p. 182.

33 Dennis Hollinger, "The Church as Apologetic" in Phillips and Okholm (eds), *Christian Apologetics*, pp. 183, 192.

34 Newbigin, *The Gospel in a Pluralist Society*, p. 182. Cf. also Knight, *A Future For Truth*, p. 202.

35 Newbigin, *The Gospel in a Pluralist Society*, p. 182.

the denial of all imperialisms, for at its center there is the cross where all imperialisms are humbled and we are invited to find the center of human unity in the One who was made nothing so that all might be one. The very heart of the biblical vision for the unity of humankind is that its center is not an imperial power but the slain Lamb.[36]

The church community came about through the witness of an oppressed, marginalized community through proclamation and dialogue—a community which passed through the gates of suffering. Middleton and Walsh claim that "[p]ostmodernists are right: the voices of the marginalized, of those who have been left outside the story line that has been dominant in the West, need to be heard."[37] It is this crucible of suffering which gives this community, the church, a unique position to identify with the other, the other suffering, the other oppressed, the other marginalized.

In the book of Acts I see the voice of the oppressed and marginalized in the dynamic Christian community. Although I will not provide a detailed account or historical analysis of the narrative in the book of Acts, a brief look at the development of the Christian church through suffering will prove helpful to my point. We see the beginning of Christian suffering with the imprisonment of Peter and John in Acts 4:3. Nevertheless, the text seems to indicate that such opposition actually contributed to Christianity's growth: "But many who heard the message believed, and the number of men grew to about five thousand" (4:4). Despite continued ongoing threats and the command to suppress their proclamation of the gospel by the Sanhedrin, they remained persistent (cf. 4:18-21, 29).

Continuing in chapter 5, we find the jealous Sadducees arresting the apostles and putting them in public jail (vss. 17-18). In 5:40, the text indicates that they were flogged. However, the apostles still counted it a privilege to be worthy of such suffering for the sake of Jesus Christ (vs. 41).

Stephen, the first recorded Christian martyr, was falsely accused of blasphemy and dragged out of the city and even stoned to death while maintaining a prayerful attitude of forgiveness toward his perpetrators (7:54-8:1). The text indicates that this was directly followed by a great persecution of the church at Jerusalem, followed in turn by a scattering of Christians throughout Judea and Samaria (8:1). In 8:3 we find Saul continuing his attempts to destroy the church community by dragging off men and women to prison. He sustained such persecution and threats of murder to Christians until his conversion in Acts chapter 9. Following the conversion of Saul there was a short time of peace for the church. However, it is significant to note that throughout such time of persecution, the community of the church had grown from a small number in the upper room to believers in Judea, Galilee, and Samaria (cf. 9:31).[38]

In chapter 12 we notice that persecution begins again under King Herod. James (the brother of John) is executed and Peter is put in prison. In chapter 13, the Jews

---

36 Ibid., p. 159; cf. Rhodes, *Where Nations Meet*, pp. 59–60.

37 Middleton and Walsh, *Truth is Stranger Than It Used to Be*, pp. 189–90.

38 See Conrad Gempf, "Acts," in *New Bible Commentary*, ed. D.A. Carson, et al. (Leicester: InterVarsity, 1994), p. 1081.

stirred up persecution against Paul and Barnabas. In 14:19 it indicates that Paul was even stoned and left for dead. In chapter 16, we find Paul and Silas stripped of their clothes, beaten. flogged, and put in prison. The text indicates that Paul was at times miraculously set free by divine intervention, but this in no way minimizes the physical and emotional suffering and public humiliation he and his ministry partners had to face. Chapters 19 onward continue to emphasize Paul's expanding gospel ministry while continuing to endure mob persecution as seen in Thessalonica, Berea, Corinth and Ephesus. In Acts 21-22 Paul was beaten by the crowds, arrested, and endured a series of trials before his eventual and final house imprisonment in Rome.

Of course, this example of persistence and forgiveness of others through suffering does not simply begin with the apostles. They were emulating the behavior they witnessed in Jesus himself. But the remarkable point I am trying to emphasize as well, is not simply that Christians were oppressed, persecuted and marginalized, but they extended their embrace to their oppressors, and also to others who were persecuted and marginalized. Christianity began with those who were culturally marginalized, bearing effective witness to the gospel message cross-culturally. The Hellenistic Jewish Christians were discriminated against, yet still bore a strong witness to unbelieving Hellenistic and Hebrew speaking Jews (cf. Acts 6:1-7:53). Even in the "wake of Stephen's martyrdom" they still carried the mission of the church "across the cultural thresholds of Samaria" and to the remote parts of their known world.[39]

Reflections on Early Christianity in Dialogue With Deconstructionism

The early expansion of Christianity was certainly no kind of imperialistic take-over. Early Christianity expanded in the context of suffering and service and embrace of the other, not in power or rulership. This in itself is a noteworthy apologetic and needed endeavor for Christians today in view of postmodern deconstructive concerns. As James Sire puts it:

> When a group of Christians lives out their faith in communal worship of God and in care for each other, when they love those around them, especially the outcasts of society, when they serve instead of rule—that is, when Christians show the marks of genuine Christian community—it is indeed powerful argument for the truth of the Christian faith.[40]

The "theology of embrace" advanced by Croatian theologian Miroslav Volf, holds great promise for peace among various races, cultures and subcultures in the postmodern ethos. Volf suggests that the biblical narrative of the Prodigal illustrates a hopeful point of departure. In the story of the Prodigal, Volf submits:

---

39 Larkin, *Acts*, p. 98.
40 James W. Sire, *Why Should Anyone Believe Anything at all?* (Downers Grove: InterVarsity, 1994), pp. 205–6.

[T]he open arms of the father became for me the picture of who God is, how God had acted toward sinful humanity.... At the center of Christian faith lies not so much liberation, but the embrace of the wrongdoer. That was where the idea of a "theology of embrace" was born. It is simply the Prodigal's father not giving up his relationship with his son—in spite of the wrongdoing of the younger son. When that son returns, the father runs toward him without having heard a single word from that son. He shows his son grace and acceptance because he was and he is and he remained his son even through the wrongdoing. That is what we see on the cross.

But it doesn't stop there. The God who runs toward us—the wrongdoers—also demands we do the same with those who have wronged us. So there is a social meaning to the cross. Divine grace obligates.[41]

Kenneth E. Bailey also rightly challenges us to rescue this story of the prodigal "from familiarity and from its traditional cultural captivity."[42] Bailey claims that the "cutting edge" of this parable has been "dulled" because we have read it simply in view of our "own cultural presuppositions." Contrary to expectations, the father in the parable gave the inheritance to his son, which brought shame and embarrassment to his family before the community. Jesus is certainly not using an oriental patriarch as the model for God here. Here he has broken the rules, so to speak, of Middle Eastern patriarchy. Instead, "Jesus elevates the figure of father beyond its human limitations and reshapes it for use as a model for God."[43]

Evangelical deconstructionist theologian, B. Keith Putt, suggests that Jesus himself emulated deconstructive thought.

Through extravagance and the metaphorical twist, Jesus deconstructed the systems of thought prevalent in first-century Israel in order to reorient those structures. If structures are allowed to ossify, they become idols, closed systems that are apothesized and defended as holy objects.[44]

Although I would say it is obviously anachronistic to claim that Jesus used "deconstruction" in his use of parables, I am sympathetic with Putt's correlation of Jesus' iconoclasm with respect to radical postmodern concerns.

My purpose has not been to diverge from an examination of the theme of suffering in Acts. I am simply suggesting that the parable of the prodigal stages an apologetic theology of gracious embrace and forgiveness extended by the Christian community

---

41 Miroslav Volf, "The Clumsy Embrace: Interview by Kevin D. Miller," *Christianity Today* (October 26, 1998): 66. See also Miroslav Volf, *Exclusion and Embrace: A Theological Exploration of Identity, Otherness, and Reconciliation* (Nashville: Abingdon, 1996).

42 Kenneth E. Bailey, "The Pursuing Father: What We Need to Know About This Often Misunderstood Middle Eastern Parable," *Christianity Today* (October 26 1998): 34.

43 Ibid.: 34, 35.

44 B. Keith Putt, "The Constructive Possibilities of Imagination as Prolegomena to Philosophy of Religion" (Ph.D. diss., Southwestern Baptist Theological Seminary, 1985), p. 210 as quoted in Millard J. Erickson, *Postmodernizing the Faith* (Grand Rapids: Baker, 1998), pp. 132–3.

to its oppressors as also seen in the Acts narrative. This is an example of the kind of awareness that deconstructionist thought may stimulate for further apologetic dialogue. I am not advocating an overall endorsement of deconstructionism but I am suggesting that many of the basic concerns expressed by the deconstructionist may be addressed by examining the nature and development of the early Christian community as expressed in the teachings of Jesus and seen throughout the book of Acts.

John Caputo claims that deconstruction cultivates "special skills" to help awaken us to the demands of the other, and provides "provocative implications for theological reflection." This is something which is lost, Caputo adds, through hasty and unsubstantiated attacks on Derrida by the Anglo-American "analytic" philosophical establishment which makes "philosophy tedious and culturally irrelevant."[45] Indeed Caputo is correct in stating that Derrida's deconstructionism has been widely misunderstood. Many do feel threatened by a style of thinking which is not their own, or that of the academic "establishment" by which they have been trained or are a part of. But can deconstruction really awaken us to the demands of the other—the oppressed, the suffering, the marginalized? I believe it can. As Bailey mentioned with regard to the often-misunderstood parable of the prodigal, it may awaken us to our prejudices and misconceptions which have become false "truths" for us in the past. It may help us identify what it is we have "left out." As Andrew Gustafson aptly notes:

> All religious conceptions leave something out. Some leave out more than others, certainly, but none are perfect—and we know this formally. Deconstruction continually examines our conceptual presuppositions and attempts to shake up old patterns of thought in hopes that hidden remainders will become uncovered. Deconstruction is about trying to remember what we usually forget, the "other" that is "out." And there is always something we leave out.[46]

Deconstruction does not define the metanarrative of the suffering, marginalized, Christian community as developed in the book of Acts. However, it certainly helps re-sensitize us to the realities of that community and challenge us to live in view of that non-totalizing metanarrative today. It helps us remember that Christian love does not remain closed to its own community. It is only when our "comfortable dwelling" begins to be "deconstructed" that we can begin to see and feel the "claims of the other upon our lives."[47]

---

45 John D. Caputo, *The Prayers and Tears of Jacques Derrida: Religion Without Religion* (Bloomington & Indianapolis: Indiana University Press, 1997), pp. 15, 16.

46 Andrew Gustafson, "Apologetically Listening to Derrida," *Philosophia Christi* 20/2 (1997): 25.

47 Norman Wirzba, "Love's Reason: From Heideggerian Care to Christian Charity," in *Postmodern Philosophy and Christian Thought*, ed. Merold Westphal (Bloomington: Indiana University Press, 1999), p. 261.

Paul at Athens (Acts 17: 16-34)

Arrival at Athens

When Paul arrived in Athens in A.D. 49 or 50, it was still a great intellectual and cultural center under Roman rule. The text tells us that Paul was greatly perturbed (παρωξύνετο, vs. 16) by the preponderance of idols there. In fact, this is the same word which occurs in the Septuagint (Deut. 9:18; Ps. 106:29; Is. 65:3) depicting the Lord being provoked to anger over the idolatry of his people.[48] Despite Paul's apparent deep provocation, however, he does not lash out in angry outbursts of judgment and condemnation. Instead, he begins to dialogue in the synagogue and the marketplace. He put himself in the hub of philosophical discussion. As Luke tells us: "All the Athenians and the foreigners who lived there spent their time doing nothing but talking about and listening to the latest ideas" (Acts 17:21). After Paul began "preaching the good news about Jesus and the resurrection" (vs. 18) he was verbally harassed by Stoic and Epicurean philosophers. But, Paul had an opportunity to defend his perspectives at the renowned Areopagus. I will not here expound on whether the "Areopagus" referred simply to "Mars Hill," to the judicial council of Athens, or was perhaps a general term referring to both. However, it does not seem apparent from the text that Paul was formally arrested. Instead it simply seems that Paul was "invited to expound his teaching before the body which was responsible to decide whether it contravened public weal or not."[49]

Paul's Speech

When Paul began his speech he started by respectfully recognizing the religious endeavors of the Athenians: "I see that in every way you are very religious" (vs. 22). Paul made this statement with sincerity, graciousness, tact, and coherence, not with empty flattery.[50] Paul's genuine courtesy should not be confused with endorsement in any sense. He used this conversational note of commendation as a contact point to seek some common ground with the Athenians. He then addressed the meaning of the "unknown God" (vs. 23) and submitted that this is none other than the Christian God, the Creator and Sustainer of the universe. Paul next appeals to common human limitations with respect to this God. He does not live in any humanly fabricated structure, nor is He in any way dependent upon humans. He created and established all orders of things pertaining to human life and existence. He therefore cannot be construed as some imposition of power by one dominant cultural group upon another. This God "is not Middle Eastern or Greek, Jew or Gentile, but the God of all

---

48 See Ned B. Stonehouse, *Paul Before the Areopagus* (Grand Rapids: Eerdmans, 1957), p. 6.

49 F.F. Bruce, *First Century Faith* (Leicester: InterVarsity, 1977), p. 40.

50 Larkin, *Acts*, p. 255.

nations."[51] As D.A. Carson comments: "Thus not only is there no room for racism or elitist tribalism, but one of the entailments of monotheism is that if there is one God he must in some sense be God of all, whether acknowledged or not."[52]

Not only is this God the one God of all, He is also near to all. To support his claims, Paul quoted from two Greek poets. The first is from Epimenides the Cretan, "For in him we live and move and have our being" (vs. 28). The original context of this quote is Epimenides denouncing his fellow Cretans for their impious claim to have discovered the tomb of Zeus on Crete.[53] Paul in a sense, "plunders the Egyptians" by using this quote in correspondence to his previous comment expressing the immanence of the Christian God. Paul then continues with a second quotation from a student of Zeno, the Cilecian poet Aratus, "We are his offspring" (vs. 28b). The original quotation, influenced by Stoicism, also refers to Zeus.[54] Since human beings are contingent beings, created by God, they are His "offspring." Certainly Paul did not wish equate Zeus with the Christian God. Richard N. Longenecker summarizes this well:

> By such maxims, Paul is not suggesting that God is to be thought of in terms of the Zeus of Greek polytheism or Stoic pantheism. He is rather arguing that the poets his hearers recognize as authorities have to some extent corroborated his message. In his search for a measure of common ground with his hearers, he is, so to speak, disinfecting and rebaptizing the poets' words for his own purposes. Quoting Greek poets in support of his teaching sharpened his message. But despite its form, Paul's address was thoroughly biblical and Christian in its content.[55]

Paul's Apologetic Connection Through Listening and Dialogue

It is clear in Paul's continued kerygmatic proclamation in this passage that he does not "forsake Biblical ground to meet the Epicureans and Stoics on philosophical turf."[56] But this does demonstrate Paul's willingness to dialogue and engage those he differed with. It also demonstrates that Paul effectively "listened" to those with contrary philosophical perspectives by being aware of their writings. According to D.A. Hayes, if one knows the minor poets of literature and is able to make offhanded quotations from them, this one is also likely to know the major poets of the same literature:

> If he read Menander, he would read Euripides. If he read Epimenides, he would read Aristophanes. If he read Aratus, he would read Aeschylus.... The aptness of these quotations to the subject in hand would seem to prove that they are far from being

51 Rhodes, *Where Nations Meet*, p. 63.

52 Carson, *The Gagging of God*, p. 500.

53 Marilyn McCord Adams, "Philosophy and the Bible," *Faith and Philosophy* 9/2 (1992): 137.

54 Ibid., p. 138.

55 Longenecker, *The Acts of the Apostles*, p. 476.

56 Adams, "Philosophy and the Bible," 142, 143.

accidental acquisitions on the part of Paul, and would rather evidence a wide acquaintance with the literature from which they so aptly are chosen.[57]

Yet Paul, in a certain sense of the term, "deconstructs" and cleanses these quotations of their pantheistic contexts and applies them to his establishment of common ground with the Athenian philosophers. As Marilyn McCord Adams argues: "It is precisely because the lines of the sermon are polyvalent, admitting as they do of multiple readings, that the speech affords any possibility of apologetic success."[58] Paul, in using these quotations and acknowledging common ground, demonstrated humility and the keen ability to listen to his host culture.[59] Although not referring to Paul at Athens, John Howard Yoder's comments are still applicable to the apologetic challenge exemplified by Paul:

> The evangelical strategy does not accept being walled into a ghetto by the outside world. Not only does it accept the language of the environs: it seizes it, expropriates it, and uses it to say things that could previously not have been said in its prior language; nor could they have been said by anyone else using the wider world's language. It proclaims the God of Abraham as no less the God of the philosophers; it does so not by filtering abrahamic language through philosophical funnels, but by pre-empting the philosophers' language in order to say with it things they had thought could not be said. It refuses to be submitted for validation to the canons of intelligibility or credibility that were in force before it happened.[60]

Often, we perceive the Athenian address as simply "Paul vs. the philosophers." However, Paul's address also had a conciliatory tone. As Adams suggests, Paul appealed to his audience to learn from one another and come to some agreement on the issues he was raising. As she observes:

> He wants the Stoics, with their refined conception of God, to receive instruction from their Epicurean colleagues regarding the evils of popular religion, presupposing as it does the god can be influenced by the "bribes" of incense and sacrifices (17:24–25). Yet, in their turn, the Epicureans should take a page from the Stoics as well as from popular religion, and withdraw their mistaken notion that the gods are remote, utterly uninvolved in our world, whether for good or ill.[61]

---

57 D. A. Hayes, *Paul and His Epistles* (New York: The Methodist Book Concern, 1915), p. 100. This, I believe shows the subtle academic profundity of Paul's quotations. Hayes' point simply shows that Paul could have quoted the "great" poets as well—but he was able to aptly quote even minor poets to support his point.

58 Adams, "Philosophy and the Bible," 144. On this she cites C.F. Barrett, "Paul's Speech on the Areopagus," in M.E. Glasweel and E.W. Fashole-Luke, *New Testament Christianity for Africa and the World: Essays in Honour of Hamy Sawyer* (London: SPCK), pp. 72–3.

59 John Howard Yoder, "On Not Being Ashamed Of The Gospel: Particularity, Pluralism, and Validation," *Faith and Philosophy* 9/3 (1992): 285.

60 Ibid., p. 296.

61 Adams, "Philosophy and the Bible," 144–5.

Interestingly, Paul is not simply promotiong dialogue with other philosophies, but also creating elements for further dialogue even among the groups he was in dialogue with.

Apologetic Reflections in View of Deconstructionist Concerns

Paul's apologetic approach of listening and conciliatory dialogue in Acts 17 is an important example for my development of postmodern deconstructive sensitivities. Paul demonstrated respect for the Athenians and took their religion with the utmost sincerity.[62] He affirmed their shared humanity, while also clearly acknowledging diversity.[63] Yet, Paul did not back down on his communication of the grand narrative of the gospel and the resurrection of Jesus. He did not do so out of arrogance or the desire to oppress others, but he communicated the gospel in love, "seeking to extend the Good News of salvation to all who suffer under the tyranny of sin."[64]

Again, I am affirming an apologetic approach of dialogue in view of the concerns expressed by postmodern deconstructive theology. Paul's example may be used as both a model of this strategy and a springboard for discussion and engagement with postmodern deconstructive masters of suspicion today. Although the pluralistic world that Paul was addressing is different from the pluralistic world of today, there are similarities that are worthy of application and dialogue as I consider the relevancy of this passage to my apologetic task. Paul was preaching good news to the Epicureans and the Stoics who were simply living under the whims of chance and fate. Paul was proclaiming the reality of a gracious, forgiving, Creator who sustained all. For moderns who view the universe as a series of impersonal forces this is good news as well. For the postmodern, "this gracious, personal God breaks the bonds of pantheistic "karma."[65]

Douglas Groothuis recognizes that Paul consistently engages in dialogue with unbelievers throughout the book of Acts. Yet, ironically in my estimation, Groothuis believes it would have been "intellectually suicidal and counterproductive" if Paul had used the strategies put forward by postmodernists of today.[66] We should not blindly endorse some extreme subjectivistic patterns of radical postmodernism.

---

62 Although in recent decades Paul is still accused of being too particularistic, as Miroslav Volf notes. Volf effectively summarizes and responds to this criticism: "[Paul's] egalitarianism stops at the boundary of Christian faith. He is unduly privileging the Christian way of salvation and thereby denying radical equality. The trouble with this objection is that so far no persuasive alternative to overcome particularism has been proposed. No one has shown how one can intelligently hold to a nonparticularist universalism. As it happens, every claim to universality must be made from a particular perspective." Volf, *Exclusion and Embrace*, p. 46.

63 See Hiebert, *Missiological Implications*, p. 114 for a discussion along these lines regarding the value of a critical realist perspective in responding to other relgions.

64 Hiebert, *Missiological Implications*, p. 115.

65 Larkin, *Acts*, p. 257.

66 Groothuis, *Truth Decay*, p. 179.

But in my estimation, Groothuis too hastily labels all postmodernist thought as theologically pernicious. Moderate postmodernist thought which calls for dialogue and engagement with the other, multicultural respect, and the acknowledgement of culturally conditioned presuppositions are undeniably positive "strategies" for apologetics. Paul "plundered" the Athenians without violating them. He engaged them through dialogue and demonstrated respect. These are the ideals I desire to propose and emulate in the next chapter.

Chapter 11

Apologetic Engagement and Dialogue

It should be clear to the reader at this juncture that a "progressive" evangelical position holds no interest in the hegemony of fundamentalist traditionalism. Paul Lakeland's *Postmodernity: Christian Identity in a Fragmented Age* concedes that both evangelicals and liberals alike acknowledge the "pluriformity" of postmodernism. But, according to Lakeland, "the former encounters the otherness of postmodernity as challenge to be overcome, while the latter finds it a fact to celebrate."[1] In my estimation, Lakeland has overstated theological liberalism's joyful acceptance of postmodernism, due to close ties of theological liberalism to modernism and the ideals of the Enlightenment project.[2] I believe he also understates and over-simplifies the "evangelical" position by failing to recognize the pluriformity of evangelicalism today. As I have noted in a previous chapter, some evangelicals would not see postmodernism as something to be overcome, but something to be critically appropriated. I am advocating, for example, a progressive evangelical apologetic process which desires genuine conversational engagement with postmodern deconstructive tendencies in theological thought. I have obviously not concurred with all deconstructive agendas; nevertheless, I do believe active dialogue with such views can offer tremendous possibilities for evangelical apologetic methodological renewal. As D.A. Carson rightly points out, if as Christians we acknowledge that "the new hermeneutic, deconstruction, and postmodernity say important and true things" we will "gain a hearing among some who would otherwise shut us out."[3]

I agree with Kevin Vanhoozer who argues that Christians should engage the "new" deconstructive masters of suspicion because as Christians we are obliged to be intellectually honest and charitable to other positions. It is important to assume a learning posture to those we may disagree with. Additionally, deconstructive tendencies have not only influenced academic thought, the interdisciplinary effects of postmodernity have spurred a cultural crisis which it is essential to grapple with

---

1   Paul Lakeland, *Postmodernity: Christian Identity in a Fragmented Age* (Minneapolis: Fortress, 1997), p. 112.

2   Once again, I am not saying that modernism and postmodernism are necessarily always opposed or contradictory. As J. Wentzel van Huyssteen reminds us, "postmodern thought is undoubtedly part of the modern, and not only modern thought coming to its end." J. Wentzel van Huyssteen, *Essays in Postfoundationalist Theology* (Grand Rapids: Eerdmans, 1997), p. 278. I am simply saying that it appears that Lakeland has overstated and/or generalized the case when he speaks of liberalism's enthusiastic reception of postmodernism.

3   D.A. Carson, *The Gagging of God: Christianity Confronts Pluralism* (Grand Rapids: Zondervan, 1996), p. 102.

for effective ministry in this age.[4] With these purposes in mind, I wish to further develop an "open dialogue" approach to an apologetic process in response to postmodern deconstructive theological concerns. I will first suggest the value of active engagement and dialogue in this regard; and second, I will espouse the importance of critical appropriation of deconstructionist concerns.

Engaging and Listening to Deconstructive "Makers" of Theology

The "Prophetic" Voice of Atheism

Before scholars were even concerned with the implications of postmodernism and deconstructionism for theological thought, neo-evangelical theologian Bernard Ramm[5] argued in favor of an evangelical engagement with atheistic thinkers in *The Devil, Seven Wormwoods, and God* (1977). Ramm claimed that theological inquiry demands that "we give the devil his due." Since God is sovereign over all, Ramm argued, he can use anybody "including Wormwoods and the devil's hacks, to say something in the furtherance of the truth and for the better understanding of the truth."[6] It seems evident from his use of such derogatory vocabulary as "the devil's hacks" that he was not attempting to build conversational bridges with such atheistic thinkers or their followers. His audience was clearly fellow evangelicals. Nevertheless, his effort demonstrated a desire to facilitate a change from the separatist thinking often characteristic of evangelical thought, and did make some attempt at "fence–mending" with regard to non-evangelical and atheist thinkers as well.[7] Lest we forget that God communicated truth through Balaam's donkey, and in some manner as well through the supposed apparition of Samuel to Saul with the medium at Endor; God can use anybody (or any thing?) to communicate his messages![8]

---

4   Kevin J. Vanhoozer, *Is There a Meaning in This Text?* (Grand Rapids: Zondervan, 1998), p. 174.

5   Ramm is commonly considered "neo-evangelical" since his theological posture moved toward conversation *with* rather than isolation *from* modern cultural thought. Neo-evangelicalism emerged in the mid-twentieth century as a reaction to the separatism characteristic of evangelical fundamentalism. See Gary Dorrien, *The Remaking of Evangelical Theology* (Louisville: Westminster John Knox, 1998), pp. 123–9; and Stanley J. Grenz, *Renewing the Center* (Grand Rapids: Baker, 2000), pp. 85–6.

6   Bernard Ramm, *The Devil, Seven Wormwoods, and God* (Waco: Word Books, 1977), p. 23.

7   Ibid., pp. 15, 23.

8   In fact, as Gerald McDermott points out: Balaam himself "spoke the truth about the future of Israel despite his becoming a symbol of avarice and idolatry." Gerald R. McDermott, *Can Evangelicals Learn From World Religions?: Jesus, Revelation and Religious Traditions* (Downers Grove: InterVarsity, 2000), p. 83. Whatever we make of the troublesome passage of the medium of Endor in 1 Sam. 28, we can certainly agree that despite the prohibition against consulting mediums and spiritists, some degree of prophetic message was conveyed through

But it is my desire to move a step beyond Ramm. I desire to begin such "fence–mending" through a constructive apologetic dialogue which precludes derisive, categorical labeling. My presupposition, like that of Ramm's, is that God is sovereign and he can communicate through whomever he chooses. Apologetic dialogue and engagement may both start and keep the conversation going. On the other hand, ascribing labels prior to conversational engagement suppresses and even closes off dialogue.

I submit that Merold Westphal's proposals on the religious appropriation of the masters of suspicion (Marx, Nietzsche, Freud) are quite helpful in this regard. Westphal boldly suggests that we can read the atheistic masters of suspicion as a "Lenten" spiritual exercise for both "self–examination" and "sanctification."[9] However, Westphal contends that the atheism which is primarily represented in these "masters" is not the evidential atheism typical of Anglo-American thought, but an atheism "of suspicion." Evidential atheism is concerned with the lack of evidence necessary to postulate the existence of God; whereas, an atheism of suspicion is primarily concerned with uncovering the spurious motives and self-interests which lie behind belief in God. Westphal submits that scornful refutation of the masters of suspicion usually stems from the failure to effectively distinguish between these two types of atheism.[10] I am suggesting the application of this same line of thought to the postmodern deconstructive "makers" of theology in order to generate further apologetic dialogue. In my view, it is necessary to humbly take the concerns expressed by postmodern deconstructive theology seriously. In doing this, it may awaken us out of our "atheistically religious" dogmatic slumbers.[11] It is this type of "prophetic

---

Saul's consultation with the medium and with what Saul at least believed was an apparition of Samuel.

9   Merold Westphal, *Suspicion and Faith* (New York: Fordham University Press, 1998), pp. 9–10. In a later work, Westphal promotes this strategy again with major postmodern philosophers. See his *Overcoming Onto-Theology: Toward a Postmodern Christian Faith* (New York: Fordham University Press, 2001), especially note p. xi.

10   Westphal, *Suspicion and Faith*, pp. 12–16. A similar distinction is made by Garrett Green in his book, *Imagining God*. Westphal's "atheism of suspicion" would be akin to what Green calls the "atheism of the imagination." Likewise, Westphal's "evidential atheism" is what Green describes as "skeptical atheism." Green submits that "the skeptical atheist characteristically *refutes* religion, while the imaginative atheist is more likely to *reinterpret* it." Garrett Green, *Imagining God: Theology and the Religious Imagination* (San Francisco: Harper and Row, 1989), p. 25.

11   By "atheistically religious," I am referring to the false piety and hypocrisy characteristic of the Christianity which deconstructive theology is confronting. Westphal provides an application of this to the same critique posed by the masters of suspicion: "The God of the Bible is conspicuously on the side of the poor and oppressed. When we are not on their side and when we make it clear by the juxtaposition of our lives and our worship that we attribute the same indifference (or worse) to God, we also make it clear that our worship is directed to some other god." Westphal, *Suspicion and Faith*, p. 208.

consciousness" that, Westphal submits, can "lead to the collapse of irreligion posing as religion, creating a space wherein true faith might flourish."[12]

Andrew Gustafson expresses a similar sentiment when he submits that Derrida, as with Kierkegaard before him, "practices the art of philosophy as prophecy, pointing out the problems, difficulties and strange predicaments which we face in communicating, thinking, reading and writing."[13] The prophet's task, Gustafson claims, is primarily to remind people of what they have a tendency to forget. In reminding us of our inadequacies and ongoing problems, Derrida writes in a prophetic mode. He is a "philosopher sage who draws us into a mode of being which pays special attention to our language and thinking."[14] I concur with Gustafson's view as it pertains to theological reflection. I am suggesting that the voices of deconstructive thought are prophetic where they "draw us into a mode of being" which reminds us of our *religious* inadequacies, and challenge us to pay special attention not only to our language and thinking as Gustafson suggests, but also to reflect on any activities or actions which may suppress and/or oppress the other.

However, acknowledging this "prophetic voice" of deconstructive atheism does not mean that I would suspend the practice of critical response and correction altogether. Atheistic suspicion may discredit the theistic believer and the church community—even if the theists views are, themselves, true.[15] So, while atheistic suspicion provides a service by revealing the duplicity of certain beliefs and/or the persons holding such beliefs, it provides a disservice if it leads to the denial of any notion of truth in the content of those beliefs simply because of duplicitous motives. But timing is critical. If the Christian responds with adamant, critical refutation and neglects to understand the use of atheistic suspicion, the possibility of apologetic dialogue may be lost.

Applied to the subject at hand, I am suggesting that it is essential to acknowledge and, when appropriate, to legitimize the concerns of the postmodern deconstructive masters of suspicion. Then we should reflect on these concerns with respect to our own religious hypocrisies through a process of critical reflection. When needing to express disagreement, it should be expressed through dialogue and interactive questions, instead of monological diatribes. Westphal reminds us of Jesus' teaching to us, lest we become hypocrites, to take care of the speck in our neighbor's eye after removing the logs of "self deception" in our own pseudo-pious ways. If we do this, then perhaps "there will no longer be the need to do so, our lives having already refuted them more effectively than our arguments ever could."[16] In my estimation, if we apply this apologetic process, acknowledging a "prophetic" voice to deconstructive atheism, it will greatly aid us in forming a theology, which as

---

12 Ibid., p. 119. Cf. also Ibid., p. 284.

13 Andrew Gustafson, "Apologetically Listening to Derrida," *Philosophia Christi* 20/2 (1997): 27.

14 Ibid., p. 27.

15 See Westphal, *Suspicion and Faith*, p. 13.

16 Ibid., pp. 60, 17.

Anthony Thiselton submits, "seeks to recover elements of the authentic and the genuine from among the chaff of self-interest, manipulation, and power–claims."[17]

With an apologetic of suspicion, however, also comes certain dangers. If such notions of suspicion do not operate within some framework of Christian faith, then suspicion may continue ad infinitum, eliminating any prospect of religious insight, hope, or commitment to our lives. In a paper on "The Dialectics of Trust and Suspicion," Patricia A. Sayre wisely notes: "Without religion, suspicion gains the upper hand; our doubts can never be stilled, and our preoccupation with our own sinfulness becomes in effect a rejection of redemption."[18] Westphal as well points out that a degenerative suspicion without any Christian faith will result in a reductionistic cynicism where nothing remains except "self-interest, self-righteousness, and self-deception," hence, making the cure for such self-deception "as deadly as the disease."[19]

The Importance of Dialogue

As I have previously contended, the art of dialogue with both texts and persons is essential for a postmodern deconstructive apologetic. I noted in the last chapter how a dialogical process was modeled by the Apostle Paul in Acts 17. Paul's conversation with the Stoic and Epicurean philosophers was personal, and he clearly demonstrated through his appropriation of philosophical quotations his previous engagement with non-Christian philosophical texts.

Likewise, I am proposing an interactionist apologetic methodology or an "open-dialogical" apologetic which includes what may be called "apologetic listening."[20] We must be willing to carefully listen to and read the concerns and ideas of postmodern deconstructive thought, in order to be both academically responsible and charitable. By doing this, "the Evangelical Philosopher can be a witness for Christ in a way which speaks much better for Christ than spreading philosophical hearsay and gossip."[21] Good apologetic listening, however, assumes time for sustained reading and reflection. To apply apologetic listening to the field of postmodern deconstructive theology requires rigorous thinking, intellectual humility, and cultural sensitivity. It

---

17 Anthony C. Thiselton, *Interpreting God and the Postmodern Self* (Edinburgh: T&T Clark, 1995), p. 16.

18 Patricia A. Sayre, "The Dialectics of Trust and Suspicion," *Faith and Philosophy* 10/4 (1993): 581. See also Westphal, *Suspicion and Faith*, pp. 284–8.

19 Westphal, *Suspicion and Faith*, pp. 286, 284.

20 I am indebted to Gustafson, "Apologetically Listening to Derrida," 15–42, for the idea of the term, "apologetic listening." I also credit David K. Clark's *Dialogical Apologetics: A Person-Centered Approach to Christian Defense* (Grand Rapids: Baker, 1993), for the notion of "dialogical" as applied to apologetics. Cf. this notion of "apologetic listening" to the "hearing," "scrutinizing" and "responding" put forward in Stanley J. Grenz and John R. Franke, *Beyond Foundationalism: Shaping Theology in a Postmodern Context* (Louisville: Westminster John Knox Press, 2001), pp. 159–60.

21 Gustafson, "Apologetically Listening to Derrida," p. 17.

calls for genuine pastoral care to listen to the problems of others, even those defiantly stated at times. It requires responding with insight to others at a personal level as they struggle with the ideas of Christian faith. These are the minimum necessary ingredients for effective apologetics in view of deconstructive concerns. An effective "apologetic listening" methodology in this regard, requires a personal wrestling with the issues brought forward by deconstructionists we have examined.[22]

Merold Westphal, in his book *God, Guilt and Death*, elucidates the art of good academic listening:

> If I am a good listener, I don't interrupt the other nor plan my own next speech while pretending to be listening. I try to hear what is said, but I listen just as hard for what is not said and for what is said between the lines. I am not in a hurry, for there is not pre-appointed destination for the conversation. There is no need to get there, for we are already here; and in this present I am able to be fully present to the one who speaks. The speaker is not an object to be categorized or manipulated, but a subject whose life situation is enough like my own that I can understand it in spite of the differences between us. If I am a good listener, what we have in common will seem more important that what we have in conflict.[23]

I will not assess the merits of whether one can be "fully present," as Westphal submits, in the Derridean sense. However, it is my desire to heartily affirm Westphal's injunction to us on the nature of good listening, especially in view of postmodern deconstructive concerns. In fact, if we apply Westphal's thought here, we would have a deconstructive listening to deconstructive theology itself. The art of listening to the unsaid and concentrating on what is said "between the lines," is the art of deconstruction applied to listening behavior. I have attempted, in this book, a proposal for apologetic listening while practicing apologetical listening. I have sought to both advocate *and* practice a methodology that approaches the topic of deconstructive postmodern theology with deconstructive postmodern sensitivities and sympathies.

Yet I am not simply espousing the practice of listening without dialogue. Instead, I am advocating an "interactionist" apologetic. Interaction assumes dialogue, and dialogue involves a mutual exchange—a two-way conversation. The word "dialogue," unfortunately, has fallen on ambiguous ground. Theologian David K. Clark notes that we live in an age where "dialogue" is chic and this word, like "postmodernism" is overused and often ground into meaninglessness. Dialogue, as I am using the term, refers to mutual interactive communication between individuals or groups, is practiced either verbally or in writing, is academic or casual, and assumes mutual respect of persons. Additionally, the dialogue partners (individually and/or collectively) must respectfully acknowledge their differences (cultural, social,

---

22 See Alister McGrath, *Intellectuals Don't Need God & Other Modern Myths* (Grand Rapids: Zondervan, 1993), p. 191.

23 Merold Westphal, *God, Guilt and Death: An Existential Phenomenology of Religion* (Bloomington: Indiana University Press, 1984), p. 12.

religious, etc.) and limitations as well as demonstrate a genuine desire to learn from the other.[24] Apologetic interactionism, then, will help us to become aware of our own cultural biases to suppress certain themes or impose other themes onto our Christian theological expressions.[25]

In his work *Dialogical Apologetics*, David K. Clark advances a cumulative case apologetic through a dialogical methodology. Clark espouses the "Classical Method" to present a cumulative case for Christianity by means of his dialogical apologetic process. This method begins with natural theology to establish theism, then uses evidences and arguments to establish specific truths of Christianity.[26] Although I differ from Clark in his espousal of the necessity to make a cumulative case, I enthusiastically support his articulation of the purpose of a dialogue-based, person-centered methodology. Clark rightly asserts that a dialogical apologetic is oriented toward the service of the other. Clark says:

> *Dialogical* here means, not just conversation with individuals, but audience sensitivity, a trait that can characterize writing and public speaking as well. It is *person-centered* because it stresses the critical personal dynamic of these encounters. Apologetics happens in dialogue, meetings of real people who approach each other with loads of baggage. This luggage—intellectual, attitudinal, cultural, and emotional—is complex and cannot be ignored.[27]

An interactionist apologetic will engage the thinking of the postmodern deconstructive thinker with an orientation to serve and understand, not dominate and control. It does not seek to manipulate the agenda of the conversation typical of "monological proclamation."[28] This takes careful cooperation and the skillful art of asking questions of the other which do not seek to threaten, and responding to the questions of the other without being threatened oneself. Westphal submits that these questions may be akin to those asked by an attorney during cross examination, "but they will not be asked in a prosecuting manner"—without issuing manifestos or making accusations. "They will rather be asked as a confessor or therapist asks them. For the purpose is not to win the case but to free understanding from self-deception."[29]

---

24 See Clark, *Dialogical Apologetics*, p. 117.

25 See Gary Dorrien, *The Word as True Myth: Interpreting Modern Theology* (Louisville: Westminster John Knox Press, 1997), pp. 206–7. Although Dorrien is more specifically referring to interactionist hermeneutical theories, and not to my notion of interactionist apologetics, I find his insights helpful and applicable.

26 This should be distinguished from the "Cumulative Case Method" as presented in Steven B. Cowan (ed.), *Five Views on Apologetics* (Grand Rapids: Zondervan, 2000). Where the Classical method would use more formal argumentation from the establishment of theism to particular Christian truth claims, the Cumulative Case method advances a mosaic of informal arguments the whole of which, it is said, provides a better comprehensive explanation of life than its alternative hypotheses. See Cowan, *Five Views*, pp. 15–16, 17–18.

27 Clark, *Dialogical Apologetics*, p. 112.

28 Ibid., pp. 116–17.

29 Westphal, *God, Guilt and Death*, p. 12.

For Clark, a dialogical apologetic is used to build a cumulative case for Christianity. What I am suggesting, however, is an ongoing dialogical–interactionist apologetic that opens up conversation in order to remove barriers of dominance and suppression so that Christianity may be seen by the other as a genuine life option. This is an apologetic that seeks to learn from the non–believer, opening up conversational bridges to communicate the message of the Christian gospel. I certainly acknowledge the value of presenting a "case" for Christianity through compassionate dialogue, gracious attitudes, and benevolent actions, both in academic writing and verbal exchange. At times, historical evidences and philosophical arguments may be presented in the context of certain academic dialogues, typical of classical apologetics. Yet, in my model, I would not insist on the *necessity* of such evidences and arguments to affirm a cumulative case for Christianity.

"Plundering the Egyptians": A Critical Appropriation of Deconstructionist Concerns

The Non–Violent Nature of "Plundering"

The interactionist apologetic engagement I am advocating is not simply lending a compassionate, listening ear to the intellectual troubles of those who hold perspectives different to my own. Nor is it simply dialogue with only a view toward understanding the other. This is certainly a part of it, but not all of it. Rather, what I am suggesting is a critical appropriation of deconstructive *concerns*. It is not only listening to the prophetic voice of atheism, it is also, in a sense, "plundering" its goods, developing its goods, and redistributing its goods in order to glean further apologetic insights for our current intellectual climate. I must understandably use extreme caution with this metaphor. "Plundering" in most contexts, connotes violence toward the other. Can I then avoid the violence of this metaphor and continue to use it?

I am proposing a notion of "plundering" which is an adaptation of that developed by Augustine in his *On Christian Doctrine* (*De Doctrina Christiana*) circa 397:

> Moreover, if those who are called philosophers, and especially the Platonists, have said aught that is true and in harmony with our faith, we are not only not to shrink from it, but to claim it for our own use from those who have unlawful possession of it. For, as the Egyptians had not only the idols and heavy burdens which the people of Israel hated and fled from, but also vessels and ornaments of gold and silver, and garments which the same people when going out of Egypt appropriated to themselves, designing them for a better use, not doing this on their own authority, but by the command of God, the Egyptians themselves, in their ignorance, providing them with things which they themselves were not making a good use of ....[30]

---

30 Augustine, *On Christian Doctrine*, Book II, Chapter 40. 60. Nicene and Post-Nicene Fathers: First Series, ed. Philip Schaff (Peabody: Hendrickson, 1994), p. 554.

These ill-used "things," for Augustine, included "liberal instruction," some "excellent precepts of morality," and even some truths pertaining to the worship of God.[31] However, Augustine strongly insists that this plundering follow a separation in spirit "from the miserable fellowship of these men" who are plundered.

I offer a modification of Augustine's model for our efforts at facilitating a progressive evangelical interactionist apologetic. My notion of "plundering" assumes that dialogue and engagement has, in some sense, already taken place. Is this stretching the context of the metaphor too far? I believe not. When we consider the original context of the metaphor as given in both Exodus 3:22 and 12:36, one notices that the "plundering" of the Egyptians occurred not in the context of violent burglary, but in the context of "favorable disposition:"

> Exod. 3:22 Every woman is to ask her neighbor and any woman living in her house for articles of silver and gold and for clothing, which you will put on your sons and daughters. And so you will plunder the Egyptians."

And in verse 12:36:

> The LORD had made the Egyptians favorably disposed toward the people, and they gave them what they asked for; so they plundered the Egyptians.

This "plundering," in my estimation, seemed to imply at least some previous dialogue and relationship. Yet, I do not deny Augustine's emphasis on the Israelites' "separation in spirit" from their oppressors even before the commencement of the physical Exodus. As Alister McGrath comments on Augustine's passage: "Israel was oppressed while in Egypt; on escaping, the people left behind those burdens, yet carried off the treasures of their former oppressors."[32] Nonetheless, the text remains clear that the Israelites asked for favors and the Egyptians favorably granted them. Although the text in Exodus 12:36 shows that the LORD was, in some fashion, instrumental in the cause of this favorable disposition, it does not negate, at a proximate causal level, that the Egyptians generously gave with willing hearts. Without pushing the metaphor too far, I am suggesting "plundering" from postmodern deconstructive theological thought, in the context of dialogue, with some "favorable disposition" as well.

Additionally, Augustine's passage implied a forthright rejection of the "dross" and the safekeeping of the "silver" in non-Christian philosophical thought. I certainly would affirm the value of applying what is true and useful from the "prophetic voice" of deconstructionist theology. Yet, it is my desire to take a step beyond this. I wish to read between the lines of the "dross"—that which is perceived to be false, irreligious, and even perhaps threatening in postmodern deconstructive theology—in

---

31 Ibid.

32 Alister McGrath, *Historical Theology* (Oxford and Malden, Mass.: Blackwell, 1998), p. 92.

order to seek to identify the underlying concerns of its authors.[33] With this proposed methodology, then, it is my desire to sympathetically acknowledge, interact with, and respond to these deep-seated concerns.

Of course, this "plundering" of non-Christian thought occurs prior to Augustine. For example, in a previous chapter I examined Paul's "plundering" of the Greek poets, Epimenides and Aratus, at the Areopagus meeting in Acts chapter 17. Gerald McDermott's work, *Can Evangelicals Learn From World Religions?*, points out that such "plundering" continued through church history following Augustine as well. McDermott submits that Augustine used the resources of Neo–Platonism, Aquinas drew from Aristotle, Calvin made use of Renaissance humanism with an "admixture of (classical) pagan thinking," and Barth even recontextualized Martin Buber's notion of the "I and Thou."[34] A more contemporary example I will consider in the next chapter is C.S. Lewis's *Till We Have Faces*—a "Christian" reworking of the classical myth of Apuleius, "Cupid and Psyche."[35] McDermott's thesis is that if Christians down through the centuries have learned from those outside of their particular Christian perspectives in order to understand God's Word, then we can also learn, through critical appropriation, from religions such as Buddhism, Daoism, Confucianism, and Islam.[36] Grenz heartily affirms this attitude in his work, *Renewing the Center: Evangelical Theology in a Post-Theological Era:*

> Only by tackling the task of critical engagement that takes seriously the postmodern condition and draws creatively from postmodern sensitivities for the sake of the advancement of the gospel in the world can this generation of evangelical theologians truly claim to stand in the legacy of their forebears, whose theological program involved an apologetic appropriation of the philosophical sensitivities of their day.[37]

I am proposing an apologetic methodology which is certainly in accord with McDermott and Grenz, but my efforts in this work are more specifically focused on dialogue with postmodern deconstructive theology.

---

33 These "concerns" may include, as I previously noted, issues such as justice, oppression, suppression, equality, etc.

34 McDermott, *Can Evangelicals Learn From World Religions?*, pp. 122–32, also previously on p. 109.

35 C.S. Lewis, *Till We Have Faces: A Myth Retold* (San Diego, New York, and London: Harcourt Brace Jovanovich, 1956).

36 McDermott, *Can Evangelicals Learn From World Religions?* p. 212. McDermott provides a chapter on each of these religions, describing various areas from which we may learn as Christians. Also see Michael S. Jones, "Evangelical Christianity and the Philosophy of Interreligious Dialogue," *Journal of Ecumenical Studies* 36/3–4 (Summer–Fall 1999): 383, 386.

37 Stanley J. Grenz, *Renewing the Center* (Grand Rapids: Baker, 2000), p. 22.

Critical Appropriation and Recontextualization

As I intimated in the "dross" and "silver" metaphor, by "appropriation" I mean borrowing and applying those elements from deconstructionist thought that are pertinent to our theological concerns, while withholding our assent from those elements which are not. I desire to engage in compassionate listening to the underlying concerns which are the impetus behind those elements that are rejected. Hence, this is not an appropriation which mandates closure, but it is an appropriation which remains open-ended for ongoing dialogue and relationship. All this implies mutal respect in the course of communication. Yet, in order to continue dialogue it is important to identify and articulate both likenesses and differences.[38] So, this is not simply "appropriation"—but it is "critical" appropriation. Discernment and careful analysis are presupposed with such an appropriation. This is not simply saying "yes," it is sometimes saying, "yes, but...", and at other times it is saying "no"— all the while seeking to keep the conversation going. We must exercise caution, lest our enthusiasm for appropriation loses its "critical" focus. I am by no means advocating blind appropriation simply for the sake of continued dialogue. I fully acknowledge that the "stumbling block" of the gospel (1 Cor 1:23) does not simply disappear through our proposed interactionist apologetic.[39] The Christian gospel may still offend in spite of a myriad of approaches used to maintain dialogue and mend fences. The key is to maintain constructive dialogue following such "offence" where possible. As Grenz warned, "evangelicals must guard against the temptation to conclude too quickly that they know exactly where this offence lies, and thereby too readily discount the postmodern critique."[40]

Critical appropriation will also entail at times, critical recontextualization. Westphal views this as the "negative side" of critical appropriation. He claims that the need to recontextualize "stems from not sharing the same assumptions or the same agenda." So, for Westphal, we simply agree to disagree and re-locate.[41] We may accept the language of our environs, but we are not blocked into a corner by it. Instead we can, as theologian John Howard Yoder submits, seize it and expropriate it and use it to say things that could not previously have been said in the prior language.[42]

But as Westphal concurs, appropriation is not simply refutation, it also implies acceptance. It finds agreement at certain points, yet it concedes that it will be

---

38 See Gary L. Comstock, "Is Postmodern Religious Dialogue Possible?," *Faith and Philosophy* 6/2 (1989): 195.

39 See Grenz, *Renewing the Center*, p. 22. See also Merold Westphal, "Appropriating Postmodernism," in *Postmodern Philosophy and Christian Thought*, ed. Merold Westphal (Bloomington: Indiana University Press, 1999), p. 2.

40 Grenz, *Renewing the Center*, p. 22.

41 Westphal, "Appropriating Postmodernism," p. 2.

42 John Howard Yoder, "On Not Being Ashamed of the Gospel: Particularity, Pluralism, and Validation," *Faith and Philosophy* 9/3 (1992): 296.

expressed differently within different contexts.[43] I would contend, however, that a critical recontextualization need not be regarded as the "negative side" of critical appropriation, but rather a positive application of the deconstructive theologian's concerns without taking on his or her complete agenda. Furthermore, I would suggest that recontextualization *inevitably* occurs at any level (and at many levels) of critical appropriation, whether or not one happens to share the same basic assumptions or agenda. This is clearly one of the issues to which deconstructive postmodernism has already alerted us, as noted in my previous considerations. This is simply acknowledging the truth of individual and community-related interpretive frameworks and acknowledging the fact that all elements of human understanding are filtered through one's own perspective, having the "contour and flavor" of that perspective.[44] Acknowledging this is what Graham Ward calls the "process of negotiation." This negotiation is suspicious of intentions: both one's own and another's. But this "slippery" movement of "negotiating the past, the heritage, in a present appropriation—can be legitimate; for every movement is always and only a movement such as this. This is the economy of *différance*."[45]

I agree that all readings, conversations, and any form of communication involves interpretation, and hence recontextualization. However, I would distinguish between *passive* and *active* recontextualization. *Passive* recontextualization may be equated with interpretation, and interpretation occurs prior to virtually every aspect of thinking, and life-application. As James K.A. Smith asserts: "Life itself is a hermeneutical venture, and it is so because of the nature of human be-ing as finite, as located and situated."[46] What I am proposing, with a *critical* recontextualization, is the practice of *active* recontextualization in dialogue with postmodern deconstructive theology. I previously made a case for a non-violent plundering of deconstructive thought. Can I make a similar case for the non-violence of critical recontextualization? I would say, "yes," as long as it is done within the context of respectful dialogue. Of course, violence cannot be equated with simply a failure to please the dialogue partner. Profound differences may result in some level of discomfort or offence. Again, Merold Westphal, in an interview conducted by Gary Percesepe, provides some excellent insights relevant to this point in question. Westphal concedes that Marx, Nietzsche, Freud, Foucault or Derrida, would not be "entirely pleased" if we reject their atheism, while at the same time we recontextualize their insights for our Christian hermeneutical perspective. Although some may call this interpretive

---

43 Westphal, "Appropriating Postmodernism," p. 2.

44 McDermott, *Can Evangelicals Learn From World Religions?*, p. 18.

45 Graham Ward, *Barth, Derrida and the Language of Theology* (Cambridge: Cambridge University Press, 1995), pp. 174–5.

46 James K.A. Smith, *The Fall of Interpretation: Philosophical Foundations For a Creational Hermeneutic* (Downers Grove: InterVarsity, 2000). Smith's thesis links interpretation to the goodness of creation and argues that "hermeneutical mediation is the necessary accompaniment of the finitude of human life" (p. 27). Hermeneutics is not, Smith contends, part of the "postlapsarian curse coming on the scene after Eden but is instead part of the original goodness of creation found in Eden as well" (p. 60).

"violence," Westphal admits, it is not necessarily so because it does not cut off "conversational possibilities"—but instead, opens them up. Westphal illustrates this in the following mock "dialogical" response from the Christian to the differing party:

> "Look, I agree with you about these insights, in so far as they have real force. Would you agree with me that they work just as well, or even better in the Christian context in which I'm placing them? In so far as it is obvious that our deepest and most fundamental disagreement is over the reality of God, is it possible to find a way to talk about that? Or must we at least for the time being just lay that aside and talk about the best way to pursue these other insights."[47]

It is important to emphasize that with this interactionist apologetic proposal, I am not simply suggesting a critical recontextualization which gleans the good, rejects the bad, then says, "Let's talk about it." Although I am recommending gleaning the "good," and rejecting the "bad," I am also proposing the acknowledgement of the deep-seated concerns of the other which have shaped the thoughts and motives behind that which I have rejected as the "bad."[48] My recommendation concurs with Westphal's challenge to distinguish between evidential atheism and atheism of suspicion. We must not assume that the atheist simply rejects belief in God due to the lack of historical, scientific, or philosophical evidences. Rather than issuing a simple, blanket rejection of the deconstructionist's "atheism" we need to ask interactive questions that may uncover that particular notion of "God" that the atheist is rejecting. Is perhaps the atheist simply rejecting a false idol of "God" which has nothing to do with the Christianity as seen in the Acts narrative?

As noted French philosopher, Jean-Luc Marion, submits in his *God Without Being*, "the 'death of God' presupposes a determination of God that formulates him in a precise concept; it implies then, at first, a grasp of the divine that is limited and for that reason intelligible."[49] I do not wish to argue for the complete converse of Marion's argument, namely, that the theist's or Christian's concept of God is totally unintelligible simply because God's existence is affirmed.[50] "Unintelligible"

---

47 Gary Percesepe, "Against Appropriation: Postmodern Programs, Claimants, Contests, Conversations," in *Postmodern Philosophy and Christian Thought*, p. 79.

48 I acknowledge that this presupposes some interpretive framework by which to make such judgments, which itself may result in faulty interpretation. Does this necessarily imply an endless chain of distorted interpretations without any possibility of any sort of foundation or objectivity? I will address this question in chapter 13 in the discussion of apologetic groundwork.

49 Jean-Luc Marion, *God Without Being*, trans. Thomas A. Carlson (Chicago and London: The University of Chicago Press, 1991), p. 29. Cf. comments by Smith, *The Fall of Interpretation*, p. 189, note 2.

50 Augustine discusses a variation of this tension in terms of the "unspeakable" nature of God: "Thus there arises a curious contradiction of words, because if the unspeakable is what cannot be spoken of, it is not unspeakable if it can be called unspeakable. And this opposition of words is rather to be avoided by silence than to be explained away by speech. And yet God,

is considerably different to *not completely* or *partially* intelligible. What Marion effectively points out, however, is the atheist's categorical denial of "God" is a denial of a pre-ordered, pre-conceived concept. Unfortunately, this denial may stem from the atheist's perceptions of a believer's spurious motives and self-interests behind his or her belief in God. In my estimation, if we are able to uncover these elements through painstaking effort in conversation and/or critical academic engagement, then it is compassion, not violence, which has prevailed.

In my view, critical appropriation through active recontextualization is an effective, creative resource for Christian spiritual renewal and apologetic methodology. This is what I have attempted to model in several themes I have already discussed. For example, I have recontextualized Derrida's notion of the "messianic," Taylor's "mazing grace," and Cupitt's "solar living" and "poetical theology," to name a few. Such a critical appropriation helps us move beyond our often narrow cultural confines which often dull our sensitivities. It provides us with occasions by which we may open ourselves to the other and be challenged to move beyond expected "norms"—to move beyond a static Christian spirituality which has often marked the modernist need for dominance, finality and control. Jesus, who ate with "tax collectors and sinners," often departed from the norms by recontextualizing. I previously mentioned, based on the study of Kenneth E. Bailey, that Jesus performed a "deconstructive recontextualization" (my choice of words) of Middle Eastern patriarchy with the parable of the prodigal son in Luke 15.[51] I would argue as well that a practice of critical appropriation and recontextualization, can help stir us out of intellectual complacency and widen our otherwise narrow notions of God. Such a "stirring" can certainly occur through this type of apologetic engagement I have espoused in the context of ordered academic dialogue, presentation, or conversation. But, I would earnestly propose that it can also happen, as Jesus himself reminded us, through the power of story, and through the use of myth and imagination. It is now to these matters which I turn in the following chapter.

---

although nothing worthy of His greatness can be said of Him, has condescended to accept the worship of men's mouths, and has desired us through the medium of our own words to rejoice in His praise." Augustine, *On Christian Doctrine*, Book I, Chapter 6. 6, p. 524.

51 See Kenneth E. Bailey, "The Pursuing Father: What We Need to Know About This Often Misunderstood Middle Eastern Parable," *Christianity Today* (October 26 1998): 35.

Chapter 12

Apologetic Imagination

The Power of Imagination, Myth, and Story in Apologetic Dialogue

The Need for Imaginative Expression in Apologetics

As I discussed in a previous chapter, the Christian apologetic task may broadly be divided into what has been defined as *negative* and *positive* apologetics. Again, this has nothing to do with what is good or bad in apologetic methodologies, but it pertains to approaches and strategies. Negative apologetics provides responses to objections to Christianity. Positive apologetics takes the initiative to show, illustrate, or articulate the Christian faith. I have argued that an interactionist apologetic must not take one approach and exclude the other. It must seek interaction and dialogue at both levels, depending on the context.

I will also reiterate another point. Romanticism's reaction to modernist ideals is crucial for understanding the beginnings of postmodern thought. The world, for the romantic, is not simply some object "out there" to be controlled, but it is dynamic, creative and unrestrained. Since I take the postmodern dethronement of Enlightenment rationalism seriously, I am proposing that positive apologetics must not be construed simply as logical, well-reasoned argumentation typical of classical and evidential apologetic systems. This does not imply that I am obliged to uncritically accept romantic ideals. But in order to critically appropriate and recontextualize postmodern deconstructive theology, it is necessary to develop skills of imagination and creative application. Alister McGrath aptly notes that the Enlightenment appealed to human reason, whereas romanticism appealed to human imagination "which was capable of recognizing the profound sense of mystery which arises from realizing that the human mind cannot comprehend even the finite world, let alone the infinity beyond this."[1]

Cupitt's "poetical theology" certainly challenged us in this regard. Strict logical, linear approaches will not suffice in a postmodern context. An arena for positive apologetics which is often overlooked, with great potential for dialogue with deconstructive theology, is the use of story, imagination and myth. McGrath claims that "[o]ne of the saddest features of some modern apologetic writing is that it makes its appeal purely to reason and neglects the human imagination—perhaps one of

---

1   Alister E. McGrath, *The Making of Modern German Christology 1750–1990* (Grand Rapids: Apollos, Zondervan, 1994), p. 38.

the most powerful allies at the disposal of the apologist."[2] Yet, it is not my desire to present the use of "apologetic imagination" in contrast with apologetic engagement and dialogue, or simply to present it as another option. Instead, I am suggesting that the use of narrative and imaginative elements may help us *in* our engagement and critical appropriation of deconstructive concerns. Story can provide profound imaginative Christian expression apart from a one-voice authority expressed in linear, logical fashion. Through the use of the imagination, the theologian can creatively "recreate" images of theological expression lest they simply become abstractions, separated from real life:

> Definitions are closed off and imprison people in formulas; images are open-ended and invite their hearers to imagine them and be captured by them. We must avoid sounding like theological dictionaries and instead be able to appeal to the imaginations of those to whom we speak. The well-honed and carefully chosen word must be used to convey images of grace to our hearers.[3]

By "imagination" then, I am simply using the term in its simplest sense: the capacity of one's mind to create images not immediately present to the senses.[4] But this does not mean that the imagination begins with a blank slate, or that it is not in any way conditioned by its culture or environs.[5] Although the image created through the imagination may not be immediately present to the senses, the imagination may allow us to see or feel something that *is* present to the senses in a fresh way. The use

---

2   Alister McGrath, *Intellectuals Don't Need God & Other Modern Myths* (Grand Rapids: Zondervan, 1993), p. 194. Also cf. Louis A. Markos, "Poetry-Phobic: Why Evangelicals Should Love Language That is 'Slippery,'" *Christianity Today* (October 1, 2001). Markos claims that evangelicals mistakenly ascribe more "validity to scientific, rational discourse than [they] do to the ambiguous, irony-rich language of the arts." Markos contends that this artistic language of the Bible is actually more meaningful precisely because it is "slippery"— maintaining that "vital sense of play" to incarnate transcendent truths through images. Hence, it more effectively captures the inherent mystery of the Incarnation itself. (p. 66).

3   McGrath, *Intellectuals Don't Need God*, p. 195.

4   It is not my intention to develop a meticulous definition of "imagination" in view of romantic critical theory. For example, Samuel Taylor Coleridge (1772–1834) recognized three types of imagination: primary, secondary, and fancy. See Verlyn Flieger, *Splintered Light: Logos and Language in Tolkien's World* (Grand Rapids: Eerdmans, 1983), especially pp. 24–5.

5   When we read a novel, the people, the places, and the voices are not attainable through our senses, but we in some sense, still "hear" them and "see" them. Certainly we use our sense of sight to see the text itself. The sounds, smells, the climate of the room in which we are reading, our personal background and current state of mind all affect our interpretation of the pictures and events the author is presenting. Additionally, the grammatical and type style of the text may affect how we read and interpret the story. Each of these factors influence this image-making faculty we possess to continually re-create images in our minds.

of the imagination is key to help us to re-express or recontextualize an old truth with new insight. It is not static, but dynamic.[6]

In previous chapters I considered the example of Jesus himself as a model of such creative recontextualization through his imaginative use of the parable of the prodigal. Of course, the Bible is full of other various literary and imaginative genres which would include poetry, wisdom literature, proverb, apocalyptic imagery, and narrative. To read and understand the Bible itelf presupposes the value and need for a "multifaceted" use of the imagination which "appeals to our human taste for a story, and to our delight in other unifying symbolic elements such as archetypes."[7]

A genuine Christian imagination can join the "prophetic voices" of theological deconstruction to challenge us with renewal and stir us from a static, oppressive, religious complacency. The use of imagination can help deconstruct Christian cliché and help us recapture with delight that which has become commonplace. It aids us, like deconstructionism, in providing a "detachment" and "upside-down view" necessary to "circumvent the ruts, the tags, the clichés everywhere awaiting us."[8] In my estimation, if we are to genuinely meet and address the concerns posed by postmodern deconstructive theology through critical appropriation and recontextualization, we must appeal to human experience through imaginative forms. One example of a scholar who applied such a remarkable use of the imaginination in this regard was C.S. Lewis. Lewis was by no means postmodern in his orientation, but there is a great deal we can glean from his insights that contribute to this discussion.

C.S. Lewis: From Rationalism to Imagination

A Change in Apologetic Strategy C.S. Lewis (1898–1963), the famous Oxford literary scholar and Christian apologist, was noted for rationalistic apologetic methods. However, some have argued that his methods radically changed after a meeting of the Oxford Socratic Club on 2 February, 1948. At this meeting, the philosopher G.E.M. Anscombe debated Lewis over his rationalistic argumentation used in his book *Miracles*, published eight months before. Lewis argued against the self-contradictory character of naturalism, expressed in favor of the existence of God. Anscombe submitted that Lewis's work was riddled with ambiguity, confusion and imprecision in its philosophical terminology, which in her estimation rendered his entire thesis suspect. Although the audience disagreed as to the winner of the

---

6   Clyde S. Kilby, "Christian Imagination," in *The Christian Imagination: Essays on Literature and the Arts*, ed. Leland Ryken (Grand Rapids: Baker, 1981), p. 37. For a discussion on basic functions of the imagination in the Christian context, see Richard Bauckham and Trevor Hart, *Hope Against Hope: Christian Eschatology at the Turn of the Millennium* (Grand Rapids: Cambridge, U.K.: Eerdmans, 1999), pp. 84–8.

7   Colin Duriez, "The Romantic Writer: Lewis's Theology of Fantasy," in *The Pilgrim's Guide: C.S. Lewis and the Art of Witness*, ed. David Mills (Grand Rapids and Cambridge, U.K.: Eerdmans, 1998), p. 99.

8   Kilby, "Christian Imagination," p. 45.

debate, it seems clear that Lewis certainly thought he had lost.[9] One of Lewis's friends and biographer, George Sayer, recounts the devastating effects of this evening for Lewis:

> [Lewis] told me that he had been proved wrong, that his argument for the existence of God had been demolished. This was a serious matter, he felt, because, in the minds of simple people, the disproof of an argument for the existence of God tended to be regarded as a disproof of the existence of God. He wanted to mount a counterattack, but he thought that would be dangerous to do so unless he were quite sure of its validity.[10]

Sayer surmises that this debate, although quite humiliating for Lewis, was for his ultimate good; Lewis had grown too proud with his logical prowess.[11] Following this, Lewis did not write another apologetics work of this type. Sayer even contends that Lewis never wrote another theological book from this point forward.[12] Others have claimed that this event prompted Lewis to turn from philosophical apologetics and devote himself to fiction.[13] I would be inclined to agree with this if we mean by "philosophical apologetics," an apologetics of only the rational, logical sort. However, in my view, I am not convinced that Lewis desired to radically separate apologetics from fiction. This presents a false dilemma to which one need not make a concession. I indeed contend that this event was a pivotal point leading to a change in Lewis' orientation to and reliance upon reason. It did not lead to the abandonment of apologetics altogether, but it did bring about a radical change in his apologetic methodology. Lewis, while not repudiating his earlier apologetic works, began to focus his energies on what I would call the use of apologetic imagination. Lewis scholar, Peter J. Schakel, puts it well: "His turning to myth is not a rejection of his earlier mode, but an effort to go beyond it and to offer a reader not "knowledge" of God but a "taste" of Divine Reality."[14]

---

9   See Peter J. Schakel, *Reason and Imagination in C.S. Lewis* (Grand Rapids: Eerdmans, 1984), p. 148, and George Sayer, *Jack: C.S. Lewis and His Times* (San Francisco: Harper and Row, 1988), p. 186.

10   Sayer, *Jack*, pp. 186–7.

11   Ibid.

12   Ibid., p. 187.

13   Katherine Harper, "G[ertrude] E[lizabeth] M[argaret] Anscombe (1919–)," in *The C.S. Lewis Readers' Encyclopedia*, ed. Jeffrey D. Schultz and John G. West Jr (Grand Rapids: Zondervan, 1998), p. 81.

14   Schakel, *Reason and Imagination in C.S. Lewis*, pp. 149–150. The quote is from p. 150. For an example of where Lewis himself uses this "tasting" imagery, see C.S. Lewis, "Myth Became Fact," in *God in the Dock: Essays on Theology and Ethics*, ed. Walter Hooper (Grand Rapids: Eerdmans, 1970), p. 66. Such a notion one may find reminiscent of Schleiermacher's insistence that "true religion is sense and taste for the Infinite." Although I find no evidence to indicate that Lewis was directly influenced by Schleiermacher, the latter's reconciliation of religion and is certainly appropriate in this regard. Religion and art "can hardly be quite alien, because, from of old, what is greatest in art has had a religious character." Friedrich Schleiermacher, *On Religion: Speeches to its Cultured Despisers*, trans. John Oman (New

In my estimation, the "taste" metaphor provides vivid imagery. It embodies both experiential and intellectual apprehension. Nothing is so experientially close and "real" as that which comes to the taste buds. For example, if I were to recommend for one's eating pleasure, the qualities of a certain apple, I could describe the fruit as reddish on the outside and crisp, juicy and sweet on the inside. Such descriptions may help a little. But, if I challenged one instead to imagine the fragrance, the taste, and the sweetness in one's mind as if he or she were actually eating the apple—it would be much more helpful. Lewis's positive, post-rationalist apologetic attempted to do just this. It made imaginative appeals through the the use of myth and story to convey the Christian gospel in a way that rationalistic propositions could not.[15] In my view both Lewis's self-perceived defeat and subsequent methodological re-orientation are precusory, yet ideologically parallel with the the postmodern critique of the dethronement of reason. This is why I have chosen him as a conversation partner in this chapter.

The Use of Myth in Positive Apologetics In *The Word as True Myth*, Gary Dorrien submits that Lewis's prominence as a Christian apologist "owes much to the fact that he approached the myth question with greater openness and discernment than most theologians."[16] Before I discuss the advantages of Lewis's notion of myth for my proposed interactionist apologetic, it is essential that I define the meaning of "myth" that I am proposing. By myth, I am not simply suggesting what Gene Edward Veith would call "magical realism." That is, employing a narrative technique "for achieving verisimilitude … [to] create the illusion of reality for things that are definitely *not* real."[17] Although I will argue that magical realism itself is one aspect of myth and it can be a very valuable means to convey spiritual reality to a materialistic culture, I cannot simply reduce myth to this literary technique alone. Granted, the notion of "myth" often simply implies that which is untrue or unhistorical. But, this is not necessarily so. Broadly, myth involves a complex network of stories which "fire the imagination"—some may be historical events, others may be fantasy—which some regard as expressions of the meaning of reality and human life.[18] Stephen Bertman, a classicist at the University of Windsor, notes: "[W]hat we disparage as mythology the Greeks and Romans would have called their most ancient history, no less valid

---

York, Hagerstown, San Francisco, and London: Harper and Row, 1958), pp. 39, 29. Cf. Nicola Hoggard Creegan, "Schleiermacher as Apologist: Reclaiming the Father of Modern Theology," in *Christian Apologetics in the Postmodern World*, ed. Timothy R. Phillips and Dennis L. Okholm (Downers Grove: InterVarsity, 1995), pp. 63–4.

15 See Duriez, "The Romantic Writer," p. 100.

16 Gary Dorrien, *The Word as True Myth: Interpreting Modern Theology* (Louisville: Westminster John Knox Press, 1997), pp. 236–7.

17 Gene Edward Veith Jr., *Postmodern Times: A Christian Guide to Contemporary Thought and Culture* (Wheaton: Crossway, 1994), p. 131ff.

18 Alan W. Watts, *Myth and Ritual in Christianity* (Boston: Beacon Press, 1968), p. 7. See also Stratford Caldecott, "Speaking the Truths Only the Imagination May Grasp: Myth and 'Real Life'," in *The Pilgrim's Guide*, pp. 87–93.

for the distance that separated them from the events their stories described. Myths embodied truths that transcended time. As such, they deserved special reverence."[19] I heartily agree with Peter Schakel's proposal that Lewis's understanding of myth may be defined as follows: "[A] use of narrative structure and archetypal elements to convey through the imagination universal or divine truths not accessible to the intellect alone."[20]

This multi-dimensional understanding of myth was key for Lewis's understanding and expression of the Christian faith. For Lewis, myth was even a vehicle by which God revealed Himself in the person of Jesus Christ. Lewis explains this in his well-known essay, "Myth Became Fact:"

> The heart of Christianity is a myth which is also a fact.... It *happens*—at a particular date, in a particular place, followed by definable historical consequences. We pass from a Balder or an Osiris, dying nobody knows when or where, to a historical Person crucified (it is all in order) under Pontius Pilate. By becoming fact it does not cease to be myth: that is the miracle.... To be truly Christian we must both assent to the historical fact and also receive the myth (fact though it has become) with the same imaginative embrace which we accord to all other myths. The one is hardly more necessary than the other.[21]

For Lewis, the Christ-story first appeared in mythical form, then through a "long process of condensing or focusing" became "incarnate as history." To insist upon the actual historical occurrence of the Incarnation does not negate its mythic quality for Lewis: "...the Myth remains Myth even when it becomes Fact."[22] A host of myths, histories and philosophies through the ages provided fragments of the myth which became fact. The Word became flesh; God became man. But, the myth which became fact "is not 'a religion,' nor 'a philosophy.' It is the summing up and actuality of them all."[23] For Lewis, the incarnational idea of the death and resurrection of a god has been "true" as myth throughout history. In Christianity, however, this myth became realized temporally, historically, hence fulfilling all other myths.[24]

For Lewis, his understanding of the mythical-historical nature of Christianity stirred his desire to plunder elements of "untrue" myth even further. It may be said that Lewis drew from what he viewed as an "enlightened paganism."[25] Lewis made a great contribution to Christian apologetics not only through his logical, rational works, but also through his greatly imaginative works. One writer remarks that Lewis's conversion to Christ "not only freed his mind from the bonds of a narrow

---

19 Stephen Bertman, "Modern Values and the Challenge of Myth," *Imprimis* 22/3 (1993): 3.

20 Schakel, *Reason and Imagination in C.S. Lewis*, p. 26. Cf. C.S. Lewis, *Miracles: A Preliminary Study* (New York: Macmillan, 1947), p. 134, note 1.

21 Lewis, "Myth Became Fact," pp. 66–7.

22 Lewis, *Miracles*, pp. 133–4, note 1.

23 C.S. Lewis, *Suprised By Joy: The Shape of My Early Life* (New York and London: Harcourt Brace Jovanovich, 1955), p. 236.

24 Dorrien, *The Word as True Myth*, p. 237.

25 Duriez, "The Romantic Writer," p. 107. This idea would be similar to the notion of the "prophetic voice of atheism" which I advocated in the previous chapter.

stoicism; it freed his heart to embrace fully his earlier passion for mythology." His realization of Christianity as the myth which became historically realized helped reopen that "enchanted world of his childhood."[26] I have argued that Lewis's radical change in methodology came much later than his conversion, but I would agree that his conversion began the process which began promoting that change. It certainly seems that Lewis's understanding of Christianity as a myth which became fact, combined with the "crisis" challenge from G.E.M. Anscombe later in life, greatly roused his pursuit of myth to promote Christian faith.

Lewis's profound notion of myth helped him to produce convincing stories which continue to function as "good dreams" to help prepare others for the gospel of Jesus Christ. These stories picture and promote redemptive activity in magical other worlds, renewing our sense of wonder and mystery, preparing minds dulled from modernism.[27] J. Richard Middleton and Brian J. Walsh affirm this: "It is only when we can imagine the world to be different from the way it is that we can be empowered to embody this alternative reality which is God's kingdom and resist this present nightmare of brokenness, disorientation and confusion."[28] It is this aspect of myth, which Veith has described as "magical realism."[29] It is "magical" in the sense that it uses story and imagination to create new fantasy worlds. It is "realism" because the fantasy worlds which are created are mini-pictures of reality. It is a "subcreation," that is, a secondary world that we may enter by means of the imagination providing us with a renewed sense of multi-dimensional reality. Hence, its purpose is not escapism, but its opposite. Magical realism seeks to put us in touch with a forgotten, neglected reality of God's creation.[30] In speaking of dramatic theology, Kevin Vanhoozer puts it this way: "We need more imagination, not less, for the best imaginative literature does not remove us from the real but allows it to take residence in it. ..."[31] This is an adequate description of fantasy literature and its use as an apologetic in view of postmodern deconstructive concerns. Mythical fantasy can help recontextualize the familiar and restore that which is oppressed or suppressed

---

26 Louis A. Markos, "Myth Matters," *Christianity Today* (April 23, 2001): 35.

27 J.I. Packer, "Still Surprised by Lewis," *Christianity Today* (September 7, 1998): 58 and Markos, "Myth Matters" 36.

28 J. Richard Middleton and Brian Walsh, *Truth is Stranger Than It Used to Be: Biblical Faith in a Postmodern Age* (Downers Grove: InterVarsity, 1995), p. 192.

29 Veith, *Postmodern Times*, p. 131ff.

30 This notion of "subcreation" belonged to J.R.R. Tolkien, but heavily influenced Lewis's perspective on fantasy as well. See Duriez, "The Romantic Writer," p. 105. See also J.R.R. Tolkien, "Tree and Leaf," in *The Tolkien Reader* (New York: Ballantine Books, 1966), pp. 33–90. For another pertinent reference with regard to postmodernism, theology and literary fantasy see George Aichele Jr, "Literary Fantasy and Postmodern Theology," *Journal of the American Academy of Religion* 59 (1991): 323–37.

31 Kevin J. Vanhoozer, "The Voice and the Actor: A Dramatic Proposal about the Ministry and Minstrelsy of Theology," in *Evangelical Futures: A Conversation on Theological Method*, ed. John G. Stackhouse Jr (Grand Rapids, Leicester, and Vancouver, B.C.: Baker, InterVarsity, and Regent College Publishing, 2000), p. 91.

by modern rationalistic assumptions. In this sense, myth can deconstruct the hidden realities behind the mask of the ordinary. Myth then functions as something which can provide healing to eyes blinded by the sinful myopia of our selfishness and reductionistic materialism.[32] Lewis discusses this with such profundity it is worthy of this long citation:

> The value of the myth is that it takes all the things we know and restores to them the rich significance which has been hidden by 'the veil of familiarity.' The child enjoys his cold meat (otherwise dull to him) by pretending it is buffalo, just killed with his own bow and arrow. And the child is wise. The real meat comes back to him more savoury for having been dipped in a story; you might say that only then is it the real meat. If you are tired of the real landscape, look at it in a mirror. By putting bread, gold, horse, apple, or the very roads into a myth, we do not retreat from reality: we rediscover it. As long as the story lingers in our mind, the real things are more themselves. This book applies the treatment not only to bread or apple but to good and evil, to our endless perils, our anguish, and our joys. By dipping them in myth we see them more clearly.[33]

Perhaps Lewis's most remarkable works in this regard were his children's stories, *The Chronicles of Narnia*, and a work we have alluded to previously, his reworking of the myth of Cupid and Psyche, *Till We Have Faces*. It may be helpful to illustrate this value of myth by citing several examples of Lewis's artistry from each of these works. I will limit my illustrations to two: one from *The Chronicles of Narnia*, book one, *The Lion, the Witch and the Wardrobe*, and one from *Till We Have Faces*.

The Lion, the Witch and the Wardrobe   In *The Lion, the Witch and the Wardrobe*, Lewis creates a new world revealed to four children through the passageway of an old wardrobe in the house of an elderly Professor. Lucy is the first to enter and return from this world of Narnia. Upon her return, she attempts to describe this wonderful new place to the other children. The children are very skeptical, but they decide to give it a try. Unfortunately for Lucy, all they find is a "perfectly ordinary wardrobe" with hooks hanging in the back. For the other three children, this exciting world of Narnia was simply non-existent. But for Lucy, the forest, the snow and all the sights and sounds were so real. What had happened? Then one day while playing hide-and-seek in the old house, Edmund hides in the wardrobe and he also passes into Narnia. After he emerges with Lucy, however, he continues to deny its existence. The other two children, Peter and Susan, become distraught with the silly delusions of their siblings—so they approach the old Professor for advice. To their surprise, he asks them how they know that their sister's story is not true. The Professor suggests that there are three possibilities:

---

32 Duriez, "The Romantic Writer," pp. 102–5.

33 C.S. Lewis, "Tolkien's *Lord of the Rings*," in *On Stories: And Other Essays on Literature*, ed. Walter Hooper (San Diego, New York, and London: Harcourt Brace and Company, 1966), p. 90.

Either your sister is telling lies, or she is mad, or she is telling the truth. You know she doesn't tell lies and it is obvious that she is not mad. For the moment then and unless any further evidence turns up, we must assume that she is telling the truth.[34]

Even though Lucy's testimony seemed to run contrary to any notion of reality they preconceived, the Professor challenges them to remain open to the possibility of Lucy's testimony—and he even suggests that it may indeed be true! In one sense, the Professor's logical presentation of three possibilities is simply an imaginative appeal to promote rationalist apologetics. However, it is not limited to this by any means. Stephen B. Smith points out that this illustration demonstrates Lewis's use of pre-apologetics in the story. He suggests that *The Chronicles of Narnia* are attempting to "break the enchantment of worldliness, including the deep naturalistic prejudice against the supernatural"—to help pre-dispose one to the reality of the Christian story.[35] One must not close himself or herself off from the possibility of Christian reality simply due to empirically based, modernist prejudices. Lewis reminds us that an imaginatively centered apologetic must challenge the typical norms of acceptability and remember that reality is much greater than our restricted vision.

Near the end of *The Lion, the Witch, and the Wardrobe*, we find another illustration which challenges our "normal" perspective of the here and now. The great lion Aslan, King of Narnia, was voluntarily killed in the stead of a traitor by the evil White Witch of Narnia. Suddenly, he appeared again, "larger than they had seen him before"—Aslan was alive! The children were astonished, both glad and afraid at the same time.

"Aren't you dead then, dear Aslan?" said Lucy.

"Not now," said Aslan.

"You're not—not a—?" asked Susan in a shaky voice. She couldn't bring herself to say the word *ghost*.

Aslan stooped his golden head and licked her forehead. The warmth of his breath and a rich sort of smell that seemed to hang about his hair came all over her.

"Do I look it?" he said.

"Oh, you're real, you're real! Oh, Aslan!" cried Lucy and both girls flung themselves upon him and covered him with kisses.

"But what does it all mean?" asked Susan when they were somewhat calmer.

"It means," said Aslan, "that though the Witch knew the Deep Magic, there is a magic deeper still which she did not know. Her knowledge goes back only to the dawn of Time. But if she could have looked a little further back, into the stillness and the darkness before Time dawned, she would have read there a different incantation. She would have known that when a willing victim who had committed no treachery was killed in a traitor's stead, the Table would crack and Death itself would start working backwards."[36]

---

34 C.S. Lewis, *The Lion, the Witch, and the Wardrobe* (New York: Macmillan, 1950), p. 45.

35 Stephen M. Smith, "Awakening from the Enchantment of Worldliness: *The Chronicles of Narnia* as Pre-Apologetics," in *The Pilgrim's Guide*, pp. 169, 170.

36 Lewis, *The Lion, the Witch, and the Wardrobe*, pp. 159–60.

The parallels to the narrative of the resurrection of Christ and the atonement are obvious, but not exact. Lewis has "subcreated" a different world with its own story, history, and theology. This subcreation though creatively points to and reminds us of a greater reality that has often been brushed aside. This dialogue reminds us well of our own limitations. Our knowledge is not only limited by our predispositions, it is also limited to our temporal nature. It challenges us to consider what there is beyond ourselves in the "stillness and the darkness" beyond Time itself. The dialogue stimulates us to think of the origin of death, and what it would mean if the consequences of death could work "backwards." Again, through the use of magical realism, Lewis nurtures the apologetic imagination which "does not so much impose Christian truth on people as draw them into that truth in such a way that they can appreciate and appropriate it."[37]

Till We Have Faces Perhaps Lewis's most subtle yet also most profound imaginative apologetic is found in *Till We Have Faces*. This new myth, which Lewis recreates from the old, does not make the more obvious parallels which we find in *The Chronicles of Narnia*. Due to the scope of this chapter, I will risk an injustice to this richly complex tale by only briefly describing the plot of the book leading up to the portion we cite for apologetic consideration. Reminiscent of the children's disbelief at the magical world of Narnia, here is another example where Lewis challenges the reader to consider a reality which is beyond that of the mere senses, dictated by reason.

The story takes place in the imaginary country of Glome. It is told in the first person by the King of Glome's daughter Orual. Orual is the simple-looking caretaker of her young beautiful stepsister Psyche. As Psyche matures, she is worshipped as a goddess instead of the nature goddess Ungit. Of course Ungit will have nothing of this—so Ungit requires the sacrifice of Psyche to her "brute" son. Orual, desiring to bury Psyche, instead finds Psyche alive and well, but clothed in rags. Although her appearance seems otherwise, Psyche claims that she is actually wearing beautiful clothing given to her by her marvelous husband in whose wondrous palace she lives and sleeps.[38] Here is just a glimpse of the dialogue which ensues:

> "Where is the palace? How far have we to go to reach it?"
> She gave one loud cry. Then, with white face, staring hard into my eyes, she said, "But this is it, Orual! It is here! You are standing on the stairs of the great gate."[39]

---

37 McGrath, *Intellectuals Don't Need God*, p. 194.

38 See Charles A. Huttar, "*Till We Have Faces*: A Myth Retold," in *The C.S. Lewis Readers' Encyclopedia*, eds Jeffrey D. Schultz and John G. West Jr (Grand Rapids: Zondervan, 1998), pp. 403–404.

39 C.S. Lewis, *Till We Have Faces: A Myth Retold* (San Diego, New York, and London: Harcourt Brace Jovanovich, 1956), p. 116.

Orual had been under the influence of her master teacher, the Fox, the Stoic, the keeper of Enlightenment reason and logic.[40] This palace that Psyche was describing did not fit within the walls of reason—for Orual it simply could not be. In fact, since it was unbelievable from Orual's perspective, it must also be terrible. Nevertheless, Orual begins to doubts herself, remembering that in Glome the gods are so close that anything was possible. Psyche recognized Orual's suspicion of her own disbelief:

> "So," she said, "you do see it after all."
> "See what?" I asked. A fool's question. I knew what.
> "Why, this, this," said Psyche. "The gates, the shining walls—"
> For some strange reason, fury—my father's own fury—fell upon me when she said that. I found myself screaming (I am sure I had not meant to scream), "Stop it! Stop it at once! There's nothing there!"
> Her face flushed. For once, and for the moment only, she too was angry. "Well, feel it, if you can't see," she cried. "Touch it. Slap it. Beat your head against it. Here—" she made to grab my hands. I wrenched them free.[41]

Orual must learn to move beyond her sole reliance on reason and make herself unselfishly open to that which is beyond the veil of her own predispositions and self deceptions. When she removes this veil and honestly confronts herself, she can gain a "face" by which she may finally "encounter **God** face-to face, without defenses, excuses, or pretenses."[42] Once again, this is simply one example among many in this profound work, where Lewis is challenging the reader to "taste" divine reality through the use of imagination and myth. This apologetic does not come in a nice, tidy rationalistic argument. Distinctions between rationality and the imagination are not always clearly drawn. Instead, Lewis writes in a way which addresses the whole person. The sense of fragmentation and separation which Orual feels is something many people can identify with. As Schakel notes, "the efforts of its characters to find unity of reason and imagination, of the physical and the psychological, can speak meaningfully to a reader who would reject the more explicitly Christian implications."[43]

Story and Narrative in Apologetics

I am not implying that we must necessarily create the kinds of stories and "myths" that Lewis created to convey theological realities. I am simply pointing to his work as a model of the type of imaginative apologetic that can be used, through myth and story, in view of and response to postmodern deconstructive theological concerns. I have previously noted that a "deconstruction" brings with it the assumption of

---

40 See Huttar, "Till We Have Faces," p. 404; and Thomas Howard, *The Achievement of C.S. Lewis: A Reading of His Fiction* (Wheaton: Harold Shaw Publishers, 1980), pp. 165–9.

41 Lewis, *Till We Have Faces*, p. 118.

42 Huttar, "Till We Have Faces," p. 405. Bold print in original citation.

43 Schakel, *Reason and Imagination in C.S. Lewis*, p. 162.

a "reconstruction" or rediscovery of that which was previously concealed. In my view, this principle may be applied to persons as well as texts. Human creativity and imagination are often suppressed to give way to that which is esteemed as rational and scientific, hence ignoring the total personhood of the individual. A progressive evangelical apologetic must seriously engage the use of imagination and myth, "alongside and interwoven with the conceptual and the empirical in ways that it has not often been hitherto."[44] Kuhn's *Structure of Scientific Revolutions* alerted us to the fact that what is most often esteemed as objective and scientific is actually rooted in creativity and the imagination. We would do well to not only acknowledge and admit this, but warmly embrace it as a quality of our humanness in our efforts to create an apologetic which is whole-person centered.[45] A story allows one to be carried forward into a world which may open up the possibility for what McGrath calls a "willing suspension of disbelief." It works quite unlike traditional apologetic argumentation where each segment of a complex, interrelated network can be specifically analyzed. With the sense of mystery that accompanies narrative, the imagination becomes engaged. As images unfold, ideas may be explored, and McGrath adds, "potential difficulties are neutralized or evaded—all within the course of the telling of a story."[46] Although I would challenge McGrath's assumption that story may alleviate or "neutralize" all potential difficulties, I certainly agree that power of story breaks down barriers which cannot be otherwise broken simply through rational argumentation.

Of course, narrative is much more than story expressed through magical realism. As Lewis reminded us in "Myth became Fact," Christians have personally appropriated a myth which has become their own personal narrative. Yet, it is a personal narrative expressed in the context of community. The biblical narratives of God's engagement with Israel and the church display the personal character and purposes of God. As Christians, we enter that world, identify with that world, and become incorporated into that community narrative, coming to know the God portrayed in that narrative.[47] As a result, we become storytellers as we recount our pilgrimage with God, "cast in categories drawn from biblical narrative, as well as the didactic sections of Scripture."[48]

In the previous chapter on Derrida, I mentioned James K.A. Smith's proposal of an "ev-angelical" theology of story telling—proclaiming healing and helping

---

44 Trevor Hart, "Imagining Evangelical Theology," in *Evangelical Futures: A Conversation on Theological Method*, ed. John G. Stackhouse Jr. (Grand Rapids, Leicester, Vancouver, B.C.: Baker, InterVarsity, and Regent College Publishing, 2000), p. 199.

45 See Hart, "Imagining Evangelical Theology," pp. 198–9.

46 McGrath, *Intellectuals Don't Need God*, p. 195.

47 Henry H. Knight III, *A Future For Truth* (Nashville: Abingdon Press, 1997), p. 102.

48 Stanley J. Grenz, *Renewing the Center* (Grand Rapids: Baker, 2000), p. 202. Cf. also Knight III, *A Future For Truth*, p. 102; and Clark H. Pinnock, *Tracking the Maze: Finding Our Way Through Modern Theology From An Evangelical Perspective* (San Francisco: Harper and Row, 1990; reprint, Eugene: Wipf and Stock Publishers, 1998), pp. 164–5.

stories.[49] Stories are what point us to relationships and community—strong ideals in the postmodern context.[50] Middleton and Walsh strongly affirm this in their *Truth is Stranger Than it Used to B*e:

> Having experienced our own diaspora, a postmodern scattering, we can rejoin the biblical story as the early church did only if we too have prophetic discernment of where we have come from and where we are, an alternative vision that will animate our praxis and a dream of a new order that will captivate our imaginations…. The good news of the gospel, the reopening of the human story, is received as a gift of the sovereign God …. And the reception of that gift transforms our reality from a series of postmodern theater pieces or sideshows into the ongoing drama of God's redemption of the world.[51]

This "drama" of God's redemptive activity is played out in the great mythic events of the incarnation and resurrection. Such mythic events provide superb Christian imagery and vivid, symbolic metaphors for inspiring hope and triumph in life. Theologians Stanley Hauerwas and Philip D. Kenneson tell us, for example, that the "resurrection reminds us that we do not live in a world ultimately determined by violence, but in a world ultimately determined by God's non-violence exemplified in the cross of Jesus."[52] As with other religions, Christianity contains many such symbolic elements that we may embrace and apply. Nevertheless, I unreservedly concur with Lewis that these are myths which actually occurred as temporal events in history and "became fact." Clark Pinnock affirms this as well when he states that Christianity is "more than fact without being less." Christianity "contains all the symbolic wealth that myths contain"—it is a myth which becomes fact "without ceasing to be myth."[53]

While affirming this perspective, however, I would express two cautions. First, as Lewis submits, God can certainly reveal himself to us through our imaginative faculties, but that does not mean we can claim absolute knowledge of any such

---

49 See again, James K.A. Smith, "How to avoid not Speaking: Attestations," in *Knowing Other-Wise: Philosophy at the Threshold of Spirituality*, ed. James H. Olthuis (New York: Fordham University Press, 1997), p. 230.

50 The reader will notice some obvious parallels here with postliberal perspectives (e.g. Hans Frei, George Lindbeck) and its embrace of narrative theology. It is beyong the scope of this work to elaborate on these themes which have been adequately addressed elsewhere. For some helpful introductions, see Gabriel Fackre, "Narrative Theology: An Overview," *Interpretation* (October 1983): 340–52; Alister McGrath, *A Passion For Truth: The Intellectual Coherence of Evangelicalism* (Downers Grove: InterVarsity, 1996), pp. 119–61; and Ed L. Miller and Stanley J. Grenz, *Fortress Introduction to Contemporary Theologies* (Minneapolis: Fortress, 1998), pp. 200–16. For a dialogue between evangelicals and postliberals see Timothy R. Phillips and Dennis L. Okholm (eds), *The Nature of Confession: Evangelicals & Postliberals in Conversation* (Downers Grove: InterVarsity, 1996).

51 Middleton and Walsh, *Truth is Stranger Than It Used to Be*, p. 191.

52 Stanley Hauerwas and Philip D. Kenneson, "Jesus and/as the Non–Violent Imagination of the Church," *Pro Ecclesia* 1/1 (1992): 85.

53 Pinnock, *Tracking the Maze*, p. 164.

revelation. The "doctrines" we derive from true myth are still "*less* true" than reality itself. They are our "translations into our concepts and ideas of that wh. God has already expressed in a language more adequate, namely the actual incarnation, crucifixion, and resurrection."[54] It is important that we acknowledge the limitations of doctrinal knowledge claims—understanding they are "less true" than reality itself. Yet, the fact that we cannot claim absolute knowledge of doctrine, does not deny the possibility of any knowledge claims whatsoever. A community narrative which seems pragmatically justified can point to a reality beyond itself. But it is often through myth and metaphor that this reality beyond is actualized in our personal experience.[55] We should strongly emphasize our limitations and cultural conditionedness without reducing our position to conceptual relativism. But how then do we make a choice between apparently competing narratives without succumbing to classical foundationalism or a Christian "neo-Wittgensteinian fideism?"[56] I will explore this further in the following chapter on apologetic groundwork.

Second, I am not suggesting that because we believe in the factual content of certain mythic events of Christianity, that we would use such beliefs as a means to suppress and discourage continued dialogue with other perspectives. I have clearly expressed my commitment to dialogue in this interactionist apologetic model. In fact, it is this commitment to dialogue, critical appropriation, and openness to conversational points of contact which distinctly separates my position from the postliberal perspective and its adoption of a purely descriptive, linguistically constructed, narrative approach to theology. The pure narrative theology of postliberalism tends to reduce truth to the internal consistency of the community narrative, refusing to identify points of dialogical contact in culture and experience.[57]

The Role of Imagination and Myth in the Formation of an Apologetic of Promise and Hope

Images of Hope

I have proposed that imagination is a part of our humanness for living in this world. I would equally contend that hope is a genuine aspect of our humanness. Without

---

54 C.S. Lewis in a letter dated 18 October, 1931 in *They Stand Together: The Letters of C.S. Lewis to Arthur Greeves* (1914–1963) ed. Walter Hooper (London: Collins, 1979), p. 425 cited in Schakel, *Reason and Imagination in C.S. Lewis*, p. 110. The "wh." abreviation for "what" was Lewis's.

55 See J. Wentzel van Huyssteen, *Essays in Postfoundationalist Theology* (Grand Rapids: Eerdmans, 1997), p. 187.

56 David K. Clark, "Narrative Theology and Apologetics," *Journal of the Evangelical Theological Society*, 36/4 (1993): 510–11, and J. Wentzel van Huyssteen, *Essays in Postfoundationalist Theology* (Grand Rapids: Eerdmans, 1997), p. 186.

57 Gerald R. McDermott, *Can Evangelicals Learn From World Religions?: Jesus, Revelation and Religious Traditions* (Downers Grove: InterVarsity, 2000), p. 38.

hope comes despair—creating an imbalance in our humanness. And if despair is left to go its own course without a corrective—it can cause severe psychological disorders. Hope and imagination work together. Without the faculty of imagination, I submit, one cannot hope. I would define hope as the confident expectation of future blessing enabling satisfaction for living in the present. Hope, in its simplest form, is the notion that life in some way will improve. Things may get worse first, but ultimately things will get better. This hope is formulated through the (re)creation of images in the mind. In *Hope Against Hope: Christian Eschatology at the Turn of the Millennium*, Richard Bauckham and Trevor Hart offer the following insights:

> Hope is among those capacities or activities which mark off the territory of the distinctively human within our world. The quest for meaning, truth, goodness and beauty is closely bound up with hope as an activity of the imagination in which we seek to transcend the boundaries of the present, to go beyond the given, outwards and forwards, in search of something more, something better, than the given affords us.... Humans, we might say, are essentially insatiable, driven forwards by a desire for contact with a reality the fullness of which constantly eludes us.[58]

Such images of hope occur within what Garrett Green calls a temporal mode of physical nonpresence. Just as the imagination is needed to "visualize" or construct past occurrences, the "anticipatory use of the realistic imagination" is used in the case of future realities. This is done "by means of extrapolations from past experience, anticipations of new developments, and hypotheses about future states of affairs."[59] We build future realities, in some sense, by a multiplex of comparisons and contrasts with past and present realities. What prevents such images of future blessing from simply becoming illusions of grandeur and mere fantasy? At some point, I would concede that these images merge into magical realism. The imagination is restrained, however, to some extent at the "level of intent." As Green suggests: "We commonly distinguish ... between scientific projections of the future and science fiction."[60]

In my estimation, Green's example breaks down from a postmodern perspective. "Scientific projections" are paradigmatically based, and they do not have the corner on all reality in the present or past, nor will they in the future. In this sense, the postmodern deconstructionist would not necessarily render greater truth-making qualities to scientific projections as to projections made at the level of science fiction.

---

58 Bauckham and Hart, *Hope Against Hope*, p. 52.

59 Garrett Green, *Imagining God: Theology and the Religious Imagination* (San Francisco: Harper and Row, 1989), p. 64. Cf. also Bauckham and Hart, *Hope Against Hope*, pp. 81, 87.

60 Green, *Imagining God*, p. 64. However, I would not deny that our projections of hope are in some senses "fictional worlds," since they are built upon our interpretations which are incomplete. However, these "fictional worlds" are meaningful because we can naturally compare and contrast them with the world with which we are already familiar. See Clarence Walhout, "Narrative Hermeneutics," in Roger Lundin, Clarence Walhout, and Anthony C. Thiselton, *The Promise of Hermeneutics* (Grand Rapids and Cambridge, U.K.: Eerdmans-Paternoster, 1999), p. 82.

However, Green's notion of "level of intent" does express an accurate distinction. The intention of the hope which I am describing, is an intention in some manner to accurately describe future reality, not simply create a chimerical fantasy. Of course, my view of the source for these images of future blessing is significant in this regard. These images of hope are mediated to us through a Christian eschatological realism, which maintains that there is an "undeniable givenness to the universe" that is "seen through the lenses of the gospel." Hence, the intention is to help construct or interpret a world which may reflect God's eschatological purpose for creation using images which will function in an anticipatory manner providing hope for that which is nonpresent reality.[61] This "givenness," however, is not to be confused with a modernist epistemology of mastery. Instead, as Middleton and Walsh affirm, I am submitting that this "givenness to the universe" expresses the reality of creation given as a gift from God to which we must listen, and which we must interpret. Yet, the creation itself stands apart from our attempts to interpret and represent it.[62] The images we use to interpret this creation, although incomplete, are used to motivate us in life, to give us hope, constantly pushing us forward to a reality which is incomplete. This hope is not an anthropocentric hope (either individually or socially) grounded in human potential, but it is a hope beyond hope grounded in the eschatological promise of God.[63]

Often traditional evangelical apologetic theology stresses so much the value of historical evidences, that both the future and the present existential benefits of the here and now are neglected in forming an apologetic. But how can hope of a future blessing in any sense be an "apologetic"? If hope is part of our humanness, then the provision of hope is a reason to believe—and in this sense, a provision of hope functions as an apologetic. Yet, if we agree that we cannot obtain or claim absolute

---

61　Grenz, *Renewing the Center*, pp. 245–6. Grenz submits that this is not a modernist, anthropocentric metanarrative or utopia typical of that which postmodernism rejects. Instead, this is a Christian theocentric eschatology—putting God at the end of the human narrative. Hence, human identity is found in the God who promises and the God who orders the *telos*. Grenz, *Renewing the Center*, p. 217. However, this does not speak to the completeness in which we understand such promises. Christian continental philosopher, Merold Westphal, also provides some pertinent comments in this regard in his introduction to *Overcoming Onto–Theology: Toward a Postmodern Christian Faith* (New York: Fordham University Press, 2001), see, for example, pp. xii–xv. As Westphal submits: "The Christian story legitimizes only one kingdom, the Kingdom of God. In the process it delegitimizes every human kingdom, including democratic capitalism and the Christian church, just to the degree that they are not the full embodiment of God's Kingdom" (p. xv).

62　Middleton and Walsh, *Truth is Stranger Than It Used to Be*, p. 168. Cf. Bauckham and Hart, *Hope Against Hope*, p. 107.

63　Stanley J. Grenz and John R. Franke, *Beyond Foundationalism: Shaping Theology in a Postmodern Context* (Louisville: Westminster John Knox Press, 2001), p. 251. For a treatment of the use of images of hope in Christian eschatology, see Bauckham and Hart, *Hope Against Hope*, pp. 109–73.

knowledge of eschatological reality due to the enigma of life, in what sense can we speak of genuine hope? With this question in mind I turn to our next section.

Hope and the Enigma of Life

With a lack of insistence on absolute knowledge of eschatological reality it does not diminish a Christian view of God, but rather enhances it. Expressing the limits of human wisdom is certainly characteristic of the injunctions expressed in Old Testament wisdom literature. Qoheleth tells us in Ecclesiastes 3:11 that God has "set eternity in the hearts of men; yet they cannot fathom what God has done from beginning to end." This does not mean that we have no power of reason whatsoever, nor that we cast aside typical proverbial wisdom since life is a grand mystery. One must understand cause and effect and the basic rules of practical living. On the other hand, experience tells us that we can never understand life with complete certainty. We must remain open for mystery, for the paradoxes of life. We can never claim absolute wisdom, because our life is not determined by self-mastery.[64] As the biblical narrative is a compelling plot which "entails coherence as well as surprise" so is God's continued work in the narrative of our lives.[65] God is beyond our limited understandings and intellectual notions. The real God is an iconoclast—and a Creator of paradoxes. But in my view, this does not diminish the God of Christian theism, it gives credence to him. Richard P. Hansen helpfully suggests that paradox helps us see God less as our individual map book for life, and more as the reason for our journey. Paradox can both reveal and hide, affirm, yet invite reflection—it "beckons us into Mystery, and offers a wholesome reminder that God is infinitely greater than our ideas about God."[66]

This notion of a limited human wisdom is easily coupled with the notion of biblical faith. The women and men of faith as recorded in the Epistle to the Hebrews, for example, lived in light of the hope of echatological realism. Their hope was derived from images given from an incomplete narrative—but a narrative derived from a personal, communicative God in whom they implicitly trusted.[67] Life was an

---

64 See Gerhard Von Rad, *Wisdom In Israel* (Nashville: Abingdon Press, 1972), p. 106. Cf. pp. 108–9. Also see Bauckham and Hart, *Hope Against Hope*, p. 43. George Aichele, Jr speaks to this when he states that the theologian, as other postmodern intellectuals, "engages in an ongoing and endless conversation with those of other traditions, and with the classic texts, a conversation with no expectation of ultimate and decisive truth, but with confidence that criteria of relative, de facto adequacy permit meaning to emerge." George Aichele Jr, "Literary Fantasy and Postmodern Theology:" 332–3.

65 Fackre, "Narrative Theology," 345.

66 Richard P. Hansen, "Unsolved Mysteries: Biblical Paradox Offers an Alternative to 'How to' Sermons," *Leadership* 21/1 (2000): 56, 60.

67 "All these people were still living by faith when they died. They did not receive the things promised; they only saw them and welcomed them from a distance. And they admitted that they were aliens and strangers on earth. People who say such things show that they are looking for a country of their own. If they had been thinking of the country they had left,

enigma, a mystery, a wandering of sorts for these women and men, yet they moved forward through images of promise—and in their wandering, created a human narrative of hope for those who follow their example. It is important to retain a sense of sublime mystery while imagining God's coming kingdom:

> And imagine we must. Our imaginative projections of the perfect society are influenced by our sensitivity to the needs of our present context, to the crisis posed by future consciousness. Our thoughts are conditioned and finite, to be sure. Nonetheless, we understand God's salvation as fulfillment, as meeting the actual needs of us creatures as experienced historically. This means that the content of God's eschatological kingdom—who and what will be there—will be made up of the very course of historical events in which we are presently engaged.[68]

One may notice parallels between Moltmann's theology of hope and Peters' notions expressed here. For Moltmann, a hope which traditionally looks to a world beyond, "must be supplemented by hope for the transformation and renewal of the earth."[69] However, Moltmann's eschatological theology of hope must not be simply construed as simply a status quo utopia. Moltmann insists that a Christian eschatology is grounded in the person and history of Jesus Christ, and this is the "touchstone by which to distinguish the spirit of eschatology from that of utopia."[70] Once again, this believing hope advocated by Moltmann, provides many creative resources for the imagination:

> It constantly provokes and produces thinking of an anticipatory kind in love to man and the world, in order to give shape to the newly dawning possibilities in the light of the promised future, in order as far as possible to create here the best that is possible, because what is promised is within the bounds of possibility.[71]

But if we readily acknowledge the limits of human wisdom and reasoning, and concurrently affirm a notion of hope in eschatological reality—do we simply abandon ourselves to the frustration of the enigmas of daily life? Is there any hope for hope today? Can such a notion of eschatological hope, as with memories, ironically lead to a sense of despair in the present? Memory can bind one to the past which is no longer present, just as hope projects one into the future which is not yet present. Cannot both memories and hopes cheat one of the possibility of happiness in the

---

they would have had opportunity to return. Instead, they were longing for a better country—a heavenly one." (Hebrews 11:13–16a)

68 Ted Peters, *God—The World's Future: Systematic Theology for a Postmodern Era* (Minneapolis: Fortress, 1992), p. 366.

69 Jürgen Moltmann, *Theology Today*, trans. John Bowden (London: SCM Press Ltd., 1988), p. 23.

70 Jürgen Moltmann, *Theology of Hope*, trans. James W. Leitch (London: SCM Press Ltd., 1967), pp. 34, 17.

71 Ibid., pp. 34–5.

present?[72] Moltmann issues an emphatic "No." Hope itself *is* the "happiness of the present." It is hope which

> pronounces the poor blessed, receives the weary and heavy laden, the humbled and wronged, the hungry and the dying, because it perceives the parousia of the kingdom for them. Expectation makes life good, for in expectation man can accept his whole present and find joy not only in its joy but also in its sorrow, happiness not only in its happiness but also in its pain. Thus hope goes on its way through the midst of happiness and pain, because in the promises of God it can see a future also for the transient, the dying and the dead. That is why it can be said that living without hope is like no longer living.[73]

As I noted previously, in the book of Ecclesiastes, Qoheleth reminds us of our troublesome plight as humans in the life of the unknown. Life is indeed a mystery. Yet, as Moltmann affirms, hope although built on a futurist eschatology, is not simply relegated to some "object" of future fulfillment—it involves the happiness of the present as well. We continue to wander, search, and err in the midst of the often troublesome paradoxes of life in hope of what is to come, yet because of this hope, we may also find satisfaction in the present.[74] It is this sense of life's enigmatic, wandering "absence" that Middleton and Walsh call "postmodern homelessness." During this time of exile in the wilderness, a time "in the margin," we realize that complete construction and control must be abandoned in order to receive the gift of God's sustenance moment by moment. But we cannot hold on to this gift as our own construction. If we are "at–home" in our own constructions we will be perpetually homeless without hope.[75]

> This world cannot be our home when we seek to secure it as such. Home is gift to be received. This gift is still offered to us in a postmodern context populated by disappointed, wandering, homeless nomads. Grasping the gift will invariably result in its loss. Receiving

---

72 Ibid., p. 26.

73 Ibid., p. 32. I recognize that Moltmann's context is different to our own. Moltmann's particular applied understanding of eschatological hope is greatly political in motivation and heavily influenced by Ernst Bloch's Marxist revisionist philosophy. Yet, I readily acknowledge the value of his thinking for the development of a renewed sense of the importance of community centered eschatology in progressive evangelical thought. See Grenz and Franke, *Beyond Foundationalism*, p. 247. For a constructive critique of Moltmann's theology of hope, see Stephen N. Williams, "The Problem with Moltmann," *European Journal of Theology* 5/2 (1996): 157–67.

74 In contrast to Moltmann's world or political hope as motivation for living joyfully in the here and now, is the autonomous hope of Don Cupitt. Although I would not adhere to Cupitt's radical subjectivism and, in my estimation, extreme anti-foundationalism, Cupitt points us to the value of enthusiastically living in the present through his notion of Solar Living. Unlike Cupitt, Moltmann's perspective of hope is not simply self-abandonment to the present, but it is seeking to "lead existing reality towards the promised and hoped-for transformation." Anthony C. Thiselton, *Interpreting God and the Postmodern Self* (Edinburgh: T&T Clark, 1995), pp. 126, 145. The quotation is taken from Moltmann, *Theology of Hope*, p. 18.

75 Middleton and Walsh, *Truth is Stranger Than It Used to Be*, pp. 155, 157–9, 161.

the gift and heeding its call to suffering service can provide us with a profound sense of home even in the midst of exile and animate our lives with a hope of a final restoration, a final and joyous homecoming.[76]

As Christians, then, we are expectant pilgrims and wayfarers in the eschatological reality to come, but we also find hopeful satisfaction in the soujourn itself because God gives us gifts for the journey and personally provides us with comfort.[77] As Mark C. Taylor effectively reminds us, this wilderness journey will be a wandering with "erring." Hope may be found in the wandering, yet, contra Taylor, not by warmly embracing nihilism, but by receiving the gracious gifts of God's sustenance in life through the power of story and the use of the imagination which convey images of a greater reality to come. This is where the value of magical realism would support this perspective of hope.[78]

Unlike Taylor, we cannot contrive any real hope from the notion of endless wandering. Grace can indeed be found in "mazing"—but grace cannot be reduced to "mazing" with no hope of fulfillment. Similarly, I have noted positive elements to Derrida's notion of the messianic as an ever-occuring hope. Although one may affirm an eschatological reality without complete closure, allowing for growth or development, I would affirm a "passion for the promise" in expectation of real fulfillment. Everything to come is not an endless *viens* ("come") as put forward with both Caputo and Derrida.[79] If the good, the hope, the truly just—is always to come, and always "impossible" but never arriving—"how is it that evil and violence are not conflated with goodness and thereby put on equal footing?"[80] We must affirm an eschatology which both "resists premature closure," yet, also refuses "premature consolation that pre–empts grief." For such a facile, premature optimism does not recognize evil for what it is.[81]

We can also gain positive insights with respect to this notion of positive sojourning from James K.A. Smith's "Augustinian" creational hermeneutic. Smith submits that hermeneutical, interpretive structures honor diversity, and are fundamentally good because they are a part of our created humanness as given by God. They are indeed

---

76 Ibid., p. 161.

77 Steven Bouma-Prediger, "Yearning for Home: The Christian Doctrine of Creation in a Postmodern Age," in *Postmodern Philosophy and Christian Thought*, ed. Merold Westphal (Bloomington and Indianapolis: Indiana University Press, 1999), pp. 193–4.

78 See Clarence Walhout, "Narrative Hermeneutics," in Lundin, Walhout, and Thiselton, *The Promise of Hermeneutics*, p. 130. Walhout aptly follows this thought by submitting that when we, as Christians, engage in reading fictional narratives we are participating "in this unending and hopeful exploration of the possibilities of living in the world and thereby in our own living to discover and enjoy more fully the faces of others and the face of the Other. (p. 130)

79 John D. Caputo, *The Prayers and Tears of Jacques Derrida: Religion Without Religion* (Bloomington & Indianapolis: Indiana University Press, 1997), p. xxi.

80 Shane Cudney, "Religion Without Religion": Caputo, Derrida, and the Violence of Particularity," *Faith and Philosophy* 16/3 (1999): 398.

81 Bauckham and Hart, *Hope Against Hope*, p. 42.

finite, but they are "grounded in creational finitude." Since finitude is grounded in what it means to be essentially human, these structures are not inherently violent or evil. "Rather than construing creation and finitude as a fault (*culpa*), no matter how happy (*felix*), a creation theology challenges us to see in our finitude a gift that is not to be despised but rather enjoyed and even celebrated."[82] Such a creational hermeneutic is in contrast to present and eschatological immediacy models which view the necessity of interpretation as a result of the fall; and a violent mediation model (Heidegger, Derrida) which views interpretation as constitutive of our humanness but structurally violent.[83]

Smith's creational hermeneutic is in accord with the interactionist apologetic model I am advocating. If we acknowledge hermeneutics as part of the creative nature of our humanness and not necessarily violent, instead of closing off possibilities for dialogue, it opens them up. As Smith states: "Interpretation is not a sign of falling into the Garden; rather it is an invitation to commune with the other."[84] As we acknowledge our common finitude in being human, our eyes are opened to the reality that God's grace transcends the bounds of race, culture, and nation. This reality can be marvelously demonstrated as a positive apologetic, as I argued in chapter 10 ("Lessons From the Book of Acts"), in ethnically and culturally heterogeneous church communities. We can, as a diverse group of wayfarers and sojourners, learn from each other, embrace each other, and reach out to strangers and outcasts. In this way, we model an understanding of ourselves not as masters and controllers, but as stewards of creation for the Creator.[85] Such an example provides an apologetic of hope and promise amidst the enigmatic difficulties of life for both those within the community and those to whom the community extends its welcoming arms. As we acknowledge our finitude as pilgrims in the process of life, we continually draw upon the use of the imagination to help push us forward into the mystery of the beyond, to the mystery of the God who created us.

I noted above that I would not ascribe carte blanche to Derrida's notion of the messianic, nor to Taylor's endless erring and "mazing" and infinite deferral of the Parousia.[86] Nevertheless, I readily acknowledge many positive insights these concepts provide in terms of one's perspective of hope and promise. Taylor certainly reminds us that "to err is human." We do wander through life's many paradoxes,

---

82 James K.A. Smith, *The Fall of Interpretation: Philosophical Foundations For a Creational Hermeneutic* (Downers Grove: InterVarsity, 2000), pp. 59, 159, 77. The quote is from p. 77.

83 Ibid., pp. 22, 23, 26. Cf. Kevin J. Vanhoozer's discussion in, *Is There a Meaning in this Text?* (Grand Rapids: Zondervan, 1998), p. 294. Vanhoozer, like Smith, examines various options in response to interpretive differences "Between Dogmatism and Skepticism."

84 Smith, *The Fall of Interpretation*, p. 113.

85 See Stephen A. Rhodes, *Where Nations Meet: The Church in Multicultural World* (Downers Grove: InterVarsity, 1998), pp. 124, 17, 135.

86 Mark C. Taylor, *Tears* (Albany: State University of New York Press, 1990), p. 84. Cf. Brian D. Ingraffia, *Postmodern Theory and Biblical Theology* (Cambridge: Cambridge University Press, 1995), p. 234.

interpreting and deciphering, always with inconclusive understandings. Our wisdom is limited; we are finite beings. Unlike Taylor, as said earlier, we cannot embrace nihilism and hopelessness, but we find hope in our wandering derived from the promises of God. We do not wander aimlessly with hope to "draw near to the sacred by patiently awaiting what never arrives."[87] We faithfully look for fulfilled promises of living in the fullness of God's loving presence. But our finitude limits us and keeps us, at times, from immediate happiness in the journey. So we continue to yearn with a "burning heart" in spite of hardship, loss and sorrow—for "Something more, Something else, Something better."[88] The apologetic behind this notion of longing, lies not merely in the longing itself, but also in a question which follows the longing: Is this longing pointing to something yet to be discovered not yet fulfilled? As Alister McGrath asks: "Can we really dismiss this human longing for something which seems to lie beyond us as a delusion, however pleasant, which merely distracts us from the harsher truths of real life? Or might this sense of longing be a signpost, pointing us to that promised land?"[89]

Smith's creational hermeneutic submits that our finitude is part of our created nature. I believe that we can apply the notions of this creational hermeneutic to a progressive evangelical eschatology. We can simultaneously acknowledge that aspects of promise can be fulfilled, while at the same time affirming that we are a people endlessly hoping and always learning and developing. A critical recontextualization of Derrida's notion of the endless *viens*—the messianic which never arrives—provides some keen insights at this juncture. As Christians, we must be hopeful people, yet cautious in our personal claims to understand reality lest we make idols out of our own desires. Our faith should be characterized by humility and sensitivity to the limits "and situatedness of our thinking" and "should be able to adopt an eschatological metaphysics of absence with an attitude of waiting 'until he comes.'"[90]

This perspective is not a far cry from the doctrine of unending growth (*epectasis*) envisaged by some of the Greek fathers—including St. Gregory of Nyssa.[91] Gregory, drawing from Paul (Phil. 3:13), submits that

---

87 Taylor, *Tears*, p. 12. Cf. Ingraffia, *Postmodern Theory and Biblical Theology*, p. 234.

88 Mark Buchanan, "Stuck on the Road to Emmaus: The Secret to Why We are not Fulfilled," *Christianity Today* (July 12 1999): 56. This "yearning" is what C.S. Lewis described in his personal journey as *Sehnsucht* or Joy. See, for example, Lewis, *Suprised By Joy*, pp. 7, 17–18.

89 Alister McGrath, *The Unknown God: Searching For Spiritual Fulfillment* (Grand Rapids: Eerdmans, 1999), p. 17. See also p. 10.

90 Andrew Gustafson, "Apologetically Listening to Derrida," *Philosophia Christi* 20/2 (1997): 18.

91 I am indebted to an article by Bishop Kallistos (Timothy) Ware for pointing me in this direction. Kallistos Ware, "God of the Fathers: C.S. Lewis and Eastern Christianity," in *The Pilgrim's Guide*, pp. 53–69.

in our constant participation in the blessed nature of the Good, the graces that we receive at every point are indeed great, but the path that lies beyond our immediate grasp is infinite. This will constantly happen to those who thus share in the divine Goodness, and they will always enjoy a greater and greater participation in grace throughout eternity.[92]

However, Gregory does not deny the possibility of any eschatological fulfillment. Those who are pure in heart will indeed see God (Matt. 5:8), but it will be according to one's capacity as to how much of God's unlimited greatness he or she can sustain. For the "incomprehensible nature of the Godhead remains beyond all understanding."[93] Although it is important to see, according to Gregory, that understanding one's limitations does not squelch one's perpetual hope, because God has created us with a never-ending hunger for Himself. "To those who have tasted and seen by experience *that the Lord is sweet* (Ps. 33:9), this taste becomes a kind of invitation to further enjoyment. And thus the one who is rising towards God constantly experiences this continual incitement towards further progress."[94]

Christian apologetics is built on the hope of the reality of its expressed truths, especially the life and death of Jesus, the resurrection, and the privilege of Christians to share in the blessings derived from such expressed realities. However, the Christian's claims to detailed accuracy must be modest. The images we derive from the multifaceted biblical narrative, our personal experiences and culture, and many other factors are still "less true" than reality itself. But I am submitting that they are partially right, and they are pointers or signposts to a reality beyond our immediacy. This is where the human reality of hope is crucial for an apologetic of the imagination. Some may counter and say that the notion of hope is simply a projection of a desired reality, but has nothing to do with reality itself. It is simply a great projection of one's longings. Simply because we long for water does not guarantee the existence of a nearby well. But, the apologetic key lies not simply at the point of desire, but at the point of need. If we are thirsty, it does not necessarily point to a nearby fountain, but it does point to a felt and perceived need. And in the case of water, it points to a natural need for personal survival. With this model, the apologetic lies not in an evidential statement of fact, but in the possibility of the signpost. Our sense of

---

92 St. Gregory of Nyssa, "The Doctrine of Infinite Growth, Commentary on the Conticle, sermon 8, 940C–941C," in *From Glory to Glory: Texts From Gregory of Nyssa's Mystical Writings*, ed. S.J. Herbert Musurillo (New York: Charles Scribner's Sons, 1961; reprint, Crestwood: St. Vladimir's Seminary Press, 1979), pp. 211–12. Cf. also pp. 56–7 in the same work.

93 Ibid., p. 212.

94 Ibid., p. 213. Kallistos Ware points out that this notion of eternal life is similarly expressed in the imaginative work of C.S. Lewis when discussing the eternal realm of Narnia near the end of *The Last Battle*: Narnia is described both like the the layers of an onion and the successive chapters of a Great Story respectively, with each circle larger than the previous one, and every chapter "better than the one before." Kallistos Ware, "God of the Fathers: C.S. Lewis and Eastern Christianity," p. 68. Cf. C.S. Lewis, *The Last Battle* (New York: Macmillan, 1956), pp. 180, 184.

longing for something beyond, something profound and satisfying, *may* point to something in reality. Christians submit that this is a pointer to a personal God who created humans with such a longing to seek Him.[95] This "what if" possibility itself provides an occasion for apologetic dialogue. But do I need a basis for such a claim? Does this necessitate a complete surrender to foundationalism? I will discuss this further in the next chapter.

---

95 McGrath, *The Unknown God*, pp. 20–22, 25. Cf. also p. 32, 71.

Chapter 13

Apologetic Groundwork:
Are Any "Foundations" Possible?

I have chosen to include a chapter on "apologetic groundwork" near the end of this work instead of at the beginning where, normally, the topic of "groundwork" would seem most appropriate.[1] This is strategic for two reasons. First of all, I wish to distinguish between the prolegomena and research used for this book, and the consideration of "groundwork" or basis for the type of apologetic methodology I am advocating in the course of this book. Second, since this book is attempting to suggest apologetic methological proposals in view of postmodern deconstructive concerns, it is important that I engage the thinking that is expressing these concerns before suggesting a methodological framework by which to continue apologetic dialogue with those holding such perspectives. In this sense, I have attempted to practice what I am proposing before making the proposal itself.

The question that is most pertinent at this juncture may be: How does one move beyond advocating a progressive evangelical concern for dialogue in the context of plurality, to making a choice between competing narratives? I want to readily acknowledge my finitude and cultural conditionedness without conceding to conceptual relativism. Accordingly, I am not advocating a modernist, strong foundationalist theology nor a Christian "neo-Wittgensteinian fideism."[2] So, how can one even make these claims and rejections, while at the same time deny foundationalism? It is well beyond the scope and intention of this work to pursue a detailed philosophical articulation of a Christian epistemology, the topic of which has been competently addressed in other works.[3] Nevertheless, I will offer several

---

1   Charles Winquist notes that modern philosophy (and I would add modern theology) strategically begins by searching for the "roots or foundations of knowledge." Then he adds: "The image of the root, the radix, of consciousness was a severe image of a taproot from which a tree of knowledge could spread." Charles E. Winquist, *Desiring Theology* (Chicago: University of Chicago Press, 1995), p. 9.

2   David K. Clark, "Narrative Theology and Apologetics," *Journal of the Evangelical Theological Society* 36/4 (1993): 510–11 and J. Wentzel Van Huyssteen, *Essays in Postfoundationalist Theology* (Grand Rapids: Eerdmans, 1997), p. 186. Van Huyssteen uses "neo–Wittgensteinian fideism" to refer to a nonfoundationalist narrative theology, where religious beliefs are simply accepted within the context of an internally consistent language game.

3   For example, see W. Jay Wood, *Epistemology: Becoming Intellectually Virtuous* (Downers Grove: InterVarsity, 1998), and R. Douglas Geivett and Brendan Sweetman (eds),

proposals in line with a "soft" or "modest" foundationalism as helpful apologetic groundwork for the discussion at hand.

The Meaning of Foundationalism

In order to proceed, I first need to describe the meaning of foundationalism as I am using the term. Foundationalism in its classical philosophical sense refers to, in the tradition of Descartes, the indubitable grounding of one's beliefs. In his classic work, *Reason Within the Bounds of Religion*, the Christian philosopher of religion, Nicholas Wolterstorff, defined foundationalism's goal as "to form a body of theories from which all prejudice, bias, and unjustified conjecture have been eliminated." In order to reach this goal, Wolterstorff adds, "we must begin with a firm foundation of certitude and build the house of theory on it by methods of whose reliability we are equally certain."[4] Some beliefs are rooted in a basic, immediate fashion, other beliefs are nonbasic or mediate. Such nonbasic, mediate beliefs are justified on the "foundation" of more basic beliefs which are grounded in self-evidential reason. These nonbasic beliefs are deductible from basic beliefs or supported by them with high probability.[5]

It is this notion of classical or strong foundationalism and its quest for indubitable certitude, which stands under severe criticism in the postmodern ethos. I find it ironic, yet insightful, that Benno Van den Toren argues that foundationalism is also the "hidden premiss of postmodern thought in its relativistic forms."[6] Van den Toren's accusation pertains to the possibility of foundationalism as a theoretical noetic structure, not to the assumed truth of the premise stated. In other words, many moderns assume the truth of foundationalism; whereas postmoderns would not assume its truth, but would assume the need to disprove its assumed truth. In this, it betrays the "hidden premiss" to which Van den Toren is referring. There is something to be said about Van den Toren's point, but more needs to be said about what "brand" of foundationalism is being disputed.

Contemporary Perspectives on Religious Epistemology (New York and Oxford: Oxford University Press, 1992).

4   Nicholas Wolterstorff, *Reason Within the Bounds of Religion* (Grand Rapids: Eerdmans, 1976), p. 24. Cf. also Kelly James Clark, *Return to Reason* (Grand Rapids: Eerdmans, 1990), pp. 132–54; and Stanley J. Grenz and John R. Franke, *Beyond Foundationalism: Shaping Theology in a Postmodern Context* (Louisville: Westminster John Knox Press, 2001), p. 23.

5   Wood, *Epistemology,* pp. 78, 85. Cf. Kevin J. Vanhoozer, *Is There a Meaning in This Text?* (Grand Rapids: Zondervan, 1998), pp. 286–7; and Benno Van den Toren, "A New Direction in Christian Apologetics: An Exploration with Reference to Postmodernism," *European Journal of Theology* 2/1 (1993): 55–6. See also Grenz and Franke, *Beyond Foundationalism*, pp. 29–35, for discussion on how Enlightenment foundationalism has influenced modern theology.

6   Van den Toren, "A New Direction in Christian Apologetics," 56.

For example, David K. Clark submits that it is not typically epistemic foundationalism (of which he claims "classical foundationalism" is a form) which postmodernists resist, but another form known as *modernist foundationalism*. Modernist foundationalism does not speak to individual convictions and beliefs as with epistemic foundationalism, but speaks to a universal grounding of knowledge and rationality in logic and language.[7] Although these clarifying distinctions may be helpful for identifying nuances of foundationalism, I would not view these differences in the substantial way Clark seems to describe them. From my perspective, as I have attempted to show in this work, postmodern thinkers do reject the classical, epistemic foundationalism in the vein of Descartes. In my estimation, it is this individually focused epistemic foundationalism that has pre-empted the more universally structured modernist foundationalist notions as well.

The Demise of Classical Foundationalism

Although classical foundationalism has been severely criticized in recent years, it lingers on in modernist assumptions. But Wolterstorff maintains, as with many others, that foundationalism "is in bad shape" and should be given up "for mortally ill" and we must "learn to live in its absence."[8] Due to the limits and scope of this book I will not detail the problems with classical foundationalism which have also been adequately articulated elsewhere.[9] Throughout this book, I have cited sympathetic perspectives to the demise of classical foundationalism stemming from Kierkegaard's religious subjectivism, Nietzsche's perspectivism, Gadamer's "fusion of horizons," Kuhn's paradigm shifts in the philosophy of science, Wittgenstein's notion of "language games," and structuralist and deconstructionist accounts of "knowledge" with all of its limitations. Each of these mark in some way the historical/cultural/linguistic rootedness of our beliefs and expressions of our understanding of reality.[10] W. Jay Wood observes the implications of this:

---

7   David K. Clark, "Relativism, Fideism and the Promise of Postliberalism," in *The Nature of Confession: Evangelicals and Postliberals in Conversation*, eds Timothy R. Phillips and Dennis L. Okholm (Downers Grove: InterVarsity, 1996), p. 118.

8   Wolterstorff, *Reason Within*, p. 52. Cf. also Stanley J. Grenz, *Renewing the Center* (Grand Rapids: Baker, 2000), pp. 190–91. Grenz cites Merold Westphal who declares that the indefensibility of foundationalism "is so widely agreed that its demise is the closest thing to a philosophical consensus in decades." Merold Westphal, "A Reader's Guide to 'Reformed Epistemology,'" *Perspectives* 7/9 (November 1992): 10–11 in Grenz, *Renewing the Center*, p. 190.

9   See again, for example, Wood, *Epistemology*, pp. 88–98; and also Michael Peterson and others, *Reason and Religious Belief: An Introduction to the Philosophy of Religion* (New York and Oxford: Oxford University Press, 1991), pp. 119–22. For a more detailed, analytic discussion of foundationalism and its inherent problems, see William P. Alston, "Two Types of Foundationalism," *The Journal of Philosophy* 73/7 (1976): 165–85.

10   Wood, *Epistemology*, pp. 96–7.

What this means is that strong foundationalists are wrong to suppose that they have demonstrated the norms on the basis of which all justified thinking takes place. And with the loss of a transcendental point of view ("a view from nowhere") there is no way to secure an ironclad guarantee that the rational standards one does invoke precisely mirror a mind-independent world.[11]

In this book I have made a modest effort to suggest a model of interactive, critical appropriation of postmodern deconstructionist concerns as a means for Christian apologetic dialogue. Can I continue these efforts in view of the postmodern critique of foundationalism? J. Wentzel van Huyssteen, in his book, *Essays in Postfoundationalist Theology*, affirms this possibility: "It therefore is possible to appropriate postmodern thought in a constructive way by interpreting it as a reflection on the potential, nature, shortcomings, and darker sides of modernity."[12] If one indeed agrees with van Huyssteen, that one such "darker side" or at least "shortcoming" of modernity is that of classical foundationalism, then I can move forward. It is this radical questioning and constant interruption of ingrained modernist assumptions—"through relentless criticism of intellectual conceit and uncritical dogmatism"—which, in my estimation, can open new possibilities to continue the apologetic conversation rather than cutting it off.[13]

But must we necessarily deny all foundational knowledge and "objectivity" in order to make this move? Wolterstorff, calling for the death of foundationalism, does not deny objective reality, nor does he repudiate truth as a "legitimate and attainable goal of inquiry" but he is simply asserting "that theorizing is without a foundation of indubitables."[14] But without such "indubitables" how do we continue to make Christian religious claims?

Rodney Clapp has metaphorically equated the foundationalist agenda to children playing on a safe, slippery slide. Some children prone to relativism may tire of the rules of the safe, slippery slide and wander into unsafe traffic. However, Clapp observes that the foundationalist's suppositions are mistaken. Safety cannot be secured absolutely. Knowledge is limited and always involves perspective. It is not

---

11 Ibid., p. 97.

12 J. Wentzel Van Huyssteen, *Essays in Postfoundationalist Theology* (Grand Rapids: Eerdmans, 1997), p. 279. Van Huyssteen refers to H.P.P. Lötter, "A Postmodern Philosophy of Science?" *South African Journal of Philosophy* 13/3 (1994): 159.

13 Van Huyssteen, *Essays in Postfoundationalist Theology*, p. 78. It is essentially this postmodern sympathy we have expressed in our critique of the Enlightenment project throughout this work.

14 Wolterstorff, *Reason Within*, pp. 52–3. For a philosophically astute descussion on the philosophical notions of objectivity and realism, see Paul K. Moser, *Philosophy After Objectivity: Making Sense in Perspective* (New York and Oxford: Oxford University Press, 1993). Moser submits that those things which are "objective" are those things which exist independently of one's conception of them. Whereas, "objective knowledge" would be knowledge of such "conceiving–independent things."(p. 4) This provides a helpful clarification which is often overlooked. There is a critical difference between affirming objective reality and affirming knowledge of that reality.

completely safe living at the top of the slide merely focusing on the slippery slope toward complete assurance. Instead, we must dismount the slide and be freed to assess the danger in its various forms in our sinful, fallen world.[15] In my estimation, Clapp's metaphor still betrays at least some closet, although modest, foundationalist notions. The freedom to assess "the danger" assumes some notion of "foundational" objectivity from which to make such assessment. I believe this expresses what is best described as a "soft" foundationalism.

A Plea for Soft Foundationalism

Although I agree with the postmodern critique on the demise of classical foundationalism, I would not completely deny the possibility of intellecutal foundations altogether. Instead, I would affirm what David K. Clark has called a "chastened foundationalism"[16]—often referred to as "soft" or "modest" foundationalism.[17] A soft foundationalism readily acknowledges the limits of human reason, while not giving in to a complete skepticism. It does not claim invincible certainty, but modestly purports "only prima facie certainty." Religious beliefs are not "foundational" to the degree of complete immunity to all doubt, "but they are perfectly acceptable unless one has good reason for thinking they have been undermined."[18] A similar thought is expressed by Michael S. Jones, in an article

---

15 Rodney Clapp, "How Firm a Foundation: Can Evangelicals Be Nonfoundationalists?," in *The Nature of Confession*, p. 89.

16 Clark, "Narrative Theology and Apologetics," p. 512.

17 Wood notes that this form of foundationalism is also called "minimal," "modest," or "mitigated" foundationalism in *Epistemology: Becoming Intellectually Virtuous*, ed. C. Stephen Evans, Contours of Christian Philosophy (Downers Grove: InterVarsity, 1998), p. 85. It should be noted, however, that not all would equate "modest" with "minimal" foundationalism in a strictly philosophical sense. For example, see Julie Gowen, "Foundationalism and the Justification of Religious Belief," *Religious Studies* 19, (September 1983): 393–406. As Gowen states: "Minimal foundationalism has a clear epistemic advantage over modest foundationalism in that those beliefs which are properly basic can be immediately justified in the weak sense (i.e. they may, or even must, receive some of their warrant from other justified beliefs)." (p. 403). For the purposes of this book as it pertains to our theological apologetic investigation in relation to deconstructionism, I will use the designation "modest foundationalism" in the more general sense as mentioned in Wood, *Epistemology*, p. 85 (as noted above) and also David K. Clark's assessment of Plantinga's Reformed epistemology, in "Relativism, Fideism and the Promise of Postliberalism," p. 116. It would also be helpful to compare this notion of modest foundationalism with the "critical realism" advocated by N.T. Wright in *The New Testament and the People of God: Christian Origins and the Question of God*, vol. 1 (London: SPCK, 1992), pp. 32–7.

18 Wood, *Epistemology*, pp. 98–9. Wood points out that the Scottish commonsense philosopher, Thomas Reid, an early critic of Descartes, represents much that is typical of the modest or soft foundationalist perspective (p. 99). Kelly James Clark discusses this in a section titled "Reid and Rationality" in his *Return to Reason*, pp. 143–51.

discussing evangelicals and interreligious dialogue. Jones effectively describes this as a "deabsolutized epistemology." This does not necessarily imply that we cannot know the truth but it does mean it may be the case that we may not know what we believe to be true, is in fact true. As Jones claims: "A belief may or may not be true regardless of whether or not one can know that it is true."[19] As one may see, this perspective is substantially aligned with the modified reformed epistemological apologetic I espoused in chapter 9, and the critical realist model discussed in chapter 10, in relation to the problem of incommensurability.

Properly Basic Beliefs

This deabsolutized, soft foundationalism does not completely dismiss the quest for basic beliefs. However, Enlightenment foundationalism and its demand for epistemological certitude with regard to what may be counted as properly basic is rejected. Religious beliefs may not be assigned a shelf on a superstructure of belief.[20] Instead, I am suggesting that there are indeed some basic beliefs all humans have which provide avenues for some degree of common parlance and ethics.[21] The notion of human reasoning (not to be confused simply with scientific reasoning) may be considered one such avenue—even though the criteria which define the content of that reasoning will differ.[22] If I did not acknowledge this, I could not assume any

---

19 Michael S. Jones, "Evangelical Christianity and the Philosophy of Interreligious Dialogue," *Journal of Ecumenical Studies* 36/3–4 (Summer–Fall 1999): 386–7.

20 Grenz and Franke, *Beyond Foundationalism*, p. 47. Reformed epistemologists, such as Alvin Plantinga, would affirm that belief in God existence is itself properly basic. See Plantinga, "Is Belief in God Properly Basic?," in *Contemporary Perspectives on Religious Epistemology*, pp. 133–41; reprinted from *Nous*, 15 (1981). Also see Peterson and others, *Reason and Religious Belief*, pp. 122–27.

21 For example, I would acknowledge such things as personal existence, and some (however abstract and to whatever degree) moral sensibility. Some may suggest that moral assertions are not in any sense foundational, but simply facts for living. Yet, as James Sire wisely notes, the fact of a moral judgment does not guarantee its authenticity. If everyone believes that the world is flat, this does not make the world flat. Sire argues that the distinction between right and wrong must point to a foundational value beyond general opinion. See James W. Sire, *Why Should Anyone Believe Anything at all?* (Downers Grove: InterVarsity, 1994), pp. 166–71. In my critique of Mark C. Taylor, I cited "four commonsense notions" which Griffin claims are practically acknowledged by all humans. See David Ray Griffin, "Postmodern Theology and A/Theology: A Response to Mark C. Taylor," in *Varieties of Postmodern Theology*, ed. David Ray Griffin, SUNY Series in Constructive Postmodern Thought (New York: State University of New York Press, 1989), pp. 35–40.

22 As Thomas Nagel submits, "reasoning in its own right defeats efforts to depict it as subordinate to something else that discredits its pretentions. It rears up its head to pass judgment on the very hypothesis that was designed to put it in its place. It inevitably reappears because any such hypothesis invites the question, 'What reason do we have to think the world is really like that?' The alternatives always have to compete with the possibility that things are more or less as they appear to be—a possibility that can often be defeated, but only for reasons

level of understanding of what I am writing in this book itself. In my view, if we deny all common ground possibilities of this sort it makes a *reductio ad absurdum* precluding any notion of human dialogue. This foundationalism is soft, however, because these basic beliefs are not used to stack belief upon belief in order to justify a complex belief system.

So, I deny that beliefs work in a classical foundationalist fashion. Instead, our beliefs are more contextually shaped by webs of relationships in various areas of thought. Grenz and Franke suggest that Christian doctrine is a "belief mosaic" and the constructive work of theology leads to a multi-patterned mosaic of interconnected pieces "rather than merely to a collection of beads on a string."[23] When we examine these beliefs and recommend them to others, we must be careful not to "suppose that another person's web must be just like our own."[24] But, to argue that our Christian beliefs are contextually shaped by a web of various modes of thought (e.g. history, reason, imagination, community) and that they even function to regulate behavior within that community does not negate the reality of those beliefs. As I have submitted in this book, such a coherence of beliefs involves the willingness to continually test, reinterpret and recontextualize certain beliefs in the process of critical dialogue and appropriation. It is this "willingness" that assumes the "soft" foundational assumption of justice in a non-oppressive setting by which such critical dialogue can take place.

Coherentism and Eschatological Realism

The theological coherentist, soft foundational perspective put forward by Grenz and Franke, as they themselves note, was greatly influenced by the theological methodology of Grenz's doctoral mentor, Wolfhart Pannenberg.[25] Pannenberg's theological coherentist method rests on his presupposition of the grounding of the unity of truth in God. Pannenberg, drawing from Augustine, submits that God "is the truth that is identical with itself and therefore immutable, and truth which embraces all that is true and includes it in itself."[26] The coherent gathering of this truth, however, is eschatologically based, not foundationally based. Therefore, its expression is subject to multiple limitations and "conditions of finitude." Recognizing this finitude along with the "inappropriateness of all human talk about God is an essential part of theological sobriety." Dogmatic theology cannot provide "concrete reality to the truth of God" presented in "packaged formulas." Does this negate the "objective" reality of God or Christian beliefs? No. Neither does it rule out personal experiences

---

that make it less credible than one of the alternatives." Thomas Nagel, *The Last Word* (Oxford: Oxford University Press, 1997), p. 95.

23 Grenz and Franke, *Beyond Foundationalism*, p. 51.

24 George I. Mavrodes, *Belief In God* (New York: Random House, 1970), pp. 88–9.

25 See Grenz and Franke, *Beyond Foundationalism*, pp. 43, 50; and also, Grenz, *Renewing the Center*, p. 195.

26 Wolfhart Pannenberg, *Systematic Theology*, trans. Geoffrey W. Bromiley, 3 vols., vol. 1 (Grand Rapids: Eerdmans, 1991), p. 53.

with God in the events of history. But, the belief statements that we make are demonstrated true as their reality rests "on anticipations of the totality of the world and therefore on the as yet nonexistent future" of history which is incomplete. [27]

Grenz and Franke's eschatological realism has also been obviously influenced by Pannenberg (and to some extent by Moltmann as well, as it pertains to hope in the promises of God). Grenz and Franke characterize their modest, erring, eschatologically centered theological epistemology as a nonfoundationalist "pessimistic hope." Enlightenment foundationalism attempts and fails to provide an anthropocentrically based hope. Instead, true Christian hope must be *theo*centric—not drawing from human potential, but from hope in God. "Christian hope is pessimistic, because it is not based on what humans might potentially do but solely on what *God* will do. And when considered from the human perspective, what God promises to accomplish can only be dismissed as *un*realizable."[28] Hence, the "objective" reality we attempt to describe is an active approximation, but cannot be equated with absolute reality. The only completely "objective" reality lies in the eschatological future of God's creation.[29] This notion is similarly expressed in Van den Toren's goal-oriented theological epistemology: "I have argued for an epistemology, which is different from both modernism and relativistic postmodernism. Contrary to both traditions I take it that truth is not primarily to be found as the *foundation* of a process of reasoning, but that it is the *goal* of the process."[30]

Epistemology in Process

In a similar vein, Middleton and Walsh creatively call for "epistemological stewardship." Since the knowing process is a gift from God in creation, and the knowing process involves human limitations, an "arrogant epistemology of mastery" cannot be justified. They insist that any form of knowing is "provisional, open to correction, redirection, and deepening." Instead of being called to master and harness the world and all its available knowledge, we are invited to share it relationally as "image-bearing rulers." Hence, we listen to the other, respecting the other as fellow image bearers. This is not a static epistemology, but an epistemology in process—a "sojourning epistemology" that is on its way home. For now, however,

---

27 Pannenberg, *Systematic Theology*, vol. 1, pp. 54–5. Cf. Grenz, *Renewing the Center*, pp. 196–7; 232–5.

28 Grenz and Franke, *Beyond Foundationalism*, p. 251; also see p. 250.

29 Stanley J. Grenz, "Articulating the Christian Belief-Mosaic: Theological Method after the Demise of Foundationalism," in *Evangelical Futures: A Conversation on Theological Method*, ed. John G. Stackhouse Jr. (Grand Rapids: Baker, 2000), p. 136.

30 Benno Van den Toren, "A New Direction in Christian Apologetics," 57. We may notice a parallel as well with Kierkegaard's expression of truth as a process: "… truth becomes an approximation whose beginning cannot be posited absolutely, precisely because the conclusion is lacking, the effect of which is retroactive." Søren Kierkegaard, *Concluding Unscientific Postscript*, trans. David F. Swenson, with introduction and notes by Walter Lowrie (Princeton: Princeton University Press, 1941), p. 169.

we see through the glass dimly, awaiting the newness and healing of a sin-marred creation.[31]

Christian philosopher, Kelly James Clark, acknowledges this type of modest epistemology in his devotionally based apologetic work, *When Faith is Not Enough*. He reminds us that truth is slippery, yet we trod along the best we can. We acknowledge God's guidance along the way and assume "there is something called Truth" but we recognize that it is often elusive. As Clark continues:

> Such is the adventure and terror of life. We follow the lights as best we can. We accept as true what, given our best judgments, seems to us to be true. We stand ready and willing to criticize our comfortable beliefs as we receive more insight. We remain open to the possibility that we have wandered into a thicket and need to be redirected. Our hope is to continue following the clues into the arms of God. Choosing to follow a path makes faith precarious and risky. And so it is—there is no escaping it. This path, like all other paths, entails risk. Make no mistake about it: belief in God is risky business.[32]

We do stumble, we err, and we wander along the best that we can, not alone, but in the community of Christian faith, in humility listening to others and recognizing our limitations. In this dialogical sojourning, I honestly believe in the central claims of the Christian gospel, and I believe that critical, non-manipulative, imaginative dialogue will help us communicate this gospel to others. However, I would not boast an apologetic which claims exhaustive, absolute knowledge of God. Nor would I reject *all* of the claims made by other religious perspectives. There is certainly no room for what Harold Netland calls "arrogant triumphalism." Instead, both humility and respect need to characterize our dialogue with those of other faiths, despite conflicting truth claims.[33]

Limited Objectivity and Provisional Truth Claims

It is mistaken to assume that "complete objectivity" is needed to maintain apologetic dialogue. As we have seen, the notion of "complete" objectivity is erroneous. As Christians, we necessarily operate from within a tradition and mosaic of cultures, subcultures, and religious beliefs. Postliberal theologian George Lindbeck effectively

---

31 J. Richard Middleton and Brian Walsh, *Truth is Stranger Than It Used to Be: BiblicalFaith in a Postmodern Age* (Downers Grove: InterVarsity, 1995), pp. 168–71. Cf. also Terry C. Muck, "After Selfhood: Constructing the Religious Self in a Post-Self Age," *Journal of the Evangelical Theological Society* 41/1 (1998): 118–19; and Wright, *The New Testament and the People of God*, p. 63.

32 Kelly James Clark, *When Faith is Not Enough* (Grand Rapids and Cambridge, U.K.: Eerdmans, 1997), pp. 104–5.

33 Harold Netland, "Religious Pluralism and Truth," *Trinity Journal* 6 (1985): 8. Netland points out that simply because we show humility and respect for religious views which differ from our own, does not mean we gloss over the differences. (p. 8) In fact, Netland submits: "We do the religious traditions an injustice if we distort or reinterpret basic beliefs so as to minimize differences" (p. 7).

brings this to our attention. Lindbeck says that we Christians think, look, and argue only within our faith—and there is no way to get outside this faith to objectively compare different options.[34] Of course, we may agree that we cannot "objectively" place ourselves outside our faith. But this seems to assume that we must have complete objectivity in order to compare (at least *justifiably* compare) our faith with others, and it also assumes that we must get outside the faith in order to do this.[35] I agree, we are culturally and religiously conditioned within our traditions. Our apologetic listening will be "filtered through our particular Christian-theological hearing aid."[36] But, as I have attempted to show in this interactive apologetic model, it does not negate the possibility of reasonable dialogue and comparison of religious options from a variety of angles.

The Christian faith does involve truth claims about reality, hence the need for a soft foundational perspective that assumes the possibility of human dialogue and understanding, while at the same time acknowledging its limitations. A deabsolutized, interactionist apologetic is processional. It is objectively "grounded" in the eschatological realism purported by the soft foundational perspective we have examined, but it does not demand absolute knowledge claims placed in hermetically sealed arguments. It does not insist on finality, but it seeks continual growth and engagement within human finiteness. It is an apologetic which affirms that learning, growing, and developing is part of our created nature. As James K.A. Smith pointed out, we must not equate finitude with evil or violence, but as part of our created humanness.[37]

To apply an adaptation of Smith's hermeneutic to a theological-apologetic epistemology, I would maintain that our knowledge is incomplete, yet we work towards understanding through creative dialogue with others while acknowledging

---

34 George Lindbeck and others, "A Panel Discussion," in *The Nature of Confession*, p. 252.

35 Nicholas Rescher rightfully admits that we cannot deny that all human endeavors take place within a cultural, historical context. But simply stating that "the affirmation of a fact must proceed from within a historio-cultural setting does not mean that the correctness and appropriateness of what is said will be restricted to such a setting. The fact that we make our assertions within time does not prevent us from asserting timeless truths." Nicholas Rescher, *Objectivity: The Obligations of Impersonal Reason* (Notre Dame and London: University of Notre Dame Press, 1997), p. 61. Cf. Douglas Groothuis, *Truth Decay: Defending Christianity Against the Challenges of Postmodernism* (Downers Grove: InterVarsity, 2000), p. 191–2. Groothuis cites this quotation in his critical response to Rorty's ethical reflections.

36 Grenz and Franke, *Beyond Foundationalism*, p. 159. Also see Van Huyssteen, *Essays in Postfoundationalist Theology*, pp. 244–6. Van Huyssteen provides cogent insights on the nature of a contextually rooted postfoundational view of rationality which encourages cross-contextual dialogue.

37 James K.A. Smith, *The Fall of Interpretation: Philosophical Foundations for a Creational Hermeneutic* (Downers Grove: InterVarsity, 2000), p. 159. Yet, Smith is careful to point out that interpretive structures, while not inherently evil, may *become* so in a fallen world (pp. 159, 162).

the context of our Christian community. This "working towards" is part of the cultural mandate given to us as gifts in creation—a creation which demands the stewardship of interpretation of the world by continually "tilling the ground." Such a perspective does not imply that all truth is arbitrary, since there is a phenomenological givenness to the world which all humans share. Smith illustrates this idea with a tree. The tree outside is phenomenologically "outside"—it is not something I can manipulate to my own whimsical interpretations. If I interpret the tree as simply an imaginary picture and I attempt to run through it, my interpretation will simply be shown wrong.[38] These elements of phenomenological givenness are akin to what we previously suggested are the basic commonsense beliefs which virtually all humans share, providing avenues for some degree of common parlance and dialogue in the pursuit of understanding.

In a similar fashion, Kevin Vanhoozer applies Plantinga's notion of proper basicality to the act of interpretation: "*Interpreting—that is, ascribing intended meanings to discourse—is properly basic.*"[39] With a soft foundational perspective, I would submit that a translinguistic reality exists in the eschatological reality of God. Interpretation is a process, a process within a community by which we make modest atttempts to express this reality. This does not guarantee that I will produce propositions or expressions which always accurately conform to this reality. Deconstructionists have certainly heightened my awareness to my own limitations in this regard. However, to move from "naiveté to stubborn skepticism is at best a dubious achievement... its all-or-nothing insistence on knowledge, resembles an epistemological tantrum that refuses to accept the human condition."[40] Vanhoozer's position is noticeably similar to Smith's creational hermeneutic:

> Humans are neither like angels, knowing things immediately, not are they dumb brutes, who are unable to work out their differences except through force. We do not have absolute knowledge, only *human* knowledge—the kind of knowledge humans were designed to have. We have, that is to say, *adequate* knowledge—all the knowledge we need to fulfill our vocation as human beings and interpreters. In the context of hermeneutics, this means that we have the epistemic abilities to respond to the communicative overtures of an author enacted in the text in the appropriate manner. Skepticism, insofar as it dissents from this view in its all-or-nothing insistence on knowledge, resembles an epistemological tantrum that refuses to accept the human condition.[41]

Both Smith and Vanhoozer effectively challenge us with a realist hermeneutic based in our created humanness and its finitude. This is not a hopeless search, but a search which can be fulfilling as we understand the value of the searching itself and the God-

---

38 Ibid., p. 169. Smith adds that interpretation is "the only game in town, but there are rules to the game—not rules concocted by a council and printed in a rule book but a rule as simple as this: you have to play on the field, staying within the boundaries. And it is the same field for all of us" (pp. 174–5).

39 Vanhoozer, *Is There a Meaning in This Text?*, pp. 288–9. The italics are Vanhoozer's.

40 Ibid., p. 300.

41 Ibid. Cf. also pp. 464–5.

given gift of the interpretive process of life. A soft foundational perspective does not deny objectivity and reality, but is arguing for modesty and humility in expressions of knowledge claims of that reality. Hence, this perspective is both modestly skeptical and modest in its knowledge claims. I addressed this problem in the chapter on Derrida in the context of religious claims. The deconstructionist correctly argues that when we speak of God, our discourse will necessarily use a system of signifiers. When we speak, we use generalities and particularities. Language continually makes promises on the one hand, but always presents barriers on the other. But the question is whether or not these barriers may be overcome. For the deconstructionist, it is impossible to deliver the metaphysical "letter" because the postal system is flawed—due to contextuality, ruptures in communication, and misunderstandings.[42]

However, it is my contention that our inherent incapability to comprehend all truth and reality, does not negate the possibility of apprehending portions of that truth and reality in the deliberative action of God to communicate it.[43] Fallibility does not preclude the ability to communicate in a modestly effective manner. Communication is simply not an all or nothing affair. Communication and understanding do occur in everyday human life with flawed communicators. Christian philosopher Dallas Willard rightly submits that "communication occurs constantly where infallibility is completely out of the question." As Willard notes, even if the speaker is infallible, as we submit God is, this does not guarantee the infallibility of the hearers. Yet we know that communication still reliably occurs when the speakers are fallible. If we hear our children, for example, we recognize their voices in a variety of settings. We would generally understand what they are saying, and we may often recognize their voices even if we cannot understand *what* they are saying.[44]

A soft, modest foundational perspective, I submit, takes seriously the problems of context and meaning brought to the forefront with deconstructionist theological concerns. Admittedly, I am espousing an interactionist apologetic that attempts "to recover elements of the authentic and the genuine from among the chaff of self-interest, manipulation, and power-claims."[45] My proposal is admittedly given in a

---

42 Again see James K.A. Smith, "How to avoid not Speaking: Attestations," in *Knowing Other-Wise: Philosophy at the Threshold of Spirituality*, ed. James H. Olthuis (New York: Fordham University Press, 1997), pp. 219–32. Cf. also Smith, *The Fall of Interpretation*, pp. 119–20.

43 Robertson McQuilkin and Bradford Mullen, "The Impact of Postmodern Thinking on Evangelical Hermeneutics," *Journal of the Evangelical Theological Society* 40/1 (1997): 75. Huston Smith notes: "Perspectivalism becomes absurd when the obvious fact that we look at the world from different places, hence different angles, is transformed into the dogma that we therefore cannot know things as they actually are." From my perspective, I would insert, *partially* "as they actually are." The Religious Significance of Postmodernism," *Faith and Philosophy* 12/3 (1995): 416.

44 Dallas Willard, *In Search of Guidance* (Ventura, California: Regal Books, 1984), p. 226.

45 Anthony C. Thiselton, *Interpreting God and the Postmodern Self* (Edinburgh: T&T Clark, 1995), p. 16.

Christian context without deconstructionist suspicion having ultimate priority.[46] Yet, it is an apologetic with a "fallibilist epistemology" that understands the "fallibilist and provisional nature" of theological truth claims. In my view, this represents an epistemology which is arguably more holistic in terms of the human person. It honestly acknowledges the limitations of truth claims while at the same time, it recognizes the role of experience, personal commitment and interpretation. Such a modest, postfoundational perspective is careful to guard against "an overly narrow and rationalistic conception of rationality."[47] Nicholas Rescher, in his *Objectivity: The Obligations of Impersonal Reason*, also concurs: "To insist on reasoning as the sole and all-comprising agency in human affairs is not rationalism but a hyperrationalism that offends against rationality as such."[48] Instead, as Van Huyssteen insists, and I concur, rationality must be regarded as the quest for intelligibility and "understanding at the deepest level"—and it is "complex, many-sided, extensive, and as wide-ranging as the domain of intelligence itself."[49] Such a quest draws upon more than simply the purely cognitive dimensions of our humanity. Intelligibility involving religious matters must not be reduced to mere scientific rationality and empirical hypotheses—they are more humanly complex than this. There is indeed some epistemological correspondence with scientific investigation, but religious reflection cannot be limited to science. Christian faith is not only a way of examining the world, but it expresses a personal trust in a personal God. This is a broader more complex rationality, according to Van Huyssteen, but it is certainly not less rational.[50]

---

46 See Patricia A. Sayre, "The Dialectics of Trust and Suspicion," *Faith and Philosophy* 10/4 (1993): 581.

47 Van Huyssteen, *Essays in Postfoundationalist Theology*, pp. 228–9. Cf. also pp. 256, 258–61.

48 Rescher, *Objectivity*, p. 213.

49 Van Huyssteen, *Essays in Postfoundationalist Theology*, p. 229. On a similar note, Marilyn Gaye Piety challenges scholars, in her reading of Kierkegaard, to a more advantageous interpretation of human rationality. We must appreciate reason informed by subjective passion as an inherent part of human knowledge. "Kierkegaard's interpretation of human rationality provides us with a positive alternative to the traditonal conception of reason as disinterested and dispassionate." Marilyn Gaye Piety, "Kierkegaard on Rationality," *Faith and Philosophy* 10/3 (1993): 366, 369, 375. Merold Westphal also contends that we should not let issues of subjectivity be rendered unimportant in any objectivist culture whether it be "Hegelian, positivistic, technocratic, or whatever, that is systematically prejudiced against religious experience in general and the life of Christian faith in particular." Merold Westphal, "Religious Experience as Self-Transcendence and Self-Deception," *Faith and Philosophy* 9/2 (1992): 189.

50 Van Huyssteen, *Essays in Postfoundationalist Theology*, pp. 260–61; 264–5. Cf. also John G. Stackhouse Jr., *Can God Be Trusted?: Faith and the Challenge of Evil* (New York: Oxford University Press, 1998), pp. 168–9. Stackhouse contends that putting faith in God is like putting faith in a lifetime lover, which "is why the Old and New Testaments frequently picture God's relationship to God's people in terms of engagement and marriage." Yet as

Granted, it appears that Van Huyssteen often confuses empiricism and rationalism. One may also contend that Van Huyssteen's description of "rationality" provides too much breathing room in view of its basic use and definition as it is used historically. Nonetheless, his application of this term to the notion of intelligibility is quite helpful. We do need to move beyond a mere understanding of the "intelligible" as only that which fits within a scientific or Enlightenment foundationalist scheme. That which is seen as "true" is often only equated with that which may be deemed as "objectively true" as it relates to a narrow modernist epistemology. Christianity does not consist in emotionless, completely unbiased assertions of truth pertaining only to material "objects." In this sense it is *not* objective. This does not mean objectivity is at fault, as Rescher concurs, but it is "a perfectly objective recognition that objectivity has certain limits."[51] As Kierkegaard reminds us, Christianity is subjective.[52] Wherever we speak of relationship, which we definitely want to affirm in Christianity, we must speak in terms of subjectivity. However, if "objective truth" refers to a mind-independent, linguistically-independent reality which only God completely knows and understands, as I have contended, then I may agree to such a notion of "objective truth." This would parallel the eschatological realism that Grenz and Franke and others have espoused as I previously discussed. Alister McGrath suggests that if the word truth continues to be problematic, we may try another approach: "Instead of asking whether Christianity is *true*, the postmodernist might be asked whether it can be regarded as *credible*."[53]

Philip D. Kenneson is an evangelical theologian who denies the notion of objective truth altogether. In my estimation, Kenneson's denial is hasty and simplistic, assuming a notion of objectivity based only in a modernist epistemology. Kenneson states, for example, that "Truth is merely the word for the way the world really is which we are trying to picture or mirror with our knowledge." And, objective truth is knowledge which has a status of true that "does not ultimately depend on the testimony of any person or group of persons." A modest epistemology still claims that

---

Stackhouse notes, we recognize that in the trust we give, we do not know everything before we decide to trust (p. 169).

51 Rescher, *Objectivity*, p. 213. Also see Wright, *The New Testament and the People of God*. Wright implores us to abandon the hard and fast distinction between "objective" and "subjective" in favor of a more "nuanced," relational, "storied" epistemology that reflects our humanity (pp. 44–5).

52 See Kierkegaard, *Concluding Unscientific Postscript*, pp. 178–9.

53 Alister McGrath, *Intellectuals Don't Need God & Other Modern Myths* (Grand Rapids: Zondervan, 1993), p. 181. For a lucid, balanced defense of the notion of objectivity in view of a myriad of modern and postmodern objections, again see Nicholas Rescher, *Objectivity: The Obligations of Impersonal Reason* (Notre Dame and London: University of Notre Dame Press, 1997). Rescher points out a "curious inversion" of the objective/subjective distinction in historical thought. Before Kant, "for something to obtain *objectively* was for it to exist as an object of thought (as an idea or other item of mental representation), while for it to obtain *subjectively* or *formally* was for it to exist as an actual subject in the real world, independently of whatever mental representation might be connected to it" (p. 215, note 2).

there is objective truth but we can only partially and progressively attain knowledge of that truth. Nevertheless, Kenneson is correct in expressing that many problems have arisen due to the false dichotomy between "objective" and "subjective," hence, creating the need to "try on a different model of truth."[54]

Truth is not simply objective nor subjective in the traditional sense—it is both, and more. As Miroslav Volf reminds us, it is not only what the mind grasps in its adjustment to reality or thinks coherently, it also involves the character of one "willing and capable of pursuing and accepting the truth." Simply because the Christian is committed to the Jesus who claims to be the Truth, does not imply that Christians can claim to "possess" the absolute truth themselves. In our coming to know the truth, we come to know only "in part" as we "see through a mirror dimly." "There is an irremovable opaqueness to our knowledge of things divine. Equally, there is an irremovable opaqueness to our knowledge of things human."[55] This does not minimize our humanness, it is simply the expression of our humanness properly situated in its finiteness before the presence of an all-knowing God—which should engender us to both humility and openness.[56]

Kenneson submits that we need to stop our preoccupation with objective truth and move on to living and demonstrating our "truth" before the world in church community.[57] With my understanding of the abuses of the notion of modernist objective truth, I would concur. I testified to the value of this in chapter 10 with the example of the early Christians in community. Rodney Clapp, in accord with Kenneson in this regard, asserts:

> We do better, I think, to come down from the foundationalist slide, recover an eschatologically informed epistemology and place that epistemology firmly in the bed of ecclesiology. It is the community called "church" that teaches people the language and culture that enables them to know Jesus as Lord. And it is the church in the fullness of its life—not primarily its arguments—that draws others to consider the Christian faith.[58]

Although I am in full agreement about the value of example in the diverse community of the Christian church as a primary positive apologetic, I believe that it is not only the "church" which "teaches people the language and culture" enabling belief, but also the "church" learning from others. I am calling for the church to be engaged in

---

54 Philip D. Kenneson, "There's No Such Thing As Objective Truth, And It's a Good Thing Too," in *Christian Apologetics in the Postmodern World*, ed. Timothy R. Phillips and Dennis L. Okholm (Downers Grove: InterVarsity, 1995), pp. 157–9.

55 Miroslav Volf, *Exclusion and Embrace: A Theological Exploration of Identity, Otherness, and Reconciliation* (Nashville: Abingdon, 1996), pp. 269–71. The quote is found on p. 271.

56 Muck, "After Selfhood," p. 119.

57 Kenneson, "There's No Such Thing As Objective Truth," pp. 169–70. Cf. also Dennis Hollinger, "The Church as Apologetic: A Sociology of Knowledge Perspective," in *Christian Apologetics in the Postmodern World*, pp. 182–93 (especially note pp. 192–3).

58 Clapp, "How Firm a Foundation," p. 90. Cf. Sire, *Why Should Anyone Believe Anything at all?*, pp. 204–6.

mutual, interactive learning with others through a process of critical appropriation and recontextualization in epistemological humility. It is my contention that this will provide a holistic, human-centered apologetic most appropriate to deconstructionist concerns.

Conclusion

This work has made a modest effort to provide some advances in apologetic methodological reflection in view of postmodern deconstructive concerns. These apologetic proposals are agreeably modest; nevertheless, it is my hope they will help stimulate continued discussion and progress in critical, interactionist apologetic dialogue.

The first chapters were primarily devoted to historical and intellectual description with brief critical interaction. I attempted to answer the question: What is it that "makes" postmodern deconstructive theology? I investigated its roots and provided some representative examples in Lyotard, Derrida, Foucault, Taylor, Rorty, and Cupitt. I made an effort to practice critical appropriation, identifying the underlying concerns I saw emerging from these representative views. I tried to respond to these concerns by re-thinking and re-working, at points, an evangelical apologetic methodology.

In the process of this effort, I have wrestled with the approach I was promoting. As I progressed in the book, I moved into a multi-layered, critical dialogue, human person centered approach as an apologetic for Christian reality. The notion of apologetics itself implies an advocation and/or defense of beliefs to other persons. Yet, in much of traditional apologetics, the plethora of rational arguments bathed in natural theology seem to neglect or forget the real human person—a person with creative longings and genuine emotional and physical needs. I do not wish to downplay my confidence in Christian claims to the temporal, real, factual states of affairs in the world. But these "confidences" do not simply stem from rational, historical, or philosophical argumentation, but from a mosaic of human sources—including experience, literature, and the imagination.

I agree with Alister McGrath when he says "A theology which touches the mind, leaving the heart unaffected, is no true Christian theology."[1] I have applied this thinking to apologetics, prompted by postmodern deconstructionist concerns, and put forth a variation of what David K. Clark calls a "dialogical" apologetic. This is an apologetic which makes service to the other central to the apologetic practice. Effective apologetics happens in interactionist dialogue with real people—people with cultural, intellectual, and emotional baggage. An interactionist, conversational apologetic of this nature acknowledges the complexity of humans and their differences.[2]

---

1   Alister McGrath, *A Passion For Truth: The Intellectual Coherence of Evangelicalism* (Downers Grove: InterVarsity, 1996), p. 178.

2   David K. Clark, *Dialogical Apologetics: A Person-Centered Approach to Christian Defense* (Grand Rapids: Baker, 1993), pp. 110, 112, 115. Cf. also David K. Clark, "Narrative

Although it is possible that postmodernist deconstructionism as both a cultural and intellectual "movement" may lose relevance in coming years, I nonetheless contend that the principles I have suggested from this study will continue to be academically relevant to Christian apologetic methodology. I have stressed that listening and dialogue are central. We must listen to the concerns of those whose views are different—even drastically different to our own, understanding that the "prophetic" voice of the deconstructive "masters of suspicion" may remind us of our own religious duplicity which closes us off from the sensitivities of others. We listen, we interact, and we evaluate. We may not agree with the views we encounter, we may even adamantly disagree. But rather than closing off dialogue, through the process of critical appropriation and recontextualization we may instead provide avenues by which to continue conversational opportunities by addressing the latent concerns behind the views.

Additionally, I argued that an apologetic of critical appropriation and recontextualization of postmodern deconstructive theology does not simply happen through the meduim of traditional propositional discourse. It is also necessary to develop skills of imagination and creative application. We can engage others through the use of imaginative stories which provide images of hope—hope rooted, in my view, in an eschatological reality. But this is not a reality which we can immediately grasp and control, it is a struggling hope amidst the wanderings we face in the mystery of life.

Perhaps the crux of my efforts are a challenge and call for apologetic humility: humility in our claims to knowledge and humility in our expression of what we perceive to be knowledge. Guarding our perceived knowledge from pride, jealousy and arrogance is crucial. This is articulated well by Christian philosopher Dallas Willard:

> For in general knowledge tends to be destructive when not held in a mature personality thoroughly permeated by love and humility. Few things are more terrifying in the spiritual realm than those who absolutely know, but are in fact unloving, hostile, proud, superstitious, and fearful. That Aaron and Miriam could be jealous of Moses is a certain indication that God could never trust them with the kind of knowledge He gave freely to Moses. That Moses was untroubled by their attack, and glad to share the prophetic ministry just as surely indicated that he could be trusted with knowledge.[3]

If we, as Christians, are truly to be "trusted with knowledge" we must transcend barriers of bigotry, oppression and suppression of the other and we must be devoted to listening—listening to diverse cultures, listening to those of differing religious traditions, listening to those of the opposite gender, and be willing to be corrected by

---

Theology and Apologetics," *Journal of the Evangelical Theological Society* 36/4 (1993): especially 512-14.

　　3　Dallas Willard, *In Search of Guidance* (Ventura: Regal Books, 1984), pp. 130-31.

them while being submissive to God's revelation in Christ and Scripture.[4] Of course, no matter what efforts we make, some will still sneer. Yet, we will trust and pray, as with Paul at Athens, so others may say, "We want to hear you again on this subject" (Acts 17:32). And with God's grace, may some become followers and believe.

I believe Kevin Vanhoozer provides an excellent caution to those who keep the Scripture close to their heart for faith and practice:

> Readers who take pride in their readings seek to "master" the text and so risk elevating their commentary over the text in importance. Pride neglects the voice of the other in favor of its own.[5]

May we ever guard against such temptation. May the Truth always overshadow our pride, and may our quest for certainty never be a substitute for the Truth.

---

4 See D.A. Carson, *The Gagging of God: Christianity Confronts Pluralism* (Grand Rapids: Zondervan, 1996), p. 552. Cf. pp. 97-8. See also pertinent comments in this regard made by Miroslav Volf on gender and "self-enclosed identity," in *Exclusion and Embrace: A Theological Exploration of Identity, Otherness, and Reconciliation* (Nashville: Abingdon, 1996), p. 176

5 Vanhoozer, *Is There a Meaning in This Text?*, p. 463.

Bibliography

Adams, Marilyn McCord, "Philosophy and the Bible," *Faith and Philosophy*, 9/2 (1992): 135–50.

Aichele, George Jr, "Literary Fantasy and Postmodern Theology," *Journal of the American Academy of Religion,* 59 (1991): 323–37.

Allen, Diogenes, *Christian Belief in a Postmodern World* (Louisville: Westminster/ John Knox, 1989).

Alston, William P., "Two Types of Foundationalism," *The Journal of Philosophy*, 73/7 (1976): 165–85.

Altizer, Thomas J.J. (ed.), *Deconstruction and Theology* (New York: Crossroad, 1982).

Augustine, *The City of God*, trans. by Marcus Dods, vol. 2, in Philip Schaff (ed.), Nicene and Post-Nicene Fathers: First Series, Peabody: Hendrickson (1994).

———, *On Christian Doctrine*, trans. by J.F., Shaw, vol. 2, in Philip Schaff, (ed.), Nicene and Post–Nicene Fathers: First Series, Peabody: Hendrickson, (1994).

Bacon, Francis, *Novum Organum*, vol. 30, 54 vols, Robert Maynard Hutchins (ed.), Great Books of the Western World, Chicago: Encyclopaedia Britannica, Inc. (1952).

———, *Of the Proficience and Advancement of Learning: Divine and Humane*, vol. 30, 54 vols, Robert Maynard Hutchins (ed.), Great Books of the Western World, Chicago: Encyclopaedia Britannica, Inc. (1952).

Bailey, Kenneth E, "The Pursuing Father: What We Need to Know About This Often Misunderstood Middle Eastern Parable," *Christianity Today* (October 26, 1998).

Barrett, William, and Henry D. Aiken (eds), *Philosophy in the Twentieth Century*, vol. 3 (New York: Random House, 1962).

Barth, Karl, *Evangelical Theology: An Introduction* (Grand Rapids: Eerdmans, 1979).

Bartholomew, C.G., "Three Horizons: Hermeneutics from the Other End—An Evaluation of Anthony Thiselton's Hermeneutic Proposals," *European Journal of Theology*, 5/2 (1996): 121–135.

Bauckham, Richard, and Trevor Hart, *Hope against Hope: Christian Eschatology at the Turn of the Millennium* (Grand Rapids, Cambridge, U.K.: Eerdmans, 1999).

Berkhouwer, G.C., *Man: The Image of God*, trans. by Dirk W. Jellema, Studies in Dogmatics (Grand Rapids: Eerdmans, 1962).

Berry, Philippa, and Andrew Wernick (eds), *Shadow of Spirit* (London and New York: Routledge, 1992).

Bertman, Stephen, "Modern Values and the Challenge of Myth," *Imprimis*, 22/3 (1993): 1–3.

Blaser, Klauspeter, *Les Théologies Nord-Américaines* (Genève: Labor et Fides, 1995).

——, "Variété des Théologies Postmodernes et Crise des 'Fondationalismes,'" in Pierre Gisel and Patrick Evrard (eds), *La Théologie En Postmodernité* (Genève: Labor et Fides, 1996), pp. 191–211,

Bloesch, Donald G., *Essentials of Evangelical Theology: God, Authority, & Salvation*, vol. 1 (San Francisco: Harper & Row, 1978).

——, *God the Almighty: Power, Wisdom, Holiness, Love* (Carlisle: The Paternoster Press, 1995).

Bock, Darrell L., *Purpose Directed Theology: Getting Our Priorities Right in Evangelical Controversies* (Downers Grove: InterVarsity, 2002).

Boice, James Montgomery, and Benjamin E. Sasse (eds), *Here We Stand: A Call from Confessing Evangelicals* (Grand Rapids: Baker, 1996).

Brown, Colin, *Philosophy and the Christian Faith* (Downers Grove: InterVarsity, 1968).

Bruce, F.F., *First Century Faith* (Leicester: InterVarsity, 1977).

Buchanan, Mark, "Stuck on the Road to Emmaus: The Secret to Why We Are Not Fulfilled," *Christianity Today* (July 12, 1999).

Bulzan, Daniel, "Apophaticism, Postmodernism and Language: Two Similar Cases of Theological Imbalance," *Scottish Journal of Theology*, 50/3 (1997): 261–87.

Byrne, James M., "Foucault on Continuity: The Postmodern Challenge to Tradition," *Faith and Philosophy*, 9/3 (1992): 335–52.

Cahoone, Lawrence (ed.), *From Modernism to Postmodernism: An Anthology* (Cambridge, Mass.: Blackwell, 1996).

Caputo, John D., "The Good News About Alterity: Derrida and Theology," *Faith and Philosophy*, 10/4 (1993): 453–70.

——, *The Prayers and Tears of Jacques Derrida: Religion Without Religion* (Bloomington & Indianapolis: Indiana University Press, 1997).

—— (ed.), *Deconstruction in a Nutshell: A Conversation with Jacques Derrida* (New York: Fordham University Press, 1997).

Caputo, John D., and Michael J. Scanlon (eds), *God, the Gift, and Postmodernism* (Bloomington and Indianapolis: Indiana University Press, 1999).

Carrette, Jeremy R., *Foucault and Religion: Spiritual Corporality and Political Spirituality* (London and New York: Routledge, 2000).

Carson, D.A., *The Gagging of God: Christianity Confronts Pluralism* (Grand Rapids: Zondervan, 1996).

Clark, David K., *Dialogical Apologetics: A Person-Centered Approach to Christian Defense* (Grand Rapids: Baker, 1993).

——, "Narrative Theology and Apologetics," *Journal of the Evangelical Theological Society*, 36/4 (1993): 499–515.

Clark, Kelly James, *Return to Reason* (Grand Rapids: Eerdmans, 1990).

——, *When Faith Is Not Enough* (Grand Rapids and Cambridge, U.K.: Eerdmans, 1997).

Comstock, Gary L., "Is Postmodern Religious Dialogue Possible?" *Faith and Philosophy*, 6/2 (1989): 189–97.

Cowan, Steven B. (ed.), *Five Views on Apologetics* (Grand Rapids: Zondervan, 2000).

Cowdell, Scott, *Atheist Priest?: Don Cupitt and Christianity* (London: SCM Press Ltd, 1988).

———, "Radical Theology, Postmodernity and the Christian Life in the Void," *The Heythrop Journal*, 32/1 (1991): 62–71.

Craig, William Lane, *Apologetics: An Introduction* (Chicago: Moody Press, 1984).

Cress, Donald A., "Editor's Preface," in *René Descartes: Meditations on First Philosophy* (Indianapolis: Hackett Publishing Company, Inc, 1979).

Cudney, Shane, "'Religion Without Religion:' Caputo, Derrida, and the Violence of Particularity," *Faith and Philosophy*, 16/3 (1999): 390–404.

Cupitt, Don, *Taking Leave of God* (London: XPress Prints, SCM Prints Ltd, 1980).

———, *Sea of Faith* (London: British Broadcasting Company, 1984).

———, *The Long-Legged Fly* (London: SCM Press Ltd, 1987).

———, "Unsystematic Ethics and Politics," in Philippa Berry and Andrew Wernick (eds), *Shadow of Spirit*, (London and New York: Routledge, 1992).

———, *The Last Philosophy* (London: SCM Press, Ltd, 1995).

———, *After God: The Future of Religion* (London: Basic Books, 1997).

———, *The Religion of Being* (London: SCM Press, 1998).

Derrida, Jacques, *Of Grammatology*, trans. by Gayatri Chakravorty Spivak, Baltimore: Johns Hopkins University Press, 1976, originally published as *De la grammatologie* (Paris: Les éditions de Minuit, 1967).

———, *Writing and Difference*, trans. by Alan Bass, Chicago: University of Chicago Press, 1978, originally published as *L'ecriture et la difference* (Paris: Editions du Seuil, 1967).

———, *Positions*, trans. by Alan Bass (Chicago: The University of Chicago Press, 1981).

———, *Margins of Philosophy*, trans. by Alan Bass, Chicago: University of Chicago Press, 1982, originally published as *Marges de la philosophie* (Paris: Les éditions de Minuit, 1972).

———, "Circumfession: Fifty-nine Periods and Periphrases," in Geoffrey Bennington and Jacques Derrida, *Jacques Derrida*, trans. by Geoffrey Bennington (Chicago: University of Chicago Press, 1993), originally published as "Circonfession: cinquante-neuf périodes et periphrases," in Geoffrey Bennington and Jacques Derrida, *Jacques Derrida* (Paris: Editions du Seuil, 1991).

Descartes, René, *Meditations on First Philosophy*, trans. by Donald A. Cress (Indianapolis and Cambridge: Hackett Publishing Company, Inc., 1979).

Desmond, William, *Beyond Hegel and Dialectic: Speculation, Cult and Comedy* (Albany: State University of New York Press, 1992).

———, *Perplexity and Ultimacy: Metaphysical Thoughts from the Middle* (Albany: State University of New York Press, 1995).

Dockery, David S., "The Challenge of Postmodernism," in David S. Dockery (ed.), *The Challenge of Postmodernism: An Evangelical Engagement* (Grand Rapids: Baker, 1997).

Dorrien, Gary, *The Word as True Myth: Interpreting Modern Theology* (Louisville: Westminster John Knox Press, 1997).

———, *The Remaking of Evangelical Theology* (Louisville: Westminster John Knox Press, 1998).

Dreyer, Jaco S, "The Researcher: Engaged Participant or Detached Observer," *Journal of Empirical Theology*, 11/2 (1998): 5–22.

Echeverria, Eduardo J., "Do Human Rights Spring from Our Nature as Human Beings? Reflections on Richard Rorty," *Philosophia Christi*, 20/1 (Spring 1997): 41–53.

Ellis, John M., *Against Deconstruction* (Princeton, New Jersey: Princeton University Press, 1989).

Erickson, Millard J., *Concise Dictionary of Christian Theology* (Grand Rapids: Baker, 1986).

———, *The Word Became Flesh* (Grand Rapids: Baker, 1991).

———, *The Evangelical Left: Encountering Postconservative Evangelical Theology* (Grand Rapids: Baker, 1997).

———, *Christian Theology*, 2nd edn (Grand Rapids: Baker, 1998).

———, *Postmodernizing the Faith* (Grand Rapids: Baker, 1998).

———, *Truth or Consequences: The Promise and Perils of Postmodernism* (Downers Grove: InterVarsity, 2001).

Ewald, François, "Une 'Folie' Doit Veiller Sur La Pensée," *Magazine Littéraire*, (March 1991): 18–30.

Fackre, Gabriel, "Narrative Theology: An Overview," *Interpretation* (October 1983): 340–52.

Faesen, Rob, S.J., "What Is a Mystical Experience? History and Interpretation," *Louvain Studies*, 23/3 (1998): 221–45.

Flieger, Verlyn, *Splintered Light: Logos and Language in Tolkien's World* (Grand Rapids: Eerdmans, 1983).

Flynn, Thomas R., "Partially Desacralized Spaces: The Religious Availability of Foucault's Thought," *Faith and Philosophy*, 10/4 (October 1993): 471–85.

Foucault, Michel, *Madness and Civilization: A History of Insanity in the Age of Reason* (Cambridge, U.K.: Cambridge University Press, 1965).

———, *The Order of Things: An Archaeology of the Human Sciences* (London: Routledge, 1970), originally published as *Les mots et les choses: Une archéologie des sciences humaines* (NRF editions, Gallimard, 1966).

———, *Power/Knowledge: Selected Interviews and Other Writings 1972–1977*, Colin Gordon (ed.), trans. by Leo Marshall, Colin Gordon, John Mepham, and Kate Soper, (New York: Pantheon Books, 1980).

———, "Nietzsche, Genealogy, History," in Paul Rabinow (ed.), *The Foucault Reader* (New York: Pantheon Books, 1984), pp. 76–100.

————, "The Repressive Hypothesis," in Paul Rabinow (ed.), *The Foucault Reader* (New York: Pantheon Books, 1984), pp. 301–29.

————, "We "Other" Victorians," in Paul Rabinow (ed.), *The Foucault Reader* (New York: Pantheon Books, 1984), pp. 292–300.

————, "What Is an Author?," in Paul Rabinow (ed.), *The Foucault Reader* (New York: Pantheon Books, 1984), pp. 101–120.

————, "Excerpt from the History of Sexuality, vol. 1," in Graham Ward (ed.), *The Postmodern God: A Theological Reader* (Oxford: Blackwell, 1997), pp. 116–123.

Gabus, Jean-Paul, *Parole de Dieu, Paroles d'hommes* (Paris: Les Bergers et les Mages, 1998).

Gadamer, Hans-Georg, *Truth and Method*, 2nd edn (New York: Continuum, 1989).

Geisler, Norman L. (ed.), *Biblical Errancy: An Analysis of Its Philosophical Roots* (Grand Rapids: Zondervan, 1981).

Geivett, R. Douglas, and Brendan Sweetman (eds), *Contemporary Perspectives on Religious Epistemology* (New York and Oxford: Oxford University Press, 1992).

Gempf, Conrad, "Acts," in G.J. Wenham, J.A. Motyer, D.A. Carson and R.T. France (eds), *New Bible Commentary* (Leicester: InterVarsity Press, 1994).

George, Timothy, "If I'm an Evangelical, What Am I?," *Christianity Today* (August 9, 1999): 62.

Gisel, Pierre, "Modernité et/ou Postmodernité," *Foi & Vie*, 97/2 (1998): 75–81.

Gisel, Pierre, and Patrick Evrard (eds), *La Théologie En Postmodernité*, Lieux Théologiques (Genève: Labor et Fides, 1996).

Goold, Patrick, "Reading Kierkegaard," *Faith and Philosophy*, 7/3 (July1990): 304–15.

Gowen, Julie, "Foundationalism and the Justification of Religious Belief," *Religious Studies*, 19 (1983): 393–406.

Green, Garrett, *Imagining God: Theology and the Religious Imagination* (San Francisco: Harper and Row, 1989).

Green, Joel B. (ed.), *Hearing the New Testament* (Carlisle: The Paternoster Press, 1995).

Gregory of Nyssa, St., "The Doctrine of Infinite Growth, Commentary on the Conticle, Sermon 8, 940c–941c," in Herbert Musurillo, S.J. (ed.), *From Glory to Glory: Texts from Gregory of Nyssa's Mystical Writings* (New York: Charles Scribner's Sons, 1961); reprint (Crestwood: St. Vladimir's Seminary Press, 1979).

Grenz, Stanley J., *Revisioning Evangelical Theology: A Fresh Agenda for the 21st Century* (Downers Grove: InterVarsity, 1993).

————, *Theology for the Community of God*, Carlisle: Paternoster, 1994.

————, *A Primer on Postmodernism* (Grand Rapids: Eerdmans, 1996).

————, *Renewing the Center* (Grand Rapids: Baker, 2000).

Grenz, Stanley J., and John R. Franke, *Beyond Foundationalism: Shaping Theology in a Postmodern Context* (Louisville: Westminster John Knox Press, 2001).

Grenz, Stanley J. and Roger E. Olson, *Twentieth Century Theology: God and the World in a Transitional Age* (Downers Grove: InterVarsity, 1992).

Griffin, David Ray, William A. Beardslee, and Joe Holland, *Varieties of Postmodern Theology* (Albany: State University of New York Press, 1989).

Groothuis, Douglas, "Postmodernism and Truth," *Philosophia Christi* 2/2 (2000): 271–81.

————, *Truth Decay: Defending Christianity Against the Challenges of Postmodernism* (Downers Grove: InterVarsity, 2000).

Gustafson, Andrew, "Apologetically Listening to Derrida," *Philosophia Christi*, 20/2 (1997): 15–42.

Habermas, Jürgen, *The Philosophical Discourse of Modernity*, trans. by Frederick Lawrence (Cambridge, Mass.: The MIT press, 1987).

Hall, Christopher, *Reading Scripture with the Church Fathers* (Downers Grove: InterVarsity, 1998).

Hansen, Richard P., "Unsolved Mysteries: Biblical Paradox Offers an Alternative to 'How to' Sermons," *Leadership* (Winter 2000): 54–60.

Harper, Katherine, "G[Ertrude] E[Lizabeth] M[Argaret] Anscombe (1919–)," in Jeffrey D. Schultz and John G. West Jr (eds), *The C.S. Lewis Readers' Encyclopedia* (Grand Rapids: Zondervan, 1998).

Hart, Kevin, *The Trespass of the Sign* (Cambridge: Cambridge University Press, 1989).

Hauerwas, Stanley, and Philip D. Kenneson, "Jesus and/as the Non–Violent Imagination of the Church," *Pro Ecclesia*, 1/1 (1992): 76–88.

Hayes, D. A., *Paul and His Epistles* (New York: The Methodist Book Concern, 1915).

Hebblethwaite, Brian, *The Ocean of Truth: A Defence of Objective Theism* (Cambridge: Cambridge University Press, 1988).

Hegel, G.W.F., *The Philosophy of Right*, vol. 46, 54 vols, Robert Maynard Hutchins (ed.), Great Books of the Western World (Chicago: Encyclopaedia Britannica, Inc, 1952).

————, *Phenomenology of Spirit*, trans. by A.V. Miller (Oxford: Oxford University Press, 1977).

Heidegger, Martin, *Being and Time*, trans. by John Macquarrie and Edward Robinson (New York: Harper and Row, 1962).

————, "The Fundamental Question of Metaphysics from an Introduction to Metaphysics," in William Barrett and Henry D. Aiken (eds), *Philosophy in the Twentieth Century*, vol. 3 (New York: Random House, 1962), pp. 219–50.

————, "On the Essence of Truth," in *Basic Writings*, David Farrell Krell (ed.), (San Francisco: HarperCollins, 1993).

Helberger, Sara, "Bringing the Academy into the Electronic Era," *Harvard Alumni Review* (February, 1998), http://www.williams.edu/mtaylor/interviews/pages/980201_harvardalumni_001.html (26 Sept. 2005).

Heller, Scott, "From Kant to Las Vegas to Cyberspace: A Philosopher on the Edge of Postmodernism," *The Chronicle of Higher Education* (May 29, 1998), http://www.williams.edu/ mtaylor/interviews/chron.html (26 Sept. 2005).

Henry, Martin, "God in Postmodernity," *Irish Theological Quarterly*, 63/1 (1998): 3–21.

Hiebert, Paul G., *Missiological Implications of Epistemological Shifts: Affirming Truth in a Modern/Postmodern World* (Harrisburg: Trinity Press International, 1999).

Hoksbergen, Roland, "Is There a Christian Economics?: Some Thoughts in Light of the Rise of Postmodernism," *Christian Scholar's Review*, 24/2 (1994): 126–42.

Hottois, Gilbert, *De la Renaissance à la Postmodernité*, 2nd edn (Paris-Bruxelles: De Boeck Université, 1998).

Howard, Thomas, *The Achievement of C.S. Lewis: A Reading of His Fiction* (Wheaton: Harold Shaw Publishers, 1980).

Hunter, James D., "What Is Modernity? Historical Roots and Contemporary Features," in Paul Sampson, Vinay Samuel and Chris Sugden (eds), *Faith and Modernity* (Oxford: Regnum, 1994), pp. 12–28.

Hutchins, Robert Maynard (ed.), *Biographical Note: René Descartes, 1596–1650*, Great Books of the Western World (Chicago: William Benton, 1952).

Huttar, Charles A., "Till We Have Faces: A Myth Retold," in Jeffrey D. Schultz and John G. West Jr (eds), *The C.S. Lewis Readers' Encyclopedia* (Grand Rapids: Zondervan, 1998).

Huyssteen, J. Wentzel Van, *Essays in Postfoundationalist Theology* (Grand Rapids: Eerdmans, 1997).

Hyman, Gavin, *The Predicament of Postmodern Theology: Radical Orthodoxy or Nihilist Textualism* (Louisville: Westminster John Knox Press, 2001).

Ingraffia, Brian D., *Postmodern Theory and Biblical Theology* (Cambridge: Cambridge University Press, 1995).

Jones, Michael S., "Evangelical Christianity and the Philosophy of Interreligious Dialogue," *Journal of Ecumenical Studies*, 36/3–4 (Summer–Fall 1999): 378–96.

Judson, George, "Education Life: Bridging the Gap between Religion and Technology," *The New York Times*, Section 4A, (Jan. 7, 1996). http://www.williams.edu/mtaylor/interviewstimes.html (8 Feb. 2006).

Kant, Immanuel, *Critique of Pure Reason*, trans. by Norman Kemp Smith (New York: St, Martin's Press, 1929).

———, "General Introduction to the Metaphysic of Morals," vol. 30, 54 vols in Robert Maynard Hutchins (ed.), *Great Books of the Western World* (Chicago: Encyclopaedia Britannica, Inc, 1952), pp. 385–94.

Kavka, Martin, "The Rationality of Derrida's 'Religion without Religion': A Phenomenological Gift for John D, Caputo," 1999. http://www.jcrt.org/archives/01.1/kavka.html (13 May 2003).

Keller, Catherine, "Power Lines," in Cynthia L. Rigby (ed.), *Power, Powerlessness, and the Divine: New Inquiries in Bible and Theology* (Atlanta: Scholar's Press, 1997), p. 67.

Kierkegaard, Søren, *Concluding Unscientific Postscript*, trans. with introduction and notes by Walter Lowrie and David F. Swenson (Princeton: Princeton University Press, 1941).

Kilby, Clyde S., "Christian Imagination," in Leland Ryken (ed.), *The Christian Imagination: Essays on Literature and the Arts* (Grand Rapids: Baker, 1981), pp. 37–46.

Knight, Henry H., III, *A Future for Truth* (Nashville: Abingdon Press, 1997).

Kuhn, Thomas, *The Structure of Scientific Revolutions*, 2nd edn (Chicago: The University of Chicago Press, 1970).

Kuipers, Ronald A, "Singular Interruptions: Rortian Liberalism and the Ethics of Deconstruction," in James H. Olthuis (ed.), *Knowing Other-Wise: Philosophy at the Threshold of Spirituality* (New York: Fordham University Press, 1997).

Kynes, Bill, "Postmodernism: A Primer for Pastors," *The Ministerial Forum: Evangelical Free Church Ministerial Forum* (1997): 1–6.

Lakeland, Paul, *Postmodernity: Christian Identity in a Fragmented Age* (Minneapolis: Fortress, 1997).

Larkin,, William J. Jr, *Acts*, Grant R, Osborne (ed.), The InterVarsity New Testament Commentary Series (Downers Grove: InterVarsity, 1995).

———, "The Recovery of Acts as 'Grand Narrative' for the Church's Evangelistic Task in a Post-Modern Age," Paper presented at the *Meeting of the Evangelical Theological Society* (Orlando, Florida, November 19, 1998).

Lewis, C.S. *Miracles: A Preliminary Study* (New York: Macmillan, 1947).

———, *The Lion, the Witch, and the Wardrobe* (New York: Macmillan, 1950).

———, *Surprised by Joy: The Shape of My Early Life* (New York and London: Harcourt Brace Jovanovich, 1955).

———, *The Last Battle* (New York: Macmillan, 1956).

———, *Till We Have Faces: A Myth Retold* (San Diego, New York, and London: Harcourt Brace Jovanovich, 1956).

———, Walter Hooper (ed.), *On Stories: And Other Essays on Literature* (San Diego, New York, London: Harcourt Brace and Company, 1966)

———, "Tolkien's Lord of the Rings," in Walter Hooper, (ed.), *On Stories: And Other Essays on Literature* (San Diego, New York, and London: Harcourt Brace and Company, 1966).

———, "Myth Became Fact," in Walter Hooper (ed.), *God in the Dock: Essays on Theology and Ethics* (Grand Rapids: Eerdmans, 1970).

Lewis, Gordon R., *Testing Christianity's Truth Claims* (Chicago: Moody, 1976).

Lindbeck, George, Alister McGrath, George Hunsinger, and Gabriel Fackre, "A Panel Discussion," in Timothy R. Phillips and Dennis L. Okholm (eds), *The Nature of Confession: Evangelicals and Postliberals in Conversation*, (Downers Grove: InterVarsity, 1996), pp. 246–53.

Livingston, James C., *Modern Christian Thought* (London: Collier, 1971).

Longenecker, Richard N., *The Acts of the Apostles*, vol. 9, 12 vols, Frank E. Gaebelein (ed.), The Expositor's Bible Commentary (Grand Rapids: Zondervan, 1981).

Lowe, Walter, "A Deconstructionist Manifesto: Mark C. Taylor's *Erring*," *The Journal of Religion*, 66 (1986): 324–31.

Lundin, Roger, *The Culture of Interpretation: Christian Faith and the Postmodern World* (Grand Rapids: Eerdmans, 1993).

Lundin, Roger, Clarence Walhout, and Anthony C. Thiselton, *The Promise of Hermeneutics* (Grand Rapids and Cambridge, U.K.: Eerdmans-Paternoster, 1999).

———, (ed.), *Disciplining Hermeneutics* (Leicester: Apollos, 1997).

Lyotard, Jean-François, *The Postmodern Condition*, trans. by Geoff Bennington and Brian Massumi (Minneapolis: University of Minnesota Press, 1984), originally published as *La Condition Postmoderne* (Collection Critique, Paris: Les éditions de Minuit, 1979).

———, *The Postmodern Explained* (Minneapolis: University of Minnesota Press, 1992).

McCallum, Dennis, *The Death of Truth* (Minneapolis: Bethany House, 1996).

McDermott, Gerald R., *Can Evangelicals Learn from World Religions?: Jesus, Revelation and Religious Traditions* (Downers Grove: InterVarsity, 2000).

McGrath, Alister, *Intellectuals Don't Need God & Other Modern Myths* (Grand Rapids: Zondervan, 1993).

———, *A Passion for Truth: The Intellectual Coherence of Evangelicalism*, (Downers Grove: InterVarsity, 1996).

———, *Historical Theology* (Oxford and Malden, Mass.: Blackwell, 1998).

———, *The Unknown God: Searching for Spiritual Fulfillment* (Grand Rapids: Eerdmans, 1999).

McGrath, Alister E., *The Making of Modern German Christology 1750–1990* (Grand Rapids: Apollos: Zondervan, 1994).

McQuilkin, Robertson, and Bradford Mullen, "The Impact of Postmodern Thinking on Evangelical Hermeneutics," *Journal of the Evangelical Theological Society*, 40/1 (1997): 69–82.

Marion, Jean-Luc, *God without Being*, trans. by Thomas A. Carlson (Chicago and London: The University of Chicago Press, 1991).

Markos, Louis A., "Myth Matters," *Christianity Today* (April 23, 2001): 32–39.

———, "Poetry-Phobic: Why Evangelicals Should Love Language That Is 'Slippery,'" *Christianity Today* (October 1, 2001): 66.

Marshall, I. Howard, *The Acts of the Apostles*, vol. 5, 20 vols, Tyndale New Testament Commentaries (Leicester: InterVarsity Press, 1980).

Matthews, Eric, *Twentieth-Century French Philosophy* (Oxford: Oxford University Press, 1996).

Mavrodes, George I., *Belief in God* (New York: Random House, 1970).

Megill, Allan, *Prophets of Extremity: Nietzsche, Heidegger, Foucault, Derrida* (Berkeley and Los Angeles: University of California Press, Ltd, 1985).

Merquior, J. G., *Foucault* (London: Fontana Press, 1991).

Michener, Ronald T., "The Relation of Faith and Reason in Paul's Defense of the Gospel in Acts 17:16–34," M.A. thesis (Western Seminary, 1987).

Middleton, J. Richard, and Brian Walsh, *Truth Is Stranger Than It Used to Be: Biblical Faith in a Postmodern Age* (Downers Grove: InterVarsity, 1995).

Miller, Ed L., and Stanley J. Grenz, *Fortress Introduction to Contemporary Theologies* (Minneapolis: Fortress, 1998).

Mills, David (ed.), *The Pilgrim's Guide:.C..S. Lewis and the Art of Witness* (Grand Rapids/Cambridge, U.K.: Eerdmans, 1998).

Moltmann, Jürgen, *Theology of Hope*, trans. by James W. Leitch (London: SCM Press Ltd, 1967).

———, *Theology Today*, trans. by John Bowden (London: SCM Press Ltd, 1988).

Monteil, Pierre-Olivier, *La Grâce et le Désordre* (Genève: Labor et Fides, 1998).

Moore, Stephen D., *Poststructuralism and the New Testament* (Minneapolis: Fortress Press, 1994).

Moreland, J.P., *Scaling the Secular City* (Grand Rapids: Baker, 1987).

———, "Philosophical Apologetics, the Church, and Contemporary Culture," *Journal of the Evangelical Theological Society*, 39/1 (1996): 123–40.

Moser, Paul K., *Philosophy after Objectivity: Making Sense in Perspective* (New York and Oxford: Oxford University Press, 1993).

Muck, Terry C. "After Selfhood: Constructing the Religious Self in a Post-Self Age," *Journal of the Evangelical Theological Society*, 41/1 (1998): 107–22.

Mudimbe, V.Y., *The Invention of Africa: Gnosis, Philosophy, and the Order of Knowledge* (Bloomington and Indianapolis: Indiana University Press, 1988).

———, *The Idea of Africa* (Bloomington and Indianapolis: Indiana University Press, 1994).

Müller, Denis, *L'éthique Protestante Dans la Crise de la Modernité* (Paris: Labor et Fides, 1999).

Murphy, Nancey, *Beyond Liberalism & Fundamentalism: How Modern and Postmodern Philosophy Set the Theological Agenda* (Valley Forge: Trinity Press International, 1996).

Murphy, Nancey, and James W. McClendon Jr, "Distinguishing Modern and Postmodern Theologies," *Modern Theology*, 5/3 (1989): 199–212.

Nagel, Thomas, *The Last Word* (Oxford: Oxford University Press, 1997).

Nault, François, *Derrida et la Théologie: Dire Dieu après la Déconstruction* (Paris: Les éditions du Cerf, 2000).

Netland, Harold, "Religious Pluralism and Truth," *Trinity Journal* 6 (1985): 74–87.

Neusner, Jacob, *Invitation to the Talmud: A Teaching Book*, revised and expanded edn (San Francisco: Harper and Row, Publishers, 1973).

Newbigin, Lesslie, *The Gospel in a Pluralist Society* (Grand Rapids: Eerdmans, 1989).

Niemeier, Jan, "Paul, Liberty, and Foucault—an Assessment of Postmodern Ethics in the Light of Paul's Concept of Freedom," B.A. thesis in theology (Livets Ord University: Uppsala, Sweden, 1999).

Nietzsche, Friedrich, *Thus Spoke Zarathustra*, trans. by R.J. Hollingdale (London: Penguin Books Ltd, 1961).

———, *The Gay Science: With a Prelude in Rhymes and an Appendix of Songs*, trans. by Walter Kaufmann (New York: Vintage Books, 1974).

———, "On Truth and Lie in an Extra-Moral Sense," in Walter Kaufmann (ed.), *The Portable Nietzsche* (New York: Penguin Books, 1976).

————, *The Antichrist*, in Walter Kaufmann (ed. and trans.), *The Portable Nietzsche* (New York: Penguin Books, 1976).

Norris, Christopher, *Derrida* (London: Fontana, 1987).

Oden, Thomas, *After Modernity What? Agenda for Theology* (Grand Rapids: Zondervan, 1990).

Oden, Thomas C., "Post–Modern Evangelical Spirituality," paper presented at the *Meeting of the Evangelical Theological Society* (Washington D.C., November, 1993).

Okholm, Dennis L. and Timothy R. Phillips (eds), *More Than One Way?: Four Views on Salvation in a Pluralistic World* (Grand Rapids: Zondervan, 1995).

Olson, Roger E., "Back to the Bible (Almost): Why Yale's Postliberal Theologians Deserve an Evangelical Hearing," *Christianity Today* (May 20 1996).

————, "The Future of Evangelical Theology," *Christianity Today* (February 9 1998).

Olthuis, James H. (ed.), *Knowing Other-Wise: Philosophy at the Threshold of Spirituality* (New York: Fordham University Press, 1997).

Packer, J.I. "Still Surprised by Lewis," *Christianity Today* (September 7, 1998), 54–60.

Pannenberg, Wolfhart, *Theology and the Philosophy of Science*, trans. by Francis McDonagh (Philadelphia: The Westminster Press, 1976).

————, *Systematic Theology*, vol. 1, 3 vols, trans. by Geoffrey W. Bromiley, (Grand Rapids: Eerdmans), 1991.

Percesepe, Gary John, "The Unbearable Lightness of Being Postmodern," *Christian Scholar's Review*, 20/2 (1990): 118–35.

Peters, Ted, *God—the World's Future: Systematic Theology for a Postmodern Era* (Minneapolis: Fortress, 1992).

Peterson, Michael, William Hasker, Bruce Reichenbach, and David Basinger, *Reason and Religious Belief: An Introduction to the Philosophy of Religion* (New York and Oxford: Oxford University Press, 1991).

Phillips, Timothy R. and Dennis L. Okholm (eds), *Christian Apologetics in the Postmodern World* (Downers Grove: InterVarsity, 1995).

————, eds, *The Nature of Confession: Evangelicals & Postliberals in Conversation* (Downers Grove: InterVarsity, 1996).

Pierard, Richard V., "Evangelicalism," in J.D. Douglas (ed.), *New 20th-Century Encyclopedia of Religious Knowledge* (Grand Rapids: Baker, 1991).

Piety, Marilyn Gaye, "Kierkegaard on Rationality," *Faith and Philosophy*, 10/3 (1993): 365–79.

Pinnock, Clark H., *Tracking the Maze: Finding Our Way Through Modern Theology from an Evangelical Perspective* (San Francisco: Harper and Row, 1990); reprint (Eugene: Wipf and Stock Publishers, 1998).

Plantinga, Alvin, "Is Belief in God Properly Basic?," in R, Douglas Geivett and Brendan Sweetman (eds), *Contemporary Perspectives on Religious Epistemology* (New York and Oxford: Oxford University Press, 1992), pp. 133–41; reprinted from *Nous*, 15 (1981).

Plantinga, Alvin, and Nicholas Wolterstorff (eds), *Faith and Rationality: Reason and Belief in God* (Notre Dame: University of Notre Dame Press, 1983).

Rabinow, Paul (ed.), *The Foucault Reader* (New York: Pantheon Books, 1984).

Ramm, Bernard, *Varieties of Christian Apologetics* (Grand Rapids: Baker, 1962).

———, *The Devil, Seven Wormwoods, and God* (Waco, Texas: Word Books, 1977).

Raschke, Carl, *The Next Reformation* (Grand Rapids: Baker, 2004).

Reijnen, Anne Marie, "Variété Des Vérités," *Analecta Bruxellensia*, 4 (1999): 49–61.

Rescher, Nicholas, *Objectivity: The Obligations of Impersonal Reason*, Notre Dame and London: University of Notre Dame Press, 1997.

Rhodes, Stephen A., *Where Nations Meet: The Church in Multicultural World* (Downers Grove: InterVarsity, 1998).

Rogovoy, Seth, "Mark Taylor: Cyberprofessor from Hell or Visionary Educator," *Berkshire Eagle* (February 3, 1996) http://www.berkshireweb.com/rogovoy/interviews/taylor.html (26 Sept. 2005).

Rorty, Richard, *Philosophy and the Mirror of Nature* (Princeton: Princeton University Press, 1979).

———, *Consequences of Pragmatism* (Minneapolis: University of Minnnesota Press, 1982).

———, *Contingency, Irony, and Solidarity* (Cambridge: Cambridge University Press, 1989).

———, *Essays on Heidegger and Others: Philosophical Papers Volume 2* (Cambridge: Cambridge University Press, 1991).

———, *Objectivity, Relativism, and Truth* (Cambridge: Cambridge University Press, 1991).

———, "Feminism, Ideology, and Deconstruction: A Pragmatist View," Hypatia, 8/2, (Spring, 1993), http://gort.ucsd.edu/jhan/ER/rr.html (9 June 1999).

———, "First Projects, Then Principles," *The Nation* (22 December 1997), http://www.physicsforums.com/archive/t-2693_%22First_Projects,_Then _Principles%22_by_Richard_Rorty.html (29 Sept. 2005).

Sampson, Paul, Vinay Samuel, and Chris Sugden (eds), *Faith and Modernity* (Oxford: Regnum, 1994).

Saussure, Ferdinand de, *Course in General Linguistics*, trans. by Roy Harris, Charles Bally and Albert Sechehaye, (eds) (Chicago and La Salle: Open Court, 1986).

Sayer, George, *Jack: C.S. Lewis and His Times* (San Francisco: Harper and Row, 1988).

Sayre, Patricia A., "The Dialectics of Trust and Suspicion," *Faith and Philosophy*, 10/4 (1993): 567–84.

Schakel, Peter J., *Reason and Imagination in C.S. Lewis* (Grand Rapids: Eerdmans, 1984).

Schleiermacher, Friedrich, *On Religion: Speeches to Its Cultured Despisers*, trans. by John Oman (New York, Hagerstown, San Francisco, and London: Harper and Row, 1958).

Sire, James W., *Why Should Anyone Believe Anything at All?* (Downers Grove: InterVarsity, 1994).

Smith, David Lionel, "Imagologies and Other Philosophical Conversations with Mark C. Taylor," interview by David Lionel Smith (Jan. 1997) http://www.Williams. edu/mtaylor/interviews/pages/970101_masshumanities_001.html (29 Sept 2005).

Smith, Huston, "The Religious Significance of Postmodernism," *Faith and Philosophy*, 12/3 (1995): 409–22.

Smith, James K.A., "The Art of Christian Atheism: Faith and Philosophy in Early Heidegger," *Faith and Philosophy*, 14/1 (1997): 71–81.

———, *The Fall of Interpretation: Philosophical Foundations for a Creational Hermeneutic* (Downers Grove: InterVarsity, 2000).

Solomon, Robert C., *From Rationalism to Existentialism: The Existentialists and Their Nineteenth-Century Backgrounds* (New York: Humanities Press, 1972).

———, *Continental Philosophy since 1750: The Rise and Fall of the Self* (Oxford: Oxford University Press, 1988).

Stackhouse, John G. Jr, *Can God Be Trusted?: Faith and the Challenge of Evil* (New York: Oxford University Press, 1998).

———— (ed.), *Evangelical Futures: A Conversation on Theological Method* (Grand Rapids: Leicester; and Vancouver, B.C.: Baker, InterVarsity, and Regent College Publishing, 2000).

Steinkamp, Fiona, "Gender and Postmodern Communication," *The Monist*, 80/3 (1997): 448–71.

Stonehouse, Ned B., *Paul Before the Areopagus* (Grand Rapids: Eerdmans, 1957).

Stossel, Scott, "A Conversation with Richard Rorty," *The Atlantic Monthly Company* (23 April 1998),

http://www.theatlantic.com/unbound/bookauth/ba980423.htm, online interview currently only available with subscription. Brief excerpt available at: http://www.erraticimpact.com/ ~20thcentury/html/rorty_richardhtm (27 Jan. 2006).

Strug, Cordell, "Kuhn's Paradigm Thesis: A Two-Edged Sword for the Philosophy of Religion," *Religious Studies*, 20 (June 1984): 269–79.

Taylor, Mark C., *Deconstructing Theology* (New York: Crossroad, 1982).

———, "Text as Victim," in Thomas J.J. Altizer (ed.), *Deconstruction and Theology* (New York: Crossroad, 1982), pp. 58–78.

———, "Deconstruction: What's the Difference?" *Soundings*, 66 (1983): 387–403.

———, *Erring* (Chicago: The University of Chicago Press, 1984).

———, "Masking: Domino Effect in on Deconstructing Theology: A Symposium on Erring: A Postmodern a/Theology," *Journal of the American Academy of Religion*, 54 (1986): 547–57.

———, *Altarity* (Chicago: The University of Chicago Press, 1987).

———, "Non-Negative Negative Atheology," *Diacritics*, 20/4 (1990): 2–17.

———, *Tears* (Albany: State University of New York Press, 1990).

———, "Reframing Postmodernisms," in *Shadow of Spirit*, Philipa Berry and Andrew Wernick (eds) (London and New York: Routledge, 1992).

———, *Hiding* (Chicago: University of Chicago Press, 1997).

———, "Betting on Vegas," in John D. Caputo and Michael J. Scanlon (eds), *God, the Gift and Postmodernism* (Bloomington and Indianapolis: Indiana University Press, 1999), pp. 229–44.

Thielicke, Helmut, *Modern Faith and Thought* (Grand Rapids: Eerdmans, 1990).

Thiselton, Anthony C., *The Two Horizons* (Grand Rapids: Eerdmans, 1980).

———, *New Horizons in Hermeneutics* (Grand Rapids: Zondervan, 1992).

———, *Interpreting God and the Postmodern Self* (Edinburgh: T&T Clark, 1995).

Tilley, Terrence W., *Postmodern Theologies: The Challenge of Religious Diversity* (Maryknoll: Orbis Books, 1995).

Tolkien, J.R.R., "Tree and Leaf," in *The Tolkien Reader* (New York: Ballantine Books, 1966).

Tracy, David, "Theology and the Many Faces of Postmodernity," *Theology Today* 51/1 (1994): 104–14.

Van den Toren, Benno. "A New Direction in Christian Apologetics: An Exploration with Reference to Postmodernism," *European Journal of Theology*, 2/1 (1993): 49–64.

Vanhoozer, Kevin J., *Is There a Meaning in This Text?* (Grand Rapids: Zondervan, 1998).

Veith, Gene Edward Jr, *Postmodern Times: A Christian Guide to Contemporary Thought and Culture* (Wheaton: Crossway, 1994).

Vergote, Antoine, *Modernité et Christianisme: Interrogations Critiques Réciproques* (Paris: Les éditions du Cerf, 1999).

Volf, Miroslav, "The Clumsy Embrace: Interview by Kevin D. Miller," *Christianity Today* (October 26, 1998): 65–9.

———, *Exclusion and Embrace: A Theological Exploration of Identity, Otherness, and Reconciliation* (Nashville: Abingdon, 1996).

Von Rad, Gerhard, *Wisdom in Israel* (Nashville: Abingdon Press, 1972).

Ward, Glenn, *Teach Yourself Postmodernism* (London: Hodder Headline Plc, 1997).

Ward, Graham, *Barth, Derrida and the Language of Theology* (Cambridge: Cambridge University Press, 1995).

Ward, Keith, *Holding Fast to God: A Reply to Don Cupitt* (London: SPCK, 1982).

Watts, Alan W., *Myth and Ritual in Christianity* (Boston: Beacon Press, 1968).

Wells, David F., *No Place for Truth or Whatever Happened to Evangelical Theology?* (Grand Rapids: Eerdmans, 1993).

West, David, *An Introduction to Continental Philosophy* (Cambridge: Blackwell, 1996).

Westphal, Merold, *God, Guilt and Death: An Existential Phenomenology of Religion* (Bloomington: Indiana University Press, 1984).

———, "The Ostrich and the Boogeyman: Placing Postmodernism," *Christian Scholar's Review* 20/2 (1990): 114–17.

———, "Religious Experience as Self-Transcendence and Self-Deception," *Faith and Philosophy*, 9/2 (1992): 168–92.

———, *Suspicion and Faith* (New York: Fordham University Press, 1998).

————, *Overcoming Onto-Theology: Toward a Postmodern Christian Faith* (New York: Fordham University Press, 2001).

————, (ed.), *Postmodern Philosophy and Christian Thought* (Bloomington, Indiana: Indiana University Press, 1999).

Wilkins, Steve, and Alan G. Padgett, *Christianity and Western Thought: A History of Philosophers, Ideas and Movements*, vol. 2 (Downers Grove: InterVarsity, 2000).

Willard, Dallas, *In Search of Guidance* (Ventura, California: Regal Books, 1984).

Williams, Stephen N., "The Problem with Moltmann," *European Journal of Theology*, 5/2 (1996): 157–67.

Winquist, Charles E., *Desiring Theology* (Chicago: University of Chicago Press, 1995).

Wittgenstein, Ludwig, *Lectures and Conversations on Aesthetics, Psychology and Religious Belief*, Cyril Barrett (ed.) (Berkeley and Los Angeles: University of California Press, 1972).

————, "Tractatus Logico-Philosophicus," in Lawrence Cahoone (ed.), *From Modernism to Postmodernism: An Anthology* (Cambridge, Mass.: Blackwell, 1996), pp. 198–9.

Wolter, Allan B., "Bacon, Francis," in *Encyclopedia of Philosophy*, Paul Edwards, (ed.), vol. 1 (New York: Macmillan Pub. Co. and The Free Press, 1967), pp. 235–42

Wolterstorff, Nicholas, *Reason Within the Bounds of Religion* (Grand Rapids: Eerdmans, 1976).

Wood, Jay W., *Epistemology: Becoming Intellectually Virtuous* (Downers Grove: InterVarsity, 1998).

Wright, N.T., *The New Testament and the People of God: Christian Origins and the Question of God*, vol. 1 (London: SPCK, 1992).

Yoder, John Howard, "On Not Being Ashamed of the Gospel: Particularity, Pluralism, and Validation," *Faith and Philosophy* 9/3 (1992): 285–300.

Index